The *BATTLE* of the B(

King James II.
from the Painting by Sir Godfrey Kneller in the National Portrait Gallery.

THE BATTLE OF THE BOYNE

TOGETHER WITH AN ACCOUNT BASED ON FRENCH
AND OTHER UNPUBLISHED RECORDS OF THE WAR
IN IRELAND (1688–1691) AND OF THE FORMATION OF
THE IRISH BRIGADE IN THE SERVICE OF FRANCE

By Demetrius Charles Boulger 🦢 🦢 🦢

ILLUSTRATED WITH MANY PORTRAITS FROM PRIVATE
COLLECTIONS REPRODUCED IN PHOTOGRAVURE

The Naval & Military Press Ltd

in association with

The National Army Museum, London

Published jointly by

The Naval & Military Press Ltd

Unit 10 Ridgewood Industrial Park,
Uckfield, East Sussex,
TN22 5QE England

Tel: +44 (0) 1825 749494
Fax: +44 (0) 1825 765701

www.naval-military-press.com
www.military-genealogy.com
www.militarymaproom.com

and

The National Army Museum, London

www.national-army-museum.ac.uk

Contents

CHAPTER   PAGE

I. THE ARRIVAL AT ST. GERMAINS   9

II. KING JAMES GOES TO IRELAND   39

III. A GREAT VICEROY   60

IV. KING JAMES IN IRELAND   82

V. THE CAMPAIGNS OF 1689–90   120

VI. THE BATTLE OF THE BOYNE   148

VII. THE FIRST SIEGE OF LIMERICK   183

VIII. THE MOUNTCASHELL BRIGADE   207

IX. THE CAMPAIGN OF AUGHRIM   223

X. THE SECOND SIEGE OF LIMERICK   245

XI. THE CONVENTION OF LIMERICK   263

XII. THE IRISH ARRIVE IN FRANCE   283

XIII. THE FIRST ACHIEVEMENTS OF THE
BRIGADE   308

XIV. THE PEACE OF RYSWYCK   337

INDEX   374

List of Illustrations

KING JAMES II

From the Portrait by Sir Godfrey Kneller in the National Portrait Gallery   *Frontispiece*

QUEEN MARY OF MODENA

From the Painting by W. Wissing in the National Portrait Gallery   *Facing page* 34

RICHARD TALBOT, DUKE OF TYRCONNELL

From the Painting in the National Portrait Gallery   66

WILLIAM HERBERT, DUKE OF POWIS

From the Portrait at Powis Castle, in the possession of the Earl of Powis   90

THE LORD THOMAS HOWARD

From the Painting at Arundel Castle, in the possession of the Duke of Norfolk   116

PATRICK SARSFIELD, EARL OF LUCAN

From the Portrait in the possession of the Order of Franciscan Friars in Dublin   164

VALENTINE BROWNE, VISCOUNT KENMARE

From the Portrait at Killarney House, in the possession of the Earl of Kenmare   242

COLONEL JOHN BROWNE

From the Portrait at Westport House, in the possession of the Marquis of Sligo   264

JAMES, DUKE OF BERWICK

From the Portrait in the possession of the Duc D'Alba   324

CHARLES, EARL OF MIDDLETON

From the Portrait in the possession of James Paton, Esq.   338

The BATTLE of the BOYNE

Chapter I

THE ARRIVAL AT ST. GERMAINS

DURING the night of December 19–20 (N.S.), 1688, there sailed into Calais harbour an English yacht, which was engaged in its customary work of conveying travellers across the Channel between England and France. On this occasion there were twenty-six passengers on board, including an infant, and the captain, Clark by name, had never before conveyed a living freight so precious and unusual. Under different circumstances, if History had only taken a slightly altered form, the little boat might have become famous as having borne the destiny of England. But *dis aliter visum*. It took away those who were never to return, the representatives of a lost cause, the last members of the sovereign House by right divine in this United Realm. It is true the sovereign himself was not on board, but he was to follow some little time after, and for all practical purposes the yacht may be considered to have carried with it the hopes and fortunes of the Stuarts.

The little barque made a good passage, and as a piquant detail, considering who were on board, it may be mentioned that she passed unchallenged and unmolested through a fleet of fifty Dutch warships in the Downs.

The principal passengers were Mary Beatrice d'Este of

Modena, Queen of England, etc., her son, the infant Prince of Wales, William Herbert, Marquis of Powis, his wife, *née* Lady Elisabeth Somerset, Lady Sophia Bulkeley and two of her daughters, Anne, unmarried but destined to be Duchess of Berwick, and Charlotte, wife of Charles O'Brien, afterwards Viscount Clare, a hero of Blenheim and Ramillies, where he received his death-wound, not for England but for France.   There were other passengers closely attached to the Queen : her lifelong friend, Madame Davia, not yet Countess d'Almonde, *née* Anna Victoria de Montecuculli of Modena, the faithful Turini, her bed-chamber woman, the courier, or page of the backstairs, Riva, another Italian.   To these three faithful citizens of her own native town must be added Lauzun, the impresario of the scene, the man who has arranged the flight, and who in his own estimation at least is the hero of the adventure.

Before going further let us give the full list of those on board :—

FULL LIST OF PARTY ACCOMPANYING QUEEN MARY OF MODENA

	Number of Persons
Queen Mary, Prince of Wales	2
Lady Sophia Bulkeley, Miss Anne Bulkeley	2
Marquis and Marchioness of Powis	2
Victoria Montecuculli Davia, and her brother the Marquis Montecuculli	2
Lady Strickland and Madame Turini (the Queen's *femme de chambre*)	2
Father Giuduci and Sir William Waldegrave (physician)	2
Dominic Sheldon, Guttier François, Riva, Dufour, and Leyburn	5
Lord and Lady O'Brien de Clare (really Charles O'Brien, afterwards Viscount Clare)	2
Three Irish Captains (McCarthy of Petersfield probably one of them)	3
Turini, Mrs. L'Abadie, dry nurse, and a wet nurse unnamed	3
Lauzun	1
	—
	26

The passage from Gravesend must indeed have been excellent, for the child slept throughout the journey. We will now take a brief glance at the events which preceded the flight, and more especially does it concern this narrative to show how and why it was that the Royal Family of England should flee to France in the absolute conviction that protection and hospitality awaited them in that country.

The affairs of England had been the subject of the closest attention in Paris ever since the accession of James II, on the death of his brother Charles II in 1685, and still more especially since the formation of the League of Augsburg in July, 1686, by William of Orange and the Emperor of Germany. During the whole of Charles's reign French influence had been in the ascendant at Whitehall. A French mistress had ruled the King, English ministers received French pensions, and English officers and men learnt the art of war under Turenne. There was no definite agreement, but there was a very good *entente cordiale*. Louis wanted this good understanding to be converted into a regular alliance, and when James proclaimed himself a Catholic it looked for a moment as if his end would be attained. But the King's conversion raised fresh obstacles instead of removing those that already existed, and when Louis revoked the Edict of Nantes a great outcry arose in England that the country was about to be betrayed to the Pope. It was this apprehension that gave William, Prince of Orange, the chance of posing as the champion of Protestantism. He took a leaf out of Louis's own book, and began to bribe the ministers of England. Sunderland, the most notorious of them all, took one salary from France and another from Holland. To James he swore by all the saints that he was a good Catholic; to William he made no oaths, but he sent him the priceless information that Louis had engaged to invest Maestricht if the Prince of Orange made any move against England.

Although Louis XIV was then at the height of his power, the league arrayed against him was formidable, and if England were to be added to it the odds against him might become too great. So long as James, not merely his first cousin, but his guest, companion, and fellow-soldier of the days of exile under Cromwell, held the throne there was no risk of this. Indeed, if James could hold his ground there was far more likelihood of his becoming the open ally of France, and had that stage been reached the map of Europe could have been re-arranged.

But the desire to obtain the English alliance did not blind the wisest of the French ministers to James's own position. Early in 1688 it became clear in Paris that James was in great difficulties, and the impression grew that he did not know how to deal with them. He was told that Sunderland was a traitor, but he continued to entrust him with his closest secrets. This conduct was the first cause of the want of confidence felt by Louvois, the great Minister of France, who was the main prop of Louis's government, in James, which became intensified with each fresh experience. Lookers-on proverbially see most of the game, and soon it was discovered that James was not merely in difficulty, but in danger. It was then that George Skelton, James's ambassador at Versailles, alarmed at the news from London, took upon himself to ask Louvois to send over a French army to keep James on the throne. Louvois having just committed himself to the invasion of the Palatinate, declined the proposal, and James, alarmed at the effect on English opinion of the rumoured introduction of French troops into the country, recalled Skelton and sent him to the Tower. He was kept there for a short space as a prisoner, but he remained somewhat longer as its governor. It was said with some neatness at the time that James punished Skelton's indiscretion with a cell, and rewarded his loyalty with the governor's quarters.

When it became generally known that William of Orange was preparing a large fleet and army to cross into England, and that he had been invited to come over for the preservation of the Protestant cause by some of the most influential men in England and Scotland, French statesmen had to face the fact that James, far from being likely to succeed in holding his own, was confronted with the grave risk of losing his throne. This risk was increased by James's own conduct. He would not believe that those who offered him such effusive lip-service could be false. He should have sent Sunderland to the Tower, instead of loyal George Skelton.

French opinion was prepared then for the downfall of James long before the poor King realised his own position, and there was no inclination at Versailles to risk the mad adventure of keeping him on the throne by means of a French army. But, on the other hand, the fact was appreciated that while the Prince of Orange had an army in England he would have fewer troops in the Netherlands, and that then would be the time for France to press him in the Meuse valley. It was also hoped that the presence of foreign troops in England would arouse national opposition to that veiled conquest of 1688 which believers in the invulnerability of England have so consistently ignored down to the present day, and it was never conceived to be possible that the English people would make, even for the sake of a menaced Church, that tame surrender which they did to the Danes, Prussians, Huguenots and Dutchmen collected under the Orange flag in the winter of 1688–9. The French hoped then that William might well burn his fingers over his adventure, and their conception of the likely course of events was at least not uncomplimentary to the English character.

For the moment the only active part that the French authorities were disposed to take towards upholding the Stuarts was in facilitating the escape of the English Royal Family, and above all of the young Prince of Wales, and in providing them with a secure place of refuge. The darker and more uncertain the future was deemed for King James himself, the more essential did it seem from the French point of view to acquire the person of his only male heir. There was no difference of opinion on this point between Louis and his Ministers. Louvois, moved by political calculations alone, was in complete accord with the chivalric impulses of Louis XIV which led that monarch to decide on giving the most cordial hospitality to the fugitive Stuarts. Louvois gladly found the money to refurnish Vincennes which was first selected as their residence, and he went even further than his sovereign in thinking that the sooner the Queen of England and her son were safe in France the better. He was also not very sanguine about James's own chances. It was not merely that he had even in these early days no high opinion of the King's ability, but his own recent experience in interfering with the religious sentiments of a people had not been very successful, and had left him in a chastened mood.

The Louvois of 1688 was not quite the same person as he had been in 1685, when James's conversion had seemed to herald the return of England to the Catholic fold. The success of the Revocation of the Edict of Nantes and the dragonnades had not been so absolute in France as to make him think that James Stuart would succeed in a task somewhat similar to but more difficult than his own, when Protestant England was the scene in lieu of Catholic France. When George Skelton asked for French troops Louvois knew that James II had already failed. The letters from his agents in England made him think, rightly or wrongly, that for the completeness of his failure James was himself much to blame, and thus his distrust and dislike of the Stuart King dated from a time anterior to their meeting in France.

But Louvois had no doubt as to the wisdom of welcoming the Stuart family. The possession of the legitimate heir to the Crown of England was a trump card in the great game of politics. If William of Orange secured not merely his father-in-law's crown, but the persons of the King and his only direct heir, then his triumph would be doubly great and lasting. How was this to be prevented?

Fate came to the assistance of his plans in the person of Lauzun, and it was the more remarkable because Louvois was not his friend. It will be more convenient to give the story of this worthless person (*ce triste personnage* of Louvois) at a later phase of his participation in the Stuart drama, but in 1688 he had not long been released from ten years' imprisonment in the Bastille and elsewhere on condition that he did not come within two leagues of the Court. He still dreamt of great deeds, and of his return to the Court where he had once been prime favourite, but no one believed that so long as Mademoiselle de Montpensier (La Grande Mademoiselle) lived he had any chance of success. At the very moment that Lauzun was conceiving impossible adventures, Louvois needed an adventurer of good class, accustomed to Courts, but with a reputation to restore. The adventure of bringing over the heir to the English crown and his mother was made for Lauzun, and Lauzun was made for the adventure. Besides, he had some special qualifications. He knew the English language a little; he had been to London, and he had served with King James as a comrade in the trenches before Landrecies in 1655. The character of the rescuer of the wife and child of an old companion in arms, who had had the good fortune to become a monarch in the interval, was one that well accorded with the grandiose ideas of his own magnificence and importance.

On October 21, 1688, we learn from the invaluable diary of Dangeau that Lauzun left for England to offer his services to James II. A more cautious chronicler expressed the current talk of the day on the subject in the words: "Lauzun has gone to England in search of some amusement." The cynical St. Simon adds that

" the English Revolution broke out expressly in Lauzun's interests." The official biographer[1] of King James II merely states that " all things being ready by this time for the Queen and Prince's departure it fell out opportunely enough that the Count de Lozune, a French gentleman, was then at the Court of England, whither he came to offer his services to the King . . . so His Majesty accepted of his offer an other way, as thinking him a proper person to attend upon the Queen in this voyage, and that under the notion of his returning to his own country (there being no business for him in England) a yacght might be prepared and the Queen and Prince pass unsuspected in his company."

By the time that Lauzun's services were required half the month of December, 1688, had passed away. The Prince of Wales had been sent to Portsmouth, under the personal charge of Lord and Lady Powis, in the belief that the Prince of Orange intended landing on the East Coast, while the King and Queen remained in London. But when William landed at Torbay, and his patrols were riding through Dorset to Hampshire, it was seen that Portsmouth was no longer a safe place, and Lord Powis, with his precious charge, was summoned back to London. There seems no doubt that the party only escaped capture in the neighbourhood of Petersfield through the intelligence of " Mr. Macarty, an Irish Officer," and when they reached London everything was ready for the immediate departure of the Queen and her child for France.

James had made up his mind to quit England. He had entrusted his personal papers to the safe custody of the Marquis Terriesi, Envoy from Tuscany, who undertook to convey them to Italy and thence to Paris. It only remained then to arrange the details for the flight, and as it was impossible for them all to escape together, it was decided that the Queen should leave immediately

[1] The autobiography (practically speaking) based on the Stuart papers by the Rev. J. S. Clarke, 1816.

after the arrival of her child, under the escort of Lauzun. The Queen was quite willing for her son to be sent over, but her reluctance to leave her husband was only overcome by his assurance that he "would follow within twenty-four hours of her departure." It was thereupon agreed that the Queen and the Prince of Wales should start first.

According to Lauzun's own account, all the preparations for departure having been made in advance, the flight took place on the same night as the arrival of the Prince from Portsmouth, and this was the 6th (O.S.) or 16th (N.S.) of December. The threatening attitude of the mob in Southwark towards the soldiers sent to escort the young Prince into London showed that there was no time to lose, and that a wise precaution had been adopted in bringing the party from Portsmouth by a roundabout route over Kingston Bridge.

Francesco Riva, an Italian gentleman in attendance upon the Queen ever since her first arrival in England, prepared an official account of the flight, which was no doubt read by the Queen and corrected under her personal direction. It is not free from some errors and omissions, but on the whole it is the best account we possess. He states that he was sent to bring the Prince back from Portsmouth, and that the route was guarded by several regiments, notably by the Earl of Salisbury's at Guildford. He also states that the party reached Whitehall at three in the morning, and that the young Prince was kept concealed in the apartments of M. de l'Abadie, groom of the chambers, all day—de l'Abadie's wife being his dry nurse.

On the night of December 16, then, the King and Queen retired as usual to rest in Whitehall, and no one was informed that the Prince had arrived. He was kept, as described, in M. de l'Abadie's chamber, close to the royal apartment, with Lord and Lady Powis and his nurse. A quarter of an hour after retiring King James

B

got up, and the Queen rose at the same time, ready dressed for travelling. Those in the antechamber, joined by the Queen's favourite, Madame Davia, entered the room, and the King, taking the child in his arms, enveloped as it was in a bundle of linen, led the way down a back staircase and several passages to a small door on the side of the Palace nearest to the river.

Here Lauzun and his friend, M. Saint Victor, a French officer of approved courage and an expert swordsman, who may have been the original of Dumas' D'Artagnan, were waiting. Saint Victor took the child in his arms, and the King, turning to Lauzun, said briefly that he entrusted to him all he held dearest in the world. There was no time to waste, and Lauzun led the way, escorting the Queen to the boat held in readiness at the Palace stairs. The night was dark, and there was rain, with a high wind, and the crossing of the river in the obscurity was no easy matter. On reaching the Lambeth side the coaches had not arrived, and for an hour the party found such shelter as they could under the wall of Lambeth Chapel. During this hour of suspense the Queen, wrote Sir J. Dalrymple, whose literal accuracy is not remarkable, " turned her eyes, streaming with tears, sometimes on the Prince, unconscious of the miseries which attend upon Royalty, and who, upon that account, raised the greater compassion in her heart, and sometimes to the innumerable lights of the City amidst the glimmerings of which she in vain explored the Palace in which her husband was left, and started at every sound she heard from there."

Riva's account is more detailed and circumstantial. It shows that besides the comparatively small party escaping from the Palace, several of the Queen's friends had gone direct to the rendezvous at Lambeth, under the charge of Dufour, page of the backstairs, and that three carriages were in readiness. Riva, curiously enough, omits to mention the name of Saint Victor, who carried the Prince in his arms, but there is no room for doubting that he was

there. Some one described him as formerly squire to the
Duc de Vendôme.

As soon as the party had crossed the river the page
Dufour went off to call the carriages. He found the ostlers
all drinking. They had not drunk so much, however, as not
to feel a little curious as to who the travellers were, and
one came forth with a lantern to find out. By this time
most of the party had taken their seats, and Riva, appre-
hensive lest the ostler might discover the Queen, jostled
up against him, upsetting him in the narrow alley, and
extinguishing his lantern. Riva also fell and rose covered
with mud. He then jumped into the back seat of the
Queen's coach, and the party drove off. After proceeding
some distance on the Old Kent Road they were met by
Leyburn, the Queen's squire, with two horses. Riva
put on riding-boots, and mounting one of them, rode
with Leyburn as a rear-guard. It seems probable that
Saint Victor did likewise, for Leyburn led two horses.
Riva either forgot all about the French officer, or did not
wish any one to share in the credit of the successful flight
but himself. Riva, not Lauzun, much less the unnamed
Saint Victor, is the hero of the occasion in the Italian's
narrative. Some time after this incident three Irish
officers joined the party, and thus the Queen had a small
guard of trustworthy and devoted men. The names of
these officers are not given, but in all probability McCarthy
of Petersfield was one of them.

Without accident the Queen and her companions reached
Gravesend. All were got on board the yacht in safety
and without attracting notice, the little Prince being
carried on board by Saint Victor " in a bundle of soiled
linen." It had been arranged that if the captain displayed the least sign of treachery he should be thrown
overboard, but he spontaneously protested his loyalty,
and declared that the only reward he asked for was the
Queen's passport, to be preserved as an heirloom in his
family. Saint Victor returned to the shore, and when

he had seen the yacht sail with a fair wind, he rode back
to London to inform the King that all had gone off as
proposed. The King then made his own arrangements to
follow the Queen the next night. This programme could
not be carried out, for reasons that have yet to be given,
but the description of James's own adventures may be
left over for a little while.

It will not be disputed that the Count de Lauzun,
to whom, despite Riva's reticence, we give the main credit,
had managed the affair very well, and when the yacht
was moored to the wharf at Calais he counted on a very
brilliant reception at Versailles, where he hoped to pose
as the rescuer of a distressed Queen and Prince. No
doubt so good a manager carefully rehearsed the scene
in his own mind. Lauzun, the champion of distressed
royalty, was to be the centre of the picture he conjured
up as occurring at Versailles rather than the English
royalties themselves.

If such were his dreams before arriving, they were
destined to a rude disillusionment on landing. Awaiting him
was the lieutenant of the Governor of Calais and Picardy,
the Duc de Bethune-Charost, and the first question
addressed to him was an enquiry for the names of his party.
Lauzun, conceiving it to be necessary for the success of his
project that the Queen's presence should not be known,
or at least that he should, before divulging it, get his own
courier off first to carry the news to Versailles, declined to
give them. He replied in general terms that he was the
Count de Lauzun and that he had some ladies with him
under his protection. The lieutenant reported the reply
to the Duc de Bethune, who then appeared on the scene
in person. The Duc said with quiet irony to the Count
that if he did not give him the ladies' names he would have
to ask them himself.

Concealment being no longer possible, Lauzun admitted
that it was the Queen of England whom he was escorting,
and the Duc de Bethune, having welcomed Her Majesty

to France in the name of his royal master, sent off an express courier to convey the news in his own name, and not Lauzun's, to Versailles.   At the same time he informed the Queen that as there was no suitable accommodation for her at Calais, carriages would be provided as quickly as possible to drive her to Boulogne, where the Duc d'Aumont held his château in readiness for Her Majesty's reception. On December 22 the Queen reached Boulogne, where she found it reported that her husband had been captured during his attempt to follow her, and thrown into prison. The poor Queen, whose affection for her husband was immense and only stimulated by his misfortunes, declared that she would return at once to England to " share his martyrdom."

This step was naturally not at all to Lauzun's liking, as it threatened to upset not only his own plans, but those of his Government, and he employed all the arguments he could think of to dissuade the Queen from taking it. He succeeded so far as to induce her to consent to wait for the receipt of further and more definite news.   Expresses were sent off to Paris to warn Louis of this inclination, and orders were issued thereupon to hasten the preparation of St. Germains.   Indeed, it was clear that the sooner the Queen took the road for Paris the better for the full satisfaction of French political requirements.

But snow covered the country, the highways were in a bad state, and above all the definite instructions of the Great King had not been issued.   As a matter of fact, there had been a change of plan at the eleventh hour.   Orders had been given to prepare Vincennes, but Vincennes was inconveniently situated with regard to Versailles, and St. Germains was substituted for it at the last moment.   But many preparations had to be made there, and King Louis had decided to send his own carriages to Boulogne for the Queen's journey.   All these arrangements filled up the fortnight between the landing at Calais and the departure from Boulogne.

Madame de Sévigné mentions in one of her letters that "the King is sending three of his carriages with ten horses apiece, litters, pages, footmen, guards, and officers to Boulogne for the Queen of England's journey." Another chronicler avers that Louis sent pioneers to make a straight road across the country, but this need not be accepted too literally. Mary of Modena had brought away but a slender wardrobe, and while at Boulogne she was visited by the Duchess of Portsmouth (Charles II's mistress), who placed her wardrobe at the Queen's disposal. The Duchess was not received on this occasion, or, indeed, until some months later when the Stuart Court was formally established at St. Germains, but the Queen accepted some of the articles which were most indispensable to her. At last, on January 4, 1689, the Queen left Boulogne in the King's carriages, and along the whole of the route she was received with royal honours. At Beaumont, where she passed the night of the 5th, the joyful news reached her that her husband had landed at Ambleteuse the day before, and her anxiety as to his personal safety being thus removed, it was with better heart she set out on the last stage of her journey to the château, which was to be her home for thirty years.

Whatever political motives may have inspired Louvois, King Louis was actuated by a chivalric desire to succour a brother sovereign in distress when he gave shelter to the exiled Stuart King and his family. Never was royal hospitality bestowed with more cordiality, generosity, and tender regard for the feelings of those who had lost the state to which they were born and had inherited by right divine, than by the King of France on this occasion to King James and Queen Mary. He had marked out a line of conduct for himself in this rôle of combined host and protector that remains a model for all time, and he never swerved from it under the very different circumstances of the closing ten years of his reign. When he first received the exiles he was the Roi Soleil and the arbiter of Europe, but the misfortunes and calamities of the Spanish Succession War produced no change in his attitude or action.

When he learnt that the Queen had left Boulogne, he sent the Marquis Dangeau and other high courtiers to offer her a welcome in his name at Beaumont, and on the following day he drove out to Chatou, a league west of St. Germains through the forest, to await her arrival. He was accompanied in his carriage by Monseigneur (his eldest son, the Dauphin) and by Monsieur (his brother, the Duc d'Orleans), and the whole Court followed in coach and carriage to witness the meeting. Arrived at the extremity of the forest the courtiers, descending from their carriages, which lined both sides of the avenue, formed a circle, while in the centre remained the King's state carriage drawn by a team of ten horses. Shortly it was announced that the carriages of the Queen of England were in sight, and at once the King got out of his carriage, leaving the Princes, as etiquette required, to await his return.

In the first carriage were the Prince of Wales, Lady Powis, Madame Davia, and the nurses, and as the King approached the ladies were about to bring out the baby, when he stopped them with a gesture, and entering the carriage took the child in his arms, praised his beauty, and kissing him declared that he would be his protector. Then, leaving him, he found that the Queen had descended from her carriage, and hastening towards her at the little running pace, which conveys in France the height of welcome and *empressement*, and which no one but a French courtier could execute without losing dignity, the King welcomed her with both hands, kissing her lightly on both cheeks and declaring that he and everything he possessed was at her disposal.

Then, leading the way, he escorted the Queen, carrying on an animated conversation all the time, to his own carriage, into which she entered, and here Monseigneur and Monsieur were duly presented to her. The cortège then proceeed to the château, where everything was in readiness, including a guard of honour of the Maison du Roi. King Louis did the honours in person, escorting the Queen to her chamber, where on the table was placed a beautiful casket containing sixty thousand francs for her personal requirements. All the furnishing had been done by Tourolle, the King's own *tapissier*, and when the King took his departure it was with the expression of the hope that " Her Majesty, his dear sister, would find herself quite at home."

The next day there was a repetition to some extent of the same scene when King James arrived, for he was only twenty-four hours behind the Queen, and as he travelled with less ceremony his movements were more rapid. In fact, the Duke of Berwick, who, as will be described later on, had escaped with the King from England, reached St. Germains in the evening of the day of the Queen's arrival, having been sent on in advance to inform her of James's journey and near approach. King James passed the night of the 6th at Breteuil, and the next morning he set out early with the intention of visiting King Louis at Versailles before proceeding to St. Germains. This detour led to some delay in his reaching St. Germains, where the King of France had gone to receive him on his arrival.

Louis, again accompanied by Monseigneur and Monsieur, proceeded to St. Germains in the afternoon of January 7 to enquire after the health of the Queen, and to receive her husband on his arrival. It was, perhaps, owing to the delayed arrival of James that Louis had half an hour's talk with the Queen in her bedroom, where she was in bed, and when the King of England's approach was announced the grand saloon and staircase were so crowded with courtiers that Louis could not get through the crush in time to reach the courtyard, *cour d'honneur*, where he had intended to receive his guest. He was consequently obliged at the last moment to change the place of reception to the entrance of the Salle des Gardes.

Here he received James in the most cordial manner, embracing him several times, and having talked with him for a little while with great animation, he led him, holding his hand in his own, to his wife's chamber, where he addressed the Queen in these words : " Madam, I bring you a man whom you will be very glad to see." Then, making the excuse that he would go and see the young Prince, gracefully to leave the restored husband and wife alone for a little time, he retired. On his return James came out to escort him to his carriage, but Louis stopped him. " No, you are to-day my guest. To-morrow you will come and see me at Versailles as we have arranged. I will do you the honours as you will do them to me the next time I come to St. Germains, and afterwards we shall live together without ceremony." The main facts in this description are taken from Dangeau's Memoirs.

Madame de Sévigné described these scenes in a letter dated three days later.

" Le Roi fait pour ses Majestés anglaises des choses toutes divines, car n'est-ce point être l'image du Tout Puissant que de soutenir un roi chassé, trahi et abandonné comme il est ? La belle âme du Roi se plait à jouer ce grand rôle. Il fut au devant de la reine avec toute sa maison et cent carrosses à six chevaux. Quand il aperçut le carrosse du Prince de Galles il descendit et ne voulut pas que ce petit enfant beau comme un ange, à ce qu'on dit, descendit ; il l'embrassa tendrement ; puis il courut au devant de la reine qui était descendue ; il la salua, lui parla quelque temps, la mit à sa droite dans son carrosse et lui présenta Monseigneur et Monsieur qui furent aussi dans le carrosse et la mena à St. Germain où elle se trouva toute servie comme la reine, de toutes sortes de hardes et une cassette très riche avec six mille louis d'or.

" Le lendemain le roi d'Angleterre devait arriver. Le roi l'attendait à St. Germain. Il y arriva tard parcequ'il venait de Versailles. Enfin le Roi alla au bout de la salle des Gardes au-devant de lui. Le roi d'Angleterre se baissa fort comme s'il eût voulu embrasser ses genoux. Le Roi l'en empêcha et l'embrassa à trois ou quatre reprises fort cordialement. Ils se parlèrent bas un quart d'heure. Le Roi lui présenta Monseigneur, Monsieur, les princes du sang, et le Cardinal de Bonzi. Il le mena ensuite dans la chambre de la reine qui eut peine à retenir ses larmes. Ils furent quelque temps à causer, puis le Roi les mena chez le Prince de Galles où ils furent encore quelque temps et les y laissa ne voulant point être reconduit, et disant au roi Jacques : ' Voici votre maison ; quand j'y viendrai vous m'en ferez les honneurs, et je vous les ferai quand vous viendrez à Versailles.' "

Although the story is well known, it is not possible to omit all account of King James's own escape from England. Unlike the Queen's, his adventure was full of excitement, and it was only at the second attempt that he got in safety out of the country.

True to his promise to the Queen, he made all his arrangements to follow her the next night as soon as Saint Victor brought the news of her departure from Gravesend. Among his final acts of authority was to write an order to Lord Feversham (Duras), commanding his troops, to make no further opposition and to disband his men. His own departure was fixed for the night of December 20 (N.S.), and about midnight he left Whitehall accompanied by Sir Edward Hales and M. de l'Abadie, his groom of the chamber and the husband of the Prince of Wales's dry nurse. They took the first hackney coach they saw and drove to the horse ferry. Here M. de l'Abadie left them, and the King with his companion or companions, for there seems no reason to doubt that Saint Victor, although un-named, was with him, entered the boat to be rowed across to Vauxhall. The tide ran strong, and the King helped the boatman by himself taking a pair of oars. On the southern side horses, held by Sir Edward's quartermaster and a man who knew the road to act as guide, were in readiness, and the whole party reached the Medway at Alford bridge about

seven in the morning without molestation. Here a relay of
fresh horses, provided by Mr. Ralph Sheldon, one of James's
equerries, was in waiting, and Faversham was reached at
ten o'clock. The custom-house hoy had been hired,
apparently by Sheldon, to convey the party to France, but
when the passengers were on board the master stated that
he had not enough ballast on to put to sea. The King as
a practical seaman saw that this was true, but the delay
proved fatal, and a comparative trifle not merely prevented
the escape, but placed the King's life in jeopardy.

The boat dropped a little down the river to fill up with
sand, and after some hours' labour the work was finished,
and everything was again ready for a start, when three
boats filled with armed men arrived from Faversham and
boarded the hoy. Resistance being out of the question,
it was hoped that the King might not be recognised, and
indeed he was not until brought back to Faversham, where
he had some narrow escapes from mob violence, which it
is unnecessary to describe. On December 26 the King
was back in Whitehall. To the astonishment of the Prince
of Orange, and perhaps also of the King himself, his return
was made the occasion of much public rejoicing. In London
there were " such bonfires, ringing of bells and all imaginable
marks of love and esteem as made it look more like a day
of triumph than humiliation."

It was under the impression caused by this incident that
the Prince of Orange resorted to extreme measures.
He sent his Dutch Guards, under Count Solmes, to turn
out the King's Guards at Whitehall, and although the
stout-hearted old Earl of Craven would have fought to
maintain his post, James forbade useless bloodshed. When
the Palace was entirely in the hands of the Dutch, the
King retired to rest and went fast asleep. But his trials
for the day were not over. A peremptory order came late
at night that the King should leave before nine the next
morning for Ham, and despite his protests the Earl of
Middleton was forced to convey the news to his royal

master while he slept. The scene has been often described how, kneeling beside the King's bed, he whispered the message in his ear.

James protested merely against the choice of Ham as " an ill winter house and at that time almost unfurnished," and said he would much prefer to return to Rochester, where the Prince had expressed a regret that he had not stayed. This reasonable wish was conveyed to the Prince of Orange, then at Sion House, and he consented to the change. He was probably glad of it, for at this period his greatest desire was to get James safely out of the country. At the same time he sent James a blank pass for one person to leave the country, ostensibly for a messenger to proceed from him to the Queen in France; but it is impossible not to see in it the conveyance of a hint to the King that he might himself be off.

When James got to Rochester the second time there was further evidence to the same effect, for while the front of his residence was closely guarded with sentinels, the back door, and that the one nearest to the river, was left unguarded and ostentatiously open. For three nights, December 29–31 (N.S.), King James slept at Rochester while his friends were completing their plans for his escape. There were among them men whom we shall meet under different circumstances—General Sutherland, Sir John Talbot, and Lord Griffin; but the two officers who arranged for the shallop to be ready to carry the King to France were Captains Trevanion and Macdonnell (probably Ronald Macdonald), and as he was one of the party it is not unreasonable to suppose that the young Duke of Berwick took some active part in it as well. Berwick does not seem to have been with the King on the first journey to Faversham. He had been with Lord Feversham's army, and probably had not got back in time.

On the night of January 1, 1689 (N.S., or December 22, 1688, O.S.), the King retired as usual, but as soon as all was quiet Captain Macdonnell came to him, and leading him out by the back door and through the garden brought him to the place where Captain Trevanion was waiting by the boat. James, the Duke of Berwick, the two captains and a Mr. Biddulph got into the boat, which was pulled down the river to join the smack off Sheerness. The wind and tide were so much against them that they could not reach her, and the King's party was obliged to take shelter on board the " Eagle " fireship commanded by an officer of whose loyalty James felt assured. When it became broad daylight on January 2 the smack was discovered at no great distance sheltering in the Swale, and although it was still blowing half a gale the King insisted on going on board her. The next night had to be passed in shelter under the lee of the Essex shore, and the following day they got as far as the buoy of the Red Sand, where they waited throughout the night.

The wind having by this time greatly fallen they set sail early in the morning of the 4th, and making a quick passage, although not able to get into Calais, reached Ambleteuse in safety the same day. Owing to the delay in getting out of the Thames provisions ran short, and Captain Trevanion, an officer of the Royal Navy, cooked a rasher of bacon for the King in a pan with a hole in it, and gave him to drink " out of an old furred can tied round with a cord." Yet such is the force of need that James declared that he had never enjoyed a meal more heartily in his life.

And so King James landed in France on Old Christmas Day, 1688, equivalent to January 4, 1689, or fifteen days after the arrival of his wife and son at Calais as described. By a curious circumstance his younger natural son, then called Lord Henry FitzJames, who was serving as a midshipman in the English Navy, was landed by Lord Dartmouth's order from a man-of-war at Boulogne on the same day, and joined his father and the Duke of Berwick a few hours later. The Duke of Berwick was at once sent off to carry the news of the King's landing to Versailles and

St. Germains, and was received by the Queen during the evening of the day of her arrival.

One other passenger connected with these incidents claims notice. The Count de Lauzun, after the Queen took up her residence at Boulogne, left for Paris, and was ordered to Versailles to give King Louis an account of the Queen's escape. On January 1, 1689, he was given an audience of three-quarters of an hour. Madame de Sévigné, who was personally well-disposed towards him, treated the episode as almost heroic, and wrote the words : " Lauzun a trouvé le chemin de Versailles en passant par Londres." There was one person, however, who refused to change her opinion about him—the Grande Mademoiselle, the lady who had caused Lauzun to be put in the Bastille.

King Louis, before he gave the Count permission to come to Court, wrote to his cousin to inform her of his intention to do so on account of his fine conduct in rescuing the Queen of England, and he begged the lady not to be cross about it. She could not oppose the King, but she did not change her views about Lauzun, for, as Voltaire wrote : " Les Françaises portent rancune," and when he sent her a letter advising her of his return not merely to France but to the King's favour, she threw it in the fire. Her relentless attitude towards the man who had once enjoyed her special favour, and who had been named in her first will as her sole heir, strengthens the presumption that they had been secretly married. The Count was five years her junior, which may perhaps explain much that is mysterious in regard to the breach in their relations. Although Lauzun was allowed to present himself at Court, he was not restored to all his old privileges ; for instance, he did not receive the right of the *grande entrée*, and when he was created a Duc by the special request of Queen Mary a little later, it was in the restricted form, not carrying with it a French peerage (*paire de France*), and thus giving him no higher precedence.

King James paid his return visit to King Louis at Ver-

sailles on the day following his arrival at St. Germains.
He arrived there at four o'clock, but earlier in the day
an amusing little incident had occurred which brings out
the severe etiquette of the French Court and the curious
anomalies that arose from the presence of a new King
and Queen. The Dauphiness, the wife of Monseigneur,
was the first lady of the French Court, and as she was
a German Princess not altogether happy or at her ease
in her surroundings, she clung to all her privileges with
rigid tenacity. She had taken no part in the meetings
at St. Germains, and the uppermost question in her mind
was how she could avoid calling first on the Queen of
England. Queen Mary was also very sensitive about her
own dignity, and when she was informed that the Dauphiness was indisposed and confined to her apartments,
she decided to find out how far the illness was true or
simulated. She therefore instructed her Grand Chamberlain, the Marquis of Powis, to drive over to Versailles,
in the morning of January 8, and enquire in Her Majesty's
name as to the health of the Princess. He was also instructed to make a point of seeing her.

The Marquis of Powis was one of the most distinguished
members of the English aristocracy, and he and his wife,
Lady Elisabeth Somerset, had kept aloof from the
scandalous Court life of Charles II's reign. His loyalty
and devotion to his sovereign were beyond question,
and he had left behind him a fine estate, producing one
of the greatest incomes in England at that period, to follow
King James to France. But he was only a Marquis,
and the Dauphiness had her reasons for not wishing to
be seen. When Lord Powis reached Versailles he was
received by the Chamberlain and other dignitaries forming
the Court of the Princess, and in reply to his enquiries
he was informed that the Dauphiness was still indisposed
and confined to her apartments. Lord Powis replied
by begging permission to be received, as his royal mistress's
concern was so great that she would be content with

nothing short of a personal report from himself. The request was passed up to the wife of the heir of France with the lord's name; but when she heard that his title was only that of Marquis she retorted that she could not receive persons with a half-and-half sort of title, and that only Dukes could be admitted to her apartments. Her true reason will be made clear in the sequel, but the direct consequence of her refusal to receive the Marquis of Powis was that four days later James raised him to the rank of a Duke.

It was some hours after this that King James, attended by the Duke of Berwick, arrived at Versailles, where he was received by King Louis, and after some conversation, visited in their turn in their separate apartments the Dauphiness (who was in bed), the Dauphin, and Monsieur. Strict formality was observed as to the King's reception in each quarter of the Palace, and as to the exact point to which the particular Prince of the Blood on whom he called was to escort him on retiring. The two Kings then rejoined company, and passed through the grand saloons engaged in animated conversation, and the observant Dangeau reports that James displayed a complete knowledge of art, china, faience, and furniture.

The Queen's first visit to Versailles was delayed by the fact that her new dress was not ready; but when it was she drove over in state, accompanied by the Duchess of Powis and her two ladies-in-waiting, Lady Sophia Bulkeley and Countess d'Almonde (the Montecuculli), to call upon the Dauphiness. Out of consideration for her indisposition the Queen had waived the right to receive the first visit, but we are told that when she entered the Princess's bedchamber and found her up and dressed, she was somewhat taken aback. Louis had accompanied the Queen into the room, but as the Princess could not sit down in the King's presence, he considerately withdrew. The formalities were thus got over; but in this case no cordial relations were established, and indeed the Dauphiness, who died in 1693, took very little part in the ceremonies of the French Court during the last few years of her life. On the other hand, she wrote a good deal about it, and always as a severe and caustic critic, in the letters to her relations in Germany.

Many questions of etiquette arose during the first few days after the formation of the Court at St. Germains, and they were not so easily solved as on the earlier occasion of Stuart exile when Henrietta Maria abode there. Charles I's wife was not merely a Frenchwoman, but she was *fille de France* (that is, Princess of France), and easily accommodated herself to the French etiquette in which she had been brought up. But Queen Mary was not French, and the Court etiquette to which she had been accustomed was that of England, which differed materially from what was the vogue at Versailles. Two striking differences offered thorny problems in those early days.

In England the Queen did not kiss men, even Princes of the blood. In France Princes of the blood had the right to kiss the Queen of France. When Queen Mary omitted to kiss Monseigneur and Monsieur at their first meeting they were quite huffed.

A more difficult matter related to the Queen's reception of Princesses and Duchesses. By French etiquette Princesses and Duchesses were offered seats by the reigning Queen, but they were not kissed by her. By English etiquette Princesses and Duchesses were kissed by the Queen, but not offered seats. Henrietta Maria had adopted the French mode; but she had sought to extend it by kissing those Duchesses whose husbands were Marshals of France (Duchesses-Maréchales), and also the ladies of the Court (Household). This innovation was purely personal, and had not been continued after her time.

In the first receptions Queen Mary followed the English etiquette, which led to some confusion and much heart-burning among the great French ladies whose highest privilege was to be seated. The Queen had the good

c

sense to see that the position was strained and would soon become intolerable. So she referred the point at their next interview to Louis, who had been rather upset by the representations made to him on the subject. Louis liked above all things a Court in which everything went smoothly on the surface; at the same time he did not see how as host he could say anything to the Queen on the subject. Mary d'Esté, therefore, gave him sincere pleasure when she addressed him in the following words almost immediately after the first complaints began to reach his ears :—

" Dites-moi comment vous voulez que je fasse. Si vous voulez que ce soit à la mode de France je saluerai qui vous voudrez ; pour la mode d'Angleterre c'est que je ne baisais personne."

In a few delicately turned sentences King Louis intimated that, if it would not be personally irksome to the Queen, it might be as well to adopt French etiquette as had been done by Henrietta Maria. Thus were the troubled waters calmed. Monseigneur and Monsieur received the sisterly kiss, and the Princesses and Duchesses were to be offered their seats on visiting the Queen at St. Germains.

Louis certainly deserved this little consideration to be shown to him in return for all that he had done for the Stuarts ; but his opinion of Queen Mary d'Esté, which had from the first been favourable, was immensely raised by the good sense and feeling she displayed on this occasion. He repeatedly expressed the opinion in the hearing of his chief courtiers that she was " the model of what a Queen should be, and that she bore her misfortunes heroically." For the harmony of Versailles it was satisfactory that she made the same favourable impression on all the Court. Madame de Sévigné gave what may be called the verdict of society in the following description :—

" La reine est maigre, avec des yeux qui ont pleuré mais beaux et noirs, un beau teint un peu pâle, la bouche grande,

Queen Mary of Modena.
from the Painting by W. Wissing in the National Portrait Gallery.

de belles dents, une belle taille, et bien de l'esprit ; une personne fort posée qui plait fort."

There were other and more serious matters to be settled
with the new Court before the relations of the two Kings
could be regarded as placed on a permanent footing. The
Stuart sovereigns were literally penniless. Queen Mary
had brought away with her a considerable portion of her
jewels. But James had carried off nothing save the Queen's
bodkin with a great diamond in the button of it, and his
coronation ring. At least he had saved them at Faversham
on his first flight, and it is probable that he retained them
about his person. Reference has been made to the present
of 6000 pistoles in the cassette on the Queen's dressing-
table. It remained to equip King James, whose wardrobe
had to be replenished, for he had only the clothes he escaped
in, and to provide the means of maintaining the Court
of St. Germains. The arrangement was come to that
Louis should give James a sum of fifty thousand écus for
his outfit, and that he should receive a pension of fifty
thousand francs a month. Louis wanted to give him a
larger sum, but, to James's credit let it be said, he refused
to accept more than the lowest sum that would suffice to
maintain his Court. The Court itself was carried on on
the most economical lines, and the French officers who
happened to dine there reported that the King of England
kept a very poor table (*une table très médiocre*).

For the first month after the arrival at St. Germains the
guard of honour was provided by a section of the Maison
du Roi, under the command of Lieutenant Saint Vians
(Marquis de Saint Viance), who gained so much favour
with James that he rarely drove out without him. But
many followers of the Stuarts had by that time come over
from England, and about January 20 Lord and Lady
Dover and Lord Dumbarton landed at Calais. Lord
Dumbarton had commanded a regiment in the English
army under King James, and he brought with him a
hundred Irish soldiers from a corps that had been dis-

banded. It was necessary to give these men employment, and it was also desirable that the French King's personal guard, which was composed of the noblest names of France, should not be diverted to duties in attendance on a foreign prince which were entirely alien to its own proper functions. Moreover, to be part of the sad Court of St. Germains, where the *cuisine* was second-rate and the cellar empty, was straining the loyalty of men who looked upon the good living and plenty of Versailles as part of their reward. Another false position was remedied when at the beginning of February, 1689, the Maison du Roi was withdrawn from St. Germains, and it was announced that the officers and troops arrived from England would be turned into a body-guard for King James. The agreeable and capable Saint Vians was permitted to remain at St. Germains, in order to train the new guard in the French fashion.

There remains, before concluding this chapter, to refer to one important personage, Madame de Maintenon. The Stuarts were installed at St. Germains in a little Court of their own ; they had also established themselves quite naturally and without friction in the eyes of the French Court. The Government, personified in Louvois, had accepted their presence for reasons of state. They were pawns in the great game of politics that might at some stage or other be of great value. But there was another person whose opinion counted, the uncrowned Queen of France, Madame de Maintenon. Her opinion might always be computed to be worth as much as a Council of State, if not more, and it was the more necessary to know what that opinion would be in this case, because King Louis was already credited by some of his courtiers with a slightly excessive zeal for the cause of Queen Mary d'Esté, and in their view of life excessive zeal could only mean that the monarch was a little *épris.* Some ill-natured wags already began to whisper what would Madame de Maintenon say if she saw all this.

Madame de Maintenon did not often attend the Court,

but she was kept well informed of what passed there, and she saw Queen Mary and became her lifelong friend. Not thus had she treated Elisabeth Hamilton, Countess de Gramont, whose Irish audacity had so far attracted the King by the force of contrast that he gave her a special villa in the park of Versailles. For her she reserved to the end the shafts of her jealousy, even when she made her second appearance at Court with much of her beauty gone and her face disfigured by blotches. But she read Queen Mary at a single interview. The poor Queen was wholly in love with her own husband; she had forgiven him all his infidelities. The only circumstance she found trying was to see his natural children around her, and to bear their presence she schooled herself as for a martyrdom. Besides, the two women had one strong connecting link, religion. They were both profoundly *dévote*.

King James, whatever his earlier failings—on coming to the throne in 1685 he had dismissed Miss Sedley, Arabella Churchill's successor as mistress *en titre*—was at this period a strictly religious man, and he looked to his Church for support and consolation. This feeling became intensified with his later misfortunes, but even in 1689, when he certainly had not given up hope of regaining his lost crown, he was prone to regard his exile as an earthly punishment for some neglect of duty or offence. One of his first visits after the formal ceremonies at Court were concluded was to Mother Agnes, the Superioress of the Grandes Carmes, who he declared had converted him; and it was a few days after this that Madame de Maintenon made one of her rare appearances in the Grand Salon at Versailles in order to be presented to King James. From those days to the end of the sad story—for the story of fallen greatness, not through any real fault of the individuals, but by the force of circumstances, is sad—the closest intimacy existed between Madame de Maintenon and Queen Mary. She was always and under every circumstance the supporter of the Stuart cause. To her, more than to any one else, was due the recognition of James III as King after his father's death in 1701.

Enough has been said for the moment in the way of detail about the arrival of the Stuart exiles in France, their reception by the King of France, and the establishment of the separate Court of St. Germains. The points that stand out in the story are the magnanimous attitude of Louis XIV, his unexampled hospitality to his guests, the rare and bounteous consideration for the deposed sovereigns displayed in his most trifling acts, and the insistence with which he required his Court to extend to them all the attributes and homage due to royalty. Even his own son and brother were not exempt from these commands. On the other hand, it says a good deal for the tact of the Stuarts that there was never at any time the smallest friction between the Courts of Versailles and St. Germains, and that they coexisted in unclouded brotherly relationship for the long period of a quarter of a century. When the relationship terminated the great King lay dying, and the most disastrous of France's many wars was closing in a peace dictated, so far as the Stuarts were concerned in it, by the conquerors.

Chapter II

KING JAMES GOES TO IRELAND

THE political considerations of the time must be taken into careful account if the true character and full import of King James's Irish adventure are to be properly appreciated. King James had lost the crown of England by his adoption of the Roman Catholic religion, but it is very doubtful if he would have lost it even temporarily if there had not been an ambitious Protestant Prince ready to take advantage of his difficulties for the attainment of his own political ends. In other words, high policy and not religion was the uppermost thought in William's mind, and it was William's disciplined army that decided the fate of England.

The Prince of Orange was quite convinced that to succeed in his great duel with his old enemy, the King of France, the co-operation of England was indispensable. Without her money, fleet and soldiers the League of Augsburg was unequal to the task it had taken in hand, and after James's accession it seemed far from improbable that the leaguers would find France and England united against them. This was the outlook which made William throw his best troops across the North Sea into England in the autumn of 1688, whilst Louis, ill-advised, was plundering the Palatinate. The first measure was a well-timed move to secure a great political result; the other was a useless military promenade only calculated to make the German enemies more bitter.

James, dispossessed of his throne, flees to France, and England, without a national army, lies at the mercy of foreign troops. It was the only means of saving the Protestant succession, but it was a humiliation for all Englishmen of patriotic feeling. James had still, notwithstanding the dislike of the mass of the nation for his religion, a strong hold on the sentiment of the country as its lawful, legitimate King, and the Jacobites of England were probably as numerous as the Williamites, but they had no organisation, no enthusiasm, and the King to whom they were attached quitted the country and left them to do as best they could for themselves. It was creditable to James's humane disposition that he would not sanction what he called "useless bloodshed," but a king who will not allow his troops to fight when they are willing must not be surprised if they are not very enthusiastic afterwards in his cause.

King James, then, was turned out of England without striking a blow, but he had not given up the hope of recovering what he had lost, and he cherished the belief that his subjects would of their own accord return to their duty and invite him back again. But this expectation was far too nebulous to suit the plans of French statesmen. The situation in their opinion was full of peril for France, and James's pious belief in the spontaneous return of his English lieges to their duty at some future date afforded them no ground for satisfaction. They also noticed that James was somewhat inert by character, and that he seemed very content with being where he was. Most of his time was given up to the practice of his religion —a devotion which, however excellent it might be, would not bring back to him his crown. It was noted that Queen Mary was more ambitious, and that she would be glad to return again to preside over the Court of Whitehall. She was ambitious not merely for her husband's sake, but for that of her son. In her, then, the French Ministers, when they recommended active measures, had a staunch ally.

The King had lost England, but he had not lost Ireland. His change of religion made him unpopular in the former country, but it ensured him the support of the inhabitants of the other. Ireland was a Catholic country, and his measures for the establishment of a Catholic Government proved as successful in Dublin as they had been a failure in London. It was perfectly clear to Louvois that James's chance lay in Ireland, the part of his kingdom which remained absolutely loyal, and it seemed also clear that if King James were at the head of an army in Ireland, the Prince of Orange would not venture to take any of his forces out of England, and thus France would have one enemy the less on her own frontier. Vauban agreed with Louvois. He said of James's chances : " Son reste est l'Irlande. Il faut qu'il y aille." The chivalrous sympathy of Louis XIV with a brother king in trouble was edifying, but the great French Minister wanted some return for the outlay, and he felt very decidedly that the Stuarts must be turned to some useful and profitable account. The general situation was far too serious to be trifled with, and France, with practically no ally but the Turk, could not throw a chance away. As Madame de Sévigné wrote : " We are now threatened with enemies on all sides, which is a little too much. We must hope that a war in Ireland will effect a powerful diversion and prevent the Prince of Orange from tormenting us by making descents."

But the thoughts of James were not set upon being an Irish king. Ireland might be useful to him, but only as a sort of indirect means of recovering England. All his steps after reaching St. Germains show this. On January 14 he addressed an open letter to the Lords and other Members of the Privy Council in England, asking them " to concert and to send in your advice as to what is fit to be done by Us towards our returning." Almost on the same day he sent Captain Michael Roth, of whom much more will be heard, to

Dublin as the bearer of the following letter to Lord
Tyrconnell :—

" I send this bearer, Captain Rooth, to you to give
notice of my being here, and to be informed how things
are with you that accordingly I may take my measures ;
hopping you will be able to defend yourself and support
my interest there till summer at least. I am sure you
will do it to the utmost of your power, and I hope this
King here will so press the Hollanders that the Prince
of Orange will not have men to spare to attack you ;
in the mean time (till I hear from you by the bearer)
all I can get this King to doe is to send 7 or 8000 muskets,
he not being willing to venture more arms or any men
till he knows the condition you are in, so that it will be
absolutely necessary that you send back this bearer as
soon as may be with one or two persons more in order
thereunto. Just before I left Rochester I had a letter
from you, as I remember it was on the 13th of December,
which told me all was quiet with you, and I hope it is so
still, and that the Prince of Orange has sent over no force
to invade you yet. For more I refer you to this bearer,
who can give you an account how we all got away and
how kindly I have been received here."

This letter shows conclusively that at the moment of
writing James had no intention of going himself to Ireland,
and, coupled with his appeal to the English peers, it seems
safe to conclude that his hope lay in his coming to terms
with his English subjects on the basis of his return to
Whitehall by their repentance for their disloyalty, and by
some agreement leaving him free to follow his own religion
while they received his further assurances that he would
not interfere with theirs.

It is well to remember what was in James's mind when
we come to consider his conduct in Ireland. Down to the
Treaty of Ryswyck James never wavered in his belief
that the English people would recall him, and in January,
1689, he was absolutely convinced that they would very

soon tire of the presence of the Prince of Orange and his foreign army. As for Ireland, he only hoped that Tyrconnell would be able to hold it against invasion. James himself had no hope of recovering England by means of an Irish army. He repelled the suggestion to take this step when first proposed in 1687-8, and he knew that in 1689 an Irish army would appear in the eyes of Englishmen just as much a foreign one as William's army of Dutchmen, Danes, Prussians and Huguenots, who at least were of the same creed and observed a stricter discipline. James was by no means the fool in all matters that Louvois took him for. He knew that to bring an unrestrained pillaging Irish army into England was the sure way to destroy all the chances which the Stuart cause possessed. Besides, let it be recorded to his credit, he loved his country better than his throne, and throughout the whole of his life he showed that by his country he meant England.

These views were quite naturally different from those held by French Ministers; but while the strategical importance of Ireland as a base against England was sufficiently obvious, they had no information as to the state of things in Ireland, and as to the forces at the disposal of its Viceroy. They accordingly supplied Captain Roth with a travelling companion in the person of the Marquis de Pointis, a naval artillery officer, who was to prepare a report on the subject.

There was a good deal of correspondence passing at this time between Ireland and France, and one matter of common enquiry was as to the treatment Louis extended to James. To some one asking this question an English officer in the entourage of the King of England at St. Germains replied in a Latin version of the scriptural text :—

> " Dixit Dominus domino meo—
> Sede a dextris meis donec ponam
> Inimicos tuos scabellum pedum tuorum."

" Sit thou on my right hand and I will make thy enemies thy footstool."

The two emissaries reached Dublin on January 18 at a critical moment. Although five-sixths of Ireland was Catholic and subject to Tyrconnell, the Protestants were drawing together at Enniskillen and Londonderry, and many of the Viceroy's own Council belonged to the same party. Among them was Lord Mountjoy, unquestionably the best general in Ireland, and supported by two of the best trained and best armed regiments in the country. Tyrconnell was afraid of his capacity and influence, but he did not know how to dispose of him.

The arrival of the King's letter provided him with an excuse. He proposed to Lord Mountjoy that he should go to St. Germains, and explain to the King that their position was such that they had no alternative to making the best terms they could with the Prince of Orange. This view entirely accorded with Lord Mountjoy's own opinion, and in order that the clearest light may be shed on this burning subject, free from all political and religious bias, I must record that Lord Mountjoy held this opinion because he believed that it was the only way to protect the Irish Protestants against the reprisals of the Irish Catholics. Lord Mountjoy fell into the trap and agreed to go. With him went as joint envoy the Lord Chief Baron, Sir Stephen Rice, a Catholic in Lord Tyrconnell's confidence. They left Dublin on January 20, in order to return by the vessel which had brought Roth and de Pointis. They reached St. Germains early in February, and Sir Stephen Rice lost no time in discharging his secret instructions, which were to assure King James that Ireland was loyal to his person, and to advise him to prevent Mountjoy's return as the Protestant leader and the most formidable enemy of his cause.

This view of the situation suited the French hopes and plans, but it was necessary to await the return of the French emissary before arriving at a final decision. On

February 21 M. de Pointis returned to Paris with the news that Lord Tyrconnell was supreme in Ireland and that he had an army of 80,000 men, adding that all that was needed to ensure a great triumph was King James's presence in Dublin. On the very day that M. de Pointis came back Lord Mountjoy was sent to the Bastille, where he remained for three years. Thus did Louvois carry the day. King James was put in the position of being unable to refuse to go to Ireland without incurring the charge of cowardice and of seeming to abuse the hospitality which had been so cordially bestowed on him and his by the French Court. But he consented to go with mixed feelings. He was being forced to a land he knew not, to strange surroundings, and called upon to deal with a complicated situation outside all his experiences. England he knew, France, the home of his childhood, he knew, but Ireland was beyond his ken. Madame de Sévigné read his mind when she wrote : " He seems to prefer to remain where he is."

But although Louvois was set upon King James's going to Ireland, he was not disposed to be very lavish in rendering him any tangible assistance, and on one point he was quite resolved. Not a French regiment should leave the country. France wanted all her troops for her own home needs. By this time Louvois had partially awoke to the stupendous blunder he had committed by the revocation of the Edict of Nantes, which dealt the power of Louis XIV a blow somewhat similar to that experienced by the Great Napoleon through the imprudent Russian campaign. His friend Vauban, at this very juncture, in also opposing the despatch of French troops to Ireland, supplied him with a memorandum estimating the direct loss that the Revocation had inflicted on the country. From this document the following passage may be taken :—

" The Revocation of the Edict of Nantes has cost France the loss of between 80,000 and 100,000 persons, and those among the most intelligent and instructed classes of the nation. She has lost at least 30 million livres of revenue. Many of her special arts and industries, much of her trade, have been ruined. The fleets of her enemies have been reinforced by 8000 good sailors. Their armies have been increased by five or six hundred of our best officers and 10,000 excellent troops."

Vauban did not exaggerate. The France of 1689 was a considerably poorer country than she had been only four years before. With enemies on all sides of her it would have been folly to send troops to Ireland. King James was to go to Ireland, but all the aid that France could give him was some arms, some money, and a few officers. Even under these heads the aid could not be very great. The French arsenals were somewhat bare, the revenue had fallen, and there were not more than enough officers to supply the armies then in the field in Flanders, Alsace, Savoy, and Catalonia. Besides, had not Pointis reported that there were 80,000 men in Ireland with the colours, and were there not several hundred English, Scottish, and Irish officers at St. Germains, with whom we shall make closer acquaintance as this narrative proceeds? Clearly there was no need for French soldiers, but even if there had been they would not have been sent. So James for very shame's sake was committed to the Irish expedition. It was one of those situations created for a man in difficulties to which he had been no willing party, but which could not be evaded. The whispering at Versailles and St. Germains that something was on the tapis for the exiled King grew into the open report—" King James is going to Ireland."

The report was first spread as the outcome of a striking incident at Versailles. King Louis was holding his Court late in the evening of one of those critical days of February, when a messenger arrived with a private letter from King James for King Louis. King Louis glanced through it, and then, wishing to give those present the latest news, handed it to the Archbishop of Rheims to read to the company. The Archbishop began to read the note aloud, but suddenly stopped short. He had come to a secret passage, and being a man of tact was trying to skip it. The King, realising his dilemma, snatched the paper from his hand, and those present were very anxious, as Dangeau remarked, to learn the secret. They were not enlightened at the time, but we need not be reticent. King James had expressed his willingness to start for Ireland.

While these important events were in progress, King James was making the best of his troubles, taking part in stag and wolf hunts in the forest of Marly, and it was noted that he was always in front with the dogs. He also supped several times with Louis at Marly, and these entertainments were always turned to account for the discussion of serious business. During this period the Duke of Berwick was coming more to the front, and acquired considerable influence in his father's councils. He had been made a Knight of the Garter before James left London, but no opportunity had offered to place his arms and banner in St. George's Chapel. Notwithstanding this defect, James gave him permission to wear the Star of the Order. About the same time Louis invested him with authority to raise a regiment to be called by his own name, and to be composed exclusively of Irish, English, and Scottish Catholics. It was to be of exceptional strength, in forty companies of 100 men each, and a rallying-place was fixed for it upon the Somme. So far as strength went the regiment never existed save on paper. There is a reference to the assembly of this corps at Rhue, near Abbeville, and to the regiment numbering 400 men besides 150 officers, all fugitives from England. There were also 300 cavalrymen or dragoons at the same place, but nothing had been decided as to their grouping.

Early in February the troops belonging to King James began to be moved from Paris and St. Germains towards the sea-coast. On February 5 young John Hamilton (the cadet Hamilton) arrived from Ireland, and on the 17th he left " with all the English and Scottish officers and soldiers " (Irish not mentioned by Dangeau) to join Berwick for Ireland. Berwick himself had left two days earlier for Orleans with marching orders for Brest, which had been fixed on for the place of rendezvous. Finally, Dangeau makes the first reference to an incident, to which fuller reference will have to be made later on, in the following passage : " The elder Hamilton (Richard) goes to Scotland to see Tyrconnell on safe conduct from Prince of Orange, and his promise not to join the troops." It need only be noted that to accord with the facts, Dangeau's entry in February must be ante-dated by nearly two months.

While these movements were in progress Louis was selecting the French officers who were to go to Ireland. The first officer chosen was the Maréchal de Camp Maumont de Fontange (wrongly spelt as Monmont), a soldier of merit. To him were joined Pusignan and Léry (Marquis de Girardin) as Brigadiers of infantry and cavalry respectively. Pointis, having been to Ireland, was sent back in charge of the cannon and munitions of war. He had under him twenty gunners, four carpenters, and two smiths. Another French officer who played a great part in the expedition was Boisseleau.

Finally, a French Lieutenant-General named Roze (not Rosen) was given the command-in-chief, and to denote his superior rank James shortly after his arrival in Ireland made him a Marshal. Roze was not French, but a Russian. His contemporaries considered him a good cavalry leader, but no general. Louis could not have made a worse choice, for to a want of true military capacity Roze added a savage nature and an inclination towards ruthless war. The Duke of Berwick said of him that " he was subject to passion even to a degree of madness."

Lauzun was to have had the command because it was thought that he would be the most agreeable person to King James, but his head had been turned by his getting back to Court, and he declined to go unless the very rarely conceded style of Captain-General were bestowed upon him. Louis declined, and Roze got the post. As some compensation for the disappointment James made Lauzun a Knight of the Garter. Louis also promised James the services of twenty captains, twenty lieutenants, and twenty cadets, but as they did not sail in the first flotilla reference will be made to them later on.

These arrangements were pushed on with the idea that James's departure should be as speedy as possible. A squadron of thirteen men-of-war, six frigates, and three fire-ships, under the command of Admiral Gabaret, was waiting in readiness at Brest. On February 25 James drove into Paris to offer up his prayers for success at Notre Dame. He then dined with Lauzun at his hotel in company with the Archbishop of Paris and M. Jeannin, and after dinner he visited the Convent of the English Sisters, called on the Grande Mademoiselle and the other members of the Royal Family who happened to be in Paris, and then drove to Versailles, which he reached at seven in the evening. Louis was waiting to receive him for what was intended and hoped to be their last interview, and for the occasion the Court had assembled in great numbers. Both Kings wore violet in mourning for the Queen of Spain, who had just died. When the hour for James's departure for St. Germains arrived, Louis made him a little farewell speech concluding with the words : " I hope, sir, never to see you again. Nevertheless, if Fortune decrees that we are to meet, you will find me always the same as you have found me." (" Je souhaite, Monsieur, ne vous revoir jamais. Cependant si la fortune veut que nous nous revoyions vous me trouverez toujours tel que vous m'avez trouvé.")

On the following day James received visits from Monsieur and Madame, and most of the princes of the blood at St. Germains. Queen Mary, who was believed to be enceinte, fainted, and James kissed all the princes of the blood.

D

On the same day James refused permission to the young
Duke of Richmond to accompany the expedition " because
he was too young and too little." There may have been
another reason for this decision, as he and his mother,
Louise de Querouaille, Duchess of Portsmouth, had been
accused of whispering against the legality of the birth of
the Prince of Wales. The young Duke had had a special
audience with Louis on the subject, and received the assurance that the King had never credited the report that he
could have said anything so baseless. Events will show
that there was not much love lost between James and his
brother's son. Indeed, the complications already existing
in the French Court by the recognition of so many of
Louis's own bastards did not need any addition through
the presence of the illegitimate offspring of foreign
kings.

On February 27 Louis drove over to St. Germains to
take farewell of his guest, whose departure was fixed for
the next morning. James had asked permission for Saint
Vians to accompany him as commander of his body-guard,
but Louis refused because he thought that Saint Vians
(apparently the Marquis de Saint Viance) had been
wounded too often. He nominated in his place d'Estrades,
another officer of the Maison du Roi, and it is curious to note
that the English papers, in describing the departure of
James, stated that he was accompanied by Marshal
d'Estrades, whom the French King had lent him to
command his army. The army rank of d'Estrades was
Maréchal de Camp, which was two grades below that of
Marshal of France, and may be considered as the equivalent
of Major-General. The Marshal d'Estrées, Governor of
Brittany, was in supreme charge of the arrangements for
the despatch of the expedition from Brest. The similarity
of names may have led to some confusion ; but d'Estrées'
part in the Irish expedition began and ended at Brest.

The parting of the two kings was naturally of the most
cordial character, and while the formalities of ceremony

had to be observed there was evidence of deeper feelings being aroused. James addressing Louis, who had just referred to his having placed 500,000 écus (an error of the chroniclers) and 10,000 muskets at his disposal, received the reply : " Sir, you have forgotten only one thing, and that is to arm me," whereupon Louis unbuckles his own sword and fastens it to James's side. Queen Mary overflows with tears, and another woman present, Madame de Sévigné, records the impression of the hour for all time : " Magnanimity could not go further, the King (Louis) has surpassed all the heroes of romance."

In the early morning of February 28, 1689, James left St. Germains in his state-coach drawn by six horses, with Lauzun in the carriage. He drove across Paris to reach the high-road for Orleans, and at Bourg la Reine, five miles south of Paris, he found his travelling carriage waiting for him. Here Lauzun and the state-coach are left behind while James goes on accompanied by Powis, Melfort, and others, with halting-places fixed at Orleans, Tours, and Angers. This programme has to be departed from, for James's carriage breaks down, and he has in consequence to accept the hospitality of the Duc de Chaulnes at Roche Bernard.

Twenty-four hours after the King left St. Germains, Lady Melfort, refusing to be left behind, followed her husband with servants in four travelling carriages, and as she was the only lady in the expedition the fact deserves special notice. Lady Melfort was Euphemia Wallace, daughter of Sir Thomas Wallace, Lord Justice of Scotland, and she gave her husband nine children, her eldest son (the second Duke) marrying eventually the widow of James's natural son, the Duke of Albemarle. D'Avaux, the French ambassador, of whom we are now about to speak, describes Melfort as in a state of constant jealousy about his wife, and the anxiety to accompany her husband in 1689 has just been mentioned. Even the Duchess of Powis, who was certainly deeply attached to her husband, remained at St. Germains, but Lady Melfort would not be consoled or left behind.

Many men of all our races and religions followed James to Brest. The Duke of Northumberland, one of the sons of Charles II, scarcely landed at Calais, hastened there to join him, and arrived in time. Lord Dover also posted there, arriving too late and having to follow by a later relay. But the only woman to sail from Brest was Euphemia, Countess of Melfort, while Queen Mary d'Esté, who would have liked to go, retired for a time to Poissy with her infant son. " She is always crying and in such a nephritic state," declares Madame de Sévigné, " that stone is apprehended." When she returned to St. Germains it was to live in close retirement, and the world was officially informed that during her husband's absence the Queen of England would receive only one day in the week.

While the parade of the affair was being carried along by the kings and the courtiers, Louis's Ministers were attending to the real business, so that the expedition to Ireland should promote the interest of France. The soldiers had been named. It was necessary to send with James a sound adviser who, while guiding his policy for practical ends, would make those ends serve French policy. Louvois chose the ablest diplomatist in his service, Jean Antoine de Mesmes, Count d'Avaux. Diplomacy was the birthright of his family. His immediate forbears had signed in the name of France treaties ranging from that of St. Germains in 1570 to that of Munster in 1648. He himself had been plenipotentiary at Nimeguen, and during ten years he was ambassador at the Hague. He therefore knew the Prince of Orange, his ambitious views and his ways of doing business, and as he was going to be pitted against that Prince, no more qualified person could have been found. Besides, the Count d'Avaux was a man of great method and common sense. His axiom was to do the work that lay ready to hand and not to take up idle schemes outside it. A better selection could not have been made.

Whoever was responsible for the Irish failure, it was certainly not the Count d'Avaux.

The Count d'Avaux received his instructions in a document signed at Marly, on February 11, 1689, by Louis and countersigned by Louvois. After mentioning that the aid rendered to the King of Great Britain in arms, munitions of war, officers, and money was as great as Louis's own excessive requirements against a great number of enemies allowed, the representative of France was warned to remember the interests of his own Government, as well as to see that King James was acting prudently for the promotion of his own. While these were general instructions, the specific point of doing all in his power in reconciling Protestants and Catholics, and especially in assuring the former that they would be safe from molestation and injury, was not to be forgotten. He was also instructed to send information as to the state of things in Ireland as frequently as possible, and to forward several copies of the same letter by different routes so as to ensure one at least of them reaching Paris. Finally, he was entrusted with the sum of 500,000 livres, of which 300,000 were to be paid to the order of James as he required, while the remaining 200,000 were to form a secret reserve, which the Count was only to disclose when he thought a real need for it existed.

The instructions to the diplomatist were supplemented by those to the general. General Maumont was their recipient, for at the time of their being drafted no officer of higher rank had been named, and after General Roze's appointment this part of the arrangement remained undisturbed. The division of responsibility between D'Avaux, Maumont, and de Pointis was to lead to some confusion and bickering among the French representatives in Ireland, but we shall come to that later on.

Maumont was to take with him 10,000 muskets, 100,000 charges of powder, the same allowance of tinder and lead. Whether it was impossible to provide the arms, or that the French intendants held them back for reasons of their own, it is certain that Maumont did not take this quantity with him. The totals given in the French War Office list are 3000 swords, 16,000 sabres, 19,000 belts, 600 pairs of pistols, 500 single pistols, 500 muskets, and 500 guns. It is very dubious if even this mixed assortment of weapons was ever sent in its entirety. De Pointis was appointed to the charge of the material, and he was to select twenty naval gunners, four carpenters, and two smiths as the nucleus of an artillery corps. Maumont was also supplied with funds. He was to take with him 300,000 livres in gold, but he was to keep the matter secret, and even if the Duke of Berwick were to ask him what the sum was he was to reply in general terms, " between 50 and 60,000 écus." A further instalment of 200,000 livres, bringing the total up to 500,000 (making altogether a million livres advanced by Louis through D'Avaux and Maumont), was to follow by the second relay, which was to consist of the Berwick regiment, etc.

Maumont had other instructions. He was not to land until he had ascertained that Ireland still held out for King James, and also that Lord Tyrconnell was loyal, for it was not known in France whether the reports of his overtures to William of Orange were genuine or not. If he was not satisfied on both these points, he was to return at once to Brest without landing arms or money. On the other hand, Maumont might promise in Louis's name that if Ireland held out till the winter he would send over French troops. Louis also hoped to be able to send another half-million livres during the summer, as he understood " money was very scarce in Ireland." With the view of promoting trade also, he removed all customs dues from Irish goods excepting wool; but wool was precisely the Irish produce for which free entry was most desired. These instructions show that Louis's personal chivalry towards James was not displayed at the cost of prudence in the regulation of the details of the enterprise.

Before he left Paris King James requested that the sum of 20,000 livres out of the sum placed in D'Avaux's charge should be sent to London for the use of Lord Preston ; and Lord Waldegrave, James's ambassador in Paris, who had married his daughter Henrietta FitzJames, undertook to see that it was safely remitted. Before his departure from Paris King James had sent Sir George Porter on a mission to Rome to interest the Pope in his cause, and he also arranged for Mr. George Skelton to proceed to Vienna on a similar errand to the Emperor. Louis provided the expenses at an agreed sum, but when James had started for Brest Skelton represented that the sum was inadequate and that he ought to be allowed more. Louis refused the request, and when the matter was reported to James at Brest he was very annoyed and angry, declaring that the allowance was quite sufficient if Skelton went alone. It seemed clear to the King that Skelton had raised his terms because he wished to take his wife. In the end Skelton went alone.

Neither of these envoys did any good. Sir George Porter remained at Rome three months, but eventually he came away quite disconsolate because the Pope was thoroughly in sympathy with the enemies of France. Skelton brought back a letter from the Emperor Leopold, to whom James had appealed not merely in the name of religion, but for the sacred cause of Kings, that gave him but little comfort. Leopold, after employing the commonplaces of civility in reference to James's deplorable experience of the instability of human affairs, went on to declare that it was due to his " listening to the fraudulent suggestions of France," and made a special grievance not merely of the French plundering of the Palatinate, but also of their concluding an alliance with the Turks. The Emperor professed sorrow at his brother's troubles, but would render no assistance in overcoming them. Skelton does not appear to have been received by the Emperor, who only recognised the Earl of Carlingford, duly accredited as James's ambassador, at his Court.

These replies could not have left any doubt in James's mind that his sole support must come from the side of France. The leaguers of Augsburg were not to be detached from one another by the difference of religion between some of their members.

As soon as it was definitely known at Brest that King James had quitted Paris, the frigate " Soleil d'Afrique " was sent, with Lord Dungan on board, to Ireland to announce the coming of the King. It was assumed that he would follow close on its heels, but the frigate returned to Brest before the fleet had departed. Contrary winds entailed ten or twelve days' further delay, but on March 15 all seemed well and anchors were raised. King James's last request before communication with the land was severed was that the French should send him some bakers and a man who could make powder. The departure was further delayed by a sharp gale, and the King's ship came into collision with that commanded by M. de Rosmadek. The consequences would have been serious but for the skill displayed by that officer. The damage having been repaired and the gale abating, sail was set at five in the evening of March 17, and within a couple of hours the flotilla had passed out of sight. The voyage was rapid and quite uneventful, and in the morning of March 22 the fleet anchored off Kingsale.

Although the bulk of the officers and men of King James's army, who had followed him to France, did not leave Brest until the second flotilla sailed under Château Renaud at the end of April, Admiral Gabaret's squadron conveyed altogether eighty-three Jacobite and French officers in addition to the King, Lady Melfort, and their servants. The following is a fairly complete and accurate list of the passengers, with many of whom we shall make closer acquaintance. Many of the Irish officers had served with Dumbarton's force in England, others had belonged to the French army, chiefly in the " gensdarmes." Others again, like Taaffe and de Lacy, had come from Lorraine and Austria to take the hazard of recovering the estates lost by their families in 1649–51. A large proportion of the officers ended their career on the field of honour during the twenty-five years covered by this narrative. In the list occurs the name of at least one traitor, the Chevalier de Murray.

List of persons who sailed with King James from Brest in March, 1689 (according to list of Marshal d'Estrées). The names are given correctly where identified; otherwise the French spelling is followed :—

Ship	Passengers
The " Saint Michel."	H.M. King James II, the Duke of Berwick and his brother, Count d'Avaux, Lord Melfort, Lord Thomas Howard, and the servants required for their service.
„ " Courageux."	Sir Stephen Rice, Chief Baron, Mr. Trinder, Mr. Collins, Lord Brittas, Capt. Edmund Burke (? de Burgh), Mr. Lane, Mr. Sarsfield, Mr. Archdeacon, Mr. Rayne, Mr. Clinton.
„ " Furieux."	Lady Melfort, her servants and suite, Mr. Drummond, son of the Scottish Chancellor (Perth), and Colonel Wauchope.
„ " François."	Captain Talbot, Lieutenant Boulger, Lieutenant Bourke (? de Burgh), Lieutenant Baker, Lieutenant Kelly and Mr. Plunkett.
„ " Apollon."	Duke of Powis and his suite, Captains McCarthy, Corbet, Dicconson, Lieutenants Tobin and McCarthy, Messrs. Nagle, O'Neill, Butler, Hussey, and Lavary.
„ " Fort."	MM. de Léry, de Pusignan, and de Pointis, Captain Nangle, Messrs. Rivedan, King, Roche, and Burke.
„ " Entreprenant."	MM. de Roze, de Maumont, Boisseleau, Colonel Hamilton (John), M. de St. Didier, Chevalier Vadré (Vaudrey ?).
„ " Sage."	Colonel Sutherland, Colonel Dorington, Captain Luttrell, Captain O'Gara, Captain Fitzpatrick, Lieutenants Binguen, Bourke, and Power, and Messrs. Nugent, Bourke, Lucas, and Corvido.

Ship	Passengers
The " Duc."	Colonel Sarsfield (Patrick), Col. McEllicott, Sir Neil O'Neil, Chevalier Baud, Captain Ulick Burke, Lieutenants Burne, Callaghan, Rayne, Murphy, Bourk, and Captain MacDonald.
„ " Faucon."	Sir — Murray, Capt. Arundel, Lieutenant Plowden, Lieutenant Baptiste.
„ " Neptune."	Major de Lacy, Mr. Taaffe, Messrs. Sarsfield, Nugent, Acton, Carroll, Nagle, and Oglethorpe.
	83 names, excluding the King and Lady Melfort.

Brief reference must be made to Scotland, the native kingdom of the House of Stuart. The Jacobite party was supreme in the Highlands, and possessed a military leader of remarkable capacity in the Viscount Dundee. But the Lowlands were Presbyterian to a man and regarded a Catholic as outside the law. The Duke of Hamilton was prominent among those who had invited the Prince of Orange over, and at his instigation the Presbyterian Lords seized the Government at Edinburgh. The Earl of Perth, the Chancellor, was captured as he was escaping in a fishing-boat and sent to Stirling Castle. Lord Dundee withdrew to the Highlands. The Duke of Gordon held Edinburgh Castle for the King, and a smaller garrison occupied the Bass Rock. While the Irish Jacobites were animated principally by love of Ireland and the desire to make her independent, the Scottish Jacobites were impelled by personal loyalty to the Stuarts.

James had a warm feeling for Scotland, almost as great as he had for England, and when he heard that a Scots Parliament had been summoned by the usurped authority of the Prince of Orange he sent a letter signed by Melfort to warn those who rebelled against his authority of the consequences of their action, and promising those who returned to their loyalty his full pardon and forgiveness. This letter, written on the " St. Michel " immediately before the fleet sailed from Brest, was entrusted to Mr. Crane, but before

it reached its destination King James's followers had
retired behind the Grampians. The embassies to Rome
and Vienna, the appeal to the subjects of " our antient
native kingdom of Scotland," were minor incidents in the
main enterprise which, thanks to French insistence, was
now to be concentrated on the complete establishment of
James's authority in Ireland, with the view of making it a
thorn in the side of the Prince of Orange. James himself
was not enthusiastic about the enterprise, and went into it
half-heartedly, and only because he could not refuse to go
without offending the French. He would have gone to
Scotland quite willingly. With regard to England he was
fully persuaded that he had only to wait with a little
patience to be recalled by his repentant subjects. But
towards Ireland he had no inclination, and when he got
there he could only think of how he might get away from
it into Scotland or England. But this is anticipating.

Chapter III

A GREAT VICEROY

WITHOUT wandering too far into other fields of history, it may be said here for the sake of clearness in the narrative that the Jacobite movement in Ireland, which began with Lord Tyrconnell's appointment to the Viceroyship in 1687, was the direct sequel to the war waged by the Irish Confederation in the royal cause of Charles I against the Parliament and Cromwell. That war, long drawn out and marked by many of the savage incidents not peculiar, as Protestant writers affirmed, to Ireland, but common to all wars in that age, had led to the wholesale confiscation of the estates of the Catholic nobility and landed gentry of the country. Then occurred the great migration of the native Irish nobility, who with only their pedigrees in their pockets and their swords by their sides left their homes to seek their fortunes in foreign lands. They went to Spain, the Netherlands, and Austria ; very few on this occasion going to France. The emigration of 1649–51, unlike its successor in 1690–1, was that of a class limited in numbers, scattered over a certain period and following different routes as opportunity occurred. If we put the emigration at a total of 5000 individuals we probably exceed the truth, but they represented the cream of the native Irish chiefs, whose ancestors had fought under Art Macmurrogh against Henry VIII and under the two O'Neils against Elizabeth.

These men had lost their estates, their castles had been destroyed, and in the pedigrees of more than one illustrious

Hiberno-Austrian family the founder of the old house on foreign soil recites as the cause of his presence, " domibus ab Cromwello raptis." The lands were given to others, and the others were " the tinkers and tailors " who had been turned into soldiers by the iron discipline of the Lord Protector. A fresh plantation of Englishry had been effected in Ireland on terms very advantageous to these new settlers. History does not contain a more striking instance of the spoils to the victors.

But the period of Republican triumph was brief, a day of reckoning came for the King-killers, and the Restoration of the Stuarts raised hope once more in the hearts of the Irish and other exiles who had lost all for their cause. The hopes of the English and Scottish cavaliers were to be realised, those of the Irish were to be dashed to the ground. Charles II publicly and solemnly declared that he would see them righted. In his speech to his first Parliament, he said : " I hope I need not put you in mind of Ireland, and that they alone shall not be without the benefit of my mercy. They have shown much affection to me abroad, and you will have a care of my honour and what I have promised them." These were fine words ; unfortunately they were not matched by acts. It would require much space to show how and why the Irish Catholics did not recover their estates. It must suffice to say here that the Cromwellian confiscations were left undisturbed. Ten years of recent occupation were held of greater force than ten centuries of prior possession. So much for Charles II and his promises.

A new situation was created with the accession of his brother, James II, in 1685. James was a declared Catholic where his brother was a concealed, and as England was essentially Protestant it was a brave thing on James's part, whatever we may think of its wisdom (all religious controversies being not merely foreign to this historical narrative but repugnant to my mind), to proclaim that his religion was different from the Church and sentiment of his

principal Kingdom.   The matter has a direct bearing
on our subject. If James had not become a Catholic there
would have been no Jacobite Movement in Ireland and
no Irish Brigade in France.

No elaboration is needed to show that the Catholics of
Ireland at once became an important political factor in the
calculations of a Catholic King, and there was a man in
James's confidence who did not fail to impress upon him
the wisdom of utilising the military resources placed at
his disposal by the religious zeal and sympathy of the Irish
Catholics. This man was Colonel Richard Talbot, whose
policy in the cause of James closely resembled that of
Strafford half a century earlier on behalf of Charles I.
Macaulay, following the English libellers of the day,
has given a very unfavourable picture of Dick Talbot,
but Macaulay's Whig prepossessions destroyed or deadened
his sense of a historian's duty, and in this particular instance
he especially allowed his pen to run riot, and he laid the
colours on thick in the conviction that no one would ever
think it worth their while to take up the cause of vindicating
Lord Tyrconnell from his scurrilous attacks. It will not be
difficult to show that, although Tyrconnell was not on
the same plane as Strafford in statesmanship, he was not
the poor creature that Macaulay's diatribes have led the
English reader so long to believe, and that he was a man of
honour and of rare devotion to his King.

The Talbots of Cartown, in the county of Kildare,
were descendants of the House of Shrewsbury. Their
establishment in Ireland dated no farther back than the
sixteenth century, but although among the latest recruits
of English immigrants they, like so many other of the
Norman settlers, had become more Irish than the Irish.
When Sir William Talbot, upon whom James I had conferred a baronetcy, was sent by the Irish Confederates to
plead their cause before the House of Commons, he made
an oration of such striking eloquence that it was decided
to send him to the Tower, " because Ireland will never be

subdued whilst it possesses such an orator." By his wife, Alison Netterville, Sir William Talbot had a large family, of whom there were eight sons and at least one daughter, Mary, who married Sir John Dungan, second Baronet, whose eldest son, William, afterwards became Earl of Limerick. Another of his sons, named Walter, was with Richard Talbot at Madrid in 1653, and afterwards served some time in the French army. The fact that Walter Dungan was only a year or so younger than his uncle Richard has led to some confusion and uncertainty.

Of the order in which these sons came by age it is impossible to speak with any confidence, except that the eldest was named Robert and succeeded to the baronetcy. Some writers have placed Richard fifth in order, but there seems no doubt that he was, as Father Anselm stated in his funeral oration before King James at the English Church in Paris, the youngest. The names of the sons appear to have been Robert, Peter, Gilbert, John, James, Thomas, Garret, and Richard. The Griffith Talbot, who died in London in 1724 at the age of eighty-two, must have been a nephew and not a brother as assumed in some of the peerages. The confusion in distinguishing among the members of the Talbot Family is excusable, seeing that there were fourteen members of the Cartown family serving James II in 1689, and all my efforts to fix the relationship of one called Buno Talbot have failed. It is also hazardous to establish the connection of Colonel Richard Talbot of the Bastille and Luzzara fame with the Duke, although there is no reasonable doubt that he was his natural son. Of Sir William's sons the only two to find a place in history were Peter, who joined the Order of Jesuits and became titular Archbishop of Dublin, and Richard, with whom we are chiefly concerned.

The date of Richard's birth is uncertain, but it is believed to have taken place in 1630, and he is supposed to have received his first commission as a cornet of horse in Charles I's Irish army when he was only eleven years of age. If such a commission was issued it is to be regarded as purely honorific, for he remained at home receiving his education, chiefly from his mother, until he was fifteen. At that age he may have joined Lord Preston's army, and was present with it at the rout outside Dublin in 1647. He was taken prisoner on this occasion, but does not seem to have been detained long (probably being exchanged or released on account of his youth), for in the following year he was one of the defenders of Drogheda against Cromwell.

He was severely wounded during the assault on and sack of the place, and left for dead on the ground. It was said that he lay there for three days, and owed his life to an Englishman called Commissary Reynolds who, noticing some signs of life in what was thought to be a dead body, took him into the town and gradually brought him round. If the story is true that Reynolds had great difficulty in saving him from a fanatical brother soldier who wished to kill him when he declared himself to be a Catholic, a guardian angel must surely have watched over the young Talbot. He is included among the twelve Irish survivors, including men, women and children, of the sack of Drogheda. When he had recovered from his wounds Reynolds provided him with a woman's dress, and in this garb he finally escaped from the town. As Talbot was considerably above the stature of even tall men—he was sometimes called Goliath at the Court of Charles II—the manner in which he escaped has sometimes roused incredulity. After the conclusion of the war in Ireland, and when leave was given to the Catholics to go abroad, Richard Talbot went to Spain. He and his nephew, Walter Dungan, were at Madrid in 1653, and when they learnt that Charles II had fixed his Court at Breda they proceeded to join him. This step seems to have been taken on the invitation of Peter Talbot, who was one of the principal advisers of the Duke of York.

At this juncture James, Duke of York was serving in the French army in Flanders under Turenne, and had greatly distinguished himself by his courage. Richard Talbot served with him, and in the royalist camp many daring schemes were suggested, and found favour with the young bloods who were growing up to manhood with the exiled princes. There was the Wogan affair, when that young officer and eight others made their way, in fulfilment of a pledge, to London, and rode through the length of England in an open manner to join the Stuart partisans in the Highlands. They reached their destination in safety, and after passing through these great dangers Wogan died through the neglect of a trivial wound.

Dick Talbot, in the full force and flush of his youth, was not to be outdone at this kind of game even by another Irishman. He went over to London, in 1655, on no Platonic mission. Nothing less than the assassination of the arch-enemy Cromwell would satisfy him. There had been a blood feud on his side since Drogheda. He crossed the Channel, he resided in London for a time, and then was arrested before his scheme had taken form in his own mind. He was brought before Cromwell himself, who cross-questioned him, and then he was consigned to prison for further examination. He had a good supply of guineas in his pocket, and induced his guards on the way to the Tower to enter a wine shop. Here he drank with them hard and fast until all except himself were under the table, whereupon he escaped while they were sleeping off the effects of their debauch. He reached Brussels on January 3, 1656, and was soon appointed to command as Lieutenant-Colonel the regiment named after the Duke of York, and composed chiefly of men from Munster.

When the Restoration took place he returned to the Duke of York, to whom he was appointed gentleman of the bed-chamber, at a salary of £300 a year. He was one of the prominent figures in the gay and giddy Court of Charles II. He made love to Elizabeth Hamilton, and then to Fanny Jennings. He was so much in love with the latter that he presumed to give her good advice—she also

E

was of the York establishment being lady-in-waiting to the Duchess—at which she took umbrage, flirted with little Lord Jermyn—the David to Talbot's Goliath—and eventually married Sir George Hamilton.

The question of the restoration of the Irish lands to their proper owners now comes up, and Talbot is accused of doing what every one else did at the time, taking bribes. When he was taxed with claiming commission on some lands that he had helped owners to recover, he replied haughtily : " At least I helped to restore lands, not to forfeit them like the Duke of Ormonde," who was accused of receiving a large extension to his estate as the price of his opposing the repeal of the Cromwellian forfeitures. Ormonde hears of this remark and accuses " the gentleman of the bed-chamber " of presumption and insolence. Talbot gives him a high answer, and tells him that Duke as he is, he is every way as good as he, and challenges him to a duel. Ormonde, the foremost man of the exiled Court, and scarcely less important at Whitehall, hurries off to Charles and asks, " Is it compatible with my dignity to fight with Colonel Talbot ? " Charles says " no," and sends Colonel Talbot to the Tower.

The offence is not deemed so very great, for in the very next year Talbot is sent to Portugal to bring back the King's bride, Catherine of Braganza. He then becomes more than ever closely connected with the Duke of York, whose household he manages ; and when that prince took command of the fleet in the war with the Dutch, he fought on board his ship at the severe battle off Lowestoft. Seven years later he was taken prisoner in the battle in Sole Bay, near Southwold. Before that incident he had married the languishing Miss (Mary) Boynton, " without knowing exactly why " (sans savoir pourquoi), in the words of Gramont, and she died in 1678 in Dublin, leaving him with a single daughter, named Charlotte, who eventually married his nephew and became Countess of Tyrconnell. We shall make her better acquaintance later on.

Richard Talbot, Duke of Tyrconnell.
from the Painting in the National Portrait Gallery.

In 1678 Talbot was in Ireland when his brother Peter was Archbishop of Dublin. They were incriminated in the concocted revelations of the Titus Oates conspiracy. Peter was accused of aiming at the establishment of Catholic supremacy, Richard of holding the Pope's commission to serve as Commander-in-Chief of the Irish forces. The allegations were really farcical and without foundation. This does not of course alter the main fact that they were both of them prominent Catholics. Rumours of Papist plots were at this time upsetting the judgment of the whole nation. The two Talbots were imprisoned in Dublin, their master, the Duke of York, was temporarily banished from the kingdom to Flanders. In the midst of this trouble Mary Boynton died, and Richard, having no further tie to keep him in Ireland, exerted his ingenuity in removing bolts and bars once more and made good his escape to France, and there a remarkable incident occurs in his life. He meets his first love, Fanny Jennings, now a widow, in Paris, and forthwith marries her, though she has not a penny and is burdened with six daughters.

We must leave Talbot for a moment to describe the fortunes of his second wife, since they were members together of the York establishment in the first five or six years of the reign of Charles II. Talbot had been genuinely in love with the sprightly Frances, and she had been well disposed to give him her hand and heart; but he had offended her when he presumed to offer her advice, because she prided herself most of all on her capacity to take care of herself. The reader of the Gramont Memoirs will know how effectively she repelled and got rid of the attentions of James himself by allowing his *billets-doux* to drop unopened from her muff. At last, in 1665, she married George Hamilton, the second son of Sir George Hamilton, Bart., who was the younger son of James Hamilton, first Earl of Abercorn. Sir George Hamilton married the daughter of Lord Thurles, and the sister of James Butler, first Duke of Ormonde, and by her he had a family of at least six sons and three daughters. The sons were in their order of birth, James, George, Anthony, Richard, Thomas, and John. Of the daughters the best known was Elizabeth, *la belle* Hamilton, who married in 1665 Philibert, Count de Gramont; but it may be mentioned that one of her sisters married Matthew Ford and the other Sir Donogh O'Brien. James was killed in 1673 in a naval battle with the Dutch, Thomas also died in a sea fight later on, while serving with the French fleet, and Elizabeth's two sisters have no place in our narrative. With Elizabeth and three of her brothers we shall come into repeated contact.

Sir George Hamilton, like Sir William Talbot, was a Catholic and one of the leaders of the Irish Confederation. He had consequently to give up his property at Roscrea, in the county of Tipperary, and he withdrew with his family to Paris in the year 1651. At that time his son George was about seven, Anthony five, and Richard three years of age. Lady Hamilton's sister was the Countess of Clancarty, and they all seem to have lived with their brother, the Duke of Ormonde, during the years of exile. This fact explains how easily the younger Hamiltons adopted France as a second home. When Charles, by his treaty with France, allowed Louis to recruit a regiment of English gendarmes, in Ireland, about 1670, George Hamilton was appointed its Colonel, and it is curious to note that the scale of pay then scheduled for officers and men served as a model for the one adopted in 1692, when the Irish brigade passed into France. In consequence of this appointment George and his wife took up their residence in Paris, where most of their children were born, and the title of Count was conferred on the Colonel, who had not then succeeded to the baronetcy.

Hamilton and his regiment played a distinguished part in Turenne's campaigns, and for a time John Churchill served under him. Hamilton was present when Turenne was killed in 1675, and the next year was himself killed at Saverne. Some months before this event Evelyn describes in his diary a journey to Dover in the company of Lady Hamilton. His comment on her is, " Lady Hamilton, a sprightly young lady (had been maid of honour to the Duchess of York, and turned Papist), accompanied Lady Berkeley and her husband, Ambassador to France and Plenipotentiary for Nimeguen." A few months later she was a widow, and Madame de Sévigné devotes some of her pity to her because she was " left penniless with six children, all of them girls." Louis probably gave her a pension, for she was still living in Paris in 1679 when Talbot, himself a widower, appeared upon the scene and married her.

On George Hamilton's death the question arose who should succeed him in the command of the regiment, and for a short space his next brother, Anthony, held the command as locum tenens. John Churchill was proposed for the post, but the stern Louvois decided that " he was too much addicted to pleasure," and bestowed it on Justin McCarthy, whom we shall know later on as Viscount Mountcashell. He was the third son of Donogh McCarthy, first Earl of Clancarty, by Elizabeth Butler, and consequently first cousin of the Hamiltons. At this time Richard Hamilton was also serving in the French army in the regiment de Roussillon. The peace of Nimeguen being signed, Louis at once reduced his army, and the regiment of English gendarmes was abolished, McCarthy and the Hamiltons returning to England.

In 1679, at the time of the marriage of Richard Talbot and Frances Hamilton, James was residing in Brussels, it having been deemed prudent to send him out of England during the excitement over what was known as the Popish plot. An alarming illness of Charles II led to his sudden return, and at the same time Talbot and his wife crossed over either with the Duke of York or immediately after-

wards. Charles recovering from his illness, it was thought
desirable that James should again quit London, and
during the last five years of his brother's life he was constantly travelling here and there, now at York on his
way to Scotland, for a brief space at Edinburgh, and again
in Flanders. In these journeys Talbot was James's constant companion and most trusted confidant, and the
relations formed in the days of exile under Cromwell
were cemented by the close association of this later period.
Talbot was not merely a brave man, but an amusing,
and his presence always cheered James in the days of his
adversity.

James, having become King, thought naturally enough
of rewarding the most faithful member of his household,
and Talbot proposed to him that the time was favourable
for the restoration of their estates to some at least of
the Irish Catholics as his brother Charles had promised.
They have met many of them abroad—Taaffes, Kavanaghs,
O'Neils, and O'Donnels, to name but a few—all dreaming
that their forfeited lands must come back to them under
a Catholic king. Talbot is also a soldier, and has military
schemes. An Irish Catholic army might prove a bulwark
of the throne, but the existing Irish army is Protestant,
with a pronounced leaning towards Presbyterianism and
Cromwellism. Talbot suggests that he is willing to purge
it of these elements, and James adopts the suggestion.

But for other reasons the Earl of Clarendon, James's
brother-in-law, the uncle of his daughters, has been
appointed Lord Deputy or Viceroy, and he is a strong
Protestant. His idea is to rule Ireland by and for the
English, and towards Talbot he has a personal repugnance,
which he seems to have transmitted to Macaulay. Talbot
is an Irishman and a Catholic, two facts which disqualify
him from all consideration in the eyes of men like Clarendon.
Notwithstanding his dislike for his associate, Clarendon
has to acquiesce in Talbot's appointment with the rank
of Lieut.-General, " to regulate the troops, and to place

and displace whom he pleased." In the royal letter of appointment he is described as " a man of great abilities and clear courage, and one who for many years had had a true attachment to His Majesty's person and interests."

It is rather difficult to discover that Talbot accomplished very much during this first commission, and it is more reasonable to suppose that he was thinking mainly of his future plans. Among his most definite measures was the attempt to disarm the militia by requiring them to deposit their arms in the residences of the captains. Both Anthony and Richard Hamilton were sent to Ireland at the same time, and associated with him in this work. In 1686 Talbot returned to London, to report what he had done and to make suggestions ; and although Clarendon did not refrain from stating that he entirely disapproved of everything in his programme, James expressed his approval of Talbot's conduct and created him Earl of Tyrconnell. In consequence of Clarendon's discontent, James began to entertain the idea of replacing him by Tyrconnell, and this intention was strengthened by Clarendon's own orders in Council, assuring the Protestants that they would be left unmolested and free from arbitrary treatment. While Clarendon reassured them, Talbot had tried to take away their arms. The Protestants were alarmed, the Catholics began to raise their heads, and all the premonitions of change and turmoil were in the air. In the preamble to Lord Tyrconnell's patent as a peer of the realm reference is made to " his immaculate allegiance and his infinitely great services performed to the King and to Charles II in England, Ireland, and foreign parts, in which he suffered frequent injuries and many wounds."

At this juncture, February, 1687, Clarendon resigns, and Tyrconnell, as we must now call him, proceeds as Viceroy to Ireland, to take up the reins of power, which he was to hold without a break (except during the King's visit) till his death, nearly five years later. They are to be the five most stirring years in Irish history, and names will be mentioned and scenes described which even to-day, after the lapse of two centuries, suffice to raise the storm of faction and bitter strife. The appointment of Lord Tyrconnell was received by the English public with some dismay, for it was fully appreciated that he was a man of action, and that he would not confine his proceedings to empty words. The observant Evelyn records that " his departure for Ireland could only herald a marked change and stormy times."

Tyrconnell, who had been half-courtier, half-soldier up to this point, had now got the chance of showing his merit on the larger stage of statesmanship; but, unfortunately, he was in his fifty-seventh year, and had lived a hard life— hard, not in Macaulay's sense, but from many wounds in honourable fray, from the time of Drogheda, and from confinements as prisoner of war or of state in many prisons. Activity and energy were especially needed in the task that lay before him ; and, owing to his physical condition, they were the qualities in which he was least well provided. On the other hand, he knew exactly what he wanted to do, and if any man could transfer the ruling power from the hands of the Protestant faction to those of the Catholic faction, he had the knowledge of Irish affairs and the courage of his opinions to do the deed.

So far as his policy in Ireland was concerned, James left the entire matter in Tyrconnell's hands, and he took no active part in the management of the Irish question until after his arrival in Dublin in March, 1689. The whole credit of success or the whole discredit of failure rested with Tyrconnell, and it is therefore important to record that King James, compiling in the closing years of his life his own authentic narrative—which, as Sir John Macpherson (the Whig) records, has never been shaken as a record of fact—declares that Ireland was certainly " never in a more flourishing way than during the time he (Tyrconnell) governed it."

The three measures that Tyrconnell took immediately

after his arrival related to the civic charters, the abuse of the pulpits as places from which politics might be fulminated, and the control and reorganisation of the army, with regard to which very little had been accomplished during his earlier missions, owing to Lord Clarendon's opposition and veto.

The civic councils, owing to the Cromwellian law unrepealed by Charles II, were entirely in the hands of the Protestants. Catholics were ineligible for a seat on them, and when the Viceroy proposed a change he was met with a defiant answer, "Here are our charters!" In very moderate language Lord Tyrconnell proposed that Catholics, not less than Protestants, should be made free of the Corporations; but when his proposal was met with defiant rejection, he resorted to the weapons left to him by the exercise of the royal prerogative, and he issued an order in Council calling in the charters. Some acquiesced without demur; others protested and took measures to defeat the Viceroy. Among the latter were Dublin and Londonderry. Dublin sent its Recorder, Sir Richard Rivers, to London to protest, but King James was in no mood for such controversies, and ordered him to return without an audience. The matter was referred to the Courts, which decided almost without debate that the King could cancel or suspend whatever charters had been granted by the Crown, and finally all had to be brought in. There was, in James's words, " no great trouble except at Londonderry (a stubborn people, as they appeared to be afterwards), who stood an obstinate suit, but were forced at last to undergo the same fate with the rest."

The calling in of the charters was the first blow at the Protestant ascendancy established by Cromwell, and in all the towns of Ireland, with the possible exception of Londonderry and Enniskillen, it was in accordance with simple justice that the Corporations should be free to Catholics and Protestants alike. The ephemeral republic of Cromwell had given an aggravated form to English ascendancy in Ireland by importing a religious test and privilege which had never before been tolerated or dreamt of.

The second matter to which Lord Tyrconnell turned his attention was the suppression of political oratory from the pulpit. An order in Council was issued, with a warning as to the penalties that persistence in this course would entail, and with a pointed " reference to a few fiery spirits in the pulpit who seek to discuss matters that do not appertain to them, and who declare that the King intends to rule by a new and arbitrary law." What King James did intend was that his Catholic subjects, who in Ireland at that time outnumbered his Protestant by ten to one, should have equal rights with the Protestants, and no one in these days would dare to call that unjust or tyrannical. Even Macaulay, the champion of militant Orangeism, did not venture to say that. He confined himself to hurling epithets of abuse and contumely at the head of the innocent and unoffending Tyrconnell.

Undoubtedly the measures relating to the armed forces of the country were the most important part of Lord Tyrconnell's programme. The regular garrison was small, and seems to have consisted in 1685 of no more than two regiments, known after the names of their respective commanders, Lord Mountjoy and Colonel Lundy. In addition there was a large militia, to which only Protestants were admitted. It might be said without much exaggeration that every adult Protestant was a militiaman, and in that capacity he had a musket and a sword, which he kept in his house. On the other hand, the Catholics were not merely excluded from all military training, but they were absolutely deprived of arms. After 1650–51 there was not a single armed Catholic in the country, and as there were neither arsenals nor factories, there were no means of replacing what had been confiscated.

In the whole range of history there is no similar case of an entire nation being placed in a state of absolute defencelessness as the Catholics were in the thirty years immediately preceding the accession of James II.

The first step towards redressing this flagrant injustice was taken when Tyrconnell ordered all the arms of the militia to be stored with the captains, and only to be distributed when the men were called out for drill. This was followed by an order to the regular troops requiring them to pay for whatever they obtained from the inhabitants, to preserve the peace and to refrain from brawling. In the same order there was a strict injunction that none of the officers should quit their garrisons, and that they should hold themselves in readiness to support the civil authorities on all occasions. At the same time more definite regulations were issued as to the pay and clothing of the troops.

Finally, two regiments of Irish Catholics—one of horse and the other of foot—were raised, and as soon as they had been recruited to full strength they were sent across to England to be trained. Several of the officers had served in the Anglo-Irish regiments in France. Richard Hamilton was appointed Colonel of the horse regiment, and Cannon (a Scot, whose correct name seems to have been Canan), of the foot. The corps was first quartered at Chester, where it underwent some preliminary training, and was then moved to Nottingham. The discipline of these troops does not appear to have been very strict, and even after Lord Dumbarton was appointed to the command of the brigade formed by these two regiments and a third one of Irish Dragoons, the order maintained among them was somewhat lax. The truth is that James did not know what to do with his Irish auxiliaries when he got them. Their presence enabled his enemies to suggest that he contemplated terrorising England with an Irish army. The unfortunate Irishmen were only home-sick, and James would have been wise if he had returned them promptly to their own country. They stayed on, were useless for all practical purposes, and were eventually interned in the Isle of Wight. Many of them escaped to France or were allowed to go there, and so they gradually filtered back to Ireland.

The mention of Richard Hamilton's name excuses a reference, as no convenient place may occur, to his breach of parole of which Macaulay, following Story, makes so much case in his description of the Boyne. In October, 1688, when it was believed that William would land on the east coast, Richard was sent to Ipswich with his regiment, which was attached to the force under Sir John Lanier. When, in accordance with James's instructions, Lord Feversham two months later disbanded his army, Hamilton came to London, arriving there after the King had gone. The Prince of Orange was anxious about Ireland, and as there were rumours that Tyrconnell would accept terms, he sought an emissary to send him a message. Who could be more suitable than Tyrconnell's own cousin, Richard Hamilton? Hamilton accepted the mission in January, 1689, and, to use Dangeau's words, he " went to Tyrconnell on the Prince of Orange's safe conduct and his promise not to join the troops." Evelyn, referring to the Boyne in July, 1690, says, " Hamilton, who broke his word about Tyrconnell, was taken," and therefore the two diarists agree. Hamilton was not to take an active part in any war, and therefore he broke his parole, to the injury of his reputation among the French authorities, who were very punctilious in such matters. But, judging him by the standard of English life, Hamilton was no better or worse than Marlborough, Sunderland, and hundreds of others. The only difference was that he broke his word to join James Stuart, all the others to betray him.

Having thus paved the way for the creation of a national Irish army, Tyrconnell set himself to the more serious task of raising a considerable force in Ireland itself, and it was rendered the more difficult by the circumstance that to a large extent it had to be done *sub rosa*. For the Protestants, who were armed, might easily become alarmed, and, taking the law into their own hands, put an end to his Government altogether. Even on his own Council, strengthened as his side was by the inclusion of Antony Hamilton and William Talbot, Tyrconnell could not be sure of a majority, and in Lord Mountjoy he had an opponent of proved skill and great reputation. The raising of Catholic regiments for service in England did not excite much apprehension among the Irish Protestants, for England could be left to take care of herself, but how would it be when recruiting was commenced on a large scale throughout the island for home service ?

Tyrconnell was too prudent to make the attempt, and all his efforts were concentrated on the concealment of his plans. Antony Hamilton was sent to Limerick to act as governor of an undefended town, which was, however, a convenient centre for rallying to the cause the powerful family of O'Brien. Justin McCarthy was sent on a similar mission to Cork. Their instructions were to incite the chiefs of the Irish families to prepare lists of officers and men who in due course might form regiments bearing their names. The Munster septs were especially appealed to, but the southern counties of Leinster and parts of Connaught (including the whole of Galway) were also included in this movement. The result surpassed Tyrconnell's expectations. An army of 50,000 men was promptly brought into existence " on paper," and the Protestant leaders had no inkling of the movement. But this army was entirely unarmed, and absolutely innocent of military training.

This result was a kind of moral support for the Viceroy, and enabled him to proceed with greater confidence in his measures for dealing with the regular troops who were armed. But in order to bring home to the levies on paper that when they were called up they would receive good pay, he issued special schedules showing how the men of the different arms would be remunerated. Soldiers in ordinary foot regiments were to receive two shillings a week for subsistence in addition to their clothes, those selected for service in the regiment of Guards were to receive two shillings and six pence, while the cavalry man was to be paid for himself and horse six shillings. These allowances were high for the times, and the Irish recruits looked forward with eagerness for the day when they would begin. Unfortunately they were fixed too high, and when the regiments were called up the foot-soldier's pay had to be reduced to one shilling and sixpence, and the Guardsman's to two shillings.

By the time that these preliminary arrangements had been completed it was known in Ireland that the Prince of Orange had landed in England, and this news was speedily followed by the tidings of the Queen's flight and the King's detention. Lord Tyrconnell decided that his only safe course was to induce the two Protestant regiments to remove to a part of Ireland where he knew that he had no influence, and to which his own plans had no reference. He visited Lord Mountjoy's camp at Mullingar, reviewed his troops, and proposed that his regiment should be sent to garrison Londonderry. Lord Mountjoy, who believed that Lord Tyrconnell might not be averse under the stress of circumstances to come to terms with the Prince of Orange, assented, but substituted the other regiment for his own. At the same time the Protestant soldiers were granted permission to leave the army and to return to their homes. This offer was made because a rumour was current that the Roman Catholics contemplated a massacre of the Protestants. The splitting up of the force rendered it no longer formidable as a danger to Tyrconnell's government, and was at once followed by the summons to the Catholic nobility and gentlemen to call out their regiments, at the same time investing them with the requisite authority to grant commissions.

Before the end of January, 1689, Tyrconnell had an Irish army of 60,000 men on the roster, but very few of them possessed arms. Some muskets had been taken from the militia, a few more had been surrendered by the troops who had resigned, and no doubt there was a small stock in Dublin Castle. The Viceroy had also called in all bayonets, swords, and firearms in Dublin, and although many were concealed, some had to be surrendered, and a little armament for the force was acquired in this manner. In December, 1688, it was reported that preparations of a hostile nature were being made at Trinity College, whereupon Captain Talbot was sent at the head of three companies to occupy the buildings, to search for arms, and to order the students to disperse to their homes, all of which was done. It was shortly after this incident that the Marquis de Pointis arrived from France, as already described, for the purpose of reporting to Louis on the situation. In the part of Ireland that he visited he found the people unanimous for King James, and signs of the levies of men in all directions. Tyrconnell was the unquestioned lord of the land, more especially since he had got rid of his rival Mountjoy by the ruse described in the last chapter.

Moreover, many of the Irish troops sent to England in the previous years were filtering back to Ireland, and these included some good officers, of which there was great lack, like Colonel Thomas Bourke, Captain Drummond, Owen McCarthy, John Scot, Gilbert Hore, William Carroll, Garret Parry, and Cornelius Mahan. It was clear to Pointis, as it is to any impartial student of the question, that Tyrconnell had got together the nucleus of an army—one, indeed, with many defects and shortcomings, but still one in which the raw material, the brawn and sinews, was first-rate—as good *char à canon* as could be found in the wide world.

Let us turn from Ireland to cite what was being written in England about the Irish army, and we will select the anonymous author of " The Popish Champion," as he was one of Macaulay's witnesses. This is what this high authority had to say about it : " The meaning of the word courage is unknown among them, and for their officers the best of them had rather creep into a scabbard than draw a sword. As for their common souldiers what are they ? but the very excrement of common prisons with which their army is cumbered not manned. . . . As for their general it is the same Tyrconnell who is famed for a coward throughout Europe." Poor scribbler ! He could not foresee the unwavering advance across the bullet-swept plain of Marsaglia, the unbroken ranks at Oberglau, or the tempestuous onset at Almanza.

What is clear, then, is that Tyrconnell, on his own resources, very limited as they were, with an empty treasury and an emptier arsenal, had set up an Irish administration such as had never before existed. He had evoked three of the strongest and noblest sentiments in the human mind, religious fervour, loyalty to the King and patriotic enthusiasm. How was this done ? Tyrconnell, by some stroke of genius, had revived the hopes of a downtrodden nation. Why did the Irish respond to the appeal again to champion the Stuarts who in the past had been so ungrateful to Ireland ? The answer is supplied in the anonymous work entitled, " A Light to the Blind," which forms the basis of Gilbert's Jacobite narrative.

The following passage has not lost its force even to-day :—

" It will be requisite in the King to restore unto the Irish Catholics their ancient estates which the Protestant usurpers have retained in possession these forty years past ; to make the parliament of Ireland absolute in enacting laws without being obliged to send beforehand the prepared bills which are destined to pass into acts by the consent of both houses of parliament for the King's precedent approbation of them, it being sufficient to have the King's assent given unto them by the voice of his Deputy after the said bills have passed both the houses ;

to make the judicature of the nation determine causes without an appeal to the tribunals of England; to give full liberty to merchants to export the products and manufactures of the kingdom and to import foreign goods without an obligation of touching at any harbour of England; to erect studies of law at Dublin; to put always the viceroydom into the hands of an Irish Catholic; to set up a silver and gold mint in the capital city; to confer the principal posts of state and war on the Catholic natives; to keep standing an army of eight thousand Catholics; to train a Catholic militia; to maintain a fleet of 24 warlike ships of the fourth rate; to give the moiety of ecclesiastical livings to the Catholic Bishops and parish priests during the life of the present Protestant bishops and ministers, and after the death of these to confer all the said livings on the Roman clergy; to make the great rivers of the kingdom navigable as far as 'tis possible; to render the chief ports more deep and thoroughly tenable against any attacks from sea; in fine, to drain the multiplicity of bogs which being effected will support a vast addition of families."

James's programme was to make Ireland the base and stepping-stone for his recovery of the Crown of England. The Irish programme was to secure Home Rule. Tyrconnell's part was to invest both projects with a character of feasibility. When the year 1689 dawned the eyes of both England and France were fixed on Ireland.

F

Chapter IV

KING JAMES IN IRELAND

AT the beginning of April, 1689, Evelyn entered in his journal: "King James was now certainly in Ireland with the Marshal d'Estrades, whom he made a Privy Councillor, and who caused the King to remove the Protestant Councillors, some whereof it seems had continued to sit, telling him that the King of France, his master, would never assist him if he did not immediately do it, by which it is apparent how the poor prince is managed by the French." As history this entry is worthless, there was not an iota of truth in it. Many of the Councillors were Protestants down to the Boyne, and some even till the Limerick Convention. It is only interesting for the undue prominence it gives to d'Estrades, not a Marshal but a Maréchal de Camp, who had been sent to train a royal body-guard at Dublin, which only got its horses on the eve of the Boyne campaign.

What purported to be the description of King James's arrival in Dublin by an eye-witness, a forerunner of the special correspondent, was hawked about the streets of London as a broadside. It read :—

"On Thursday the 14th of March (O.S.) the late King being recovered of the indisposition caused by the sea set out for Dublin, where he arrived on Saturday following, being the 16th of the month, being met and received by the Earl of Tyrconnell ten miles from Dublin, who conducted him thither, having caused all the forces to be drawn up at the entrance into the town, who saluted the late King's arrival with three volleys of shot. The Lord

Mayor, Aldermen, and Common Council also met him in their formalities. The streets were lined with the Irish Life Guards even to the Castle Gates, where the late King was conducted and lodged. The Papist inhabitants shouting, the soldiers musquets discharging, the Bells ringing, and at night Bonfires in all parts of the town.

"The next day being Sunday there was singing of Te Deum, and Processions for joy and a multitude of masses said for the advancement of the Catholic Church."

With which account we need not greatly quarrel; let us pass to more authentic records.

On the fifth day (that is March 12 O.S., 22 N.S.), after sailing from Brest the squadron, commanded by Admiral Gabaret, cast anchor in Kingsale Bay. King James landed that day, and waited while horses were obtained for the journey to Cork. This was no easy matter. No preparations had been made for the royal arrival and horses were scarce. Two days were taken in getting ten together, and thereupon the King, the Count d'Avaux, and the more important members of his suite set out for Cork. It is said that some of the French officers not wishing to be left behind seized some of the horses in the place, whereupon the natives took offence and drove their horses and ponies into the hills. The story rests on no sure basis. The statement is better authenticated that the people themselves made a free gift of fifty oxen and four hundred sheep to the French sailors. On this occasion and throughout the long struggle the best relations existed between the French and the Irish, and no credence whatever need be given to the stories to the contrary.

The original impressions of the French envoy were very much to the point, and anticipated with almost prophetic precision the causes of ultimate failure. In his very first letter to Louvois, written from Kingsale, D'Avaux wrote: "Our chief difficulty will be the irresolution of King James, who often changes his mind and then decides not always for the best." An instance of this occurred on the journey. One of the officers on board the "Faucon," the Chevalier de Murray (Sir —— Murray), was discovered to be a traitor, and King James agreed that he should be sent back to France. A day later he changed his mind and allowed him to remain as a prisoner in Cork, from which place he eventually made his escape to England. Two Protestant lords, one of whom was Lord Inchiquin (who died in 1693 as Governor of Jamaica), had been given leave by General McCarthy to quit the country before the King's landing, and on hearing of this both D'Avaux and Melfort urged the King to countermand it. He did so, but was so slow in his decision that the two noble lords escaped from Cork in an English frigate that happened to lie there. The true significance of the affair lay in the fact that they took £20,000 away with them, and that money was a very rare commodity in Ireland. McCarthy's co-operation in the flight of Lord Inchiquin is quite intelligible, for his father had been the chief commander of the Irish in the Wars of the Confederation.

At Cork Lord Tyrconnell was waiting to receive the King, and he then and there delivered an account of the state of the Kingdom to His Majesty. It was to the following effect, as expressed in the King's own words : " Lieutenant-General Hamilton had been sent down with two thousand five hundred men, as many as could be spared from Dublin, to make head against the Rebels in Ulster, who were masters of all that Province except Charlemont and Carrickfergus ; that in Munster the whole province was totally reduced by Lieutenant-General McCarthy ; that by the diligence of the Catholic nobility and gentry above fifty regiments of foot and several troops of horse and dragoons had been raised ; that he had distributed amongst them about twenty thousand muskets, most of which, however, were so old and unserviceable that not above one thousand of the firearms were found to be of any use ; that the Catholics of the country had no arms, whereas the Protestants had great plenty as well as the best horses in the kingdom ; that for artillery he had but eight small field pieces in a condition to march, the rest not mounted, no stores in the magazines, little powder and ball, all the officers gone for England, and no money in cash."

This was not a very cheering statement for a King in search of a lost throne to receive on the threshold of his enterprise, but it showed that Lord Tyrconnell did not disguise the truth for the sake of making his sovereign believe for a moment that he had done more than he had. James's comment on the report was : " there is a great deal of goodwill in the kingdom for me, but little means to execute it." He was also displeased at some of the details of Tyrconnell's administration, but he succeeded in hiding his displeasure, and raised Tyrconnell to the rank of Duke. For instance, he disliked the conferring of such high military rank as that of Lieutenant-General on Hamilton and McCarthy. It placed him in a difficulty with the French officers, who had to be raised to the same rank forthwith. He also was not pleased with the order depriving the Acts of the English Parliament of force in Ireland, but when he realised that he must bow to this popular decision among the Irish, until at least he had recovered England, he held his tongue.

In the meanwhile D'Avaux was keeping his eyes open and collecting information. On the road from Kingsale to Cork he passed a battalion of good-looking Irish troops, but armed only with cudgels (probably shillelaghs). When Louvois read the lines he wrote the caustic note : " What will these fine fellows do against the Prince of Orange's troops armed with muskets and sabres ? " At Cork D'Avaux saw some of McCarthy's troops partially armed and consequently making a better show. He again describes them as splendid men, the shortest foot-soldiers being over 5ft. 10 in., and the pikemen and grenadiers 6ft. 1 in. At Cork also D'Avaux established friendly relations with William Talbot, Tyrconnell's nephew, as well as with McCarthy, who had not forgotten " la belle France." D'Avaux whispers in his ear the project of exchanging Irish and French regiments, and that McCarthy is the man to command the former. McCarthy is delighted at the idea, and assures the French envoy that he will not say a word to either the King or Melfort, who would be sure to oppose the scheme.

The conferences at Cork cover several days while carriages and carts and horses are got together for the King's journey to Dublin. It is also necessary to provide the means for conveying there the French money and some, at least, of the arms and ammunition. During this interval James shows his hand. He has come to Ireland not to rule an Irish kingdom, but to make his way to Scotland or England for the recovery of his English Crown. Tyrconnell takes a black view of the situation in England, and is not afraid to declare his opinion that the English Crown is lost past recall for many years. James is not merely optimistic himself, but he likes those around him to paint things in rosy colours. The Secretary Melfort is at his elbow to echo his views and humour them. He, too, shares at least one of his master's opinions. He has no wish to stay in Ireland. Of what value is an Irish Crown ? Better 'twere to have none at all.

And so the war of factions begins before the Stuart King has been a week on Irish soil. Tyrconnell, who has done everything to make the adventure possible, is already cold-shouldered as an Irish enthusiast. He not merely exposes the impossibility of a descent on England, but he dwells on the difficulty of taking Londonderry. Its garrison is well armed, the best troops in Ireland are there, and they are more closely knit together than the Jacobite forces. Nor has he any exaggerated opinion of the value of his own army. There are fifty or sixty thousand men on the paper lists. He proposes to the King that this force should be reduced to 25,000 foot, 3000 dragoons, and 2000 cavalry. He does not see how more can be paid for out of the moderate sum of money brought from France. He is also disappointed with the assistance rendered by the French King. He is told that more is coming with the second squadron, and that if he can only hold out till Christmas French troops will follow. But the need is at the moment, and he wishes they had come, for with Ulster unsubdued Ireland is only half won for the Jacobite cause. Tyrconnell is an adviser whom James does not want to see every day, or for long audiences. He prefers the honeyed words and cerulean dreams of Melfort.

But at last things are as ready for leaving Cork as they ever will be in a country where D'Avaux declares it " takes three days to do what is done in one elsewhere," and King James sets out on his journey to Dublin in Lord Tyrconnell's carriage on April 1 (N.S.). On the 3rd he enters the capital in state amid popular demonstrations of extreme joy. The French ambassador, asking himself the reason of this, supplies his own answer. It is " because the Irish hope to become independent of England."

Let us quote the description of the journey given by the author of " A Light for the Blind."

" All along the road the country came to meet his Majesty with staunch loyalty, profound respect, and tender love as if he had been an angel from heaven. All degrees of people and of both sexes were of the number old and young ; orations of welcome being made unto him at the entrance of each considerable town, and the young rural maids weaving of dances before him as he travelled. In a word, from Kingsale to Dublin (which is above a hundred long Irish miles) the way was like a great fair, such crowds poured forth from their habitations to wait on his Majesty, so that he could not but take comfort amidst his misfortunes at the sight of such excessive fidelity and tenderness for his person in his Catholic people of Ireland. This was a different behaviour from that which his Majesty found from his subjects in England after the Prince of Orange's arrival. And happy would the King be if he could have preserved unto himself this island which in a few years would make a prince very powerful if due care were taken by reason that it is fertile in soil, notably productive of corn and cattle of all sorts, abounding in fish, marine and fluvial, admirably situated for a general trade, and endowed with excellent harbours from nature.

" But to go on. The King made his entry into Dublin on March 24 (O.S. April 3, N.S.) being Palm Sunday that year. He was received by the Lord Mayor, Sir Michael Creagh, and aldermen in their formalities, by the principals of the city, and by the garrison under arms, while the bells rang, the cannons roared, and the music, on stages erected in the streets, harmoniously played. And in this manner his Majesty was lodged in the royal Castle where the court of the kingdom is usually kept."

Ireland had not seen a King since Richard II, and it was not so very surprising that an emotional people should under the circumstances receive the last of the Stuarts to reign " like an angel from Heaven." Unfortunately, James was not worth all their enthusiasm. His thoughts were elsewhere. Shortly after reaching Dublin letters from Scotland with what was called pleasing news were placed in his hands, and he was all for setting off for that country forthwith. D'Avaux had to make a firm stand and tell him that it was not for visionary schemes that the King of France had taken up his cause and rendered him generous aid, but to accomplish the definite task of securing the whole of Ireland. This was the beginning of the breach between James and the French ambassador. Writing long afterwards the Duke of Berwick records in his Memoirs about D'Avaux that " the King was dissatisfied with his haughty and disrespectful manner of conducting himself," but he is constrained to add, " he was, however, a man of sense."

One of the first steps taken by the King on his arrival in Dublin was the formation of an inner and supreme

Council of three, the presence of the sovereign having nullified Tyrconnell's commission as Lord Deputy. The three were Tyrconnell, Melfort, and D'Avaux; and as the first two were bitterly opposed to each other, and as the feud extended also to their ladies, it followed that for a time D'Avaux controlled the Council. This suited neither Melfort nor James, so Tyrconnell was given a commission nominally to carry out his proposed reduction of the army, but really to get him out of Dublin. His absence was prolonged by illness, which at one time seemed likely to prove fatal.

Before Tyrconnell left the capital, however, he was to take a leading part in a ceremony that claims brief notice. The citizens of Dublin have been fêted with the entry of a King. They are now to be provided with a second show in the reception of an Ambassador. Count d'Avaux, the Ambassador of His Most Christian Majesty, has to present his letters of credence, and April 15 is the day fixed for the ceremony. The Duke of Tyrconnell calls for him at his residence, and drives him in his six-horse coach to the Castle, where the ambassador is received by the Duke of Powis, Lord Chamberlain, and conducted to the royal presence. The formal letters are presented and the usual formal speeches are made, James thanking his good brother Louis for the assurance of his friendship. The street to the Castle is lined by the Lord Mayor's Regiment (commonly called Creagh's), and the people are delighted with a show such as had never been seen in Dublin before.

From Jacobite Ireland the scene changes to Londonderry, where a small but determined force holds on to the last vestige of Protestant ascendency in Ulster. These men are formidable by the spirit which animates them. The very extremity of their situation has inspired them with a resolution to conquer or to die, and while Dublin and southern Ireland are absorbed in the delight of welcoming a King and seeing unwonted sights, the people of Londonderry are busily turning the place into some imitation of a fortress.

On February 20, 1689, the people of Derry, having got rid of the Catholics in the garrison and town, proclaimed the Prince of Orange as King William. It was then that Tyrconnell sent Richard Hamilton with 2500 men, as mentioned by him at Cork, to drive all the outlying Protestant garrisons into Derry. The first news that James received on entering the capital was that Hamilton had routed the enemy at Dromore. Hamilton reported that he had driven the enemy out of Dromore and across the Bann to Coleraine, where, however, they were so numerous and well-posted that he must await reinforcements. James at once sent General Pusignan and the Duke of Berwick with such troops as could be gathered to his aid, and resolved to follow himself in a few days with Roze and others. Both Tyrconnell and D'Avaux opposed the King's going, but he would not listen. It was at that moment that Tyrconnell was ordered to Munster, and D'Avaux, seeing that there was no use in staying behind, and that his presence might baffle Melfort's plan of getting the King over to Scotland, accompanied the royal party to Armagh.

At this stage the French envoy did two things that were not unavailing. He wrote to Louvois suggesting that Louis should get Queen Mary d'Esté to write to her husband begging him not to leave Ireland until it was completely subdued. He also called attention to the fact that while the Irish people were whole-hearted in their sympathy for France, James was only partly of the same way of thinking and Melfort not at all. Louvois records in his despatches : " Ils n'entrent pas tout à fait dans les bons sentiments des Irlandais pour la France." Insensibly French policy partook more and more of a character to help its own interests before those of James. A Franco-Irish alliance was in the air, and D'Avaux urged Louis to send over 4000 French infantry, and engaged to send back

William Herbert, Duke, of Powis.
from the Portrait at Powis Castle.

in exchange six or seven thousand of the best Irish troops under McCarthy, who was entirely devoted to him and to France. The proposal to send Irish troops was first introduced to pacify Louvois and Vauban, who had declared that France could not spare a man. D'Avaux therefore made a proposal by which France would gain two or three thousand men, and he described them as physically among the finest men he had ever seen. After a little discipline and with good arms, France might thus find the Irish as useful as the Swiss. This proposal gave a new complexion to the question, and Louvois agreed to sending over four regiments at the first favourable chance. But he insisted that the situation in the Low Countries must first be improved. The campaign of 1689 revealed that the pressure there was much diminished by the absence of William and his best troops in England.

On reaching Derry the King found that something had been accomplished by Hamilton in the way of confining the garrison to the place by the capture of Culmore Fort at the entrance to the channel leading to Derry. He had also erected two small batteries to command the channel, and had cast a boom across the passage above Culmore. The garrison, in the belief that their communication with the outer world was cut off, seemed inclined to treat for surrender, and declared that they would give up the place on terms, provided the Jacobite army did not come within a stipulated distance of the walls, and also that they were satisfied that King James was really in Ireland. The townspeople were allowed to send two delegates into the camp, where they saw the King; but they also saw a good deal more, and when they returned into Derry they reported that the enemy had no mortars or heavy artillery. It was not difficult, therefore, to persuade the citizens to hold out a little while, and the negotiations were broken off. When wanted an excuse can be found for almost any human action. The people of Derry alleged that Roze had broken the truce by coming within the prescribed limits. Apparently he had. He had marched his troops up a hill and down again.

James, finding that he was not to enjoy the cheap triumph of seeing Derry surrender at his presence, decided to return to Dublin, taking with him Roze and D'Avaux, and entrusting the joint command to Maumont and Hamilton. Major-General Pusignan was also left in charge of the infantry. The conduct of the siege was distinctly faulty, as there was not a competent engineer in the investing force, and the only mortar of any size burst after a few discharges. It was said at the time that Hamilton's military knowledge had been acquired in an infantry regiment, but it showed extraordinary neglect for any soldier to leave the camp of the besieging force quite open and defenceless. It was due to this fact that the besiegers suffered a heavy and irreparable loss in the early days of the beleaguerment.

The two French generals were watching the town from Penniburn Mill, not far from the walls, when a party from the place seeing their opportunity sallied out and cut them off. The French officers and their small escort made a brave resistance, but before a relieving force could reach them they were all killed or mortally wounded. Both the French officers were men of ability as well as courage, and what is more rare, they were very popular on account of their affability. Among others slain was at least one Irish officer of experience and distinction, Major John Taaffe, brother of the Earl of Carlingford and Count Taaffe. A few days later Captain Maurice Fitzgerald was killed in another sortie, and in the meantime no impression whatever had been made on the walls. The advantage rested with the besieged. Hamilton, from inclination or necessity, confined his attention to an investment in the hope that the garrison might be starved into surrender.

We must return to Dublin, whither D'Avaux had preceded James. The French envoy took advantage of the King's absence to reconcile Tyrconnell and McCarthy, on whom the title of Viscount Mountcashell had just been conferred. James arrived some days later for the purpose of meeting his first Parliament, which had been summoned for May 7. For this occasion a new crown had been made for the King's use, and the two Houses were opened with all possible formality. The House of Peers numbered only thirty-five, but in compensation the counties and boroughs returned not fewer than 200 representatives to the Commons. On the very day that the Parliament was opened a large French fleet sailed from Brest with reinforcements and supplies.

The commander of this fleet was the Count de Château Renaud, one of France's most distinguished seamen, and he had under his orders twenty-eight ships of the line, fifteen frigates, and fifteen fire-ships. There were on board the more or less trained English, Irish and Scottish troops who had escaped to France from England. These men had formed the bulk of James's loyal troops under Lord Dumbarton and Colonel Scott at the time of the Dutch invasion. It is declared that they numbered 3000 officers and men, and on arrival in Ireland they were placed under the orders of M. Boisseleau, governor of Cork, to undergo a course of training and to be passed into different regiments. One regiment, named after Boisseleau himself, was formed at once, and its numerical strength is given at not less than 1600 men. A certain number of French officers of higher grade arrived about the same time to replace Maumont and Pusignan. Among these we may name the Count de Gacé, Chevalier d'Escots, D'Hocquincourt, D'Amanzé and Saint Pater. These came by their King's orders, but M. d'Anglure, ex-captain in the French guards, came to serve James " through pure devotion."

Château Renaud's cruise was not without its adventure. He reached Kingsale Bay without coming across the English fleet, under Admiral Herbert, which was cruising somewhere in the Channel; but while he was engaged in the work of disembarkation news was brought that the

English fleet was in the offing. He at once stopped the work of landing and hastened out to sea. In the fight that ensued the English fleet was beaten off with some loss, and had to make for Plymouth to refit. The news of this victory reached Dublin while Parliament was sitting, and a Te Deum was sung for it in St. Patrick's Cathedral; but James was peevish and cross, and when D'Avaux informed him that the English ships had been driven off, he exclaimed with some irritation, " C'est bien la première fois donc." The French ambassador must have been puzzled by this professional spirit which asserted itself over self-interest. No one would have suffered more than King James from an English victory at that juncture, and yet he was sorry to learn of the defeat of the navy in which he had served. He even imagined all kinds of excuses for it, and fully persuaded himself, at least, that Admiral Herbert had sailed away out of loyalty to his person. It is not surprising if James became an enigma to his French allies.

But although he disparaged Château Renaud's success, he was quite prepared to turn it to account, and proposed that he should sail round Ireland and attack Derry by Lough Foyle. The French admiral's reply was that his orders were to return without delay to Brest; but if it had been possible to spare the fleet out of French waters for any length of time, the result might have justified James's strategical insight. A little later French frigates did appear on the north coast of Ireland, and the gallant Du Quesne navigated lochs and estuaries on the west coast of Scotland, where warships had never been seen since the Spanish Armada.

Before returning to the incidents at Derry, where by the tacit admission of both sides the first decisive phase in the struggle was to be enacted, we may describe what happened in James's first Parliament. Proof was furnished therein that the King and his legislative Assembly were not in accord, and that when he gave his assent to measures that could not be avoided, it was very often against his own wishes and convictions. The speech made by the King at the opening of Parliament read as follows :—

" The exemplary loyalty which this nation expressed to me at a time when others of my subjects so undutifully misbehaved themselves to me, or so basely betrayed me, and your seconding my Deputy as you did in his bold and resolute asserting my Right in preserving this Kingdom for me, and putting it in a posture of defence, made me resolve to come to you, and venture my life with you in defence of your liberties and my own Right, and to my great satisfaction I have not only found you ready to serve me, but that your courage has equalled your zeal.

" I have always been for libertie of conscience and against invading any man's right or liberty, having still in mind the Saying of the holy writ ' Do as you would be done to, for this is the law and the Prophets.'

" It was this liberty of conscience I gave which my enemies both at home and abroad dreaded to have established by law in all my Dominions, and made them set themselves up against me, though for different reasons, seeing that if I had once settled it my people in the opinion of the one would have been too happy, and, in the opinion of the other, too great.

" This argument was made use of to persuade their own people to join with them, and so many of my subjects to use me as they had done, but nothing shall ever persuade me to change my mind as to that ; wheresoever I am Master I design, God willing, to establish it by law, and have no other text or distinction but that of Loyalty. I expect your concurrence in so Christian a work, and in making laws against profaneness and against all sorts of debauchery.

" I shall most readily consent to the making such laws as may be for the good of the Nation, the improvement of trade, and relieving such as have been injured in the late Act of Settlement, as far forth as may be consistent with reason, justice and the public good of my people.

" And as I shall do my part to make you happy and

rich, I make no doubt of your assistance by enabling me to oppose the unjust designs of my enemies, and to make this Nation flourish.

" And to encourage you the more to it, you know with how great generosity and kindness the Most Christian King gave a sure retreat to the Queen, my Son and myself, when we were forced out of England and came to seek protection in his Kingdom, how he embraced my interest, and gave me such supplies of all sorts as enabled me to come to you, which without his obliging assistance I could not have done ; this he did at a time he had so many and so considerable enemies to deal with, and you see still continues so to do.

" I shall conclude as I have begun, and assure you I am as sensible as you can desire of the signal loyalty you have expressed to me, and shall make it my chief study as it has always been to make you and all my subjects happy."

This speech would have been an excellent one before an English Parliament, but in Dublin in the year 1689 it was out of place and incomprehensible to the mass of the people. The exhortation that all men should be free to follow their conscience was not to the liking of the Irish Catholics. It was not followed in England or Scotland, as James's own experience showed, for he had been deprived of his throne for exercising the very liberty that he so much vaunted. If there were no other evidence, this alone would convict James of being no statesman. The Irish members wanted to hear that all their old estates were coming back to them, and instead the King gave them a sermon on religious tolerance, which was not the general practice among either Catholics or Protestants until two centuries later.

The following passage, taken from " A Light for the Blind," shows very clearly what was in the minds of the Irish Catholics :—

" No experience will make him behave himself towards those traitors (Protestants) as he should do. He spoiled his business in Ireland by his own great indulgence towards them. He was infatuated with this rotten principle —provoke not your Protestant subjects—the which hindered His Majesty from drawing troops sooner out of Ireland into England for the security of his person and government; from making up a Catholic army in England; from accepting those forces the Most Christian King had offered him. It was this false politic which prevailed with him to declare that he had no alliance with France; that he did not believe the Dutch had any design on him till they were almost landed in England. In fine 'twas this deceitful suggestion that ruined him entirely by not mistrusting in time the loyalty of those heretics, as it was that which made King Charles the Second commit such horrid injustices in leaving the estates of his faithful Irish in the usurped possession of known rebels both to himself and to his royal father Charles the First."

The observant D'Avaux had read the situation far more correctly when he wrote, " les Irlandais sont ennemis irreconciliables des Anglais en sorte que si on leur lachait la main ils egorgeraient en peu de temps ceux qui sont icy."

Having listened to the King's homily, the Irish Parliament proceeded to conduct its business in its own way. A Bill was brought in to repeal the Act of Settlement. In the House of Lords the Bishop of Meath made a set speech against it, on the ground that it would be unjust to the actual holders who were, with the exception of five or six of the greatest or most fortunate peers—then in England with the Prince of Orange, the second Duke of Ormonde at their head—descendants of the Cromwellian settlers. The Lord Chief Justice Keating backed up the Bishop's speech with an address to the King, representing that the repeal would be " the ruin of trade and future improvements." But these efforts by the small Protestant faction to maintain the Act of Settlement were quite futile. The two Houses passed by a practically unanimous vote the law abrogating it, so that all their old

G

estates were to be repossessed by their original Catholic proprietors ousted from them in 1650-52. The decision of the Legislature was absolute, and James appended his signature because he was told that if he did not he might just as well quit the country at once. He signed, but he entered in his private diary a note which has passed into history to the effect that " it had without doubt been more generous in the Irish not to have pressed so hard upon their Prince when he lay so much at their mercy, and more prudent not to have grasped at regaining all before they were sure of keeping what they already possessed."

The Irish Parliament was in session from May 7 until July 20, and during that time it passed a very generous vote of £20,000 per month for the King's service ; but, unfortunately, this vote was meaningless, because there was no money in the treasury and no trade or commerce on which to raise taxes or customs. The small sum provided by the King of France went but a very little way, and the people, not liking the look of the small French silver coins, a royal order had to be issued showing the rate at which they were to be accepted. But the evil was far greater than uncertainty as to the value of this money. There was not enough of it or of any other. On June 18 another order was issued decreeing that a new coin of brass or copper was to pass current as the equivalent of sixpence. As time went on recourse to base money became more frequent and on a larger scale, but it was remarkable in the first instance as coinciding with the Parliament's generous paper subsidy.

Notwithstanding the adoption of a meaningless vote about liberty of conscience, and James's repeated declaration that he meant to treat the Protestants by an equal law with the Catholics, he was forced by his advisers, despite the support of Lord Melfort, to recognise the facts of the situation. He might call the Protestants his subjects if it pleased him, but that did not alter the fact that they were his enemies, and that they were treating his forces very badly in the north. On July 15 he had to sign the order calling upon the Protestants, of whom there were a good many in Dublin, to surrender their arms and horses within fifteen days. Those Protestants in Dublin who were not citizens were ordered to leave within twenty-four hours, and thus James was compelled to do at last what Tyrconnell and D'Avaux had been urging him to do ever since his arrival. During all these months, too, James absolutely refused to make a declaration of war against England. The English were his dear subjects; it was only the Prince of Orange, his nephew and son-in-law, who was " his unnatural enemy " ; but the consequence of this was that he could not grant letters of marque to Brest privateers to prey on English commerce. Neither could he fit out Irish privateers for the same purpose. To the French his policy seemed neither one thing nor the other, a mixture of senility and impracticability. As a matter of historical justice it must be mentioned that James wanted something that was not in the minds of either his French or his Irish advisers. He wished to get back to Whitehall, and he knew that to employ Irish methods would be to blast his chances of doing so for ever. Probably every day of his residence in Ireland he regretted that his obligations to the French King had deprived him of the liberty to refuse to go to that country. His changing policy, his inability to adapt himself to his surroundings, prove, not that he was the fool that D'Avaux and Louvois took him for, but that he was in a false position.

Having referred to the delicate question of the proper course for James to have pursued towards the Protestants in Ireland, it will be appropriate at this stage to deal with and demolish the monstrous charge Macaulay brings against D'Avaux of having counselled James to authorise a massacre of the Protestants. His words are :—

" With this view he (D'Avaux) coolly submitted to the

King a proposition of almost incredible atrocity. There must be a St. Bartholomew. A pretext would easily be found. . . . Any disturbance, wherever it might take place, would furnish an excuse for a general massacre of the Protestants of Leinster, Munster, and Connaught " (" History of England," Vol. V, p. 39).

This charge is a figment of Macaulayan imagination. To support it, the not over-scrupulous historian had to invent a misquotation. Let us examine the evidence.

Macaulay gives as his authority an extract from the letter written by D'Avaux to Louis XIV, dated August 10, 1689 (N.S.), and he quotes as follows :—

" J'estois d'avis qu'après que la descente seroit faite, si l'on apprenoit que des Protestants se fussent soulevez en quelques endroits du royaume on *fit main basse* sur tous généralement."

D'Avaux *never* wrote the words alleged. The following is the correct quotation of the passage :—

" J'estois d'avis qu'après que la descente seroit faite si l'on aprenoit que des Protestants se fussent soulevez en quelque endroit du royaume *on s'asseurast* généralement de tous les autres, puisqu' on ne pouvoit douter que ceux qui ne s'estoient pas encore declarez n'attendoient que l'occasion favorable pour le faire."

What D'Avaux proposed, then, was to " make sure of " or " to arrest " (*s'assurer*) the Protestants. He must be judged by what he wrote, not by what Macaulay invented, and no twisting of words can make " *s'asseurast* " mean anything more than " secure " or " arrest."

It is quite true that in Louis's reply, dated September 6, disapproving of this counsel, on the ground that the Protestants could carry out more effective reprisals, Louis uses the words " *de faire main basse*," but this remark will be explained later on. Again we must repeat D'Avaux is to be judged on his own merits or demerits. As Macaulay could have satisfied himself by carefully perusing D'Avaux's despatches, the French ambassador advocated the arrest of leading Protestants, their being disarmed, and the prevention of their sending money out of the country; but from first to last there is not a word suggesting their being killed, and losing their lives by being massacred. It is most extraordinary that Macaulay should have made so terrible a charge, and that his statement should have been allowed to pass unchallenged and unrefuted for half a century.

The essential facts on the point are those cited; but, lest it might be said that the remark attributed by D'Avaux to James himself, in his letter of August 14, bears out Macaulay's assertion, we must examine that point also. Let us premise, however, that D'Avaux can only be held responsible for what he said himself, and not for a hasty ejaculation or conclusion by the King. In his letters of August 4 and 6 to Louis, D'Avaux elaborates what he means by " s'asseurer " of the Protestants. He proposes that they should be disarmed, and that they should be dispersed in small parties throughout the prisons of different towns. His fear, as he states many times, was that in several towns, notably Dublin and Galway, the Protestants would be more than a match for the Catholics. At the same time he had pressed upon James the counsel that, in view of the imminent descent of Schomberg, the whole of Ulster outside Londonderry, Enniskillen, and the other places held by the Protestants should be laid bare, so that William's general would be unable to draw any supplies therefrom. He would have driven off the cattle, burnt the villages and crops, and generally laid waste the province. But James would not listen to this proposal, and declared he " would not pillage his own subjects." All that need be said on this proposal of D'Avaux's is that it was in accordance with the usages of war, and that its execution would have embarrassed Schomberg.

In his letter of August 14 D'Avaux describes the closing scene in the episode. He brings up again in an audience with the King the question of the measures he had previously proposed to be taken against the Protestants, and he asks James if he has come to any decision about his proposals. Thereupon James bursts out with the remark that he will be no party to " cutting his subjects' throats " (*égorger ses sujets*). James had, as we have seen, a habit of blurting out his inner thoughts, and it is a pity from the historical point of view that D'Avaux did not reply, " But I have never proposed that you should cut their throats." We must, however, remember the strict etiquette of Court life in those days. As a courtier D'Avaux could not meet the King's outburst with a flat contradiction. He could only turn the allegation aside by saying, " What I proposed was after all not so very inhuman." His actual reply really signified the same thing. It reads :—

" Je lui repartis que je ne lui proposois rien de fort inhumain, que je ne pretendois pas qu'on fist aucun mal aux Protestants qu'après qu'on les verroit se soulever, et que s'il en usait autrement la pitié qu'il aurait pour eux serait un cruauté pour les Catholiques."

Which may be translated :—

" I answered that I proposed to him nothing very inhuman, that I did not suggest any harm being done the Protestants until after they had risen in insurrection, and that if he treated them otherwise the pity shown to them by the King would be an act of cruelty to the Catholics."

What he had proposed, disarmament and imprisonment, is on record, but it suited Macaulay to ignore it, and to represent that cutting people's throats was, in D'Avaux's opinion, " *rien de fort inhumain.*" What D'Avaux meant was clearly that disarmament and imprisonment were " nothing very inhuman."

But it may be said that Louis's own use of the phrase " *de faire main basse,*" in his letter of September 6 shows that he knew what was in D'Avaux's mind. It does nothing of the kind. It was based on James's communication alleging that D'Avaux had proposed a massacre of the Protestants, and that he wished the ambassador to be restrained. But James's misinterpretation of D'Avaux's advice does not justify Macaulay's assumption. D'Avaux must be judged by his own words in the letters of August 4, 6, and 10.

At the same time James may be pardoned, as he lived in constant dread of the Irish Catholics falling upon and massacring the Protestants in Dublin. The memory of what had happened fifty years before was ever in his mind, and he knew that if such a calamity occurred he would be held responsible, and that his chances in England would be destroyed for ever. There is excuse for James in magnifying "*s'asseurast*" into "*égorger*." There is none for Macaulay in quoting "*faire main basse*" for "*s'asseurast*."

We may return to Londonderry, where Hamilton, deprived of the assistance of French officers, contented himself with watching the place. The offensive was taken by the besieged, who seized a mill on the north side of the town and protected the road to it with a palisade twelve feet high. While they were doing this Hamilton did not interfere with them, but when he found himself galled by the fire from this new post he proceeded to attack it. He had no artillery to cover the assault, for his cannon were at Culmore and in the batteries on the river. He trusted to his infantry capturing the palisade at a single dash, and it was not very surprising, considering that they rested on no sure foundation, that these hopes should be disappointed. In this assault, which occurred on May 16, he lost one hundred and fifty killed, including some good officers. We may name among them Brigadier Ramsay, Lieutenant-Colonel William Talbot, of Templeoge, and Viscount Netterville, of Douth. Sir Garret Aylmer and Captain John Browne, of Neal (Mayo), were taken prisoners, and the repulse was rendered all the more aggravating by the knowledge that the enemy had suffered very little loss.

Undeterred by this reverse, Hamilton decided to re-peat the attack in the same manner, but in somewhat larger force. Unfortunately, the movements of his troops were clearly visible from the town, and gave full notice of what was coming, and the garrison made suit-able preparations to meet the attack. The incident may be described in the words of Plunkett's narrative slightly epitomised :—

"Hamilton draws out the greatest part of the foot and orders them to attack the line. A detachment out of all the grenadiers of the army marched a little before under the leading of Captain John Plunkett, the youngest son of Mr. Nicholas Plunkett of Dunsoghly (county Dublin). After them there came the line of Colonels with their pikes in hand at the head of the infantry. On the right marched a detachment of horse under the conduct of Lieutenant-Colonel Edmund Butler, eldest son of Viscount Mountgarret. In their march they were exposed to the cannon of the windmill; they also received a shower of ball from the entrenchment in long fowling pieces without seeing an enemy. Captain Plunkett received at the first fire his mortal wound, and being carried off to his tent died an hour later. Notwithstanding their losses the loyal party went on boldly and attempted to mount the entrenchment, but their endeavours proved all in vain, by reason the work was so high that they had need of ladders to carry it suddenly. At the same time the party of horse on the right went to attack the end of the entrenchment by the river where it was somewhat lower. But on coming near they found it not practicable for cavalry. However, Colonel Edmund Butler, being extraordinarily well mounted, resolved to show the way if possible. At which clapping spurs to his charger he flies over, but was immediately taken prisoner. Captain Purcell of Thurles (Tipperary) followed, but his horse was killed, and he leaped back in his armour and so saved himself. An old gentleman, Edward Butler of Tinnahinch

(Carlow), gained the ditch, but he and his horse were both slain. The rest of the troopers retired having lost some of their men. Upon the conclusion the Irish were forced to retreat with the loss of at least two hundred men killed without doing any damage to the defendants. Among the slain in addition to those named were Lieutenant-Colonel Roger Farrell, Captain Barnewal of Archerstown (Meath), Captain Patrick Barnewal of Kilbrue, Captain Richard Grace, Captain Richard Fleming, brother of Sir John of Staholmock, and Captain William Talbot of Wexford."

These successive repulses shook the confidence of Hamilton's soldiers in their leader, and the King's confidence in Hamilton, who was freely criticised on all sides. Louvois said it was absolute folly to entrust an important siege to an officer whose only training had been in a foot regiment, adding, a little spitefully, " and not very distinguished in that." James, thoroughly alarmed by the holding out of Derry, decided to send General de Roze, on whom he conferred the rank of Marshal-General, to conduct the siege in person, and he moved northwards as many troops as possible, including some of those which had arrived with Château Renaud. Of the twenty French officers who had come with that commander ten were at once sent off to Derry. Of these two, the Chevalier de Tangy and Lieutenant Dastier, were engineers, and the first of any competence to look at the walls of Derry. Pointis, the artillerist, also went there about the same time, but he had no artillery, and as he was trying to make some use of one of Hamilton's cannon he was shot in the leg, rendered helpless for many months, and at one moment brought by the incompetence or neglect of his surgeons to death's door. This misfortune did not stand alone. Tangy, an admittedly competent engineer officer, was challenged by another French officer, named Coulanges, described by D'Avaux as incapable and mad, and in the ensuing duel was killed. Dastier was too young and inexperienced to take his place, and Massé, the artillerist who followed Pointis, was killed by a shot from the town. Clearly, as the French would say, James is to have no chance.

Up to this phase in the question General Roze, the officer lent by Louis to James as *generalissimo*, has done nothing beyond riding in the King's company on that first journey to Londonderry. He is a cavalry officer not less ignorant of sieges than the infantry officer Hamilton. Some curiosity must have been felt as to how he would fare. The curiosity must have been greater among his Irish colleagues, because his criticism of the Irish forces had been free and scornful.

Most of the officers, Irish as well as French, had deplored the lack of adequate supplies in equipping the troops for the field, and the badness of the weapons supplied to them. For instance, the Walter Butler regiment, so named after its Colonel, had no swords and no powder or ball. The Bagenal regiment had swords, but no bullets. Another regiment had swords, but of several lengths, and no belts to attach them to, consequently they carried them in their hands! A French report on the arms of the Lord Mayor's regiment (Creagh's) was to the effect that for one good musket ten were bad. Here also the swords were bad and of unequal lengths. But Roze, while dwelling on these defects of armament, did not confine himself to that point. He attacked the Irish officers, alleging that commissions had been recklessly given to tradespeople who knew nothing about the military profession, that the only officers who were of any good were those who had served in continental and the English armies. Tyrconnell did not deny that there was some truth in this statement, for one of the objects of his provincial tour had been to cancel commissions.

But the shortcomings of the officers was not the only defect in the Irish army. There were no artisans, no smiths, not even a baker. The art of making bread seems to have been unknown in Ireland, and the most urgent of the many urgent requests sent to France was one for several bakers. There was also no salt in Ireland, and the want of these simple necessaries reveals the deplorable state of the country. The one thing in which the country was rich was live stock, and the French commander records with some astonishment that every Irish soldier was by trade a butcher. Finally, in the list of Irish defects Roze reports that the beer was brewed so badly that it could not be drunk without producing dysentery, from which one man died out of ten. Nothing, he adds, but his duty to King Louis could keep him in such a country, and it was in this frame of mind that the General-Marshal proceeded to take charge of the Siege of Derry.

Roze having formed such a poor opinion of the forces at his disposal, was fully satisfied that the only way to secure Derry was to starve out the garrison, who were known by this time to be in straits, but he had thought out a cruel way of expediting the end. He gave orders that all the Protestants of the Province of Ulster—men, women, and children—were to be herded together and driven to the walls of Derry, so that the garrison might take pity on them and admit them, with the consequence that their supplies of food might be more speedily reduced. These unfortunate people were told that if they returned to the Irish lines they would be massacred. But Roze had gone in this beyond his powers, and directly contrary to a Royal Order which James had authorised Hamilton to issue, promising clemency, protection and liberty to all Protestants not in arms. The French General, by his new order, made the King appear in the light of a perjurer. James was naturally furious, and declared to his Court, " If Marshal Roze were my subject I would hang him " ; but as he was not his subject he had to write him a civil letter, telling him that " it is positively our will that you do not put your project in execution as far as it regards the men, women and children of whom you speak, but on the contrary that you send them back to their habitations without any injury to their persons."

This counter-order was highly creditable to James's humanity, and was in full accordance with Hamilton's procedure, for before Roze took up the command he used to allow fifty and sometimes a hundred a day of the aged, the young, and the sick of the townspeople to leave Derry and go to their friends elsewhere. It remains to the lasting credit of King James that, although he was himself a convert to Rome, and the most fervid of Catholics, he set himself rigidly against continuing the cruel proceedings so common to all religious wars. But James did not limit his disapprobation to a mild censure. He sent Lord Dover on a special mission to France " to endeavour with all the softness imaginable to have our dearest brother recall the Marquis de Roze as one after having done what he did at Londonderry incapable to serve us usefully. Since we will not vindicate our justice by punishing of him we must show our dislike of his procedure by having him recalled."

After this incident all Marshal Roze could think of doing was to take some steps to protect his camp, which had been left quite open, and to wait with such patience as he could command until the place should surrender through famine, and for a time he waited with considerable confidence, for a first attempt by General Kirke to throw supplies and troops into the town had failed. But at this juncture a very great disaster befell a part of the King's army, and not merely shook his position in Ulster, but everybody's confidence in the Army itself. The misfortune was all the greater because it befell Lord Mountcashell, who was the most experienced of the Irish generals, and whose regiment was one of the best trained and armed in the whole force.

At the same time that Roze was sent to Derry Mountcashell was ordered to collect a mixed force of 4000 men and proceed to capture Crum Castle, in Fermanagh, as a preliminary to attacking Enniskillen. The cavalry of his force was commanded by Anthony Hamilton, and the result showed that he was better with his pen than his sword. But although Mountcashell's force was not lacking in numbers, it had no artillery, and when its commander found that Crum was too strong for attack without cannon he drew off his troops and marched towards Newtown Butler. Hamilton, with the horse, marched in front, and Mountcashell followed with the infantry.

Now news of the intended attack on Crum had reached the garrison of Enniskillen, which was under the command of Brigadier William Wolseley, and it was decided to march out to relieve that place. Without either being aware of the fact Hamilton and Wolseley were marching against one another, and they came into contact near Newtown Butler. There was some little firing between the dragoons on either side, and then Hamilton, thinking he ought to rejoin his chief, gave an order which was, to put the matter charitably, misunderstood. Whatever the explanation the fact remains that the Irish cavalry turned right about and galloped off the field as fast as they could, and that Brigadier Hamilton galloped off with them, which was scarcely reconcilable with his own story at the subsequent court martial that he intended to rejoin Mountcashell. But the affair was even more discreditable than described, for the cavalry were seized with a panic in their flight, threw away their arms, and even abandoned their horses to escape across country.

News of the flight of his cavalry and of the advance of the enemy reached Mountcashell together, and thus before his force was engaged its confidence was seriously shaken by the overthrow of the cavalry. An honourable exception must be made for Mountcashell's own regiment, which stood firm and was cut to pieces. A French officer, Captain Marigny, of the regiment de Champagne, rallied the regiment of Lord Bophin and made a good stand with the best part of it, but the rest of the foot ran away as ignominiously as the cavalry had done. Both Mountcashell and Marigny were seriously wounded and taken prisoners. The French report of the battle is brief and sarcastic : "Lord Mountcashell deserted by his cowardly soldiers was wounded and taken prisoner." There is nothing in the rout of Newtown Butler to show that the Irish Catholic army might become an efficient war instrument. Roze saw his chance and capped the incident by declaring that if there were only capable officers in Derry they would lead out their men and drive his army away. Roze also presided at the court martial on Anthony Hamilton and Captain Lavalin, who misunderstood the order. Hamilton was given the benefit of the doubt, but Lavalin, an officer of some experience abroad, was ordered to be, and was, shot. Somebody ought certainly to have been punished for such a disgraceful affair, but the opinion of the day was that the real culprit was not Lavalin. D'Avaux, indeed, declared that all the intriguing of the day was for the purpose of saving the Hamiltons from the consequences of their failures, Anthony at Crum and Richard at Derry ; but then, they were not his friends.

The Mountcashell disaster was soon followed by another. The Derry garrison was at last in the throes of starvation, and unless supplies reached them surrender within a few days had become inevitable. General Kirke with the reinforcements and stores was still in Lough Foyle, a fresh effort was decided on to get succour up the river, and the "Dartmouth" frigate was assigned to lead the forlorn hope. It got past Culmore and the batteries without being hit (it was said that the men in them were all made drunk by the gift of a cask of brandy), and it smashed its way through the boom. Then people marvelled why Hamilton had not sunk boats or barges in the navigable channel. But regret was too late when in the wake of the "Dartmouth" came the rest of the ships with Kirke's regiments and ample supplies on board.

Roze at once accepted the situation. Derry had been

relieved. It only remained for him to draw off his army.
He retreated until he came to Drogheda at the mouth of
the Boyne, and there he halted by the King's order.
The total losses of the Irish army before Derry amounted
to 8000 men, chiefly from disease, and it was computed
that the defenders lost about 3000. But the Irish army
was completely demoralised and presented a deplorable
appearance. It is a well-known fact that the best armies
deteriorate during the long beleaguerment of a place, and
the Irish army had never been more than an army in the
making. D'Avaux wrote with more or less truth, "the
troops returning from the Siege of Derry are entirely ruined,
and it is useless to expect anything from such men."

Alarm was felt even in Dublin, where the garrison
consisted of six badly armed regiments who had never fired a
shot, and in the event of withdrawal from it becoming
necessary, Athlone and Limerick were the only places left
to retire to. But for the moment there was no real danger,
the Ulstermen had not the power to assume the offensive,
and although it was known with more or less certainty that
an army was coming from England, it had not yet arrived.
There was no need then for Roze's force to continue its
retreat south of the Boyne. At this moment further bad
news came from Scotland.

James's personal desire to go to Scotland has been
mentioned. In April he had allowed two of his officers,
both Highlanders, Sir John Maclean and Captain Ronald
Macdonald, chief of his clan, to go to Scotland and raise
there forces to help Dundee. It was also agreed that 2000
Irish troops should follow, and Dundee had specially asked
for some cavalry. This was compromised by the despatch
of the Purcell Dragoon regiment dismounted, and at the
same time Colonel Cannon (apparently Canan) with some
more of the Scottish officers in James's service left for their
native heath. This force was conveyed across on the three
French frigates already referred to as being under the
command of M. Du Quesne. Thus reinforced Dundee

gave battle to William's army, commanded by General Mackay in the pass of Killiecrankie, on July 27, and completely defeated it. But in the moment of victory the gallant Stuart leader received a severe and, as it proved, a mortal wound. Before he died he wrote a letter to his sovereign, which is interesting on account of the tribute it pays to the Irish soldiers who took part in the battle of Killiecrankie.

The following extracts will suffice :—

" I gave the enemy's baggage to the soldiers, who, to do them all right, both officers and common men, Highlands, Lowlands and Irish, behaved themselves with equal gallantry to whatever I saw in the hottest battles fought abroad by disciplined armies. . . . Therefore, Sir, for God's sake assist us, though it be with such another detachment of your Irish forces as you sent us before, especially of horse and dragoons." The death of Viscount Dundee, " last of Scotsmen and last of the Grahams," as the poet called him, was the death-blow to James's chances in Scotland. Colonel Cannon succeeded to the command, but although a good officer he did not understand the Highlanders' way of fighting and was not popular with them. He suffered a serious defeat at Dunkeld, and then the clans retired into the hills. The unfortunate Irish soldiers, in a strange land where supplies were exceedingly meagre, seem to have died almost to the last man, and literally of starvation. A certain number of the officers of Dundee's army later on reached France, where we shall meet them again.

This succession of failures and reverses brought James's fortunes to a low ebb, but before we record the remarkable improvement that took place in them during the late summer of 1689, and that was maintained until William's arrival in the following year, it will be well to describe the episodes which culminated in Melfort's removal from office and D'Avaux's departure for France.

Louis was very much concerned when he learnt, through

D'Avaux's communications, that James's councillors were divided against each other, and he exhorted his envoy "to try and impress on Melfort that the interests of his King and my own (Louis's) are the same," and D'Avaux replies that he will do his best to get on with Melfort and "to induce him to do things which shall be advantageous for Ireland and France." But a very little later he reports that Melfort is hopeless, that he has two faults characteristic of Scotsmen, " he is very hot-tempered and takes offence at trifles," and besides that, even if he gave way to him in everything, no good would follow because the Irish detested him and were clamouring for his removal from office.

Financial considerations were also the determining factors in the situation. There was practically no money in Ireland ; that brought from France was not much, and both James and Melfort seemed unable to make the most of the little they had. Besides, it was impossible to get accounts from them. D'Avaux writes in one despatch : " King James wastes his money, gives nothing for useful purposes, and thousands for useless. I have paid two hundred and fifty thousand francs to his Receiver, and I can get no information as to what has been done with it." Certainly none of the Irish commanders ever got a penny of it, and Melfort's neglect to send supplies was often the direct cause of some of the worst mishaps. Melfort's fall was deferred by the frequent illnesses of Tyrconnell, but about the time of the withdrawal from Derry he recovered sufficiently to resume his place on the Council, and a concerted effort was made to get rid of the Secretary of State, as Melfort was called.

D'Avaux undertook to bell the cat, and called upon Melfort to give some explanation in regard to what had been done with the money supplied by France. Melfort replied that this was very little, and that much more was required. The French ambassador retorted that he had allowed Protestants to leave the country with a million

H

(i.e. francs) of money, and Melfort said that they had only removed 400,000. The scene became somewhat stormy, and angry words were exchanged. Among other things D'Avaux asked Melfort to take off the import duty on French wine, and Melfort replied that he would do so if France removed her duty on Irish wool and cloth. Several Platonic ordinances had been published in both countries about the naturalisation of the two peoples in the other's country, and Louis had taken off the import duties on all Irish articles " except wool." The situation somewhat recalls the speech of Dido to Æneas: " Tros Tyriusque idem, et nullo discrimine agetur."

Immediately after this interview D'Avaux had an audience of the King, and expressed a very strong opinion that Melfort was incompetent and ought to be removed from office. James replied with some asperity that he was aware of his shortcomings, and that he would remove him if there was any one to put in his place, but unfortunately there was not. As D'Avaux then suggested, would it not be better to have no ministers here than retain one who was clearly injuring the King's cause ?

At this time letters arrived from Queen Mary d'Esté urging James to dismiss Melfort, but unfortunately the weight of the advice was diminished by an attack on D'Avaux, who was alleged to have said in his letters to France that James had no will of his own, that he was ruled in everything by Berwick, who in turn was swayed by the Hamiltons. James thereupon taxed D'Avaux in the matter, alleging that he was making charges behind his back, but he denied ever having said anything of the kind, and a search of his published correspondence reveals no evidence on the subject. What he had written was that James consulted Berwick in all matters affecting the army, and allowed him alone to make the appointments, giving as an instance of this that Berwick had made his Lieutenant-Colonel a Major-General, although a regular toper who got drunk every day. As this officer was not

Irish it is unnecessary to give his name. He may have drunk hard, but he could also fight well.

At the same time D'Avaux had written some very severe things about James in his letters to Louvois. He accused him of " sleeping when he should be awake." He also complained of James's want of appreciation of good service, instancing the case of Du Quesne, who took the Irish regiment to Scotland and captured several prizes, which he handed over to James without receiving any reward or recognition, and when he came to Dublin to have a farewell audience the King left him to pay his travelling expenses out of his own pocket. As a final censure the French ambassador declared that the King " gets angry very easily," and then " il n'agit pas avec la noblesse de cœur qu'on devrait attendre non pas d'un roi mais d'un simple gentilhomme."

This free criticism of royalty in that age was somewhat unusual and hazardous. D'Avaux was certainly bringing about Melfort's fall, but at the same time he was undermining his own position at Versailles. He did not know, of course, that quite unconsciously he was playing the game into the hands of his successor Lauzun, the next puppet of the show. Lauzun was the carrier of the tales between Versailles and St. Germains. His friend, Lord Dover, who did not care much for the French making for the moment an exception in Lauzun's favour, but who detested the Irish, brought him a supply of gossip after each mission to Dublin. Queen Mary insensibly adopted the opinion that Lauzun, who had rescued her, might prove her husband's saviour also. Sir George Porter, who had been James's ambassador at Rome (whence he reported that the Pope was all for the enemies of France), was sent by the Queen to Dublin to disparage D'Avaux and support the interests of Lauzun. D'Avaux described him as " lazy, generally disliked, and dishonest," and there is good reason for saying that the criticism was just. When Louvois got wind of the plot he warned D'Avaux to be more careful, but by that time his relations with James had become hopelessly strained, and he was only desirous himself of getting back to France.

If the objection to Melfort's remaining in office had only come from D'Avaux it is probable that James would have succeeded in putting off a decision to remove him, but the outcry among the Irish at his disregard of their interests had become loud and menacing. The climax of his shortcomings seems to have been reached when he turned a deaf ear to Sarsfield's request that 300 horses should be sent to him in Sligo. It was after this incident that Tyrconnell, with a deputation of Irish officers, presented himself to James and formally demanded Melfort's removal. To such a plain and public request as this James was unable to give any but an affirmative answer. He removed Melfort from the post of Secretary of State for Ireland, accepting Tyrconnell's nephew, Sir William Talbot, in his place, and then to show that the deposed Secretary was still in favour he made him Secretary of State for England !

The consequence of this was that while Irish affairs were left to Sir William Talbot, Melfort, although denounced on all hands, still ruled the King. The Duchess of Tyrconnell, in the absence of her husband, spoke to him for interfering in matters that no longer concerned him, and Melfort haughtily and angrily justified himself by declaring that " an angel from Heaven could not have done better than he had done," adding in what might seem to us an irrelevant manner that " those who were afraid should leave the country." Melfort might have stayed on indefinitely, and had the satisfaction of seeing D'Avaux go first, if he had not suddenly learnt that there was a plot among the Irish officers to assassinate him. His last offence had been to allow four Irish Protestant peers in Dublin and Kildare to retain strong mounted bodyguards, for which he was bribed. The imminence of the danger was brought home to him by the lawlessness of some of the

The Lord Thomas Howard (of Worksop)
from the Painting at Arundel Castle in the possession of the Duke of Norfolk.

troops in Dublin. More than one encounter took place between the bodyguard and the men of other regiments, and on September 6 he requested James's leave to return to France. He and his wife left Dublin in secret, and it was said that in their carriage they carried away a good deal of treasure. D'Avaux's comment on the news when it reached him was, " if it had only taken place three months ago it might have done some good; now it is too late." Melfort reached France in safety, and was received by Queen Mary on September 26 at St. Germains, where we may leave him for the present. He was more fortunate than poor Lord Thomas Howard, of Worksop, who sailed shortly afterwards and was lost at sea. Lord Thomas, " the best man here," according to D'Avaux, was a nobleman of great parts, but he stood aloof from political intrigues. His two sons (to whom Evelyn refers) became in turn Dukes of Norfolk.

No exact information of Lord Thomas's fate has been forthcoming, and the records at the French War Office contain nothing on the subject. The known facts are that he sailed on board a ship called " The Tempest " in company with a well-known French officer—the Chevalier de St. Didier—and that nothing was ever heard of either again. The weather was very bad at the moment of sailing from Cork, and the captain—an Englishman, who had been consul in Holland—was advised not to sail, but he refused to listen to the advice.

Melfort was one of those bad advisers with whom the Stuarts were cursed at all stages of their history. There is no evidence to show that he was a traitor like Sunderland, although one of the subsequent edicts passed at St. Germains in 1694 was " a pardon to the Earl of Melfort for acts of treason to James and his predecessor." But it is clear that he had no grasp of the state of affairs. He pursued the shadow of James's possible return to England, and neglected the substance of setting up a strong Government in Ireland. As he was a Protestant he had no sympathy with the views of Catholic reactionaries, and it was quite impossible for him to work in harmony with Tyrconnell. He had gained James's ear by flattery, and especially did he flatter him in his views about the sentiments of love and loyalty of his English subjects who rose in arms against him. At the same time Melfort was extremely jealous of his master's attentions to his wife. Much of his time was given up to watching her movements, and as Lady Melfort's main object was to amass money—a special collection being raised for her benefit among the Jacobites in Scotland—an explanation may be furnished of the fact that whatever the Secretary of State may have done with the French money, very little of it ever reached James. In James's own memoir it is stated with some bitterness that he long was charged for the maintenance of 50,000 troops whilst there were only 18,000 men with the colours. Certainly if money was diverted from its proper purpose Melfort was the only man into whose pockets it could have passed.

The disputes with Melfort had shaken the faith of the French Government in the feasibility of doing anything material from the side of Ireland. If James could only have made Ireland an independent kingdom it would have remained a thorn in the side of England, cramping her efforts as against France. But James did not show the smallest inclination to pacify the whole of Ireland, or to rest contented with it if pacified. He had his own ends in view, and they were totally disconnected with French interests. Louvois saw quite clearly what was in James's mind; he also saw that his schemes were visionary and unattainable. The Frenchman said, " England is lost, but Ireland may be won." The Stuart Prince replied, " I do not care about Ireland, but I want England." Louvois wrote peremptorily to D'Avaux on receiving these chimerical propositions : " Tell King James bluntly that if he continues to listen to bad advisers it will be useless for King Louis to waste his resources in trying to help him." And if Louvois had had his own way it is probable that the Irish adventure would have been dropped then and there.

But King Louis had passed his word to help his royal brother, and while he often heeded the wise counsels of Louvois there were times when he followed his own line and was not to be turned from his course. Provided his arms were successful in the Netherlands he was quite prepared to send some troops to Ireland to endeavour to change the fortunes of the war there. He had the assurances of his ambassador that at least an equal number of Irish troops should come over to France, and of his officers Boisseleau and Pointis that Irishmen only required good discipline and arms to make good troops. It is quite true that down to September, 1689 (the date of Melfort's departure), they had done nothing to deserve this good opinion. Defeat, disaster, and even disgrace (the affair between Crum and Newtown Butler was disgraceful) were the only records attached to their name and efforts. The army created by Tyrconnell had failed in every sense to justify its existence. It might have been termed a horde or a mob, and if James had fled with Melfort it seems only too probable that no opportunity would have been left it of redeeming the fallen reputation of the Irish people for natural courage reduced to the lowest possible ebb by the failure at Derry and elsewhere. The remarkable change that followed will be the theme of the next chapter.

Chapter V

THE CAMPAIGNS OF 1689-90

WHEN Melfort left Ireland for France it looked as if James's situation were desperate. What were the causes of the remarkable improvement that took place immediately after his departure ? They may well have been more numerous, but two at least stand out with prominence. The first was the arrival at the end of July of five competent French generals. They were intended to take the places of the unfortunate Maumont and Pusignan, and their names were Count de Gacé, M. d'Escots, M. d'Amanzé, M. Saint Pater, and M. d'Hocquincourt. All these officers held the rank either of Maréchal de Camp, or of Brigadier in the French army, and in Ireland they were promoted by King James to that of Lieutenant-General or Major-General. At the same time five of James's own officers (one Irish, two English, and two Scottish) were promoted Lieutenant-Generals, and three, including Sarsfield, became Major-Generals. The placing in command of a considerable number of superior officers, many of whom had served in war, was undoubtedly a beneficial step.

It may be doubted whether it would, by itself, have produced any great result but for the second cause. Another French officer, who did more by himself, if the test of results is applied, than all the other French officers together to help James's cause, had just at this very critical juncture brought to a completion his efforts for the formation of a new Irish army. Boisseleau was left, when James landed at Kingsale, to perform what seemed the thankless and unpromising task of drilling Irish recruits, and Boisseleau's zeal had been somewhat chilled in the first place by being left a simple Brigadier when others of his own rank got a step. Besides, Boisseleau had no control over the arms which de Pointis held in his hands and would not part with. It was not until the arrival of the Château Renaud squadron that matters improved for him, and that he found himself able to dispose of the nucleus of a regular military force furnished by the soldiers who had fled to France from England. About the time that the regiments from the force before Derry were reaching Drogheda and Dublin, Boisseleau's new army had begun to collect from the south in the camp specially prepared near Dublin not far from the Curragh in Kildare.

One of the French officers last arrived, M. d'Escots, was ordered to visit all the Irish regiments in their garrisons and to prepare a muster roll. The following is its exact text:

Positions and strength of Irish Regiments (according to M. d'Escots' report of August 29, 1689).

AT DROGHEDA

Regiment	Strength
The Grand Prior's	200 (of whom 120 armed)
Nugent	400 (of whom 168 armed)
Gormanstown	200
Slane	300
Moore	400
Louth	400
Purcell (Dragoons)	360
Westmeath (Cavalry)	200
Sutherland „	105

AT DUBLIN

Regiment		Strength
Guards		1200
Bellew		350
Clancarty		200
Barrett		400
Thomas Butler		300
Galway	Infantry	400
Mountcashell		200
Oxburgh		300
Grace		150
Kilmallock		500
Kavanagh		300

At Dublin

Regiment		Strength
Dungan		360
Simon Luttrell	} Dragoons	150
Cotter		240
Guards		200
Horse Grenadiers		50
Tyrconnell		250
Galmoye	} Cavalry	250
Luttrell		180
Sarsfield		250
Abercorn		120
Parker		400

(All the Dragoons and Cavalry not mounted)

At Camp near Dublin

John Hamilton	247
Richard Butler	321
Edward Butler	368
Eustace	454
Fitzgerald	193
Creagh	547
Bagenal	458
Boisseleau	1178
Antrim	634

At Athlone

Bophin	215
Dillon	500
Farrell	350
Clanrickarde	350

At Galway

Dominic Browne	400

At Limerick

MacElligott	450
Charles O'Brien	400
Sutherland (Cavalry)	30

At Kingsale

Nicholas Browne	450

At Cork

O'Donovan	400
Macmahon	500
Kenmare	200

AT WATERFORD

Regiment	Strength
Tyrone	400

AT WEXFORD

Westmeath (Cavalry)	80

AT CASTLE DERMOT

Dungan (Dragoons)	60

AT ROSS AND KILKENNY

Kenmare	250

AT CARLOW

Eustace	53

AT CARRICKFERGUS

McCarty Mor	200
Cormac O'Neil	300

AT NEWRY

Cormac O'Neil	250
Gordon O'Neil	100
Maxwell (Dragoons)	360
Chevalier O'Neil (Dragoons)	150 (all unarmed)

AT CHARLEMONT

Gordon O'Neil	100

These items give a grand total of 16,468 infantry, 1680 dragoons, and 2115 cavalry, or a little over 20,000 men altogether. About 14,000 of them were stationed between the line of the Boyne and Dublin. This army was not fully equipped, and many of the cavalry and dragoon regiments had an inadequate supply of horses, but it was none the less an immense improvement on the force that had carried on the siege of Derry. There was more cohesion in it, the commanding officers knew their work, and for the first time the Irish regiments presented something like a trained appearance. D'Avaux himself went to see the troops and was filled with astonishment. Whereas all his previous letters had been full of dismal forebodings, he began from the middle of September to report " great improvement and more hope generally," and at the commencement of October he declared that " the improvement in the Irish army is almost inconceivable."

The Irish public were also described as being quite pleased at their men being brought to the front, and especially at the command in Dublin being given to Simon Luttrell, an Irishman.

The improvement had not been effected a moment too soon, for a new and formidable danger confronted King James. An army of over 10,000 men, under the command of Marshal Schomberg, had landed at Bangor, in County Down, on August 23, 1689, and this force was joined by the Ulster corps from Derry and Enniskillen, raising its total strength to 16,000 men. This army was also strong in artillery, the arm in which the Jacobite side was weak and sometimes totally deficient throughout the whole of the three years' war. Schomberg's first act was to attack Carrickfergus, where Colonel McCarty Mor was in command of a garrison of 600 men. The place was well defended for ten days, and then the powder gave out; but the garrison was allowed to leave on honourable terms and to rejoin the main army. The terms of the surrender, however, were not strictly kept, and many of the men's arms were taken away from them. Macpherson also alleges that the Ulstermen drove the women through the streets stark naked. Schomberg then moved south by the coast road and came to Dundalk.

One of the opinions prevalent in James's camp was that a large portion of Schomberg's army might be induced to desert, and a proclamation was issued from Drogheda offering every soldier who deserted forty shillings and employment, and every officer a commission of equal rank. The proclamation does not seem to have been directly successful, but on the other hand 500 of the French troops (Huguenots) mutinied, and were shut up in Carlingford. A scheme was formed to rescue them, and entrusted to Colonel Stapylton and Captain Hugh Macnamara. Its failure is explained by the excessive loyalty of the Irish troops, for when on his approach being challenged Macnamara declared that he was for King William, his men angrily protested that they were for King James, thus spoiling the expedition's chances of success. When called upon to explain their conduct, they declared that they thought that their leader had turned traitor and was leading them to an ambuscade. It was an instance of the peril of not taking one's men into one's counsels.

When James heard of Schomberg's advance, he ordered his army to cross the Boyne and move northwards. At the same time he left Dublin for the front, declaring with some proper pride that " he was not going to be walked out of Ireland without having a blow for it." By calling in all the surrounding garrisons he seems to have succeeded in concentrating 20,000 men at Ardee by September 25, and the following Order of Battle shows the names of his commanders and the list of the regiments present :—

KING JAMES'S ORDER OF BATTLE (SEPT., 1689)

Right	Centre	Left
Roze	The King	Tyrconnell
Marquis de Girardin	R. Hamilton	Count de Gacé
Galmoye	Buchan, Boisseleau	Sheldon
	Wachop, D'Amanzé, Dorington	
	Infantry	
Cavalry	The Duke of Berwick	Cavalry
	M. d'Escots	
	M. Carney, Saint Pater, Maxwell, Sarsfield	
	Hugh Sutherland	

Cavalry Regiments		Infantry Regiments	Infantry Regiments
Cotter		Mountcashell	Dillon
Tyrconnell	of 3	Bellew	Kavanagh
Parker	squadrons	Nugent	Galway
Sarsfield	each	Slane	Antrim
		Edward Butler	Kilmallock
Luttrell		Richard Butler	Grace
Galmoye		Boisseleau	Eustace
Body Guard	of 1	Clancarty	Hamilton
Purcell	squadron	Oxburgh	Bagenal
Dungan	each	Creagh	Louth
Abercorn		Gormanstown	Cormac O'Neil
Sutherland		Guards	Clanrickarde

After a few days the King, finding that Schomberg would not leave his entrenched camp, marched towards him in full array and offered battle. But the Prince of Orange's general was too cautious and would not accept the challenge. On the other hand, James, having made a good show, was too cautious to attack him, and this led to a hot dispute among his Generals, some of whom declared that the loss in carrying the entrenchments would not be very great. It would be idle to attempt to decide between the two opinions. James seems to have distrusted his army, most of which, although admirably drilled, had never taken part in a regular action. He expressed the opinion that "if we only had five or six French battalions we would drive Schomberg out of Ireland," and the inference is that as he had not those battalions he could not do so. At the same time there can be no doubt, looking at the situation by the light of after events, that he had a far better chance of defeating Schomberg on October 1, 1689, than he had of vanquishing that Marshal's master in the following July, when he fought against far superior odds; nor can there be any doubt that if he had fought and won, William himself would never have ventured to cross the Irish Sea.

In James's own memoir he enters into close detail as to his movements and intentions during this brief campaign, and he attributes to Roze the caution and timidity which the friends of the French general attributed to the King. Schomberg was able to give a better justification for his inaction. He wrote to William : " So far as I can judge from the state of the Enemy, and King James's having collected here all the force that he could in this kingdom, he wants to come to a battle before the Troops separate on account of the bad season which will soon begin; for this reason it appears to me that we should lie here upon the defensive. . . . If Your Majesty was well informed of the state of our army, and that of our enemy, the nature of the country, and the situation of the two camps, I do not believe you would incline to risk an attack. If we did not succeed Your Majesty's army would be lost without resource. I make use of that term for I do not believe

if it was once put into disorder that it could be re-
established."

No doubt Schomberg's own admissions strengthen the
case of those who declare that James lost the game by his
fatal hesitation in October, 1689. The elaborate defence
left in the King's own memoirs and used verbatim in the
official Life is strong evidence that James, thinking the
matter over carefully in after years, concluded that a
mistake had been made in not attacking Schomberg, and
then threw the blame incontinently on Roze. There is
good reason to believe that James owed Roze a grudge,
for when D'Avaux suggested a month or so earlier that
he should obtain Roze's advice, the King had answered
testily that he " did not wish for the Marshal's advice."

Having decided not to attack, the King thought there
was no use in further watching his cautious opponent,
and broke up his camp, placing his troops in winter quarters
along the Boyne and near Dublin. As advanced posts the
Jacobites held Cavan, Belturbet, and Charlemont, and
James established himself in Dublin Castle for the winter.
While inaction prevailed in county Louth, Sarsfield,
having got the horses which Melfort had refused him,
made a daring raid into Sligo, and recovered the town of that
name and also Jamestown.

Schomberg, having waited some days to ascertain
whether the Jacobite army had really withdrawn, also
broke up his camp and retired on the line from Newry to
the sea. His army had suffered greatly from the ravages of
typhus and influenza. Bad food, bad water, and the heavy
rains had affected the English recruits very adversely, and the
total loss of Schomberg's army during the winter of 1689-90
was placed as high as 8000 men. It is well to remember
that Schomberg's army was mainly English—seventeen
battalions out of a total of twenty-two being English—
whereas William's army in the following year contained
a majority of continental soldiers, and indeed very few
English troops at all. It is a point of permanent interest

and significance that there was really no standing army in England of any importance in 1688. The House of Commons had prevented the creation of a regular army. This fact no doubt enabled it to oust the Stuarts, but it also admitted a foreign army. There was another consequence. At least 15,000 raw English recruits died in Ireland of the diseases inseparable from camps in those days, 8000 under Schomberg and 7000 under Ginkel, in 1691.

When James returned to Dublin, he took two steps of a more uncompromising character than any he had yet sanctioned. He ordered the complete disarming of the Protestants in Dublin, which had been up to that point very partially carried out, and he wrote a letter with his own hand to Louis begging him to send five or six veteran regiments of foot, and promising to return as many from among the best in Ireland. Up to this point he had been haggling about the exchange, but now, moved by necessity, he passed his royal word to do his part in the transaction. It was also arranged that Roze and D'Avaux should return with the Irish regiments, and that Lauzun should come over with the French to assume the supreme command. The meritorious Dangeau notes the completion of this transaction in an entry of October 29, which may be quoted : " The King has decided to send M. de Lauzun to Ireland with 7000 infantry including 15 or 1600 English, Scottish, and Irish troops now at Lille. Roze is to come back, and Lauzun is to hold the rank of Captain-General." On the following day King Louis goes to St. Germains to tell Queen Mary the news, at which she is very pleased.

Although James was at last induced to adopt some severe measures against the Protestants as a general body, he could never bring himself to be severe with individuals. His official printer was a Protestant, and a notice calling upon the Protestants to surrender arms and horses under severe penalties (this was the last of several similar notices, but it ordained harsher penalties) was sent to him to print. But somehow he forgot to print it, and the omission was not discovered for several weeks. James was urged to make an example of him; instead he accepted his excuses. Another instance was when he allowed a resident in Dublin, detected in corresponding with William's Government, to escape so that he should not be obliged to have him executed. It was not thus that William dealt with informers. When Mark Bagot was caught some months later disguised in woman's clothes in Dublin, he was hanged without mercy. From the humane point of view there is not the smallest reproach to be cast at James II.

The winter months of 1689-90, pending the arrival of the French reinforcements, were passed in absolute stagnation. The process of hibernation was not enlivened by even the quarrels of D'Avaux and Melfort, and perhaps the most exciting incident was Lord Mountcashell's escape from Enniskillen after the proposal to exchange him for Lord Mountjoy had been discussed. The Dublin Court, despite the gay spirits of the Duchess of Tyrconnell and her daughters, for three of whom she had succeeded, during her husband's Viceroyalty, in finding husbands among the Jacobite peers (Viscount Rosse, Viscount Kingsland, and Henry, afterwards Viscount Dillon), was dull, poor, and without distinction. The available resources were so meagre that even at the King's table wine had to be measured out in small glasses. All the efforts made to improve the financial situation had failed. The white metal money had fallen into even worse repute than the brass. D'Avaux's hoards, secret and avowed, had been exhausted. The only course left to support existence was to sleep through as much as possible of the winter in the hope that the spring would bring French troops and victory.

James, having made his request to the French King, seems to have thought that there was nothing more for him to do than to await Lauzun's arrival, and sank into moody inactivity. The same lethargy fell over all the Irish camps, and the improvidence that neglected to

I

prepare everything for the decisive campaign, which every one saw was to mark the year 1690, may have been the principal cause of the defeat that happened when victory seemed to be reasonably assured. As Plunkett wrote :—

" During this winter, 1689, the King and his Catholic people of Ireland were cheerful enough as having not received so great a loss from the army of Marshal Schomberg as they at first apprehended. But with all this His Majesty had little or no intelligence of what preparations were a-making in England against Ireland for the next campaign, and therefore he and his loyalists improved not their condition. There was no augmentation of troops made, as there should be, and that considerably ; no care taken in exercising the army in their respective quarters ; in providing arms and apparel, in fortifying towns and filling them with ammunition and victuals. This was not the way to secure Ireland and conquer England. Great undertakings require great wisdom, great care, great diligence. Alas, it is no children's play ! "

At the same time that it is impossible to acquit James of apathy in regard to preparations for the future, it must be noted that he passed some acts that were intended to benefit his soldiers. In December, 1689, he restored the infantry soldier his full two shillings a week, and the dragoon his six shillings, while the cavalry man was to get eight shillings. Of course it had to be paid largely in base money, but the King was not to be blamed for that, and if his promises could raise the value of a currency it would not long have been base. But what he could do in other ways to secure for the men their money's worth he did. He caused sutling houses to be opened throughout Ireland wherein good ale had to be sold by measure at two pence a pint, and he caused a notice to that effect to be placed in their windows written in English and French (Pan-Gaelics must learn with regret that there was no reference to Irish). When meat became so dear in Dublin that the price was prohibitive, although there was plenty of meat in the country, he sent the Lord Mayor an order that he was neither to tax it nor hinder its admission into the city.

D'Avaux alone was busy and attentive to the work he had in hand. He dropped the rôle of James's adviser or critic. The responsibility for his success or failure was no longer his affair ; it was passing into other hands. But he was responsible for his master's getting the pick of the Irish regiments and of the Irish officers, and this kept him busy when others were idle. As that episode forms the true birth of the Irish Brigade, we shall leave it for detailed description in a later chapter devoted to the Mountcashell Brigade.

As the Irish troops had nothing to do, it is not very surprising that quarrelling was somewhat common among them. Among the French officers more than one duel was fought, and although duelling does not seem to have been fashionable in the Irish army at this period there were several murders. One of these was the case of a non-attached French officer named Coverent (a volunteer, in fact), who was killed by an Irish dragoon named John Wall. Wall was acquitted on the ground that Coverent was not attached to his regiment and that there was nothing to show him that he was an officer. The French were very much surprised and not over-pleased at discovering that one of their officers might be killed by a private soldier, who would escape scot-free on the decision of a native court martial.

The most sensational incident, however, was the quarrel between Henry FitzJames, the titular Lord Grand Prior, and Lord Dungan, which might have had serious consequences but for the latter's great self-control and forbearance. Lord Dungan, who was one of the best of the Irish officers and who had raised his dragoons to a high state of efficiency, was at a merry soldiers' party in Dublin with other Irish officers when the Duke of Berwick and his brother Henry FitzJames entered the room. A toast was being given, and Lord Dungan, filling up a glass, handed it to FitzJames with a request to join in it. He had, perhaps, not reflected on its character, or was ignorant of the true Stuart feeling; but when he gave it as "Confusion to Melfort and all bad counsellors," FitzJames not merely refused to drink it, but declared that he regarded Melfort as a friend. High words began to pass, and before those present could intervene FitzJames had flung his glass, wine and all, in Dungan's face, spoiling his cravat and cutting his nose.

Of such an incident it was only too easy for those present to imagine the grave consequences, and while Berwick and others intervened to prevent an immediate collision on the spot a duel seemed inevitable, and this, between two such notable persons, could scarcely fail to have the effect of increasing the dissatisfaction of the Irish officers with the Court. Lord Dungan, too, had the reputation of being rather a fire-eater, and in the opinion of the most competent persons present the hours of Henry FitzJames might be counted.

But Lord Dungan was not blind to all the wide and far-reaching possibilities of the occasion, and he showed an unexpected magnanimity. He refused to regard Mr. FitzJames's act as one that called for serious treatment. It was the unreflecting step of a boy who, Lord Dungan could not forget, was also the son of his King. As far as he was concerned then, he would treat the incident as if it had never occurred. D'Avaux, who records the incident, gives the Grand Prior a very bad character, stating that he was "a very debauched young man, drinking brandy all the day, and unable for a long time at a stretch to mount his horse through intoxication." In this case perhaps D'Avaux was a little too severe, as we may have better means of judging when we meet the younger FitzJames later on at St. Germains. But attention may be called to the curious coincidence that the widow of the young Lord Grand Prior, who championed the first Duke of Melfort, was to marry the second Duke of Melfort, and that Lord Dungan and FitzJames may have ridden in some of those cavalry charges at the Boyne from which the elder did not return.

The King of France having decided at last to send troops to Ireland, it might have been thought that he would spare no pains to see that they left in such a state as should ensure the best results for himself. Under ordinary circumstances the commanding officer would have seen to this himself in conjunction with the Ministers Louvois and the young Colbert, and all would have gone off satisfactorily. In the wars of the first half of Louis's long reign, only generals of proved merit were given commands. We have now reached the period when the Great Monarch, satiated with success, seemed to think that victory would always come at his command, and that a courtier might be just as useful in the field as a trained general. Lauzun was the first of these later strategists of the boudoir who between them were to destroy the talisman of success so long in Louis's possession, and his personal triumph was the more remarkable because to a certain extent he had forced Louis to give him the command. Circumstances had aided him, Queen Mary had aided him, so had Madame de Maintenon, and *le triste personnage* of Louvois, " that Lauzun little in mind and little in body " of Count Rabutin, was entrusted with the command of the first French expedition sent across the English Channel since Louis VI besieged Dover. Every one marvelled by what dexterity he had got himself into the post ; no one presumed on the expedition succeeding because he had got it.

But while Court circles marvelled and speculated, there was one personage, the Minister Louvois, who bitterly resented the appointment of Lauzun. He had the greatest contempt for the adventurer, and he was never at any pains to conceal it. The success of the expedition depended on the way in which it was equipped as much as on the manner in which it was led. There is no reason to believe that Louvois went so far as to withhold what was asked for, but Lauzun did not know what to ask for, and Louvois did not trouble himself to supply what the ignorance of the applicant did not comprehend. Besides, James had asked for a great deal more than the French troops. He wanted arms, supplies of all kinds, and money. The following list of his requests cannot be said to err on the side of lack of comprehensiveness.

KING JAMES'S REQUESTS OF THE FRENCH GOVERNMENT (OCTOBER, 1689)

6000 French infantry armed and with their tents.
A sum of money (unspecified).
1000 barrels of powder containing 100 lbs. each, ball, tinder. etc., in a corresponding quantity.
10,000 grenades.
12,000 muskets.
3000 firelocks.
13,000 bandoliers.
Train of artillery with officers.
Some Surgeons and Armourers.
Bridges and material.
Harness.

It is difficult to state what part of the stores and arms requested ever left France or reached Ireland, for at least one ship laden with muskets and powder was captured by an English cruiser ; but certainly there were many gaps in the list. The Irish acknowledgment of the stores that came with Lauzun's expedition reads somewhat indefinitely, as " twenty-two pieces of cannon for the field, three hundred bombs of different sizes, six thousand grenades, a great quantity of ball of all sorts, and of arms and other necessaries for the troops, Irish as well as French." But there was certainly a great deficiency of powder, for the French authorities could not believe the fact that there was no saltpetre in Ireland ; and with regard to the muskets only a small number was sent, because deduction was made from James's request of the 7000 supposed to be possessed by the Mountcashell brigade, which was dispensed from bringing arms into France. It never entered the heads of the French magnates that that brigade was an unarmed force, and that if it had been made a condition that it should come " arms in hand " it would never have sailed from Ireland.

But the main request of all was complied with in its entirety. The 6000 French infantry were detached from the army in Flanders, where the withdrawal of William's best Dutch troops to England had undoubtedly weakened the forces of the Allies, and, indeed, it is proof that France then possessed no transcendent military genius, or he would have overwhelmed the enemy in the Netherlands. They were excellent and veteran battalions too, not the ordinary French line regiment. Louis himself had once drawn up a standard of comparison in his own army, and he had valued a Swiss battalion as equal to four, and an Italian, English, or Scottish to two battalions of the French line. The troops he sent to Ireland were of this higher category. They were mainly Swiss, Flemish and Walloon, the French element was practically non-represented ; but on the other hand there were no better troops for stern fighting and the hard work of a campaign to be found in France.

The seven battalions, each of which ought to have numbered no less than 1000 men, were those of Faméchon, Zurlauben (2), Forest, Courtassier, Lamarche and Mérode.

Name of Regiment	Officers	Men
Lamarche	47	1050
Tournaisis (Courtassier)	47	1050
Faméchon	55	1000
Forest	47	1050
Mérode	55	800
Zurlauben (2)	90	2000
	341	6950

There were also six artillery officers and sixty-one supernumeraries, including medical staff, and intendants of stores.

The totals quoted give the paper strength of the respective regiments ; but the returns of the number of troops who sailed from Brest with Lauzun show a total of officers and men for the seven battalions of 6547.

Nor did the French King fail to send some good general

officers. The Marquis Léry de Girardin, one of the best cavalry leaders in the French army, was appointed second in command under Lauzun with the rank of Lieutenant-General, and the Marquis de la Hoguette, reputed to be one of the bravest generals of junior rank in the French service, accompanied them as Maréchal de Camp. The French troops, however, were accompanied not, as Dangeau expected, " by 1700 Irish soldiers," but " by three or four hundred Irish and a few English." Finally, a strong protecting squadron of forty-one warships was got together at Brest, and placed under the command of Gabaret and Amfreville. While the French battalions were being got ready for their voyage from Brest, we must describe some occurrences in Ireland which were symptomatic of what was to follow.

The autumn campaign of 1689, for no better reason perhaps than that it had been free of distinct reverse, had left the impression that James's chances were far from hopeless. The events of the winter were to modify this impression and to revive despondency. The first incident occurred at Newry, an open town held by a few of Schomberg's troops. Boisseleau sent Captain Christopher Plunkett with a party of grenadiers to seize it, which was not very difficult. But for some unknown reason Boisseleau became alarmed for either the safety of this detachment or his own security, and sent a message peremptorily recalling Plunkett at once. This was particularly annoying for the Irish captain, as he had located a good deal of spoil in Newry, all of which he had to leave behind. An extraordinarily magnified report of this affair reached Paris, from which it appeared that " Boisseleau had beaten an English force, captured the Lord who commanded it and killed six English captains." The Paris world needed something definite to substantiate Sir George Porter's fairy tales that " James had 28,000 good troops and would be ready to invade England in the spring " ; and the Newry bulletin was one of the encouraging incidents put in circulation.

A few weeks after the Newry affair a small force was sent, under Brigadier Patrick Nugent, to attack Nenagh Castle in County Longford. It belonged to Sir Thomas New-comen, who had raised a regiment for William of Orange, which was in Schomberg's camp. The castle was held in his absence by his wife and a small garrison. Nugent made some demonstration before Nenagh, and the garrison marched out with the honours of war, Lady Newcomen riding at the head of her men. There was not the smallest good to be gained from this sort of demonstration, and it had not even the excuse of the MacMahon " criaghts " (irregulars or rapparees), who indulged in raids and forays for the purpose of acquiring arms. Lady Newcomen's garrison carried off theirs in glory.

The provocations at Newry and Nenagh stirred Schom-berg to action, and it was to be to some effect. In February he moved a strong party composed of the Enniskilleners and some English troops to Cavan with orders to seize and hold that place at all costs. The command was given to Brigadier William Wolseley, whose views about the Irish problem were summed up in his favourite sentence, " An Irishman is only to be taught his duty by the stick." As an officer he was very alert and his troops were excellent. D'Avaux knew perfectly well what he was writing about when he said, " Ulstermen are beyond question the best of the Irish troops," and they were the substance of Wolseley's force.

The Jacobite commander at Cavan was Major-General John Wauchope, a Scot who had been an officer in the Guards in London, and who owed his advance to his friends and kinsmen the Drummonds and Lord Middleton. He was in favour with the Duke of Berwick, who had given him the command at Cavan because he trusted his judgment. At the same time the Duke says in his Memoirs that he charged him to be on the look-out and to keep parties out lest an attempt should be made to surprise him. Wauchope replied, " All right," and for a time there seemed no reason to apprehend attack in this quarter. But in February Wolseley moved rapidly from Belturbet, and after some close fighting captured the town of Cavan and destroyed a large quantity of stores and powder in the place. The success was the greater because the Duke of Berwick, getting wind of the enemy's march, made a dash with cavalry and dragoons to help Wauchope. He arrived in time to take part in the fight, and had a horse killed under him ; but the result of the skirmish was distinctly a reverse to the royal arms, which was rendered all the greater by the loss of several good officers. Wolseley was not able to retain the town because the castle remained in Wauchope's possession, but he destroyed the magazine which had been carefully prepared in the town itself as a base for future operations. The Irish lost over 200 killed, including Brigadier Patrick Nugent, and ten of their officers besides were taken prisoners. Wolseley lost fifty killed and sixty wounded, besides three officers killed, Major Trahern, Captains Armstrong and Mayo.

It was soon after this incident that Lauzun landed, but while he was still endeavouring to get his troops conveyed with their impedimenta to Dublin, Schomberg opened the campaign by attacking Charlemont. This place was called a royal fortress, but in reality it was no more than a mediæval castle surrounded by a ditch. It was scantily provided with provisions, and the garrison numbered about 1000 men, commanded by Sir Thady O'Regan. The explanation of there being insufficient food in the place was given by some as an instance of Melfort's neglect, which was rather far-fetched, seeing that he had left Ireland six months before. A more plausible theory assigned it to there being no salt in Ireland, so that meat could not be cured. But perhaps the truth lay in the circumstance that the garrison was much too large for the dimensions of the place, and after an honourable defence of three weeks, during which every living thing, including rats and mice, was eaten up, Sir Thady O'Regan surrendered on honourable terms.

Having had his farewell audience of Louis at Marly on February 15, Lauzun posted to Brest. A favourable wind did not arise till March 17, the first anniversary of James's own departure, and it was noticed as a curious coincidence that the fleet reached Cork on the 22nd of the same month, exactly one year after the King's landing at Kingsale. The situation was reproduced in another and unfavourable sense. Lauzun, like the King, found no measures taken for his reception. There were no carriages or carts, no horses or oxen, and the roads were like the tracks of a farm-yard. James in his after apology throws the blame on Lord Dover, whom he had appointed Intendant-General at Cork, and excuses himself by saying that he had only poor tools for his service. Lord Dover and Lauzun had been friends, but the Frenchman was so angry with his reception that he quarrelled with him, and thus the situation became worse. The French army that was to turn the day against the enemy was fairly hung up half on shipboard because it could not be fed on land, and half on land clamouring to get back to the ships in order to be fed. It was a bad start.

The end of Lord Dover's connection with the Stuarts may be described. James had created him Earl of Dover, but this title was one of those never recognised in England. On arriving in Dublin Lauzun made a formal complaint against Lord Dover for his neglect at Cork. James sought the easiest way out of his troubles by giving Dover a pass to go to England, where he made his peace with William, and a few years later succeeded his elder brother as Baron Jermyn. The French were very much disgusted at this way of dealing with a man who had shown inexcusable incompetence and neglect of duty. The Marquis Sourches expressed the general opinion that Lord Dover should have been executed as a traitor. The Stuarts owed much of their troubles to ill-placed lenity.

Admiral Gabaret had also his orders to adhere to. They were to land the troops and the stores, to take the Irish regiment on board, to provide accommodation for Count

D'Avaux, General Roze (whose Marshalship expired with his leaving Ireland), Count de Gacé and a few others, and to return at once to Brest. " At once " meant by the next favourable wind for France. With a considerable English fleet at anchor off Torbay it was perilous to leave the French coast unguarded for any length of time, and Gabaret was anxious to be gone. At this juncture pressing letters came from King James urging Gabaret to defer his departure and undertake a separate adventure, for which James promised him much honour and glory. The adventure was to sail up the Irish Sea, and to prevent the departure of, or cut up, William's squadron and fleet of transports, which, by all accounts, were about to convey the host that William had levied with the intention of conquering Ireland. In October, 1689, James asked for 6000 French troops to drive Schomberg into the sea ; in March, 1690, they have come, but he then sees that they will not be enough to deal with William of Orange. Then, regardless of Louis's own needs, of Gabaret's duty, he proposes that the French fleet shall sail up a dangerous and little known sea possessing no harbours or arsenals, and risk its existence in carrying out his paper plan of preventing William landing at Carrick-fergus. And because James's appeal was not so much as listened to, and only served to hurry Gabaret's departure, it was alleged that the generous help of the French King, which was ample if properly utilised to effect the pacification of Ireland and never intended for chimerical adventures in England, was niggardly and begrudged. James's plans on the map were lauded to the skies by his courtiers as masterstrokes of strategy, whereas they were, in truth, simply impracticable. The Royal apologia for the failure in Ireland is not the least typical instance of the ingratitude of the Stuarts to those who devoted themselves to their interests, for of all the loyal champions of their cause Louis XIV is entitled to the first place.

There were others anxious to be gone besides Gabaret. D'Avaux had succeeded after many difficulties and disappointments, still to be described, in getting his Irish regiments together. All he thought of was hurrying them on board before they turned home-sick. Perhaps he had a vague apprehension that James might countermand their departure on the plea of the increased danger arising from the approach of William of Orange. From the French ambassador, then, Gabaret got no encouragement to linger. If D'Avaux could have controlled the winds there would have been but little delay, for he had the five regiments on board for the first time on April 1, ten days only after Gabaret entered Cork harbour. Between that and the 18th of the month there were frequent embarcations and dis-embarcations, but at last, on the latter date, the wind served and the French fleet sailed away with what was destined to become the first detachment of the Irish Brigade in the service of France.

Meanwhile, Lauzun had reached Dublin, and the French regiments followed as rapidly as they could over bad roads to pitch the tents, with which they had come provided, on the Curragh of Kildare. If Lauzun had been a great commander he would still have found it difficult, on the spur of the moment, to form any plan that would be at all likely to meet the many perils of the situation. The Irish army was scattered in a number of small garrisons, and although orders were issued at the end of April for a great part of it to assemble at Dundalk, it was certain that that could not be carried out for several weeks. In the meantime Schomberg had captured Charlemont, got his troops out of their winter lethargy and was fairly on the move. James, instead of getting everything ready, had been simply waiting for the French.

The whole of May and the greater part of June were absorbed in the task of gradually getting together an Irish army of 20,000 men at Dundalk. De Gacé assured King Louis, when received at Versailles on May 10, that " James had 30,000 good troops, although there was a deficiency in the supply of horses for the cavalry." Porter put them at

28,000, and the lowest estimate was that 25,000 good troops would be found north of the Boyne. When James rode into his camp on June 26 (N.S.) to inspect his army he found no more than 20,000. As an instance of the delay in assembling the Irish army it may be mentioned that Sarsfield only reached the Boyne on July 4.

Two days before James's arrival at Dundalk, William of Orange landed at Carrickfergus, bringing with him at least 20,000 regular troops and a large train of artillery. The Protestant army united mustered not less than 36,000 men, as William, resolved not to throw a chance away, called in all the outlying garrisons at Derry, Enniskillen, Newry, and elsewhere. The French reports written prior to the battle give William a total force of 9030 cavalry, 3080 dragoons, and 42,154 infantry, or over 54,000 altogether. It seems probable that the French reporters did not allow for the diminution in Schomberg's force during the winter.

North of Dundalk the road is carried through a marshy region over a long causeway, and at the southern extremity is a pass, known as " the four-mile pass," that presents many advantages for defence to the holder. If James's army had occupied this position in force it would have been in a very advantageous situation to defend itself, and the probability is that William would have been compelled to abandon the coast road and to advance by one of the inner roads from Armagh, which would necessarily be a slower and riskier proceeding. The advantages of this position were not unknown because it had been occupied during the previous campaign with Schomberg, and on the present occasion James sent a small party to seize the pass, or rather the southern end of it ; and everybody in the army understood that they were to move forward to occupy it in force on the following day. The Marquis Girardin, reporting on the battle of the Boyne, affirmed that the campaign was lost through the fatal decision not to hold this strong position.

The advance party consisted of the grenadier companies

of four regiments, commanded by Colonel Fitzgerald, of
Lord Bellew's regiment, and of sixty mounted dragoons
under Colonel Lawrence Dempsey. On arrival they found
that the other end of the pass was held by a party of about
300 English infantry and dragoons, which had been sent to
reconnoitre James's camp and obtain some information as
to the number of troops in it.

The two parties were not long in coming into collision,
and after a fierce little encounter the English were driven
back with a loss of thirty killed and two officers prisoners.
On the Irish side ten men were killed and Colonel Dempsey
was mortally wounded. He died at Oldbridge, on the
Boyne, a few days later, and his loss was not inconsiderable,
for he was an experienced officer who had gained much
distinction in the Portuguese army. But the really calami-
tous part of the affair was the capture of Captain Farlow,
who had been known to James in the old days at Whitehall.

James sent for him and had a long talk with him, and
Farlow supplied the King with as much information as he
asked for. According to this shrewd officer, who had
reason to remember the peril of the narrow way, William
had 50,000 troops, all highly disciplined and many of them
veterans. Among them were 15,000 cavalry, and the
artillery numbered thirty field-pieces. The fleet, he added,
had orders to coast down to Drogheda and lend the land
forces a helping hand. As James heard these details his
courage sank, and he at once gave orders to break up the
camp and retreat for the Boyne. Captain Farlow must have
felt some consolation for his bad luck in Four Mile Pass in
the consequences of the picture he drew before the mind
of the timid King.

James was quite justified in his decision to retreat by
a fair comparison between his army and that of William of
Orange, and if he had really retreated no one could have
thrown a stone at him, and the result of the war might have
been very different. But to run away from a good position
only to fight a few days later in a bad one is not to be ex-

plained by common sense or any of the canons of the art of war. James at Farlow's story works himself into a state of funk and runs away. Then, thinking it over, he reflects on the line of march that thrones are not recovered without risking something, and he decides to stand his ground and to fight. Throughout all these changes of view in the crisis of his struggle he could not find a definite plan, and there was no one to supply him with one. Certainly it was not Lauzun who, as Berwick said of him, " has quite forgotten all his military knowledge if he ever possessed any."

From Dundalk James moved to Ardee and then to the Boyne. His army crossed that river on July 9 (N.S.), his infantry passing through Drogheda and his cavalry by the ford at Oldbridge. Having reached the southern side of the river James's courage returned, and it was given out that the King would there await the onset of his enemy. In all these matters James decided for himself. Lauzun was apathetic and indifferent. Tyrconnell was in favour of making a fight of it, Sarsfield and the other Irish leaders had wished to make the stand at Dundalk, but they were not unwilling that it should be made on the Boyne. Even the cautious Berwick was not averse to the attempt to defend the passage of the river.

James's own version is contained in his Memoir : " What induced the King to hazard a battle on this inequality was that if he did it not there he must lose all without a stroke, and be obliged to quit Dublin and all Munster and retire behind the Shannon and so be reduced to the Province of Connaught, where having no magazines he could not subsist very long, it being the worst corn country in Ireland. Besides, his men seemed desirous to fight, and being new raised would have been disheartened still to retire before the enemy and see all their country taken from them without one blow for it, and by consequence be apt to disperse and give all for lost."

James had got himself into such a position that he must either fight a battle or evacuate Dublin, and it was his realisation of what life in Ireland would be out of Dublin that drove him to the desperate course of fighting an army immeasurably superior to his own. But of course that does not justify his conduct. Under the circumstances there was no other prudent course open to him than to leave Dublin to its fate, and to retire without fighting into the interior of the country. If he had fallen back on Athlone and secured the line of the Shannon, all the strategical advantages would have been on his side and not with the Prince of Orange. Besides, William could not remain long in Ireland. A short, decisive campaign was essential to him. Whereas James, if he had cared to do so, might have passed the rest of his life in Ireland, William could be absent for only a few weeks, or at the longest a few months, from England; and with the Irish army that fought at the Boyne preserved intact James might have prolonged the struggle, which continued as it was for eighteen months after his flight, for a very long period indeed.

When James gives as a reason for fighting the small resources of Western Ireland he overlooks the fact that that would have been a further obstacle in William's path. The Prince of Orange, thanks to the Boyne, got to the walls of Limerick, but his experience there was not of a nature to make us hesitate in saying that he would never have got there at all if Fabian tactics had been resorted to at the beginning of July, 1690. But it would have been unreasonable to expect in the King's apologia the true reason for his decision. The list contains many reasons, but the true one is left out.

We have seen from the first that James's heart was not in the Irish adventure. He was ever regretting that he had come to Ireland at all, and the latest letters from the Queen were full of forebodings that he might be detained there for ever. Any decent excuse, then, to leave it would seem preferable in such a frame of mind to taking a firm resolution for the prudent conduct of the war which would entail his remaining indefinitely in an unattractive country.

K

But the prospect became even worse, when for the comparative civilisation of Dublin there had to be substituted the wild region of Western Ireland. James found the outlook exceedingly uninviting. He had made no friends among the Irish nobles. He took none of them into his counsels. Even Tyrconnell, who knew Whitehall and was a courtier, represented a waning influence. The only men in whom he really confided were Powis, Thomas Howard, the Chief Justice Herbert, Gosforth, the Chancellor, all Englishmen, who knew nothing about Ireland, and thought solely of a royal restoration in London. Not to fight, then, meant an indefinitely long stay in Ireland; while to fight would end the matter one way or the other. Personal comfort, the desire to have an end put to an uncongenial task, had far more to do with James's proceedings at this juncture than prudence, military knowledge or even common sense.

There was another explanation of James being left to have his own way with regard to the fatal decision to make a stand at the Boyne. Among the generals on his Council of War, there was not one competent or qualified to give him advice. Lauzun was already treated with contempt as a mere cypher, and the French generals who had come with him had not yet measured the situation. D'Escots, a man of promise, had died suddenly. Girardin, or Léry, as he was sometimes called, was only a cavalry leader. La Hoguette had no local knowledge. When James expressed an opinion, therefore, it was repeated by all.

None of the Irish leaders had any influence. Sarsfield, the ablest of them, was already at loggerheads with the Stuarts. "A very brave man, no doubt," said James, "but with no headpiece." Berwick repeats or perhaps inspired this view, and says later on in his Memoirs that "Sarsfield imagined himself to be a great general." Perhaps it would have been well if Berwick had known in turn what D'Avaux had written about him, "a very brave man, but a *bad officer*, and with no common sense." Certainly there was nothing in Berwick's conduct in Ireland to reveal the future victor of Almanza, and the general who was said never to have lost a battle.

But the great defect of Sarsfield in the eyes of the Stuarts was that he was a leader of the Irish. " He has more influence in this country than all the others put together," D'Avaux had written some months earlier. Now whatever else James had failed to learn during his stay in Ireland he had at least got some first-hand information about the Irish problem, and he knew beyond possibility of self-deception that the uppermost wish of every Irishman was to be independent of and separated from England. That was a project with which James had no sympathy. He was essentially a Unionist who believed in the inviolable unity of the Empire.

Whether their schemes were feasible under any circumstances may be left to the reader's independent judgment, but that they should find an opponent in King James was certainly not the way to make the Stuarts popular in Ireland. Long before the Boyne enthusiasm for James had waned. More and more clearly did it stand revealed that the Irish were fighting for their own ends, and not for the recovery of his throne. Even Tyrconnell had declared during the crisis of the Melfort dispute that it would be better " for King James to go back to France and leave us to fight our battles in our own way and for our own ends." Sarsfield went even farther. He was openly in favour of a national Government in Ireland with a regular alliance with France. The feelings of the leaders in the Jacobite camp on the Boyne were therefore very mixed, and the ends of some of them would be served just as much by defeat as by victory. Defeat would, at least, convert a war in the Stuart interests into one for national objects.

Chapter VI

THE BATTLE OF THE BOYNE

A WITTY French writer has observed that the fight on the Boyne would have only passed in history for a skirmish if it had not been the nearest approach to a pitched battle that William of Orange ever won. Without going so far as to style it with him an "*échauffourée suivie d'une déroute,*" we need not hesitate in asserting that its significance as a trial of strength between two armed forces has been ridiculously exaggerated for party purposes. Neither side displayed any generalship to be proud of, and it was no glorious achievement for 36,000 completely armed troops with a very considerable artillery of thirty field-pieces to oust from an open position 25,000 incompletely armed troops with only six small cannon. There can be no question that James had no business to have fought at all. His fatal hesitation in postponing a decision to retreat to the west, left him no alternative save the hopeless course of trying to defend a river fordable at all points against overwhelming odds. It gave his adversary the opportunity of scoring a success without risks, and of earning a cheap renown. It provided the excuse for the celebration of an anniversary even to the present age of a so-called triumph of one Irish party over another Irish party, for which the facts of the battle supply no justification. Considering that the battle, such as it was, was won by Danes and Dutchmen, French Huguenots and Prussian Brandenburghers, it is almost ludicrous to any one who has the smallest respect for historical accuracy to see Orangemen celebrating the anniversary of the Boyne as their victory.

No visitor to the valley of the Boyne from Drogheda to Slane Bridge can have failed to notice that the left bank completely commands the right. This is especially noticeable above the ford of Oldbridge, where there are now the fine stone bridge and the William Memorial. It was on this plateau that William pitched his main camp on July 10 (N.S.) (June 30, O.S.), 1690, with his left wing stretching to the vicinity of Drogheda, held for James by a garrison of 1300 men under Lord Iveagh. It was from this spot that William surveyed the position of James's army on the opposite bank late in the afternoon of the day of his arrival, and it was here that he received the abrasion on the shoulder from a cannon shot which led to the circulation of a false rumour that he had been killed. This report reached Paris before the news of the battle, and gave rise to some premature rejoicing, including the lighting of bonfires. William's comment at the time was : " It should have come nearer," but the next day he wore a plaster on his shoulder and carried the right arm in a sling. The Jacobite gunner was not many inches off solving a grave political problem.

The River Boyne, which ran at the foot of the plateau, was easily fordable when the tide was out, and even when it was high water several fords remained passable. That of Rossnaree, five miles above Oldbridge and two miles short of Slane Bridge, which had been broken, was one available at all states of the tide. The several fords at Oldbridge were quite easy at half flood, that lower down at Donore was only available at low water. William had, in Schomberg's opinion, the choice of two courses : he might either attack and capture Drogheda, making his crossing at that place, or he might march up the river to Slane, repairing the bridge there and crossing by it and the ford at Rossnaree. William did not adopt either of his veteran lieutenant's proposals. He decided that his army should cross the river at three separate points, and that he would take advantage of his superior numbers to turn James's flanks both up and down the river. He assigned the command of the centre to the Duke of Schomberg, he took that of the left in person, and the right he entrusted to Count Meinhardt Schomberg, the Duke's son, to whom he gave as Lieutenant-Generals the services of Portland, Albuquerque and the Fleming D'Espinguen.

The last force was the first to move. " Before daybreak on July 11 " (N.S.), according to Dumont, the right wing began its march up the river. As it marched across fields it was assumed that it would reach Rossnaree about six in the morning. It was probably a little later, as the valley of the Boyne was enveloped in a dense mist which did not disperse till eight o'clock (Dumont). Opposite Rossnaree, watching the ford, was Sir Neil O'Neil at the head of the dragoon regiment bearing his name.

In order to distinguish the men of the two armies from each other—neither side having a distinct national colour—William's troops were ordered to place a green bough or sprig in their hats, and as evidence of the necessity of this precaution in an army composed of so many different races and languages it may be mentioned that Dumont, in the press of the battle when the Enniskilleners were driven back, was on the point of running his sword through one of them when he observed the green spray in his hat. James's troops, on the other hand, wore pieces of white paper in their hats to assimilate them to their French allies, whose distinguishing mark was the white cockade. This practice was not introduced for employment at the Boyne. It was in general use in the Netherlands by a tacit understanding between the belligerents, where the Dutch and Spanish troops always wore green sprigs in their hats on the day of battle, and the French pieces of white paper.

We may now turn to describe the position of James's army. The principal camp, including the King's own head-quarters, was at Ramullin on the top of the elevated ground to the right of Oldbridge. Here the hill lies back some distance from the river bank, and beyond the reach of cannon shot in the age with which we are dealing. In the little village of Oldbridge were placed two infantry regiments—Antrim's and Clanrickarde's—and on the extreme left was merely the O'Neil dragoon regiment opposite Rossnaree. The bulk of the army was drawn up along the elevated ground at a distance from the river varying from half to a full mile.

The position was absolutely unfortified, and the only defences that could be said to exist were the few cottages and garden walls in the miserable little village of Old-bridge. With regard to numbers, it is impossible to place James's army at a greater total strength than 25,000 men, including the French contingent of about 5500 strong. Neither in arms, nor in discipline, nor in experience of war could there be any comparison between the two armies. The majority of the Irish infantry had never heard a shot fired in action. The French regiments formed a *corps d'élite*, but at their head was Lauzun, of whom Berwick said : " If he ever possessed any knowledge of the military art he had completely forgotten it."

Finally, James had only eighteen small pieces of artillery (six-pounders), and of them only six took part in the battle. With regard to the supreme command, while William possessed the experience of twenty years' campaigning, and the assistance of one of the best European generals in Schomberg, the command of the Jacobite army rested with the King, who, whatever his knowledge of naval war might have been, knew nothing of land war, and whose own lack of experience and skill was not compensated for by the military ability of his lieutenants Lauzun, Tyrconnell, and Richard Hamilton.

During the evening of July 10 (June 30, O.S.), James held a Council of War, and it was decided, after the army had been assured that a stand would be made, not to fight, but to retreat. Unfortunately, this intention was not put into immediate practice. It was assumed, with that habitual procrastination which had so often proved fatal to the cause of the Stuarts, that there would be time enough in the morning. When the morning arrived the baggage was packed up and sent off to Dublin, and with it were sent twelve of James's total of eighteen pieces of artillery. The six retained were those with the French contingent, and thus on the day of the Boyne the Irish army had not a single cannon. Dumont tells us that when the sun first appeared at eight o'clock they saw that James's army had broken up their camp and were in full retreat. The effect of this spectacle on William was to make him hasten his movements.

He had intended deferring his attack until he had heard that his right wing had got over the river at Rossnaree, and more particularly until the ebbing tide had reached a point to make the ford at Donore easily practicable. But the spectacle of James's retreating army, and the thought that it might escape and draw him into the wilds of Ireland, were too much for his equanimity, and he ordered Schomberg to attack Oldbridge, while he led off his cavalry to the left with the intention of getting it over the river at some point or other below that place.

It was at this stage of the day's operations that the second mistake, which decided the course of the battle, was made by the Jacobite commanders. Sir Neil O'Neil had reported the appearance of the enemy across the river; on the opposite bank the same sun which disclosed to William the retirement of the Jacobite army revealed to James and Lauzun the movement of young Schomberg's infantry towards the right of William's battle. The nervous commanders at once jumped to the conclusion that their left would be outflanked and their line of retreat menaced. Lauzun was particularly anxious about his retreat being kept open, and, as every one knows, the general who is always looking behind him instead of in front of him never wins a battle. As soon, then, as he saw the movement of part of William's army up the river, he moved off to the left with the whole of the French contingent, which naturally took with it its six field-pieces, and as he had no cavalry, Lauzun appropriated Sarsfield's regiment of horse, and Maxwell's regiment of mounted dragoons, two of the best corps in the Irish army. The Irish army left to oppose the main attack, then, was without the French veterans, without artillery, and without three of its best regiments (Sarsfield, Maxwell, and O'Neil).

At this point not a shot had been fired, and we will reserve our own description of the encounter to quote that of Macaulay, which is the one taught to every English schoolboy, but which we hope will be relegated to the department of fiction when all the facts set forth in this chapter have been weighed and considered. Macaulay begins :—

"The first of July dawned, a day which has never since returned without exciting strong emotions of very different kinds in the two populations which divide Ireland. The sun rose bright and cloudless. Soon after four both armies were in motion. William ordered his right wing under the command of Meinhart Schomberg, one of the Duke's sons, to march to the Bridge of Slane some miles up the river, to cross there and to turn the left flank of the Irish army. Meinhart Schomberg was assisted by Portland and Douglas. James anticipating some such design had already sent to the bridge a regiment of dragoons commanded by Sir Neil O'Neil. O'Neil behaved himself like a brave gentleman, but he soon received a mortal wound, his men fled, and the English right wing passed the river.

"This move made Lauzun uneasy. What if the English right wing should get into the rear of the army of James ? About four miles south of the Boyne was a place called Duleek, where the road to Dublin was so narrow that two cars could not pass each other, and where on both sides of the road lay a morass which afforded no firm footing. If Meinhart Schomberg should occupy this post, it would be impossible for the Irish to retreat. They must either conquer or be cut off to a man. Disturbed by this apprehension the French general marched with his countrymen and with Sarsfield's horse in the direction of Slane Bridge. Thus the fords near Oldbridge were left to be defended by the Irish alone.

"It was now near ten o'clock. William put himself at the head of his left wing, which was composed exclusively of cavalry, and prepared to pass the river not far above Drogheda. The centre of his army, which consisted almost exclusively of foot, was entrusted to the command of Schomberg, and was marshalled opposite to Oldbridge. At Oldbridge had been collected the whole Irish army, foot, dragoons and horse, Sarsfield's regiment alone excepted. The Meath bank bristled with pikes and bayonets. A fortification had been made by French engineers out of the hedges and buildings, and a breastwork had been thrown up close to the outer side. Tyrconnell was there, and under him were Richard Hamilton and Antrim.

"Schomberg gave the word. Solmes's Blues were the first to move. They marched gallantly with drums beating to the brink of the Boyne. Then the drums stopped, and the men, ten abreast, descended into the water. Next plunged Londonderry and Enniskillen. A little to the left of Londonderry and Enniskillen Caillemot crossed, at the head of a long column of French refugees. A little to the left of Caillemot and his refugees the main body of the English infantry struggled through the river up to their armpits in water. Still further down the stream the Danes found another ford. In a few minutes the Boyne for a quarter of a mile was alive with muskets and green boughs.

"It was not till the assailants had reached the middle of the channel that they became aware of the whole difficulty and danger of the service in which they were engaged. They had as yet seen little more than half the hostile army. Now whole regiments of foot and horse seemed to start out of the earth. A wild shout of defiance rose from the whole shore; during one moment the event seemed doubtful; but the Protestants pressed resolutely forward, and in another moment the whole Irish line gave way. Tyrconnell looked on in helpless despair. He did not want personal courage; but his military skill was so small that he hardly ever reviewed his regiment in Phœnix Park without committing some blunder; and to rally the ranks which were breaking all round him was no task for a general who had survived the energy of his body and of his mind, and yet had still the rudiments of his profession to learn. Several of his best officers fell while vainly endeavouring to prevail on their soldiers to look the Dutch Blues in the face. Richard Hamilton ordered a body of foot to fall on the French refugees, who were still deep in water. He led the way, and, accompanied by some courageous gentlemen, advanced sword in hand into the river. But neither his commands nor his example could infuse valour into that mob of cow-stealers. He was left almost alone and retired from the bank in despair. Further down the river bank Antrim's division ran like sheep at the approach of the English column. Whole regiments flung away arms, colours and cloaks, and scampered off to the hills without striking a blow or firing a shot."

This favourite Whig description of the Boyne from the pen of the Whig writer, who fought under the Orange banner of Protestant ascendancy, is as near historical truth as a fairy tale is to the hard realities of life. We shall subject it to close dissection later on, and it will be seen that hardly one of Macaulay's details is in accord with the testimony of the witnesses on both sides. But the careful reader, who has no local knowledge and who never read another account of the battle, must have been puzzled to try and conjure up the despairing figure of Richard Hamilton on the river bank while his men bolted in one direction and the Huguenot regiments came on by the ford, not fifty yards across, which they had already half traversed when Hamilton got there. If the incident had taken place as described, Hamilton would have had small chance of taking part in those cavalry charges about which Macaulay worked up a little cheap eloquence.

As a matter of fact, Hamilton had nothing to do with the cavalry charges at all. He commanded the infantry division as Lieutenant-General. The cavalry charges occurred later in the day, and were led by the Duke of Berwick and Dominic Sheldon, while the Duke of Tyrconnell and Henry FitzJames also took part in them. Richard Hamilton had been wounded and taken prisoner by the time that William's cavalry came down from Donore on the right flank of the Irish infantry commanded by him in and behind Oldbridge.

The probability is that, having piled all the epithets of contumely and contempt on the Irish infantry as " cow-stealers," Macaulay began to reflect that there were some things about the Boyne which required a little explanation. There was the incident of Schomberg's death rallying a broken regiment, Caillemotte also was mortally wounded doing something very similar ; then, again, the awkward fact that the victorious army failed to force the Pass of Duleek and attempted no pursuit hardly tallied with the picture just given of the broken and fugitive host. Finally, Macaulay cannot have been blind to the fact that William's taking five days to cover the twenty odd miles from the Boyne to Dublin required a little elucidation, and seemed to show that the victorious William was not quite so sure as his panegyrist a hundred and fifty years later that he had smashed up the Irish army, and the later events of the campaign amply justified the Dutch Prince's view.

Macaulay could not explain, because to do so would have been to cancel what he had written, but he felt the need of a corrective for his own exuberant criticism and he supplied it in an eulogium on the Irish cavalry. We resume the quotation of Macaulay's description from the point where we broke off :—

"It required many years and many heroic exploits to take away the reproach which that ignominious rout left on the Irish name. Yet even before the day closed it was abundantly proved that the reproach was unjust. Richard Hamilton put himself at the head of the cavalry, and under his command they made a gallant though an unsuccessful attempt to retrieve the day. They maintained a desperate fight in the bed of the river with Solmes's Blues. They drove the Danish brigade back into the stream. They fell impetuously on the Huguenot regiments, which, not being provided with pikes, then ordinarily used by foot to repel horse, began to give ground. Caillemot, while encouraging his fellow-exiles, received a mortal wound in the thigh. Four of his men carried him back across the ford to his tent. As he passed he continued to urge forward the rear ranks, which were still up to the breast in the water. Schomberg, who had remained on the northern bank, and who had thence watched the progress of his troops with the eye of a general, now thought that the emergency required from him the personal exertion of a soldier. Those who stood about him besought him in vain to put on his cuirass. Without defensive armour he rode through the river and rallied the refugees whom the fall of Caillemot had dismayed. 'Come on,' he cried in French, pointing to the Popish Squadrons, 'these are your persecutors !' Those were his last words. As he spoke a band of Irish horsemen rushed upon him and encircled him for a moment. When they retired he was on the ground. His friends raised him, but he was already a corpse. Two sabre wounds were on his head, and a bullet from a carbine was lodged in his neck. Almost at the same moment Walker, while exhorting the colonists of Ulster to play the man, was shot dead. During nearly half an hour the battle continued to rage along the southern shore of the river. All was smoke, dust and din. Old soldiers were heard to say that they had seldom seen sharper work in the Low Countries. But just at this conjuncture William came up with the left wing. He had found much difficulty in crossing. The tide was running fast. His charger had been forced to swim, and had been almost lost in the mud. As soon as the King was on firm ground he took his sword in his left hand—for his right arm was stiff with his wound and his bandage—and led his men to the place where the fight was the hottest. His arrival decided the fate of the day. . . . His troops, animated by his example, gained ground fast. The Irish cavalry made their last stand at a house called Plottin Castle, about one mile and a half south of Oldbridge. Then the Enniskilleners were repelled with the loss of fifty men, and were hotly pursued till William rallied them and turned the chase back. In this encounter Richard Hamilton, who had done all that could be done by valour to retrieve a reputation ruined by perfidy, was severely wounded, taken prisoner, and instantly brought through the smoke and over the carnage before the prince whom he had foully wronged. 'Is this business over,' he said, 'or will your horse make more fight ? ' ' On my honour, sir,' answered Hamilton, ' I believe that they will.' ' Your honour ! ' muttered William. ' Your honour ! ' That half-suppressed exclamation was the only revenge which he condescended to take for an injury for which many sovereigns would have exacted a terrible retribution. Then restraining himself he ordered his own surgeon to look to the hurts of the captive. And now the battle was over. Hamilton was mistaken in thinking that his horse would continue to fight. Whole troops had been cut to pieces. One fine regiment had only thirty unwounded men left. It was enough that these gallant soldiers had disputed the field till they were left without support, or hope, or guidance, till their bravest leader was a captive and till their King had fled."

And this pretty piece of writing, with its compliments to Hamilton, who, it must be repeated, took no part in the cavalry charges, has no more applicability to the real facts of the encounter than the earlier passages in which contempt, instead of flattery, provides the key-note.

The impression at the time among Irish and French witnesses of the battle was not at all favourable to Hamilton. He was accused of making a very poor defence at the head of the infantry in the village of Oldbridge. It was alleged that his heart was not in his work, and some of the

French went so far as to declare that he was paid to prove the traitor. We do not attach any importance to this story, but there is nothing whatever to induce us to say that he played the hero. His brothers Anthony and John believed for a time that he was killed. A French officer declared a few days after the battle that he had seen him riding into Dublin in the cortège of William. With regard to Anthony Hamilton, whose name has just been mentioned, it may be stated that he did participate in the cavalry charges.

For this garbled and misleading version we wish to substitute a description of the encounter which is somewhat nearer to the literal truth, and which is based, not on the Protestant clergyman Story's version, blindly followed by Macaulay, but on the evidence of Berwick, James himself, la Hoguette, Dumont de Bostaquet, and Zurlauben.

We left Lauzun moving off to the left and William to the left also on the opposite sides of the Boyne. Their respective movements required time, and neither came into action for some hours. That is a vitally material point to which it did not suit Macaulay to make any reference. James and his staff, now without a single French officer on it, have seen William's movement down the river, and Lord Dungan, with his dragoon regiment, is deputed to move along the crest of Ramullin to keep the enemy in view and to hinder their crossing the river. It is hoped and believed that no crossing in the state of the tide will be found possible, and that in any case Lord Dungan, whose regiment is a good one, will be able to delay, if not prevent, the passage. The point desirable to be borne in mind by an impartial student is that in the first phase of the battle there is no peril on either flank for James's army. The whole fortune of the day depends on what happens at Oldbridge. If Schomberg is defeated there, it does not matter what William does lower down the river. Upstream Meinhardt Schomberg's force and Lauzun's may be considered fairly equally matched and to neutralise each other. A skilful commander, then, would have concentrated all his efforts on the repulse of Schomberg's main attack, the development of which was fully visible, and although James was hampered by the absence of artillery and of well-trained infantry, much more might have been done than was attempted to defeat it.

James's own version of the battle shows clearly that he had nothing to do with the fight in the centre of the battle, that he was only nervous for the security of his line of retreat, and that he was busily engaged in passing troops from his right to his left to reinforce Lauzun. He would have withdrawn all Tyrconnell's force from Oldbridge but for, as he says, " the cannon and baggage not being far enough advanced on their way towards Dublin." No stronger evidence could be asked for to prove that flight and not fight was in the King's mind throughout the day, and no troops could fail to be affected by the timidity of their commander.

At this critical juncture it was Tyrconnell who took upon himself the duty of arranging what should be done for the defence of Oldbridge, where, throughout the early hours of the morning, there were only the two regiments of Clanrickarde and Antrim. When he saw the preparations for the attack developing he moved down five infantry regiments under Richard Hamilton to support the two in Oldbridge, but the position was somewhat cramped, and beyond the few cottages mentioned it was quite open. The French reports absolutely negative Macaulay's assertion as to a fortification having been made by French engineers. There was not a French engineer in the force. On the sloping ground behind Oldbridge leading gradually upwards to the Pass of Duleek, Tyrconnell drew up his cavalry regiments. These consisted of Tyrconnell's own regiment, two troops of the bodyguard commanded by Berwick, Parker's regiment and Sutherland's regiment, or a total of three and a half cavalry regiments. These troops were as good cavalry as existed anywhere, but it is putting them at a high figure to say they totalled fifteen hundred sabres. The seven infantry battalions numbered four thousand, so that Tyr-

connell had five thousand five hundred men to oppose
Schomberg, who had at least fifteen thousand men under
his immediate orders.

It is impossible to form any decided opinion as to the
exact hour at which Schomberg ordered the regiments
selected to lead the attack to march down from the table-
land already mentioned to the river bank at Oldbridge, but
it does not seem to have been much before midday.
Macaulay, following Story, states ten o'clock; an Irish
writer places it as late as four. All that can be said is that
so steep is the acclivity on the left bank that it would have
taken the large body of troops employed in carrying the
passage a considerable time to deploy on the river bank
with the precision that would alone satisfy Schomberg.
This central force comprised the pick of the infantry—
the Dutch Blue Guards under Count Solmes, the Huguenot
foot under Caillemotte, the Ulster regiments, and, finally,
the English regiments. It would not be surprising if the
raw Irish infantry without cannon were shaken and un-
steady at the mere sight of this imposing array before they
met in the shock of battle. The best account of what
followed is that given in James's own narrative, which, as
he did not see this part of the battle, was supplied him by
one of the officers present, probably General Dorington,
who commanded the battalion of Guards. It reads as
follows in his own phraseology and spelling :—

" As for what pass'd at Old Brig, it seems the enemie
perceiveing the left wing and most of the foot had march'd
after Lausun attacked the regiment which was at the village
of Old Brig with a great body of foot all strangers, and soon
possessed themselves of it ; upon which the seaven battal-
lions of the first line, which were left there and drawn up a
little behind the riseing ground which shelter'd them from
the enemies cannon marched up to charge them, and went
on bouldly til they came within a pike's length of the enemie
notwithstanding their perpetual fire, so that Major Arthur
who was at the head of the first battalion of the Guards run

the officer through the body that commanded the battalion he march'd up too.   But at the same time the enemies horse began to cross the river which the Kings foot perceiveing immediately gave way notwithstanding all that Dorington and the other officers could doe to stop them which cost several of the Captains their lives as Arundel, Ashton, Dungen, Fitzgerald and two or three more, besides the Marquis de Hoquincourt, who was kill'd with several others of his brigade.   Barker Lieut.-Colonel of the Guards with Arthur the Major were both wounded of which the latter dy'd the same day."

As all the officers named were in Dorington's regiment (the Guard of James's army), it is further proof of his having supplied the King with the material for his narrative. If we compare this description with that furnished by the Williamite reports we shall conclude that up to a certain stage in the encounter the infantry offered a good resistance, and that it was on seeing that his men were not making much headway that Schomberg rushed from the high ground to rally them.   As Dumont states positively that his cavalry regiment was the first to get over the river, and that they then heard of Schomberg's death, it is perfectly clear that he was killed in the infantry encounter, and before the Orange cavalry came down on the right flank of the Irish infantry, as described in the further passage from James's narrative, which we shall quote further on.

As a further piece of evidence to the same effect, Schomberg was supposed to have been killed by Sir Charles O'Toole, a lieutenant in Dorington's regiment.   It is sufficiently clear, then, that before William's horse crossed the river the Jacobite infantry fought very well, that during that period the Protestant troops wavered, that Schomberg felt bound to hasten to join in the fray, and that he was killed and the leader of the Huguenots, de la Caillemotte, received a mortal wound at the same juncture.   It was only when the horse came charging down on the right flank that these half-trained Irish troops broke and got out of hand.

L

Let us now turn to the progress of William's left wing under his own immediate command. Owing to the tide being in there was great difficulty in finding the ford of Donore, and when found it was not fordable. Dumont's mounted regiment of French refugees led the van, and with it was the regiment of Danish foot guards. After waiting a long time William could wait no longer. Dumont's regiment was ordered to swim across, the Danes to cross in single file. On the opposite bank was Lord Dungan and his dragoon regiment. William covered the crossing with the fire of two cannon, and those of the Danes who had not entered the water were ordered to fire volleys from the bank. Lord Dungan was killed by one of the first cannon shots, several of his officers and men were also killed and wounded, and the rest of the regiment galloped off over the heights of Ramullin towards Duleek, and took no further part in the battle.

The right of the Jacobite army was thus uncovered, but it took time for William to get his troops over the river, and then to traverse the several miles between the crossing-place and the position at Oldbridge. It was during this interval, as Dumont states, that news was received " of Schomberg's death, of there having been fierce fighting, and of many of our officers having been killed and wounded."

We may now revert to the King's narrative :—

" Notwithstanding the foot was thus beaten the right wing of horse and dragoons march'd up and charg'd such of the enemies hors and foot as passed the river, but my Lord Dungan being slaine at their first going on by a great shot his Dragoons could not be got to doe anything nor did Clare's do much better (Clare's regiment was infantry). Nevertheless the hors did their duty with great bravery, and tho' they did not break the enemies foot it was more by reason of the ground's not being favourable than for want of vigor, for after they had been repulsed by the foot they rally'd again and charged the enemies hors and beat them every charg. Tyrconnell's and Parker's troops suffer'd the

most on this occasion. Powel and Vaudrey both Lief-
tenants of the Guards with most of the Exempts and
Brigadiers of both troops were slaine as also the Earle of
Carlingford, Mons d'Amande, and several other volunteers
that charged with them. Nugent and Casanone were
wounded of Tyrconnell's ; Major Mara and Sir Charles
Take killed and Bada wounded. Of Parker's the Colonel
wounded, the Lieftenant Colonel Green with Dodington
the major and many other officers killed, and of the two
squadrons of that regiment there came but off about thirty
sound men. Sunderland's [really Sutherland's] regiment—
tho' wounded himself—suffer'd not much, haveing to do
only with the enemies hors which he soon repulsed ; in fine
they were so roughly handled and overpowered by numbers
that at last they were quite broke. Lieftenant General
Hamilton being wounded and taken prisoner at the last
charge, and the Duke of Berwick having his hors shot under
him was some time amongst the enemie, he was rid over and
ill-brused ; however by the help of a trooper got off again.
Sheldon who had command of the horse had two kill'd
under him."

Dumont's account of the cavalry encounter in which he
and his regiment took a prominent part does a great deal
more than corroborate this description. He describes the
Irish cavalry as charging like madmen, and he honestly admits that his own corps was driven back. He also refers to
the Casaubon regiment (Huguenots) being repulsed with
the loss of twenty killed and wounded. Finally he mentions
the Enniskilleners being shaken, and the failure to induce
them to charge again. This was the moment when he
nearly killed one of them already referred to. Berwick
states in his Memoirs that at the Boyne he and the cavalry
" charged and charged again ten times, until the enemy
amazed at our boldness halted."

While these events had been happening in the centre and
on the right, Lauzun with King James in person had taken
up a position on the left opposite to the corps, 10,000

strong, under young Schomberg. Lauzun had 5500 French infantry, three excellent regiments of Irish cavalry and dragoons, and the only artillery with the whole army. Here then, if anywhere on the Boyne, the Jacobite army was on something like an equality with its assailant. Here, too, it did least of all. Let James tell his own story of that part of the battle which passed under his eyes, and in reading it let us bear in mind what Macpherson said of him, that with all his faults James had a punctilious regard for accuracy of fact, and that few of his literal statements have ever been controverted.

" Sir Neale O'Neal's dragoons did their part very well, and disputed the passage with the enemie almost an hour till their cannon came up and then retired in good order with the loss only of five or six common men but their Collonel was shot through the thigh and an officer or two wounded. No sooner had the enemie passed there but they stretched out their line to the right as if they designed to take us in the flank or get between us and Dublin which Mons de Lausune seeing marched with the left to keep up with them and observe their motion ; while this was a-doing the King went to the right to hasten up the troops to follow Lausune believeing the main body of the enemie's army was following their right which had passed at Slane, but when the King came up he found the Duke of Tyrconnell with the right wing of hors and Dragoons, and the two first brigades of the first line drawn up before old bridg, from which post he did not think fit to draw them, the Cannon and baggage not being far enugh advanced on their way towards Dublin. However the rest of the foot marched by their flank towards Lausune, and the King took the reserve consisting of Purcel's hors and Brown's foot with which he marched till he came up to that rear of the foot that followed Lausune, and then ordering Sir Charles Carny, who commanded the reserve, to post himself at the right of the first line of those foot to make a sort of left wing there. Then (the King) rid along the line where he found Lausune and the enemie's right

Patrick Sarsfield, Earl of Lucan.
from the Portrait in the possession of the Order of Franciscan Friars in Dublin.

drawn up in battle within half cannon shot faceing each other. The King did not think fit to charge just then being in expectation of the troops he had left at old bridg, but while he was discussing this matter with Lausune an aid de Camp came to give the King an account that the enemie had forced the pass at old bridg and that the right wing was beaten ; which the King wispering in Lausune's ear tould him There was now nothing to be done but to charge the Enemie forthwith before his troops knew what had happen'd on the right, and by that means try if they could recover the day. And accordingly (the King) sent Mons. Hoguette to the head of the French foot, made all the Dragoons to light (alight) and placed them in the intervalls between the hors and ordered Lausune to lead on. But just as they were beginning to move, Sarsfield and Maxwell, who had been to view the ground betwixt the two Armys sayd :— ' It was impossible for the hors to charge the enemie by reason of two dubble ditches with high banks and a little brook betwixt them that run along the small valley that divided the two Armys,' and at the same time the enemie's Dragoons got on horseback, and their whole line began to march by their flank to their right, and we soon lost sight of their van by a village that interposed ; only by the dust that ris behind it they seem'd to endeavour to gaine Dublin road. Upon which the King (sins he could not attack them) thought fit to march also by his left towards Dublin road too to pass a small brook at Dulick which was impracticable high up by reason of a bog. The King was no sooner on his march but the right wing's being beat was no longer a mistery for severall of the scatter'd and wounded hors men got in amongst them before they rought Dulick ; whereupon Mons de Lausune advised the King to take his own regiment of horse which had the van of that wing and some dragoons and make the best of his way to Dublin for fear the enemie who were so strong in hors and dragoons should make detachments and get thither before him which he was confident they would endeavour to doe, but that if his Majesty arrived there first he might with the troops he had with him and the garrison he found there prevent their possessing themselves of the town till Mons Lausun could make the retreat which he prayed him to leave to his conduct.

" He then advised the King, not to remain at Dublin neither but go with all expedition for France to prevent his falling into the enemie's hands which would be not only his but the Prince his Son's utter ruin, that as long as there was life there was hope and that if once he was in France again, his cause was not so desperate, they being in all probability masters at sea ; that he would give one of his hands that he could have the honour to accompany him, but he must endeavour to make his retreat in the best manner possible he could, or dy with the French if they were beaten. This advice went much against the grain, so the King demur'd to it tho' reitterated several times, but Mons. Lausun ceased not pressing him til at last he found by a more particular account in what manner the business had been carryd on the right, that all the enemie's army had passed the river which forced even their troops that were not beaten to retreat, and that by consequence it was necessary for him to doe so too."

The facts which stand out clear from the King's narrative are that neither he nor Lauzun seemed to realise that the main attack would be made at Oldbridge, that he removed at least eight regiments of Irish infantry from the centre to the left, and that in consequence of that reinforcement Lauzun's force was increased by at least five thousand men, so that it possessed a clear numerical superiority over the corps under young Schomberg.

Nicholas Plunkett's account of the battle may be given as representing what was supposed by the Irish witnesses to have been the course of the encounter, but he is so much out as to the hours of its commencement and progress that it possesses no more value for the one side than Story's does for the other.

" The King resolved in the evening on Monday (i.e. June

30, O.S. ; July 10, N.S.) to decamp that night, but un-
happily again that resolution was not executed till Tuesday
morning, July 1st, about eight o'clock, at which time the
army was commanded to march upwards by the river,
giving their right flank to the front of the enemy in order,
as 'twas believed, to go to Dublin to get a better opportunity
of defence or of giving battle. Before the army began to
move, you must know that there were two regiments of foot,
the Earl of Antrim's and the Earl of Clanrickarde's left at
the ford of Ouldbridge within some gardens of the poor
inhabitants without intrenchment or cannon to stop the
enemy a while from coming over till the infantry got clear
of the river. At the same time Sir Neil O'Neil from the left
was placed with his regiment of dragoons at the ford of
Rossnaree, a little beneath the Bridge of Slane (the bridge
being broken before) to guard that pass. This being so, the
army began their march. The Prince of Orange seeing them
in their motion of going off ordered his army (and not before) to pass the river in two places principally at the ford of
Ouldbridge and at the ford of Rosnaree. He sent Lieut.-
General Douglas and Count Schomberg, the Marshal's son,
with above ten thousand horse and foot to pass at Rosnaree
on his right. He sent a greater force under Marshal Schomberg, the general, to traverse the ford of Ouldbridge, he
himself following with the rest.

" The King observing the prince to attempt a trajection
commanded his army to halt and face to the enemy which
they did and prepared themselves to fight upon the passage
of the river. But alas ! they were deceived in this expectation, for there was no battle because they were not brought
to combat. There was only a skirmish in passing the waters
between a party of theirs and the whole army of Orange.
And because this party did not keep all the hostile troops
beyond the flood the King's host must march away and
leave the pass to the foe. If there was a settled resolution
to fight, why was not the army led down in two wings to the
river with their field-pieces as they saw the enemies forces

divided and there to stand it out for two or three hours ? The hostile cannon could not much annoy the Irish as being mounted on an overlooking ground, while the Irish artillery might play without obstruction in the faces and flanks of the enemies as they were descending to the river and crossing it.

" I am confident by the knowledge I have of the loyal troops and of their eagerness for fighting that day, if they had been managed as aforesaid, the Prince of Orange would not have persisted in traversing the water at such disadvantage as violent as he was for approaching to Dublin. Marshal Schomberg better understood the point when he made difficulty at that juncture to attempt the trajection as he saw the Irish drawn up for combat. But he was overruled by the temeraciousness of Orange which notwithstanding did succeed through the non-resistance of the loyal host which was occasioned by the ill-conduct of generals as you shall now observe. The two great wings of the Prince of Orange's army being come to the river, action was discovered to begin at four in the afternoon both at the ford of Rossnaree and at the ford of Ouldbridge. Whereupon it was ordered that five regiments of Irish foot should be in haste sent to reinforce the two before-mentioned regiments at Ouldbridge.

" At this time the Lord Dungan was commanded down from the right with his regiment of dragoons to give a check unto some advanced troops of the enemies that were ready to gain the banks at the upper end of the ford of Ouldbridge in despite of the fire that was made on them at something too great a distance by the Irish foot which were posted near the said ford. The Lord Dungan having repulsed those troops to the other side of the river marched back to his station. But in his retreat upon a high ground he was unfortunately slain by a cannon-ball. At the same juncture Sir Neil O'Neil on the left with his dragoons did wonders at Rossnaree in stopping the abovesaid ten thousand men some half an hour. But there was no care taken to sustain him and so he was forced to retreat to his line.   In this while the King's army was only spectator of this fierce conflict between a few regiments of their own and the whole hostile camp which was an unequal match.   Whence we may judge that it is easy for a host to gain the victory where little or no opposition is given and that a hundred thousand men signify nothing in the field if they are not brought to the combat.

" Immediately after Dungan's dragoons retired, Marshal Schomberg brought down to the ford of Ouldbridge the gross of his cavalry with orders to push on and suffer no check.   At this the seven regiments aforesaid of Irish foot observing they would be soon overpowered they cried to their own for horse to sustain them.   In the meanwhile they made a smart fire at the enemies and laid them in heaps as they were entering the waters.   But their crying for horse was in vain, for they received but one troop which was as good as nothing.   At this time the King, remarking from his station which was at the Church of Donore that the enemy was gaining the passes both on the right and left, sent orders to his army to retreat leaving the conduct to the Duke of Tyrconnell, and then he himself went off to Dublin, being guarded by some troops of Colonel Sarsfield's horse and by some of Colonel Maxwell's dragoons.   As the King departed the army began their retreat towards the bourg of Duleek.   The left wing with the centre went off first, which left wing was posted over against the ford of Rossnaree, the pass being first forced.   The French brigade of foot marched in the rear of the centre, bringing along with them their cannon, by the help of which they covered the infantry while the horse on the said left gave their assistance. The seven regiments of Irish foot which guarded the great ford of Ouldbridge not being supported by horse, were also forced to retreat, but were in danger to be intercepted by such of the enemy as had traversed first the river before they joined their main army, which the Duke of Tyrconnell from the right perceiving flew with his regiment of horse to their rescue, as did the Duke of Berwick with the two troops of guards, as did Colonel Parker with his regiment of horse and Colonel Sutherland with his.

"It was Tyrconnell's fortune to charge first the blue regiment of foot guards to the Prince of Orange, and he pierced through. He presently after engaged the Enniskillen horse, bold troopers. At the same time the two troops of guards and the other two regiments of Irish horse signalized themselves and were bravely opposed by their enemies. This gave opportunity for the King's infantry to get off in safety.

"By the time Schomberg was killed the Prince of Orange traversed the river with the rest of his army, who near the village of Dunore had some small engagement, for the Irish horse, especially the right wing, fought, retreating all the way, in covering the main body till they came to Duleek, two miles from the Boyne, where being pressed by the pursuit of the enemy, the Irish army halted and faced about with preparations for a bloody combat if set upon. But the Prince of Orange, observing the King's army to make so good a countenance thought it more prudent to halt and suffer them to march away. The heat of this action lasted not above one hour, when you see that it was but a skirmish between nine regiments without cannon or entrenchment, and an army of thirty-six thousand choice men for the defending and gaining a few passes upon a shallow river; and after the passes gained there happened a running fight between a few regiments of horse with the help of a brigade of foot, and all the said army of thirty-six thousand men for two miles, which shows the retreat was admirable considering the superiority of the enemy and the openness of the ground.

"There was slain of the loyalists about five hundred men. The enemy had about a thousand private men killed."

In concluding this description of the Battle of the Boyne, which incorporates the narratives of Macaulay, James II, and Plunkett, I am going to add entirely new matter from the several French reports preserved among the historical archives of the French War Department. M. Martinien informed me that I was the sixty-first student from Great Britain to examine these documents, and I was simply astounded to see how my predecessors, of whom Macaulay was the first, have left the pearls in their shells. Macaulay's abstinence is intelligible, for these contemporary reports level the whole of his historical structure with the ground.

As these texts, dealing not only with the Boyne, but with the whole of the war in Ireland, would fill a large volume, I shall only take out of them the very small quantity that suits my present purpose and the character of this work. But it will not be for want of effort on my part if these historical documents are left to fade away, as some are doing, in bad ink on bad paper.

For my present purpose I am only making use of them to show what the French commanders and their troops did, and by that light I claim to place the conduct of the Irish soldiers in an entirely new aspect.

Macaulay most certainly did look at those volumes of manuscript bound in calf for the most part with the arms of the Kings of France on the cover. He probably began with the first of them, Vol. 960, and he found there ready to his hand the letter of La Hoguette, dated Kingsale, July 14, 1690. He gives his readers the first passage in an English translation. It suited his views to the letter : " The Irish troops were not only beaten ; they were driven before the enemy like sheep." Macaulay had found all he wanted. Why should he wade for more through twenty volumes of letters and reports ? We can well imagine his closing Vol. 960 with an ejaculation of complete satisfaction, and his deciding that it would not be necessary to trouble the " Section des Archives Historiques " any further. He did not even finish La Hoguette's letter, or surely he must have paused over its closing lines. We, humbler devotees of the Muse Clio, have to be more careful.

Here is the text of the opening and final passages of La Hoguette's letter to Louvois :—

" Monseigneur,

"Je n'ay pas le temps de vous faire le destails de dèsastre qui est arrivée à l'armée du Roy d'Angleterre, lequel vient de me dire tout presentement qu'il vouloit partir tout à l'heure. J'aurai l'honneur de vous en ecrire par la première occasion. Je vous diray seulement que nous n'avons pas eté battu mais que les ennemies ont chassé devant eux les troupes irlandaises comme les moutons . . .

" J'espère que le Roi ne dèsapprouvait de ma conduite . . .

" Sa Majesté sera toujours maitre de ma vie, mais non pas de m'envoyer à la guerre avec de pareils generaux."

La Hoguette's first letter thus contained not merely the reflection on the Irish troops, but a little further on a sense of some doubt as to how his own conduct might be viewed, and finally a severe denunciation on the bad generalship, not of the Irish, mind, but of French officers. Bad generalship has lost battles far more important than the Boyne, and it was not the first, nor will it be the last time that the ex-cusers of bad leading have invented an excuse in the cowardice of the troops. But this letter was written three days after the battle by a man who had galloped over one hundred and fifty miles in the interval. We may assume, not uncharitably, that he was somewhat upset and un-nerved.

La Hoguette soon discovered that there was need to ex-plain his own conduct, and after an interval of three months he sent from Galway his full report of the battle. In this there is nothing whatever about the Irish running away. The comparison to sheep is suppressed.

On the contrary, he declares that " Tyrconnell retired in good order," and that " it was only when the two retiring bodies came into contact at Duleek that confusion ensued." He also states that " Oldbridge was held by only one battalion," as " two French battalions and another Irish battalion which had been placed there the previous evening were withdrawn early in the morning," that " the one battalion was overwhelmed by a large force collected out of sight before aid could reach it, as the five supporting battalions were too far back," and finally that " both the French and Irish troops on the left clamoured to be led to the attack of the force under young Schomberg." What a shock Macaulay spared himself by not going on to Vol. 962 !

The Report is in the main a detailed explanation of La Hoguette's own conduct as to how he got separated from Lauzun and the French troops, and found himself close on the heels of James in his flight to Dublin. There was at least one of the French colonels to insinuate that La Hoguette and other French officers had not altogether played the hero. Of these undoubtedly La Hoguette had fled the fastest and by himself. I do not say that La Hoguette was a coward. He was, like the majority of men, brave one day, and, to put it mildly, not so brave on other days. " What is rare," said Villars, in a passage worth remembering, " is the man who is always brave." The Boyne was one of La Hoguette's bad days; the Marsaglia, where he met a soldier's death, one of his good.

There were others besides La Hoguette. It has always been a mystery what the French troops did at the Boyne, and how it was that Lauzun returned to France with only six hundred men fewer than he brought with him, and the mystery is increased by the discovery that among these six hundred missing were three hundred Germans in French pay who deserted to William after the battle (Hague records). We have to thank Colonel Zurlauben for clearing up the mystery. The Zurlauben report is the cream of the documents in Paris so far as the Boyne goes. The Colonel, a veteran who had fought under Turenne, and whose regiment formed a notable portion of the Swiss contingent, the élite of the French army, declares at the commencement that " in what he writes he is actuated solely by regard for the King's service." He then exposes " the faults which are the true cause of our losing the battle." It is unnecessary to expatiate further on the incapacity of Lauzun, but the following passage places the retreat from the banks of the Boyne in an entirely new light. Here it is :—

" M. de Lauzun prit la partie de nous abandonner avec Messieurs de La Hoguette, Famechon, Chamerade et Mérode."

In other words, those valiant French colonels who urged James to flight, who saw the phantoms of William's cavalry in close pursuit, ran away. Zurlauben supplies another piquant detail. The colonels had put their regimental colours in their pockets. This is not the invention of an Irish apologist. It exists in the contemporary letter of Colonel Zurlauben in Vol. 962 of the War Archives of France.

We may borrow a little more information from Colonel Zurlauben. Who covered the retreat, and checked the Williamite pursuit at Duleek? He replies with pride, " My regiment, seconded by the Irish cavalry." Then, again, as to the confusion in the narrow pass at Duleek, he shows clearly what took place there. The Irish infantry retreating from Oldbridge and the French troops retiring from Rossnaree reached this point at the same moment. In the confusion the Irish threatened to break the formation of the Zurlauben regiment. The Colonel had to fire on them to keep them off. What he feared was that if they got mixed up with his men the maintenance of the strict order on which the holding of the enemy in check depended would be impossible. Incidentally he shows that the Irish infantry had not retired more rapidly than the French, for they reached Duleek together. The last point is corroborated, as has been shown, by La Hoguette himself, who says in his full report of October, 1690, that " Tyrconnell retired in good order, but that the two retiring wings, right and left, came into contact at Duleek, and that confusion followed." He had apparently forgotten by that time, or had the wisdom to suppress his earlier comparison of the

Irish troops to sheep. Of all the French officers at the Boyne Zurlauben was the only one summoned to Versailles to receive from the King in person his thanks and the well-earned recompense of the soldier who has done his duty. Perhaps a stronger proof of his merit was furnished when after his return to France the Irish lords offered him their best men to fill the gaps in his attenuated regiment. We shall meet him again amid the dead and dying at Blenheim.

The Battle of the Boyne having been fought and lost, there is one sequel of it that may be dealt with and dismissed before closing this chapter. Having listened to Lauzun's advice, James, accompanied by some horse, quitted the battlefield while yet the enemy was at a distance, and rode off to Dublin. He reached it the same evening, and there he found Major Wilson with letters from the Queen, and news that Marshal Luxemburg had defeated the Dutch forces at Fleurus. It was an indication of James's curious way of looking at things that the impression of his own great reverse seemed effaced by the news of this French victory, as if the French could have no other object in gaining victories than to replace him on the throne. It never seems to have occurred to him that he was expected to help French plans by gaining victories, or at least prolonging the struggle with William in Ireland. The messenger brought other messages. The Queen was calling out for her husband's return. Was he going to remain in Ireland for ever? In her view now was the time, with France victorious in Flanders, with William absent in Ireland, for James to return post haste to France, obtain the aid of Louis, which she did not doubt would be rendered, and land in force on the English coast, and march in triumph to London. It was a pretty programme, and chimed in with the views James always held. It reached him, too, at a moment when the Irish programme, in which he had never had great faith and for which he had never any liking, seemed hopelessly doomed.

But before deciding James must observe the forms. He

had only fled from the Boyne at the reiterated advice of
Lauzun. He would not flee from Ireland without the
advice of his councillors, so when he had removed some of
the dust from his clothes and refreshed himself after the
long day, during which he had undoubtedly ridden a great
deal, he called them in one by one and asked them their
opinions. There were Baron Gosworth, Sir William Herbert, the Marquis Albeville, Sir Richard Nagle, and others ;
and they one and all declared that he should lose no time in
going to France. Things were in a state of panic in Dublin
that night. Many of the Jacobite families left for the West,
and everybody believed that the foe would be at the gates
of Dublin in the morning.

James, finding everybody of his own opinion, decided to
start the next morning, but about midnight he received a
messenger from the Duke of Berwick informing him that he
had rallied about seven thousand Irish infantry at Brasil, and
that he would be glad if he would send him some horse and
dragoons, so as to enable him to make his retreat. Berwick
did not mention that Sarsfield had drawn off from both him
and Lauzun, and was rallying the cavalry on his own account.
Sarsfield's own regiment was intact, so were Maxwell's and
Purcell's dragoons. James sent his son all the cavalry in
Dublin, which was three troops of Abercorn's horse and six
troops of Luttrell's dragoons. Soon after came a more pressing message. Lauzun had joined Berwick, and as they were
not coming to Dublin, they begged that all the troops in the
city should be sent to Leixlip to join them, and that James
should not delay his own departure by a single hour.

James was nothing loath. He mounted his horse at sunrise on July 12 to ride out of the Irish capital. The Duke of
Powis, Henry FitzJames, and other members of his household, were with him, and as escort he had retained two
troops of his bodyguard ; and just as he was starting La
Hoguette arrived. He was followed shortly afterwards by
three French officers, the Colonels Chamerade, Famechon,
and Mérode, who came from Lauzun to urge the King to

hurry his departure and to escort him ; but as their horses were tired out and James had no fresh ones to give them, they were left behind. James started at five in the morning and rode leisurely to Bray, ten miles from Dublin. He left there the bodyguard to hold the bridge till twelve o'clock, while he and his few companions rode on to Arklow, where they rested two hours at Mr. Hacket's house, and then resumed their journey southwards. Two miles beyond Mr. Hacket's they were caught up by the four French officers, who declared that a party of the enemy had pursued them and was close at hand. James was incredulous, but mended his pace, and the only explanation of the French officers' story is that they had mistaken some of James's body-guard for the enemy. None of William's troops had reached Dublin when James sailed from Duncannon two days after he quitted the capital. By way of explanation it may be mentioned that Chamerade was no soldier. He was gentleman usher to the Dauphiness, and his nomination to command one of the regiments on the eve of its departure for Ireland was regarded as a Court job.

However, urged by the French officers, who were probably instructed by Lauzun to get the King out of the country before he could change his mind, the party rode all night, reaching Duncannon at sunrise on July 13. Immediately on arrival Hoguette rode up the river to Passage, where he found a St. Malo privateer of twenty-eight guns, named the " Lauzun." He induced the captain to go down the river with the tide and pick up the King at Duncannon. In the evening the ship got over the bar to the open sea, and made its way to Kingsale, where there was found a French squadron of ten frigates, under Messieurs Foran and Du Quesne. This squadron had been sent there at Queen Mary d'Esté's personal request to M. Seignellay, the Minister of Marine, so that her husband might have the means of escaping if things turned out badly.

From Kingsale James wrote letters to Tyrconnell reappointing him his Lord Deputy, and then sailed for Brest,

M

where he arrived on July 20, bringing the news of his own defeat. At Kingsale the French officers left him, returning to their regiments, which were on the march for Galway ; but another French officer, the Marquis de Léry, or Girardin, who had been with him from the beginning, joined the party there and returned to France. James reached St. Germains, as the conscientious Dangeau records, on July 25.

The elaborate defence made in the official Life shows that James realised in later years that his quitting Ireland in such hot haste after a battle at which he was present, but of which he had seen nothing, needed some explanation and excuse. The blame had then to be thrown on his councillors, who had committed the fault of showing themselves courtiers in giving the advice which they believed would be most to the King's own liking. The defence is well worth placing on record.

" Tho' this sollicitude for the King's safety which seem'd to stifle in some sort all other considerations was not pardonable but commendable in the Queen, yet those who ought to have made his own well-being and that of his Subjects, together with his honour and reputation in the world a part of their concern, should not so rashly have advised such disheartening Councels as to make his Majesty seem to abandon a cause which had still so much hopes of life in it. He had all the best ports and some of the strongest places still behind him, he had leasure enough to see if the Army (which was very little diminished by the action) might not be rally'd again, which his presence would hugely have contributed to, and his speedy flight must needs discourage them from. He might be sure his own people and especially the Court of France would be hardly induced to maintain a war which he himself so hastily abandon'd. But, on the other hand, it was not so much wonder'd that the King should be prevailed upon to do it, considering the unanimous advice of his Council, of the Generals themselves and of all persons about him (none of the Irish generals were consulted), that universal pannick fear which could make those

French officers (men of service) see visions of troops when none could certainly be within twenty miles of them, excused in great measure the King's *takeing so wrong a resolution*. However, all that would not have determined him to leave Ireland so soon had he not conceived it the likeliest expedient to repair his losses according to a certain scheme he had formed to himself, and which in realitie had been laid by the Court of France."

Leaving the last passage for later consideration, it is noteworthy that James admitted subsequently that he took " a wrong resolution " in fleeing from Ireland immediately after the Boyne. He throws the blame on his advisers. But at the moment that he took it he had persuaded himself that he was doing a wise thing, and that he would speedily find compensation for his Irish reverses in English successes. That was the " certain scheme he had formed to himself," but the allegation that it had " in realitie been laid by the Court of France " does not appear to have any basis in fact, and the quoted words are those, not of James himself, but of the historiographer, J. S. Clarke, who quotes as his authority Sir J. Dalrymple. Dalrymple declares that " in his flight he (James) received a letter written with Louis the Fourteenth's own hand, in which that Monarch informed him of the victory of Fleurus, which had put it in his power to draw his garrisons from Flanders to the coast, and of the station his Fleet had taken which prevented his enemies from succouring each other. In this letter Louis urged him to sail instantly for France, and to leave the conduct of the war to his Generals, with orders to protract it, and promised to land him in England with thirty thousand men."

The first point to note about this is that as it was received " in," that is to say during " his flight," it did not influence him to flee. He had already fled. But there is a much stronger objection to be taken. James, on reaching St. Germains, received a cool greeting from Louis. James at once made the request that Louis should lend him an army to make a descent on England, and Louis excused himself by saying that he very much regretted it, but " this is the only request he cannot concede to his dear brother." Now if James had in his possession such a letter as Dalrymple states, all he would have had to do would be to hand it back to Louis. Moreover, if Louis had written such a letter, he would not have repudiated its purport less than three weeks after it was written. There can be no doubt, then, that Louis never wrote any such letter. The probability is that the Queen placed her own interpretation on something the King of France said to her, and gave too literal expression to what she hoped he meant. There remains on record one remark of the Queen's in connection with this very victory of Fleurus which seems to bear out this interpretation—" à quoi nous servent toutes ces victoires, si le Roi perit en Irlande, qu'à me faire désespérer davantage."

As to what was thought in France about James's conduct, there is no ambiguity. Louvois roundly accused the King of having " spoiled everything by a mixture of ignorance, over-confidence, and folly." Marshal Luxemburg summed up the general verdict in a neat sentence—" Ceux qui aiment le roi d'Angleterre doivent etre bien aise de le voir en santé, mais ceux qui aiment sa gloire ont lieu à déplorer le personnage qu'il a fait." Which may be rendered— " Those who love the King of England must be very glad to see him safe and sound ; but those who think of his reputation have reason to deplore the figure he has cut."

If James's flight from Ireland lowered his reputation in France, it suffered irretrievable damage among the Irish. In the subsequent Stuart risings of 1708, 1715, and 1745 not a hand was raised in Ireland for James III. The Stuart cause was dead. The struggle in Ireland continued with varying fortunes for nearly eighteen months after his departure, but it was no longer a war for the Stuarts. The motives were vague, the views of the leaders differed ; but so far as there was an impulse it was national and not Jacobite. There was the old, unreasoning racial antipathy to the English, there was the bitter animosity of Catholic and Protestant, but sympathy with James and his family was cold and gone. The flight after the Boyne only completed an alienation that had begun as soon as the Irish people realised that James had no sympathy with the national aspirations of the Emerald Isle, and that he looked upon it as no more than the only convenient or indeed available stepping-stone for the recovery of England.

But even this might have been forgiven him if he had displayed any personal sympathy with Irishmen. He kept them almost ostentatiously at arm's length. His household was composed of Englishmen or Scotsmen—Powis, Howard, Dover, and Melfort—his favourite military men were of the same nationalities, Dorington, Sheldon, Sutherland, Maxwell, Wauchope, Buchan. He did not like Mountcashell, Sarsfield he dubbed a fool and only made a Brigadier at the instance of D'Avaux, and until Simon Luttrell was made Governor of Dublin, again through D'Avaux, there was no case of his rewarding a native of the country. Moreover, he did not like the disintegrating effect of the legislation of the Irish Parliament. He opposed as long as he dared all the proposals to separate the legislation of Ireland from England ; and when he at length gave a tardy and reluctant assent, every one around him knew that if he recovered the throne of England he would get out of his promise as well as he could.

Finally, he was by character a man of moderation in his religious policy, and this was the more remarkable because converts have always had the reputation of being excessive in their zeal. He was moderate by temper, but he was doubly moderate because he was persuaded that in that direction alone lay his chance of returning to London. He was very fearful of being implicated in Irish excesses. He knew quite well that the prejudice against the Irish in England was great, that the massacres by Cromwell had not obliterated the earlier massacres by the Irish, and that any repetition of them would intensify the feeling of disapprobation and aversion. From the first day to the last of his stay in Ireland he set himself against all extreme measures, and he refused to sanction not merely the wholesale arrest of Protestants, but even the laying waste of the Protestant districts in Ulster in order to deprive Schomberg on his arrival of the means of sustaining his army.

These views and conduct were highly creditable to James. They showed he was free from prejudice, as well as a man of humane sentiments. But they were not those calculated to evoke enthusiasm in Ireland. What the Irish Catholics wanted to be assured of was that their race and religion should be predominant in Ireland, that the tie with England should be broken, that as the Catholics had had their estates confiscated in 1651, so should the Protestants lose theirs in 1689–90, and that James Stuart should set up in Dublin the Court of an Irish King. James had no sympathy whatever with any of these projects. The idea of separation from England was hateful to him. He also knew that the scheme was quite incapable of being placed on any permanent basis. Ireland might be separated from England for a time, but by the inexorable laws of political gravitation one country must control the other by force or by mutual common sense and good feeling. But in running counter to and thwarting popular aspirations James alienated Irish goodwill and support. Before the Boyne he was already regarded with indifference. His conduct on the day of the battle, the great haste with which he put his person in a place of safety, which to the public mind could not be explained by any motive except cowardice, turned that indifference to contempt. It is very dubious whether Sarsfield ever uttered them, but the words with which he is credited—" Exchange Kings and we will fight you over again," faithfully reflected Irish opinion.

Chapter VII

THE FIRST SIEGE OF LIMERICK

THE army of " cowstealers," the rabble horde on which Macaulay pours out his vials of contempt, moved westwards unmolested and unpursued towards the Shannon and Limerick. At the same time the members of the little Court at Dublin, despite the difficulties of the route and their poverty, scorn coming to terms with the usurper and proceed as best they can to the same destination. The scattered garrisons draw to the same rallying-point, and early in August we find the Irish forces behind the Shannon. In Limerick itself are 20,000 Irish infantry, six miles away is the camp of the cavalry, some 3500 in number, under the command of the Duke of Berwick, with Sarsfield, Sheldon, and Maxwell under him, while still further off at Galway is Lauzun with his seven battalions more or less intact. In the south, Cork, Waterford, and Kingsale are held for King James, and Cork, at least, is held in some force.

With regard to Lauzun he has formed only one resolution, and that is not to risk the life of another French soldier. He has failed in his mission, and lamentably failed. He has led a French army in the field, and prevented its fighting. His own idea is to get it back to France with as few casualties as possible, so that it may win glory on other fields and under other leaders. Well may Louvois, on learning the facts, call him " a contemptible person." But if Lauzun has neither courage nor ability he has still a very high opinion of himself, and as he rides by Limerick to seek a surer shelter for himself in the far west he exclaims :

" A place that could be captured by a bombardment of roasted apples." He should have added, " if the commandant's name were Lauzun." We have a different tale to tell.

With Lauzun to Galway went Tyrconnell. He had for the moment been infected by the pessimism of his French comrade, and he had no hope that the army which had failed on the Boyne would succeed at Limerick. He had also lost the principal object for which he had been striving. The departure of James left him without a cause, and the thought occurred to him and to others if there was nothing to fight for was it worth while to go on fighting ? This thought did not then present itself to him for the first time. It had found expression in October, 1689, when James would not attack Schomberg, declaring that he needed five or six French battalions to drive him into the sea, and Tyrconnell had consulted D'Avaux as to whether it would not be better for James to return to France and leave him, Tyrconnell, at liberty to come to terms with William.

At that time Tyrconnell had some hopes about the Irish army ; now with diminished numbers and shaken confidence he could have few or none. Besides, his views about the value of French aid were modified. The French regiments had come and they had done very little. They had been present at the one battle of the war, and for all the practical good most of them had done they might just as well never have left France. Tyrconnell was despondent, and he had reason to be so. Lauzun was no cheerful colleague. The French officers and troops were sick of the business and anxious to be gone. The war in Ireland offered them no chance of glory, and none at all of spoil. Both Tyrconnell and Lauzun agreed that Limerick could not hold out, and both saw in that circumstance a new peril. Lauzun saw that it would jeopardise his departure, Tyrconnell that it would reduce his chances of arranging favourable terms with William. But even the clearness of the consequences did not inspire Lauzun with the courage

to move out with his troops to embarrass or attack the army
that beleaguered Limerick. Contemptible as his conduct
was at the Boyne, it was criminal at Galway. Tyrconnell,
having no troops under him, could do nothing, but he
vetoed Berwick's offer to lead a raid with his 3500 cavalry
on the rear and line of communication of William's army.
The solution of the situation did not rest with the timid
refugees at Galway, but with those who were playing a
man's part behind the low and feeble walls of Limerick.

When William found that the Irish army had rallied on
the Shannon he decided to move against it, more especially
as the glorified report of the fight on the Boyne sent over to
impress the English public had consolidated the position of
his Government in the principal kingdom. Some minor
successes in Ireland also encouraged the belief that the task
of dispersing the beaten Irish army would prove neither very
difficult, nor very protracted. Drogheda, where there was
a garrison of 1300 men under Lord Iveagh, surrendered
without a blow on the one condition that the men were not
to be made prisoners of war. They gave up their weapons
and were allowed to march to Athlone. A similar success
was achieved at Wexford, whence the garrison escaped,
leaving behind it only a considerable quantity of stores,
arms, and powder. The garrison at Duncannon parleyed
and surrendered with leave to march to Limerick. Waterford, where there were two regiments (Kavanagh and
Barrett), did likewise on the condition that they should
march to Cork without molestation. All these places might
have resisted, and although there is no reason to think that
they could have held out for any long period, their resistance would have caused great delay in the execution of
William's plan against Limerick. The yielding up of these
places, one after another, must have strengthened his
belief that there was no fight left in the Irish army.

At only one place did the Orange army find the opposition
that should have met it at all points. The most important
place on the Shannon above Limerick is Athlone, where

there was a bridge over the river. Through it passed the main route to Connaught, and Tyrconnell, knowing that on its preservation depended the security of Galway, had entrusted its defence to Colonel Richard Grace, an old officer of experience in the war of the Confederation and afterwards on the Continent. Colonel Grace had his own regiment, which had done well at the Boyne, and some other troops. He had also the disarmed garrison of Drogheda, of whom he may have been able to arm a few, but numerically he had but a small force to withstand the large body of troops William detached from his main body for the capture of Athlone.

This task he had entrusted to General Douglas, one of the most capable of his officers, and he placed under his orders three regiments of horse, two of dragoons, and ten of infantry, with an artillery force of ten field-pieces and two mortars. If a conclusion were formed from what had occurred elsewhere, the mere appearance of such a body of troops ought to have brought about the immediate surrender of Athlone. But as it happened Colonel Grace was a man of firm fibre, and when General Douglas summoned him to surrender he returned his compliments with an intimation that such was not his intention. Thereupon Douglas began to bombard Athlone with his ten field-pieces and two mortars, but after a week of it he found that he had made no progress, that his ammunition was being exhausted, and that he had lost between three and four hundred men by the enemy's fire and sickness. He then gave up the attempt to force the passage of the Shannon, and marched by the left bank to join the main army, which had now reached Limerick. The repulse at Athlone was the warning precursor of the greater repulse at Limerick. It was the first flicker of success that raised the hopes of those who upheld the Jacobite cause.

While William was marching towards Limerick he received news that for a moment greatly disconcerted him, and threatened to ruin all his plans. He learnt first that his army in Flanders, under the Duke of Waldeck, had been defeated at Fleurus, and then that the joint Anglo-Dutch fleet had been defeated by Tourville off Beachy Head. The latter news was the more serious because the English fleet had fought in such a manner as to raise serious doubts as to its loyalty to himself. In face of this intelligence William halted in his march, and hastened back to Dublin with the idea of returning to England. But at Dublin he received reassuring news from Queen Mary, who was carrying on the Government in his absence. The situation in the Netherlands presented no serious danger. Fleurus was another of those battles of the period destitute of results. The reported landing of French troops on English soil was insignificant. Tourville had gone back to his ports. The House of Commons had made a generous grant for the building of new ships to replace those lost in the Channel. Completely reassured William retraced his steps, resolved to bring the affair of Limerick to a head as soon as possible.

Limerick was described at this time as " a weak town having no outward works, but a toy of a palisade before a little part of the wall, nor a rampart within. The wall is of an old standing and far from being thick." This description becomes clearer when elucidated by the one given by the Duke of Berwick. He wrote : " The place had no fortifications but a wall without ramparts, and some miserable little towers without ditches. We had made a sort of covered way all round, and a kind of horn work palisaded before the great gate, but the enemy did not attack it on that side." The French report, undoubtedly drafted by Boisseleau, states that : " The fortifications were inconsiderable, the wall being made of stone, but not cemented, and without ramparts ; all the works were old and irregular in form." Boisseleau did what he could to put the place in a better state of defence, but this could not have amounted to a great deal considering the short time at his disposal.

As garrison Boisseleau had under him the whole of the Irish infantry with the exception of the three garrisons at

Athlone, Cork, and Kingsale, and Berwick places its strength at 20,000 men, adding, however, that " only half of them were armed." Tyrconnell stated that it numbered only 8000 men, and probably he was only counting armed men. One specific instance may be given. The Macmahon regiment had no arms, but it took a prominent part in the repulse of the final assault by hurling stones on the assailants.

The French reports state that there were twenty-eight Irish infantry regiments in Limerick, one cavalry regiment (Henry Luttrell's) and one dragoon regiment (Maxwell's). This list would not give a greater strength than 15,000 men.

Boisseleau, who by this time had begun to understand the Irish and to be trusted by them, was appointed Commandant, and he had under him the best of the commanding officers, Dorington and Maxwell, Gordon O'Neil and Simon Luttrell, John Hamilton and Richard Talbot the Younger, Kilmallock and Fitzgerald. With the cavalry not far off were Sheldon and Sarsfield under Berwick.

On August 18, N.S. (that is to say thirty-eight days after the Boyne), William unfurled his standard in front of Limerick, and at dawn of the following day he sent a trumpeter to summon Boisseleau to surrender on the honourable terms which he would be happy to concede. Boisseleau sent a reply, in which covert sarcasm and confidence in his own position were equally revealed, to the effect that he was very much surprised by the letter he had received, and that he hoped to deserve a better opinion from the Prince of Orange by the vigorous defence of the place, which he intended to offer with the aid of the troops of the King of Great Britain. Whereupon William gave orders for the erection of two batteries, one at Fort Cromwell of five 12-prs., and the other of four similar guns opposite the hornwork. He also dug a trench opposite the centre redoubt, the wall of which was so low that the English troops were able to throw grenades over it.

Although he began the bombardment at once, the Prince was expecting his heavy siege artillery in a few days, and once it arrived he knew that he could lay all the defences of the place level with the ground. He was full of hope of thus putting a speedy end to the siege, and when a deserter brought news to the besieged of the approaching convoy the hearts of Boisseleau and his companions-in-arms sank within them. How could the convoy approaching from Dublin be stopped ? Who was the man to stop it ? Unless it were stopped the fate of Limerick seemed sealed.

The cavalry camp lay some miles off in County Clare, but Sarsfield was in Limerick watching with eager impetuosity the lines of the leaguering army and the fire of the two batteries to which the garrison had no means of replying. He was in the town on August 21, when the deserter brought the news of the approaching convoy, and he at once undertook to make an attempt to intercept it. He rode off to the cavalry camp to obtain the loan of some cavalry for the execution of his raid, and although Berwick was not well disposed towards Sarsfield and personally piqued by the vetoing of his own plan, he could not deny Sarsfield the use of his own regiment and a few squadrons of dragoons. These troops together numbered 500 men, and with them he crossed the Shannon, by swimming, at Killaloe, some distance below Limerick, and making a wide detour through Tipperary he got in the rear of the convoy with the artillery train. It had reached its last halting-place at Ballineedy, a small ruined castle only seven miles from William's camp.

Sarsfield waited till nightfall, and then while the camp was lulled in sleep and fancied security he charged into it at the head of his horsemen, who raised the cry of Sarsfield. The guards were cut down to the last man, so were many of the waggoners, and it was also alleged some women. Then Sarsfield filled the eight battering-pieces with powder, fixed the muzzles in the ground and blew out their breaches. At the same time he destroyed all the ammunition and

stores, and the great explosion and conflagration at Ballineedy told the spectators in William's camp what had
happened. Having effected his object, Sarsfield galloped
off as hard as he could to reach the other side of the Shannon,
which he accomplished without loss or hindrance by taking
a fresh route and crossing at Banagher. In this way he
evaded the pursuit of the cavalry sent from William's camp
to meet the convoy. The blame for this mishap was cast
upon the Earl of Portland (Bentinck), who put off leaving
with his cavalry till the morning. Sarsfield had done well
at Sligo, but he did better at Ballineedy, for his daring and
successful raid was undoubtedly the cause of William's
failure to capture Limerick. The story at the time was
that " the loss of his artillery struck the Prince of Orange
into a great rage," which can well be believed. It is not
surprising that with the Irish Sarsfield became more than
ever the popular champion.

Having lost his battering-pieces William had to do what
he could with his 12-prs. and some heavier pieces that were
fetched from Waterford, and after a week's bombardment
he proceeded to attack the two advanced redoubts. One of
these, known as the Stone Fort, was captured with small
loss, and on August 27 he delivered his first assault on the
other with three regiments led by the Prince of Wurtemberg and Generals Kirke and Tettau. This force reached
the covered way, but was eventually driven out of it by the
heavy musket fire from the walls. The next day a fresh
battery of four guns was erected at a point in the centre
commanding the covered way, and a good many of the
garrison were killed there before they could be withdrawn.
During the night of the 29th, Wurtemberg got his force
to within thirty yards of the second redoubt with the idea
of attacking it in the morning. Boisseleau took his measures
to defeat it by placing 150 good marksmen under Colonel
Fitzgerald in the redoubt over night, and by ordering
Lord Kilmallock to take up a position with 300 cavalry so
that he could fall on the flank of the attacking force.

Thanks to these precautions the attack of the 30th made with Danish and Prussian troops was repulsed with considerable loss. The chief credit of this repulse was due to Lord Kilmallock's vigorous charge.

After this repulse the bombardment was resumed, and thanks to the fire of a fresh battery the advanced redoubt was completely destroyed. Notwithstanding this, the garrison continued to hold it, and were only expelled after some fierce fighting and heavy losses on both sides. Even then the besieged continued to oppose the occupation of the redoubt, and several serious encounters took place in which the Irish lost 100 killed and the besiegers 300 killed. But William caused an overwhelming force of infantry, led by all the French refugee officers, who had been under the command of Schomberg, to be thrown into the redoubt, which was then occupied. Having obtained possession of the redoubt, William at once caused a fresh battery of five 24-prs. and one 36-pr. to be erected in it, and with the fire from these guns at close range he proceeded to batter down the wall, and the little towers, described by the Duke of Berwick, from which a galling cross fire had been kept up. From this position, also, a large number of bombs were thrown into the town, setting fire to several of the houses. After this second and, as it proved, final bombardment had gone on for five days, a wide strip of the wall, not less than one hundred yards in length, had been demolished, and on September 6 all seemed ready for the assault.

But Boisseleau on his side had not been inactive. He saw that the critical hour was close at hand, and he made his preparations very quietly and very effectually to repel the great assault when it was delivered. The Irish made scarcely any reply to the bombardment, but they were hard at work on the construction of an inner defence thirty yards behind the old wall. In good positions along this rampart the French officer placed three small cannon with their muzzles pointing on the gaps through which the storming parties were sure to come, and he kept them concealed until the very last moment. At the same time he collected the whole of the garrison in the side streets in readiness to relieve and reinforce those at the front.

These preparations had scarcely been completed when William gave the order for assaulting the town at two in the afternoon of September 6. The counterscarp was the object of the first attack, and for this task William ordered up the grenadier companies of all the regiments and, as a support, several of the best Huguenot and Danish regiments. Before this onset the Irish in the covered way fell back, reaching by a cross way the Gate of St. John, which remained throughout the fight in their possession. The following account of the attack on the breach is translated from the one written by Boisseleau for the information of his Government.

" The enemy mounted the breach with great vigour, and the besieged waited the attack with great firmness, not firing a shot because they were much inferior in weapons and ammunition. When they reached the crest of the breach the three cannons loaded with bullets and shrapnel began to fire on them, and at the same time the men holding the inner rampart began to fire volleys. The enemy were much shaken by this double fire, although they had eighteen guns playing on the wall and kept up a heavy musketry fire as well. Three Irish regiments (those of the Grand Prior, Boisseleau, and another whose name escapes me), with their standards planted in front of them in the breach, held their ground with extraordinary firmness although they had no cover, and at no time was there any difficulty or hesitation in filling up the gaps. Lieutenant-Colonel Beaurepaire (of Boisseleau's regiment), several officers, and about 200 men were killed in this part of the fight, which lasted about four hours. Four hundred men of the Macmahon regiment, who had no arms, threw stones at the assailants, which seriously incommoded them.

" The besiegers strove hard, nevertheless, to establish a means of communication between the part of the covered way they had occupied and their own trenches, and as the dragoons of Maxwell and Talbot, stationed at St. John's Gate, were ready to move forward to support the defenders of the breach, the Prince of Orange directed two English regiments to attack and drive them out of their position. But these regiments were received with so much valour that they were compelled to retire in disorder, which was much increased by the accidental explosion of four barrels of powder. This killed thirty of them and made the rest take to flight in the belief that the place was mined. Thereupon Talbot attacked with great energy, and although fresh troops were brought up they were forced to abandon the whole of the covered way. Then Boisseleau ordered a general advance, driving the assailants with sword and pike through the breach back to their trenches. Although the enemy put their loss at the lowest possible total, there is no doubt that it reached 2000 killed and wounded. In the François de Cambon regiment alone there remained only six officers fit for service, and seventy-one were either killed or wounded. The other Huguenot regiment, and those of Douglas, Meath, Stuart, Cutts, and Drogheda also suffered heavily. The Danes had forty-five captains, lieutenants, and ensigns killed or disabled."

The effect of this rude repulse was that after two or three days' desultory firing, and much talk of delivering a second assault, William decided to abandon the siege and returned to Dublin on his way back to England. His army, bearing a long train of sick and wounded, followed by slow marches, having burnt their camp and accidentally the house which was their chief hospital and which contained many wounded. During the whole of the siege William lost over 5000 men, which included some of his best troops and officers. The defenders lost 1062 men and 97 officers in killed and wounded. The French report of the defence reads that " the officers in the defending force greatly distinguished themselves during a siege of twenty-one days of open trenches, and the Irish soldiers not merely fought well, but

N

sustained with extraordinary patience all the fatigues, which were very great, seeing that they were always under arms, and that they were in want of the simplest necessaries of life. Brigadier John Hamilton (the one who never served in the French army) assisted me with constancy and ability."

The following is the Duke of Berwick's description of the siege :—

" At length the enemy began to move, and proceeded from Dublin to Limerick. The same day they made their appearance the French troops retired to Galway. We left M. de Boisseleau, a Frenchman, Captain in H. M. C. Majesty's Guards and Major-General, to command in the town with all our Irish infantry amounting to about 20,000 men, of *whom, however, not more than one half were armed.* We kept the field with our cavalry, which might make up 3500 horse. We encamped at first five miles from Limerick on this (west) side of the river Shannon, which passes through it, in order to keep up a free communication with the town. In this our success was complete ; the enemy never daring to attempt investing it on our side nor even to send any party across the river, which is only fordable in some parts. The place had no fortifications, but a wall without ramparts, and some miserable little towers without ditches. We had made a sort of covered way all round, and a kind of hornwork palisaded before the great gate, but the enemy did not attack it on that side.

" They opened their trenches at a distance to the left ; they erected batteries, made a breach of 100 toises and then summoned the garrison to surrender.

" The Irish would not listen to the message ; in consequence the Prince of Orange caused a general assault to be made with 10,000 men. The trenches not being more than two toises from the palisade, and there being no ditch the enemy had mounted the breach before any alarm was given of the attack. The fire of a battery, which Boisseleau had formed on the inside, checked them for some little time, but they soon made their way into the town. The Irish forces

advanced on every side, and charged the enemy afterwards
in the street with so much bravery that they beat them
back as far as the top of the breach, where they endeavoured
to make a lodgment. Brigadier Talbot, who was then in
the hornwork with 500 men, ran round the wall on the
outside and, charging them in the rear, drove them out,
and entering by the breach posted himself there. In the
action the enemy had 2000 men killed on the spot ; on our
side there were not so many as 400. The Prince of Orange,
seeing the ill-success of this attack and that he had lost his
choicest troops in it, resolved to raise the siege. He gave
out through Europe that the continued rains had been the
cause of it, but I can affirm that not a single drop of rain
fell for above a month before, or for three weeks after. At
the time the siege was raised there remained in Limerick not
more than fifty barrels of powder, and we had not in the
whole tract of Ireland which belonged to us enough to
double the quantity."

William, disappointed and enraged with his defeat when
he counted on a sure success, had to seek some excuse or
explanation of his failure to satisfy the public opinion of
England. He found it in the weather. It was given out
that it had rained so heavily and so persistently that the
River Shannon overflowed its banks, that the country
became like a morass, and that the cavalry horses could
hardly keep their footing. It would have been a disgrace
for the victors of the Boyne to have been vanquished two
months later by the same foe over whom they had gained
a success which all the official scribes were occupied in
magnifying, but it was none at all to be beaten by King
Pluvius. From one end of England to the other the story
ran that William had retired from before Limerick in
consequence of the rain.

The Duke of Berwick, whose word is not to be disbelieved,
and who had no reason, as will be shown, to deviate from
the truth, replies to this statement with a formal contradiction : " I can affirm that not a single drop of rain fell

for above a month before or for three weeks after." If the Shannon had been swollen Sarsfield could not have crossed it twice, if the roads had been soft and sticky he could not have made the long raid through Clare and Cork to Balli-needy. Berwick had no share in the honour and glory of the defence of Limerick, he was jealous of Sarsfield's reputation, and if there had been any natural cause to diminish the merit of the defence it is only too probable that he would have said something to disparage the leaders in the city of Limerick. Far from doing so, he gives his formal word in contradiction to the story of William of Orange.

Now with regard to William's explanation there was nothing very unnatural or blameworthy in his giving it. He was in such a position of general insecurity that he was bound to try and explain away his defeat. It was also not unnatural that his heterogeneous army of veterans should welcome any excuse to explain how they had been beaten by an untrained army on which they affected to look down with contempt. The suggestion that this failure was due to the downpour of the overcharged heavens was, therefore, welcomed as a consoling palliative, which no witness that the world would be at all likely to accept as impartial seemed likely ever to dispose of. They reckoned without the Duke of Berwick.

But while it was perfectly excusable and natural for William to invent an excuse to serve his temporary need, there is no excuse for Macaulay, writing a hundred and sixty years after the event at the bar of history, to repeat and adopt blindly the temporary expedients of the Dutch Prince. He adopts the statement of Story and others in William's camp that " rain fell in torrents, that the Shannon was swollen, the ground sodden, etc." And although he cites Berwick's statement in a footnote, he passes it by as valueless, but he adopted them so blindly and readily that he did not even examine and weigh carefully what his own authorities stated. First, with regard to Story, Macaulay quotes merely

that " it was cloudy all about, and rained very fast so that
everybody began to dread the consequences of it," but he
omits to state that this was *after* the repulse of the attempt
to storm on September 6.   Story's version is that it was
apprehension of what might be the consequences of further
rains that led to the retreat of the army, not that the
attack had failed on account of the rain.   Story is a very
poor authority to lean on.   His assertion that Boisseleau
told the Irish in a speech before his departure that the
success of the defence was due to himself, and that the
Irish would not be able to defend it if again attacked, bears
the hall-mark of unveracity on its face.   Boisseleau told
William's officers on September 7, when they asked to bury
their dead, that he was ready to give them a better reception than before whenever they cared to renew the attack.
Tyrconnell had just reinforced him with a thousand
fusiliers and dragoons.

Nor does Macaulay quote his second witness, Dumont
de Bostaquet, any more accurately or fairly.   Macaulay
declares that " Dumont says that before the siege was
raised the rains had been most violent, that the Shannon
was swollen, that the earth was soaked, that the horses
could not keep their feet."   Here are the exact facts as
given by Dumont.   In the first place the statement refers
to a particular interval during the attack while a fresh
battery was being prepared.   Dumont, a Huguenot officer
already referred to at the Boyne, was sent to the river
bank to try and cross the Shannon with some cavalry.   The
reference to the ground being heavy refers only to the river
bank, and exclusively to the one day when Dumont was
seeking to cross the Shannon.   He adds : " The rain
stopped," and notwithstanding the rain, he reports " the
river had not risen."   Macaulay's reputation as a serious
and trustworthy historian has been so seriously undermined
that it would probably furnish a fruitful harvest of
misstatement and misrepresentation for a careful student
with the necessary leisure to examine all the statements in

his history seriatim, and discover how he utilised historical materials, and with what degree or deficiency of good faith. Even here, with limited opportunity for excursions from our main narrative, several gross perversions of the evidence have been exposed.

But this is not the only serious misstatement to be found in Macaulay's description. He declares that " the Irish fled into the town and were followed by the assailants, who, in the excitement of victory, did not wait for orders. Then began a terrible street fight. . . . The very women of Limerick mingled in the combat, stood firmly under the hottest fire and flung stones and broken bottles at the enemy." What are the facts ? William's troops never got past the inner temporary rampart which Boisseleau erected thirty yards behind the wall. There was no street fighting, the women were not engaged, and Macaulay's picture is one of the imagination.

Again : " In the moment when the conflict was fiercest a mine exploded and hurled a fine German battalion into the air ! " This was the affair of the four powder barrels which killed thirty men of an English regiment. If a German battalion had been annihilated, then William's loss would have to go up by nearly a thousand men. The exploding mine is a freak of pure romance.

Shortly after the raising of the siege a French fleet arrived at Galway for the purpose of conveying the French troops back to their country, and by the same order all the French officers, including Boisseleau, were to return with them. As this meant the withdrawal of all French aid, and as the stores for war were in a very depleted condition, this practical abandonment of the Irish cause filled the Duke of Tyrconnell with lively apprehension. He decided to proceed to France, to explain the exact situation, and to appeal to Louis for renewed assistance. The English army had retreated, both sides would go into winter quarters, and he could carry out his mission and be back again before the time for fresh activity had come round. But as an *avant-coureur* he sent Anthony Hamilton to France with news of the raising of the siege, and then he came to Limerick for a few days to arrange things during his absence. He first appointed the Duke of Berwick to act as Viceroy, but the French reports show that Berwick was not left supreme. In military matters he was to take counsel with Lord Clare, Sarsfield, Maxwell, Galmoye, and Sheldon. In civil matters he was to act by the advice of Albeville, Riverston, and Plowden.

General Dorington was nominated commandant of Limerick, and Sarsfield was propitiated with the assurance that Tyrconnell would bring back the patent of an Earl as his reward for the affair of Ballineedy. Having made these appointments, Tyrconnell returned to Galway, where he went on board the French fleet, and sailed away with Lauzun for France. But while Tyrconnell held the supreme place to which there was no other aspirant, he was not in complete harmony with many of the Irish leaders, who strongly dissented from his proposals to make favourable terms with William's Government. Berwick says that at this time " Tyrconnell had become fearful and heavy," and that " neither his age nor his bulk suited him for active work." He also states that Brigadier Simon Luttrell and Sarsfield proposed to him to arrest Tyrconnell, whereupon the Duke rejoined that to do so would be tantamount to committing high treason.

At the same time the Duke feigned to share their views, and suggested that they should send delegates to King James at St. Germains. This suggestion was adopted, and the two Luttrells, Henry and Simon, Colonel Nicholas Purcell and Creagh, Bishop of Cork, were sent as the independent Irish delegation to St. Germains, proceeding to France on a ship from Limerick. At the same time Berwick sent Brigadier Maxwell, an officer in his confidence, with them nominally on a mission about military matters, but really with a secret message advising James not to allow Henry Luttrell or Nicholas Purcell to return. This advice James was unable to follow, for when he suggested that the individuals named should remain in France they quietly replied that if they did not return their comrades would seize the Duke of Berwick and hold him as a hostage. Under these circumstances, James thought it best to let them return, contenting himself with sending by Maxwell an order to Berwick to leave Ireland as soon as possible.

Tyrconnell met with a good reception at the French Court and made a favourable impression there. It may be interesting to state that his wife, the Duchess, had preceded him. Her arrival at Brest on August 25, 1690, is mentioned in the French report, and she was accompanied by one of her married daughters, Lady Kingsland, and her unmarried daughters, of whom one shortly afterwards became a nun at St. Omer. The Duke's only daughter by his first wife was also with her. Tyrconnell had several audiences with Louis, who assigned him an apartment at Versailles. He also presented him with his portrait set in brilliants. At James's hands he received the Garter on the vacancy caused by the death of the Duke of Grafton at Cork. On January 1, 1691, Tyrconnell started on his return journey, taking with him some stores and arms and a few engineer and artillery officers. Louis had also given him a promise that he would send further assistance as soon as he received a message from him stating definitely what he wanted.

The reception that awaited Lauzun was a cool one, although Louis did not altogether share the views of Louvois about him. Whatever else he had failed to do, he had brought back the French regiments almost intact, and French soldiers had become so very greatly needed that this was no trifling service. On balance France had gained from her intervention in Ireland the Mountcashell brigade which had done so well in Savoy. The idea that other forces might be drawn from Ireland seems also to have taken some root, for in the first letters announcing Lauzun's intention to return it was stated, " he will bring with him 8000 or 9000 more Irish troops." But Louvois had his own opinion.

In his eyes Lauzun was " a contemptible fellow " and " a poltroon," and " the first French general to prevent the army under his orders from fighting."

Boisseleau was received in the manner to which his meritorious conduct in drilling the Irish troops and in defending Limerick entitled him.   Louis received him in audience, raised him to the rank of Brigadier, and gave him a pension of 500 crowns.   La Hoguette, too, after an interview of over an hour with Louis on October 19 (when to the surprise of Sourches and others his explanations of his own conduct in Ireland were accepted), was sent to Savoy to succeed to the command held by St. Ruth, of whom we shall be hearing more in a later chapter.   With regard to the French troops, they were to have the opportunity of gaining on other fields the reputation for prowess denied them in Ireland.

The following particulars as to the French troops brought back by Lauzun are taken from the Paris archives.   There came back to Brest with him 304 officers and 4346 soldiers fit for service.   In addition there were 747 sick officers and men, 65 artillery officers and men, and 103 officers who had been serving with Irish regiments.   During the voyage Colonel Mérode and many of the sick died, and the condition of the troops on being inspected in France is stated to have been deplorable.   Misfortune seemed to dog the expedition, for a considerable number of the Faméchon regiment were drowned by the upsetting of a boat on which they were being landed.   The French intendants reported that to recover their former efficiency most of the regiments would have to be reformed.   Boisseleau attributed this deterioration to the poverty of Ireland—" a country where there is no corn, no bread, no medicine, and where a wounded man is as good as dead."   Lauzun's corps returned then to France in October, 1690, in very much the same condition as the Mountcashell division had reached it in April of the same year.

The retreat of William's army from before Limerick,

followed by the withdrawal of the French contingent under Lauzun, marks the close of the first phase in the Irish war. When the French squadron sailed from Galway the Irish party was again left to its own unaided resources as it had been prior to James's arrival in March, 1689; but it was no longer in the same advantageous position. At the earlier date Tyrconnell held the whole of Ireland outside Londonderry and Enniskillen. He possessed Dublin and all the ports of the kingdom. He had raised an army of 50,000 men, which was not free from defects, but which was of great promise. It was ill-officered, its weapons were bad in quality and insufficient in quantity, but if a rich country like France had set itself the task of providing the means and the leaders, there was no limit to what it might have accomplished in Ireland alone.

But by the later date the situation had materially changed. The national party held the west and the south-west. It had lost Dublin and all the Leinster coast. A large hostile army was in occupation of the eastern and northern parts of the island. The Protestants had been re-armed and reorganised. The Catholics in the provinces held by William had been stripped of their lands and ruthlessly turned out of their homes. Finally, the magazines were exhausted, and the Irish leaders at Limerick were confronted with the prospect that if supplies did not come from France in the spring of the new year, there would be no powder or lead to carry on the war.

And as a warning of the grave peril that stared them in the face, came Marlborough's brief but exceedingly successful campaign in County Cork. When William returned to England and found that things were not so bad in Flanders as he feared they might be in consequence of his defeat at Fleurus, and that Admiral Tourville had not followed up his success at Beachy Head, he bethought him that it might be as well to do something to render it more difficult for the French to land troops in Ireland. He reflected that the southern ports, which they had

hitherto used, were in the hands of the Irish party, and
whether it was his own idea or that of the man to whose
command he entrusted its execution, he decided to fit out
a combined naval and military expedition for the capture
of Cork and Kingsale. Whoever conceived the expedition
there can be no dispute as to the transcendent ability of the
man to whose hands it had been entrusted. John, Lord
Churchill had been one of the last to abandon the cause of
James in 1688, not because he had any sympathy with the
Orange party, but because his wife's relations with the
Princess Anne promised to make him ultimately the most
powerful man in the kingdom. His want of sympathy with
the Dutch Prince made him a Jacobite intriguer throughout
his life, of which there will be sufficient evidence hereafter.

But in 1690 he was a Lieutenant-General in William's
service, and to attach him more closely to the new Government he was promoted Earl of Marlborough. When
William, smarting under his repulse at Limerick, conceived
the idea of applying a salve to his wounds by achieving
some further success in Ireland before the winter arrived,
he turned to Marlborough and asked him to lead an
expedition to capture Cork and Kingsale, or it may well
have been that Marlborough himself suggested the project;
but in either case Marlborough was delighted to receive
the command of his first independent expedition. There was
another interesting feature about it. It was composed exclusively of English troops. There were seven complete foot
regiments, two marine regiments, and some extra companies
of foot, and the warships and transports made up a fleet of
over eighty ships. The first and most important point to
be attacked was Cork, where seven weak Irish foot regiments
were quartered, two at least having already surrendered at
Waterford to the Orange army and been allowed to go on
the terms of the capitulation. Their strength did not
exceed 4000 men, about half that of Marlborough's land
force. The defences of Cork were even more insignificant
than those of Limerick, and when D'Avaux saw them in 1689

he had strongly advised that the walls should be levelled, and that the place should be declared incapable of defence. But this was not the Jacobite way of doing things. It was perfectly clear that Cork could not be defended; therefore a garrison should be left there to be sacrificed in attempting the impossible. The seven regiments in the place were those of Clancarty, Tyrone, Kavanagh, Mac Elligott, Macarty Mor, Barrett, and Sullivan, of which the first-named five had suffered at the Boyne. There was no artillery with the force, and only a small fort with two or three old cannon guarded the approach to the harbour. The proper and obvious course for the commander to follow was to abandon the town on the arrival of the English fleet and to retreat to Limerick. But unfortunately Colonel Mac Elligott had been blamed for surrendering Waterford without defending it, and he conceived that his honour compelled him to offer resistance at Cork, which any sensible man must have known would be useless. To make the case more hopeless it was known that General Ginkel had detached a force of 5000 men from Kilkenny to attack Cork from the land side.

On October 1 (N.S.) Marlborough's fleet arrived, and sending in his warships in single file they knocked the old fort to pieces with their broadsides as they passed by. The troops were then landed without opposition and the investment was completed. Mac Elligott held out for about a week, by which time all his powder was expended, and then he and his garrison had to surrender themselves as prisoners of war. In one of the last encounters the young Duke of Grafton (son of Charles II) was mortally wounded. On this occasion a new practice was adopted. Up to this point the garrisons which surrendered had been disarmed and allowed to go free, but a new departure was now made. The garrison was to be deported out of the kingdom and it was proposed to exchange it eventually in Flanders for Danish and Huguenot prisoners captured in France. This incident will be dealt with later on, but it represents a forgotten phase in the abstraction of the flower of Irish manhood from their native land.

Cork captured, Marlborough next turned his attention to Kingsale, but before he started one of his ships, the " Breda," of sixty guns, blew up in the harbour, everyone on board, including twenty-five prisoners, among them Colonel Charles Kavanagh, being killed, except Colonel John Barrett, and Colonel Kavanagh's young son, who were blown so far into the water that they escaped without serious injury. At Kingsale Sir Edward Scott was the commander, but although he had only a small force he was well supplied with provisions and ammunition and made a good defence. After holding out for a week and losing 300 men out of a total garrison of 1500, Sir Edward surrendered on honourable terms, he and his men marching out with arms and baggage and withdrawing unmolested to Limerick. Marlborough complimented Scott, whom we shall meet again, on the excellence of his defence. James blamed Mac Elligott very much for his want of prudence in not coming to terms, whereby a large force was sacrificed; but there does not seem any justification for his charge against Marlborough, which alleged that at Cork he would not bury the wounded prisoners when they died, so that they might spread a contagion among the survivors. The truth is probably that he had so many prisoners on his hands that he did not know what to do with them. When Marlborough returned to England in January, 1691, he brought back with him 150 Irish officers, including the Earls of Clancarty and Tyrone, who were put in the Tower pending despatch to Ostend, but transport for the poor Irish soldiers was not provided until the month of March.

Marlborough's successes on the south coast were obtained while Lauzun was on the sea between Galway and Brest, and were not known in France for many weeks later. It was clear at once that a very considerable impediment had thus been placed in the way of sending troops from France, for, as Dangeau expresses it, " no port of landing remained in the possession of the King." The efforts made to find some compensation for this blow were not very fortunate. The Duke of Berwick made a raid on Bir Castle, but owing to the unskilfulness of his gunners he failed to take it at once, and then had to retreat rather precipitately on the approach of General Douglas with large reinforcements. In Kerry another body of Irish levies was assembled with the idea of advancing upon Cork, but a rumour spreading that the English troops were approaching, the leaders thought it wise to burn the little town of Killarney, to destroy the crops, and to retire into the hills.

The year 1690 did not close, therefore, as favourably for the national cause as it might have done. Despite the success at Limerick the Irish had lost between Cork and Kingsale 5000 of their trained men. The stores were brought to the lowest point of depletion. The troops, officers and privates alike, were in rags. Their powder was reduced to a few barrels. There was no source from which their needs could be supplied save France, and to a certain extent communications with that country had been severed, or at least rendered more difficult. While everything was black around them they were confronted with the clear and certain prospect that in the spring their adversaries would resume the struggle with more troops and full supplies provided by the wealth of England.

The reader will have no doubt that at least one man rejoiced when the King's order, brought by the Duke of Tyrconnell, summoned the Duke of Berwick from this depressing scene. A few weeks later King Louis received the young Duke at Marly, and Dangeau, not then foreseeing all the importance of what he wrote, makes the conscientious entry : " He will now serve in France."

Chapter VIII

THE MOUNTCASHELL BRIGADE

IT was pointed out in a previous chapter that as soon as Count D'Avaux landed in Ireland, in March, 1689, he began to sound General McCarthy, shortly afterwards created by James Viscount Mountcashell, as to his willingness to command an Irish corps destined for the service of the King of France in exchange for French troops to be sent to Ireland. Lord Mountcashell (to give him his subsequent title) welcomed the proposal. From a passage in one of the unpublished documents in the French War Department it would even seem that he was the originator of the whole project, having written, *proprio motu*, to propose an exchange of troops as early as February, 1689, and offering himself to command the Irish contingent. Dangeau tells us that he had already served in the French army, where he was well known by the name of Mouskry, and we have already stated that he had been selected by Louvois to command the regiment of English gendarmes, on Sir George Hamilton's death, in preference to Churchill. Mouskry, a name which has puzzled many commentators, is clearly Muskerry, and Dangeau probably confounded him with his elder brother Viscount Muskerry (son of the Earl of Clancarty), who first distinguished himself in the French service, and then made himself somewhat notorious in France by his sensational departure as described by Claren-don in Vol. VII of his History. This Lord Muskerry, the first of his family to serve in France, was killed on board the "Royal Charles" in 1665, in the battle with the Dutch in the Medway, and buried in Westminster Abbey. The

McCarthys were therefore well known in France, and for the success of the scheme it was desirable that the commander, at least, of the new corps should know that country, and also be acquainted with the strict discipline that characterised the French army at the period.

It was not until after Melfort's departure and James's admission that a nucleus of trained French troops was indispensable for the expulsion of Schomberg's army that the project took a practical form. At that moment Mountcashell happened to be a prisoner in the enemy's hands; and although it was proposed to exchange him for Lord Mountjoy, the question of nominating the first commander of the corps could not be left unsettled for the arrival of that contingency. D'Avaux passed the eligibles in review, and on the whole inclined to the choice of the Duke of Berwick, although he pronounced him " very brave, but a bad officer, and with no common sense." The only fetters placed on the ambassador's independent judgment were Louvois's peremptory order that " in no case was the command to be given to any of the Hamiltons; neither was a Hamilton to be appointed Colonel of any of the regiments sent over." The question of the commanding officer was happily solved by Lord Mountcashell's escape shortly afterwards, whereupon he proceeded to Cork and took charge of the operation of preparing the brigade that was to bear his name. It is not uninteresting to note that D'Avaux, fully conscious of the jealousy of French generals for interlopers, added that while Mountcashell was a first-rate officer " his near-sightedness would effectually prevent his ever becoming a great general."

The French authorities wished that each regiment sent should be composed of sixteen companies of 100 men apiece, and although this condition could not be complied with, it explains how and why the five regiments sent from Ireland were reformed into three on arrival in France. With a view to complying with the French proposal, four regiments were first named for the service. They were those of Galway, Daniel O'Brien, Neil O'Neil, and Feilding. The way proposed for the raising of these regiments was for James to appeal to the head of a certain number of Irish families to raise a regiment, the command to be given to a junior member of the house. Letters of this nature were written to the Earl of Clanrickarde, Viscount Clare, Viscount Dillon, and probably Viscount Mountgarret. The O'Neil failed to raise a regiment and retired from the original list. Lord Clanrickarde had raised a regiment for the King's service, but the idea of sending it to France with his son and heir was not so attractive to him. His name was next eliminated.

On the other hand, Viscount Dillon was not at all opposed to his regiment going to France under the command of his second son, Arthur, who was a keen soldier. Lord Mountcashell also set himself to the task of reforming his old regiment which had suffered so heavily at Crum, and such was his popularity that in a few weeks he raised the skeleton battalion left of 300 men to one of the full strength of 1200 men. The Feilding regiment made but slow progress until Lord Mountcashell came to his brother-in-law's help, and then it reached a sufficient number to pass muster. Colonel Robert Feilding, an Englishman who had been a member of the House of Commons in the last of James's English Parliaments, had married Mary, only daughter and heir of Ulick, Marquis of Clanrickarde and widow of Charles McCarthy, Viscount Muskerry, Lord Mountcashell's elder brother, who was killed in battle in 1665 as already stated.

The O'Brien regiment was raised the quickest of all, but when a rumour got about that Lord Clare did not intend to give the command to his son the regiment declared that they would not leave Ireland unless an O'Brien were in command. The disaffected were soon pacified, when they were informed that Daniel O'Brien, their chief's son and heir, would be their Colonel. The Butler regiment was raised mainly by the influence of Viscount Galmoye, and the

o

command was taken by his kinsman Colonel Richard Butler. By March, 1690, then, the five regiments of Mountcashell, Richard Butler, Dillon, O'Brien or Clare, and Feilding, with an average strength of 1200 men apiece (excepting the last named, which mustered about 800), were ready for trans-shipment to France. With regard to its numerical strength, the return of the French officials at Brest made the total force in the brigade 5800 in round numbers.

The following list of the officers in each regiment at the time of leaving for France possesses a more than passing interest :—

THE MOUNTCASHELL REGIMENT

Colonel-in-Chief, Lord Mountcashell
Lt.-Colonel-in-Command, Lt.-Colonel Colgrave
Major Michael Roth
Major Hogan

Captains	Lieutenants	Ensigns
McCarthy	O'Brien	Mulvany
Dooley	Maccarty	Trueley
Meagher (adjutant)	Carroll	McCarthy
G. FitzGerald	FitzGerald	Roth
Browne	Sullivan	Comyn
Power	Hogan	Colgrave
Condon	Sweeney	Keogh
O'Brien	Maurice	Callaghan
	Chivers	Rayne
	Cusack	Lavallin
	Condon	
	Rayne	

THE RICHARD BUTLER REGIMENT

Colonel-in-Chief, Colonel Richard Butler
Lt.-Colonel, Lt.-Colonel Butler
Major Butler.

Captains	Lieutenants	Ensigns
Fort	Kelly	Butler
Archer	Carney	FitzGerald
FitzHarris	St. Leger	Raggett
Doran	Sutton	Stafford
Boulger	Rayne	Kerans
Kelly	Roche	Boulger, Jun.

Captains	Lieutenants	Ensigns
Lincoln	Mandeville	Kelly
Sexton	Forde	Newport
FitzGerald	Cokeley	Walsh
McKennins	Butler	Jordan
		Langton
		Fagin

Surgeon Kelly. Priest, Father Murphy.

THE DILLON REGIMENT

Colonel-in-Chief, Colonel Arthur Dillon
Lt.-Colonel, Lt.-Colonel Henry Crafton
Major Dalton

Captains	Lieutenants	Ensigns
Lally	Costello	Burke
Ro. Dillon	Lally	Dillon
O'Neale	Dillon	Knipe
FitzGerald	Sweeney	Farrell
Chris. Dillon	Blake	Lemmon
Ro. FitzGerald	Fox	Linch
Lu. Dillon	O'Rourk	MacDermot
Blake	Daly	Nolan
Macgowlie	Tyrrell	Mullalin
Tho. Dillon	Talbot	Dalton
Brabazon	Plunket	Dooley
MacDermot	Shiel	Magowley
Macdonogh	Dillon	Harvey
John Dillon	Boulger	Dophin
Rounel	Burke	Macdonogh
Morgan	Maguire	
Daly		

Surgeon Dignay. Priest, Father Dillon.

The mention of the name of the Lieutenant-Colonel in the French records as Henry Crafton (the Irish lists give it as Bourke) is particularly interesting for a different reason. The famous and unfortunate Count Lally married Félicité Crafton, and much mystery has been cast upon her identity and status in life. There seems hardly room to doubt that she was the daughter of this Lieutenant-Colonel of the Dillon regiment, in which Thomas Arthur Lally served for thirty years before Fontenoy.

THE O'BRIEN (OF CLARE) REGIMENT

Colonel-in-Chief, Daniel O'Brien, afterwards Visct. Clare
Lt.-Colonel Arthur
Major Whelan

Captains	Lieutenants	Ensigns
Skiddy	Kennedy	FitzGerald
Rowe	Coward	Burke
Callaghan	Burke	Mansfield
Roche	O'Brien	Stritch
Ryan	Callaghan	Tubbs
Lacy	Ryan	Lacy
O'Brien	Lacy	Burleigh
Barry	Egan	Raleigh
Raleigh	Lane	Macnamara
Carroll	Creagh	Harrild
Harrild	Samson	Burke
	Ryan	

Priest, Father Kennedy.

Similar particulars are not available for the Feilding regiment, but in numbers it was the weakest of all.

The condition upon which these five regiments were sent to France was that they were to enter the service of the King of France and to be entirely at his disposition to serve where he should direct, and against all his enemies "excepting it were the King of England," should the case arise. As the story develops it will be seen that there was a marked distinction in the status of the Mountcashell brigade and that of the Irish troops who followed after the Limerick Convention. The former became French troops at once; the latter were for many years nominally King James's men and subject to his orders and not to those of the King of France.

The schedule of pay was also drawn up and agreed to before the regiments left Ireland. It was based on the arrangement made when George Hamilton raised his regiment in 1671. Each private was to receive nine livres or francs per month, and the non-commissioned officers got an increase on this sum. A captain received five livres a day, a lieutenant forty-five sols (2 f. 25 c.), and an ensign thirty-six sols

(1 f. 80 c.). The pay to the infantry soldier was practically the same as that James proposed to pay him in Ireland, but in France a small deduction of 1 sol in the livre was made from the private's pay for the personal benefit of the Colonel of the regiment. Taking the strength of a regiment at 1600 this deduction meant the equivalent of £400 sterling per annum for the commanding officer. In addition he drew a regular salary of 2700 francs a year.

Before the question had been settled that those who raised the regiments should nominate their colonels, D'Avaux had been trying to get the best men in the Irish army for the posts. The Hamiltons being ineligible he asked for Lord Galway, son of the Earl of Clanrickarde. He was also not unwilling to accept the Earl of Clancarty as another on account of his high connections, although he styled him "a young fool and a little roué." And then he asked for Sarsfield, adding : " He is not a man of the birth of Lord Galway or McCarthy, but he is a gentleman distinguished by his merit, and has more credit in the country than any one else." D'Avaux's appreciation of Sarsfield had led him to obtain for him from James his first promotion as Brigadier-General, and it was on that occasion that James replied with some tetchiness : " Sarsfield is a very brave man, but has no head."

D'Avaux also asked for Lord Dungan, son of the Earl of Limerick, of whom he had a high opinion, not only for his own merit, but because his uncle Walter had served with some distinction in the French army. Finally, he wanted Dominic Sarsfield, Lord Kilmallock, to be one of the commanders. Lord Kilmallock was a man of conspicuous merit, whose career reads like a romance. He was one of those peers of Ireland who forfeited their estates for their religion in 1651. After the Restoration, on finding that his estates were not to be given back, he enlisted in an assumed name in the English Guard and served in it during the reign of Charles II, reaching the grade of sergeant by pure merit. It was only on James's flight that he went to Ireland, revealed his identity to

Tyrconnell and raised a regiment, which he soon made one of the most efficient in the army. We shall meet him again, both in Limerick and France.

When James, in addition to his regiments, was asked to part with his best officers he got quite cross, and he made at least one rejoinder to the effect that if Irish officers were wanted, " plenty could be found in the King of France's German regiments."

Although the physical qualities of the men composing the regiments were as good as they could be, James had no justification for calling the Mountcashell brigade " the best regiments in his service." They were raised for the greater part in haste, expressly for the purpose of being sent to France, and the great majority of the men had never shouldered a musket before receiving their equipment at Nantes and Bourges. It is also undoubted that owing to the hurry and to the need of making up a paper total, a considerable number of ineligibles were enrolled and many of the officers had no claim to hold a commission. The French authorities were very quick in detecting these shortcomings and rejected about one-tenth of the force, who were shipped back to Ireland. These were taken principally from the Butler and Feilding regiments, but the bulk of those returned to Ireland probably came back to France after the end of the war.

D'Avaux was somewhat to blame in this matter. In his anxiety to show what a valuable recruiting-ground Ireland might become for the French army, he wished to get together as big a total as possible. He tried hard to raise the corps to 7000 men, but he only succeeded in getting 6000 men or thereabouts. But Louvois had not been so exacting. He asked for only 4000 Irish troops in exchange for Lauzun's force, but he added that they were to be " good troops under good officers." Louvois could not get exactly what he wanted, but he obtained the best material out of which good troops and good officers could be made.

The immediate consequence of sending too many men

and regiments of unequal strength was that the French military authorities, who insisted on each regiment being composed of sixteen companies of 100 men each, decided to reduce the five regiments to three, and the Butler and Feilding regiments were at once broken up. The best of them were incorporated in the three other regiments, the Mountcashell, the O'Brien or Clare, and the Dillon. This left a surplus of six or seven hundred men, who were incontinently shipped back to Ireland. The French authorities had to seize upon any excuse they found handy for this rejection. The Butler regiment was accused of having brought over forty sergeants as valets; they were sent back. Another contingent of the Butler regiment on board a ship separated from the main squadron by rough weather was driven into La Rochelle. The local officers refused to allow them to land until they had communicated with Paris and received formal authority from the capital to do so. When this detachment reached Nantes, several weeks after the rest of the corps, they were told that the cadres were full and that there was no place for them. They, too, were sent back to Ireland.

In this manner the redundants were got rid of, and soon there were only the three regiments of 1600 men apiece and about 100 officers to each regiment. There is some reason to think that a certain number of those rejected were taken into the French navy. Immediately after his arrival Lord Mountcashell was summoned to Versailles, where Louis gave him a very good reception, making him a present of 4000 écus for his equipage, and granting him an annual pension of the same sum, which was to be in addition to his revenue as Colonel of his regiment. Certainly Lord Mountcashell was no loser by changing the scene of his service from Ireland to France.

Louis, no doubt, had not forgotten the name or the facts that there had figured in the French Army List a regiment called Muskerry from 1647–62, and another called Dillon from 1653–64.

The first Irish corps having been landed, sifted, and brigaded, it is interesting to read what the French intendants sent down to clothe the force thought of the new acquisition. Their reports are in the War Department, and they are full of detail. With scarcely a varying note the description given is unfavourable and depressing. M. Bouridal, for instance, describes them as " shirtless, shoeless, hatless, and afflicted with vermin." Lest this might be thought a reflection on the Irish of the day, I may mention that I was relieved to read in a subsequent volume exactly the same account about the French troops who returned with Lauzun. Something must be set down to the miserable poverty of Ireland—for instance, there was no straw in Cork for the French soldiers to sleep on—but on the whole the main cause of the insanitary condition of the troops was the medical ignorance and neglect of hygiene in that age.

But it may be accepted as a fact beyond dispute that the Irish troops under Lord Mountcashell arrived in France clothed in rags. It was, of course, never intended that they should bring their arms with them, but certainly the French commissariat officials were rather taken aback at their appearance. However, bootmakers were set to work to supply them with shoes, shirts were distributed, a felt hat was provided with one side turned up to the crown (to which the white cockade of the French army was attached), and lastly a grey coat or tunic was given out as the special dress of the Mountcashell brigade. There happened to be a large accumulation of this grey cloth in the French warehouses, for in the winter of the same year a quantity sufficient for 20,000 uniforms was sent to Ireland. But there is one point that lends a piquant interest to the business of clothing the Mountcashell brigade. The Irish troops clamoured for red coats, and Lord Mountcashell received an assurance that when new uniforms had to be provided they should be in red. It is curious to find these poor Irish exiles, who had gone forth from their own land because they had been persuaded that England was their natural enemy, protesting that they would wear the English national uniform and no other. Their flag also was the English flag. It was St. George's Cross, with a lion in gold, and above it a golden crown in the centre. No one thought of the Green Flag or the Harp in those days !

Having clothed and armed the new arrivals at Nantes, peremptory orders were received to march them to the front, and the French orders state quite candidly, "where they are urgently needed." It is clear from this order that the condition of the Irish troops could not have been so very bad, and that when their most glaring shortcomings had been removed by the supply of a proper equipment the Irish levies appeared in the eyes of French critics to be soldiers and not useless recruits. And so in June, 1690, the three Irish regiments were marching bravely and singing songs to the surprise of the French peasantry across Berry and Dauphine to the frontier of Savoy. The original intention had been to employ them in Catalonia under Marshal Noailles, but the army under Marshal Catinat on the Italian frontier was short in numbers and opposed by far superior forces which had been recently increased by Imperial troops brought from Hungary. Catinat, the most cautious and perhaps the ablest of all Louis's later commanders, was clamouring for reinforcements. They were sent him in the Irish contingent of 5000 men under Lord Mountcashell.

But the French authorities were not disposed to leave the sole control of the new force to the officers who had come with it from Ireland, and therefore Andrew Lee, an officer who had served with much distinction for twenty years under the French flag, and who was at the time a Lieutenant-Colonel in the Greder regiment, was appointed Lieutenant-Colonel of the Clare regiment and sent posthaste to join it at Vienne. Andrew Lee, better known in France as André, Marquis de Lée, was of Irish origin, and had joined Sir George Hamilton's regiment as an ensign.

When that corps was disbanded he remained in France, receiving a lieutenant's commission in the Furstenberg regiment. As we shall see, he was specially trusted by the French authorities, and was used by them as a confidential intermediary with the Irish officers who were strangers in France. His first employment with them was, however, in the definite capacity of second in command of the Clare regiment during the campaign of 1690 in Upper Savoy.

At this juncture Louis had four considerable armies in the field, one in Flanders under Marshal Luxemburg, another on the Rhine under Villeroi, a third in Catalonia under Noailles, and a fourth in Savoy and Piedmont under Catinat. We are only concerned with the last named. Catinat's principal opponent here was the Duke of Savoy (who played several rôles during these long wars), and he had been lately joined by his young kinsman Prince Eugene, who had so distinguished himself against the Turks that the Imperial Commander, the Duke of Lorraine, had predicted " the young Savoyard will one day be the greatest commander of the century." Savoy itself was held by the Barbets, the Vaudois Protestants, who were mountaineers and accustomed to warfare in this inaccessible and precipitous region.

The task before Catinat was one of extreme difficulty. He had himself advanced into the valley of the Po, leaving his lieutenant, de Larray, to deal with the Barbets in Upper Savoy and to keep open his communications. But when Catinat got into Piedmont he found in front of him the superior and continually increasing army of Savoy and the Empire. What was he to do ? He could only summon Larray to his aid, but Larray could not move until some new force had arrived to take his place and prevent the Barbets filling up the gap and closing in on the rear of Catinat's main army. A French army was in deadly peril beyond the Alps, and that was why the Irish soldiers were marching in hot haste across the sun-baked plains of central France to Lyons and thence to Grenoble.

They reached their destination towards the end of July. Larray, resigning the command in Savoy to St. Ruth, marched forward to the aid of Catinat, bringing him a reinforcement of 6000 troops. St. Ruth with the 5000 Irish and a few French troops was left to hold the province of Savoy and to keep the Vaudois Barbets in check. There is no necessity to describe here the battle of Staffarde, fought on August 18, 1690, when Catinat gained a decisive victory over his enemy, who, notwithstanding the reinforcement of Larray, was superior to him in numbers.

Under the date of September 21, 1690, Dangeau notes : " St. Ruth reports that in the late battle in Savoy the Irish troops had done wonders (*fait des merveilles*)," and this report was confirmed by Sourches and others. On the occasion referred to Lord Mountcashell was dangerously wounded by a musket shot in the breast.

Whereas Larry had stood on the defensive in Upper Savoy, confining his attention to keeping the road open over the Mont Cenis from Grenoble to Susa, St. Ruth, as soon as the victory of Staffarde ensured the safety of the main army under Catinat, resorted to the offensive. During the months of September and October, 1690, the Irish troops were employed under his orders in driving the Barbets northwards into Switzerland. The operations began with the attack on and capture of Chambéry, the Duke's capital. It was in the capture of this place that Mountcashell was severely wounded. Rumilly and Annécy were the next places to fall, and then St. Ruth turned into the Tarentaise, the southern division of Savoy of which the capital is Moustiers. In this district some of the most desperate fighting took place. The castles of the Marquis de Sales and other Savoy nobles, crowning peaks that seemed inaccessible, were carried by escalade one after another, and it was only the advent of winter that put an end to the operations. As the only troops employed were the Irish there was no possibility of detracting from their merit. The subjection of Savoy was the proof.

The records of the French War Department are defective in some particulars, owing to many documents having been destroyed during the Commune, and therefore it is impossible to fix the number of Irishmen who gave their lives for their new country in Savoy in 1690. But as St. Ruth was instructed, on departing for Ireland in 1691, to send back at once 500 picked Irishmen to raise the Mountcashell brigade to its proper strength, it seems safe to conclude that its loss in August, September, and October amounted to that total. The fleet which carried St. Ruth to Limerick brought back that number to Brest, but owing to the difficulty of getting out of the Shannon it only arrived in France about the same time as the battle of Aughrim was fought. There is reason to think that a large number of the men originally rejected from the Butler and Feilding regiments were among those who returned.

The French authorities were also somewhat dissatisfied with the majority of the Irish officers of regimental rank, and with the view of attracting a better class the younger sons of good families were invited to join the Mountcashell Brigade as cadets. I have before me a list of sixteen young gentlemen who sailed from Limerick in July, 1691, for the purpose. Among them was Morgan Kavanagh, aged fourteen, son of Colonel Charles Kavanagh, who was blown up in the " Breda," ship of war, at Cork. He and his cousin Maurice Eustace reached Rochefort on July 20, 1691. Having discovered the value of Irish soldiers Louis's Government became very anxious to improve the quality of the officers, who never having had any professional training, were, for the most part, not up to the standard of what the French considered an officer should be, and the institution of the cadet system was one of the first measures to that end.

The campaign of 1690 having relieved the pressure on the side of Savoy and Piedmont, Mountcashell's brigade was ordered to Roussillon to reinforce the army of Marshal Noailles, which was expected to drive the Spaniards south of the Pyrenees in 1691. The reputation gained by the Irish troops under Catinat and his lieutenants in 1690 was confirmed and strengthened under Noailles. Marshal Noailles and his son, also Marshal, had for half a century Irish troops under their command from Roussillon to Dettingen, and none of the other French generals ever spoke so ungrudgingly and warmly in their praise.

At the siege of Argelles, at the capture by assault of Valence and Roy, Mountcashell and his men confirmed the good impression they had made at Chambéry and Annécy the year before. The commander-in-chief reported two things about them that deserve mention: " They were always in good spirits," and " they were always first in the breach."

It is unnecessary to dilate or dwell upon the achievements of the Mountcashell Brigade, which was the forerunner of the larger and more famous Irish Brigade with which it was eventually amalgamated. There are only two points on which we need lay any stress. The first is that this corps had the first opportunity of showing what Irish troops with good weapons and under proper leading could accomplish. The second was that its achievements satisfied Louis and the most sceptical of his ministers that the Irish would justify their existence as the auxiliaries of France. Before, then, a single man of the Irish Brigade brought into France as the sequel of the Limerick Convention had reached that country, there were positive facts to show that Irish troops were as good as any in the world.

It is necessary to establish this point, because by some curious optical defect the English people had not seen things as they were. In their opinion, the Irish had been for a hundred and fifty years before the Boyne " cowards," " savages," and a race to be treated with contempt. They only discovered the truth when they came to be pitted against them under a hostile flag. A wiser policy in England, a less insular point of view, would have obviated the painful necessity altogether ; but things being as they were it was inevitable if

future concord and mutual respect should be attained—it
was desirable even if the Irish national character should be
established without the intervention of English criticism
or co-operation—that these Irish representatives should go
out into the wide world and display their courage and
assert their martial reputation once and for all time by
military achievements which have never been surpassed.
To Lord Mountcashell belongs the credit of having placed
the experimental employment of Irish soldiers by France
on a successful and mutually satisfactory basis.

Chapter IX

THE CAMPAIGN OF AUGHRIM

IF the Irish troops had not done wonders ("*fait des merveilles*") under French generals in Savoy, it is very dubious if Louis would have sent another man or another franc to Ireland after the return of his own troops. In the first period of revulsion after the Boyne, French opinion had taken a very unfavourable view of the Irish nation, and Madame de Sévigné, whose Jacobite enthusiasm soon waned, gave expression to it in a sentence, declaring that " the Irish were poor creatures and traitors." But a little further experience sufficed to expose the injustice of this view and to bring out the truth, which was that Irishmen could not command victory when the conditions were impossible any more than Englishmen or Frenchmen could; and there can never be any doubt that the conditions under which the Irish fought at the Boyne were as nearly hopeless as they well could be.

When the Duke of Tyrconnell arrived, then, in France, he found Louis prepared to risk a little more, if not very much, in the Irish venture. No French Minister would sanction the despatch of any more French troops, and the relief at having recovered so many of those sent did not admit of any fresh strain. But apart from an army, France could still do a good deal to assist the Irish, and Tyrconnell asked in the first place only for stores, arms, and money. He also asked for the services of a good general, and of some staff officers to aid him. Of Irish regimental officers and of men he represented that there were more than enough, although he does not seem to have made his calculations with sufficient care, for the Irish forces had been reduced by the defection of that curious adventurer, Baldearg O'Donnell, who had taken off to the wilds of Sligo 7000 of the Rapparees or irregulars, and there held a bedraggled Court of his own as if he and not James were the Irish King. His chief grievance seems to have been that the Duke of Tyrconnell had been given the title which appertained to his family. It is not surprising to find in Berwick's Memoirs expressions of surprise and disgust at the endless quarrels and divisions of Irish parties. Nor had proper allowance been made for the 4000 men captured at Cork. Tyrconnell had not taken these matters into adequate account when he declared that there was a sufficiency of fighting-men in Ireland.

But perhaps it was discreet not to ask the French King for what he was indisposed to grant, and an arrangement was come to for very generous supplies to be sent early in the new year. Tyrconnell was sent back to reanimate the Jacobite cause by bearing himself the news that French succours were to follow after him.

If the condition of the Irish troops had been bad when Tyrconnell sailed from Ireland it was naturally much worse when he got back three months later. The officers were in rags, the soldiers " miserably naked," and the sum of money he brought with him was soon dispensed in doles to relieve so much misery. At the same time all the base money was called in, and commissioners were appointed to take a list of the amounts and the holders, so that they should be indemnified whenever the King came by his own again. To men in such need the French aid seemed long in coming, and when it came inadequate ; although it was not ungenerous of its kind, and there seems no justification for the complaints, which occupy so large a space of James's Memoirs, at the hostility of Louvois to his cause. Louvois had to look after French, not Jacobite, interests, and he was a hard bargainer. When he fitted out the expedition of March, 1691, he stipulated that Tyrconnell should return

500 Irish recruits to raise the Mountcashell Brigade to its full war strength.

The general selected to take the command of the Irish army was Charles Chalmot, Marquis de St. Rhue (commonly but erroneously called in English literature St. Ruth). To a certain extent he seems to have put himself forward to secure the command, for he had extolled the valour of the Irish troops under him in Savoy, and as he was extremely popular with the Mountcashell Brigade it was assumed that he must be just the man to get on with the troops in Ireland. He was essentially a fighting general, but he had served with the cautious Catinat, and had acquired some of that great commander's skill as a tactician. Berwick says that he " was by nature very vain," but even if the remark be not merely ill-natured, as many of Berwick's were, vanity was no reflection on his military skill.

In St. Ruth, as we suppose we must call him, France sent one of the best officers at her disposal. He was immeasurably superior as a soldier to either Roze or Lauzun. He was accompanied by the Marquis d'Usson and the Chevalier de Tessé as Lieutenant-Generals, both of whom had seen much service in the French wars. Colonel La Tour was selected to fill the post of Governor of Limerick, but the only French officers beyond these who sailed for Ireland in 1691 were the few artillerists who had accompanied Tyrconnell some weeks earlier. But some civilians were sent to look after the money and the stores (among these was material for 20,000 tunics in grey or mouse-coloured cloth) sent from France, and these officials wrote some very interesting and informing reports on the state of Ireland, which have yet to be published. Adverse gales delayed St. Ruth's departure, and it was not until the commencement of May that the Chevalier de Nesmond, commanding the escorting squadron of thirty-two large ships, conceived it would be safe to make a start. More care had to be taken in these matters than previously, as it was no longer merely the straight course to the south of Ireland

P

that had to be accomplished, but the dangerous Kerry coast had to be rounded in order to reach the Shannon. At last the winds seemed propitious, after the squadron had first been driven from Brest to Belle-Isle, and about the 20th of the month St. Ruth made his formal entry into Limerick. The difficulty of communication may be gathered from the fact that although Nesmond's orders were to return without delay, he was unable to get out of the Shannon until the middle of July—in fact, only a few days before Aughrim.

St. Ruth brought with him a good supply of arms, clothes for several regiments, a large quantity of powder and ball, and a considerable amount of oats, meal, and biscuit, as well as of wine and brandy, in all of which there had been a great deficiency if not absolute dearth in Ireland. Thus for a brief space there was plenty in the land, and the long-starving troops were put into good heart for the fierce ordeal that lay before them. When St. Ruth reviewed the troops with which he was to carry on the war he was very pleased with the appearance of the infantry, which he found nearly 20,000 strong, and with the exception of a few regiments lately raised to replace those captured at Cork, they consisted of seasoned troops. The cavalry was numerically weak, although excellent in its way, but there were no means of raising more horse regiments, and the gaps made at the Boyne had never been refilled. It was an army well suited for the defence of the river line formed by the Shannon, bridged only at Athlone, Banagher, and Limerick itself. But in order to make it as efficient as possible the less trained regiments were put to garrison Limerick and Galway.

In June D'Usson reviewed fifteen battalions at Killaloe, and reported the men as good, their discipline imperfect, and their arms showing a deficiency of at least 100 per battalion. The Intendant Fumeron fixes the total strength of the Irish army at 25,000 infantry, 3000 cavalry, and 2500 dragoons. The greatest defect in the force was that there were no horses to draw the artillery, and it was added that these had been allowed to perish by neglect during the previous winter. The French reports, as a rule, bring in a statement to the effect that " the misery of the people is beyond belief."

In the meantime Ginkel had been largely reinforced from England, and recruits were sent across the Channel in hundreds and thousands with the view of being trained on the spot.

In several of his letters, written in French and preserved at the Record Office, he complains that they required a great deal of training, and that he feared the enemy would be ready to take the field sooner than himself. Although Ginkel's infantry was not quite as numerous as the Irish his cavalry force was four times as strong, and he also possessed a numerous and powerful artillery both for the field and for attacking walled places. Thanks to St. Ruth's delayed arrival Ginkel was able to take the field first, and he then marched straight for Athlone, capturing on the way the castle of Ballymore and its garrison of 500 men. Plunkett writes :—

" By the beginning of June the English army was assembled at Mullingar, and on the 6th of the same month they began their march towards Athlone, with intention to take that great pass into Connaught. On the 7th they came to the village of Bally-more, about half-way between Mullingar and Athlone. There is a fort close by it at the side of a lough, which was a little fortified by the Irish the last winter. Lieut.-Colonel Miles Bourke was now Governor thereof, in which there were about 500 soldiers. Ginkel, resolving not to leave this untaken, sent a summons that same day to the Governor, who refused to comply on good terms ; at which the general ordered a few pieces to batter the fort, which was brought down to the ground, so that the next day, the 8th of June, the garrison was forced to surrender at discretion. They were sent prisoners to Dublin, and thence all the private men were transported to the island of Lambay. There were found in this little hold only two diminutive pieces of cannon."

Fumeron is less complimentary to the defenders of Ballymore. He states that " no resistance was offered,

although there were 800 fusiliers and one month's supplies
in the place." Considering Ginkel's overwhelming force
it would be more just to regard this affair as another
instance of the Irish frittering away their chances. The
500 men placed in Ballymore could only have been put
there for the purpose of being lost.

At this supreme moment when everything called for
union in the Irish camp the cabal broke out again against
Tyrconnell. St. Ruth had pitched his camp about two
miles south of Athlone, in which he placed an excellent
garrison commanded by Colonel Nicholas Fitzgerald, and
General d'Usson was also appointed to direct the defence
with his superior knowledge. The Duke of Tyrconnell,
anxious to take part in the fray that was approaching,
accompanied the army, and pitched his camp with it. He
was not a military genius, as his critics constantly remind
us, but he was a brave man, and no skulker despite his age
and his weight. He also had his views, and sometimes, at
least, they were reasonable and judicious. Such was the
case with regard to Athlone. The previous year when
Athlone had been successfully defended by Colonel
Richard Grace, a strong entrenchment had been erected
on the southern side of the town, that is to say, on the
side now facing St. Ruth's camp. The Duke proposed that
this should be levelled as contributing in no way to the
defence, and as only serving as an obstacle to the sending
of reinforcements into the place. His advice was rejected
and gave his opponents the chance of declaring that he
was interfering in military matters of which he knew
nothing.

Having gained this first success his detractors decided
to humiliate him still further, and some of the Irish Colonels
sent him a formal notice that unless he quitted the camp
they would cut the cords of his tents. As the Duke had the
sympathies of the larger half of the army he undoubtedly
exercised great self-restraint in complying, but he said that
he would do nothing to divide the army on the eve of what

promised to be the decisive battle of the long war. He mounted his horse and, accompanied by his personal retinue, rode back to Limerick ; but if his advice had been taken with regard to the removal of the obstructing entrenchment Athlone need not have fallen, or rather it could have been easily recovered on June 30 (O.S.). In these matters St. Ruth, as he had no local knowledge and could not speak English, had largely to depend on the guidance of his Irish subordinates. While Henry Luttrell and Purcell were bitterly opposed to Tyrconnell (no doubt they guessed that like Berwick he had advised James to have them treated as Mountjoy was), other Irish commanders resented his old favouritism for the Hamiltons. But perhaps the greatest cause of confusion which led to clashing and divided counsels was St. Ruth's ignorance of English, and the little knowledge most of the Irish officers had of French.

Such was the prelude to the attack on Athlone, which may be told in Plunkett's words :—

" The English army marched to Athlone, which was invested on June 19 on the Leinster side. This part of the town was for the most part burned the last year by the Irish : yet at the present they had in it three or four companies of foot. On the 20th General Ginkel battered it for his first attempt. In the afternoon he made an attack and gained it ; a few men were killed on both sides.

" This part of the town being theirs, they raised batteries the next day against the other part that is on Connaught side. It is destitute of walls and only defended by a castle and the river, over which there runs a stone bridge into the town, the governor whereof was Colonel Nicholas FitzGerald, with a garrison of fifteen hundred men, choice grenadiers and foot. Lieutenant-General D'Usson put himself into it also. On the 22nd the whole side of the castle was beaten down so that it became unserviceable to the besieged. In a day or two after, what small works were about the castle became so far demolished that there remained no cover to the defendants except a little behind the said castle.

" This work being over, the next attempt of the besiegers was how to get possession of the bridge in order to attack the town therefrom. The dispute was exceedingly fiery, but the English gained all the arches but the last, which had been broken by the Irish. However, they carried on their endeavours so far the next day that they laid beams thereon and planked part of the beams ; yet the same day a detachment of the Irish with a surpassing audacity threw down beams and planks, notwithstanding the most terrible fire of the enemy. The next day the besiegers renewed the attempt by the help of fascines ; but it proved in vain, for the besieged burned them all. . . .

" In this perplexity Major-General Talmash principally, and seconded by the Duke of Wirtemberg and others, advised attempting to get into the town through the river by a sort of ford near the bridge. This resolution was no sooner taken than a deserter traversed the river above the town and came to the Irish camp, letting the generals know that the enemy would attack the town through the ford the next day. No notice was taken of this warning, it being judged a thing impracticable. On this very day the Irish garrison, which had behaved themselves to admiration during the five previous days and while the fury of the siege lasted, was relieved, and in their place three regiments of foot were sent, two of which, viz., Colonel O'Gara's and Colonel Anthony MacMahon's, were raised but the winter before and had been on no service. They were consequently most unfit to be put upon the defence of a place threatened with assault the next day by a daring army. Along with this relief came Major-General Maxwell for better managing the defence.

" The 30th June (O.S.) a deserter or two from the Irish camp swam the river to the English very early in the morning, and told them that the Irish felt secure and that the garrison consisted of but three ordinary regiments.

Ginkel commanded two thousand men to make ready under the command of Major-General Mackay, distributing some money among the men as a cordial.   At six in the morning Captain Sandys and two lieutenants led through the ford up to the armpits sixty grenadiers in armour, twenty abreast, followed by a great body of foot.   The garrison fired at them and the English army fired in amongst the garrison with great and small shot.   But amidst this furious storm the adventurers gained the bank through a breach, and casting before them their grenades which bursting made frightful effect among the raw soldiers not used to such squibs.

" Some of the ingressors ran immediately to the end of the bridge and helped their companions on the other side to lay beams and planks on the broken arch ; others went to assist the laying of the bridge of boats, by which the English passed into the town so fast that in half an hour all the town was their own, the garrison being forced to yield to numbers and better soldiers, and to retreat to their army.   Thus the place was lost against all expectation. Here was nothing but a concatenation of errors in all the enterprises of the loyalists, no antecedent experience rendering them wiser.   Of the Irish a few were slain, amongst whom were Colonel MacElligott and Colonel Richard Grace of Courtown ; and Major-General Maxwell was made prisoner."

The Huguenot officer Dumont de Bostaquet did not serve during this campaign, but as he got his information from some of his brother officers, his brief descriptions of the fights at Athlone and Aughrim may be introduced for purposes of comparison.   His information as to the over-confidence among the Irish leaders in the security of Athlone probably gives the true explanation of the misfortune :—

" The enemy having burnt down our work to restore the bridge thought themselves quite safe, and St. Ruth and the other generals gave themselves up to amusement not thinking that our troops could do anything for several days ; but General Ginkel, having discovered a ford, caused a strong body of infantry to cross the river and then sent over cavalry to support them, so that the enemy had to abandon this part of the town. The troops who came to their help from the camp were driven back to it in confusion."

The several accounts in the French records bear out, generally speaking, these statements. The defence of East Athlone is described as having been good, and General Wauchope is given the credit of it. It is declared that the enemy lost 500 good troops and the Irish no more than 200. In connection with this fight it is also noted that the Irish officers are improving and that the men are taking more care of their arms. With regard to the capture of Athlone itself, it is declared that the enemy were so quick in crossing the ford that the reinforcements could not get up in time, and that D'Usson, hurrying up with them, was knocked down and trampled on.

The capture of Athlone, with the best crossing over the Shannon, was a serious blow to the Irish cause, and paved the way to its final collapse. It seems probable that St. Ruth had not sufficient knowledge of the country to perceive all the importance of the position until it had been lost, and there must have been some neglect on the part of his Irish lieutenants in not impressing upon him the vital need to hold Athlone at all cost. There and not at Aughrim should the French general have made his stand.

Having lost Athlone St. Ruth felt bound to retreat, retiring down the river towards Limerick. Tyrconnell strongly urged him to return to Limerick, to refrain from coming to a general action, and to prolong the war till the following year, by which time Louis might be in a position to send troops and further aid. But for the moment no one would listen to Tyrconnell. Besides, St. Ruth was very much piqued at the loss of Athlone, for which he was inclined to blame D'Usson, who was not at his post when the final attack was made. D'Usson also was against risking everything on a pitched battle, and was sent off to Galway. St. Ruth took the view that his military honour made it imperative that he should risk a pitched battle, so he slowly retreated, looking out carefully for a favourable spot on which to make his stand. He found it near the small town and castle of Aughrim or Kilconnell.

The battle of Aughrim, unlike that of the Boyne, was a real trial of strength between the two opposing armies, and both sides could look back on the affair without having to blush for themselves or their commanders. It is always held by Irishmen that the day was won when St. Ruth was killed, and although Berwick states in his Memoirs that he did not believe Aughrim would have been a victory, he was not there, and this opinion of his, at least, is not entitled to much weight. Our other authority, the Huguenot officer, Dumont de Bostaquet, also was not present, but in his account of the battle he assigns the credit of the victory to the final charge of Ruvigny and the French Protestant cavalry.

Let us commence our account of the battle with Plunkett's narrative :—

" He (St. Ruth) marched towards Limerick until he came a little beyond the village of Aughrim, where viewing the ground he judged it convenient for his design, and so fixed there his camp in waiting for the enemy. Before his front he had a morass, over which foot could come but not horse. At each end of this morass there was a passage through which the enemy's horse could come to his right and left flank. That on the right was a little ford caused by a stream issuing from the morass. That on the left was an old broken causeway, only large enough for two horses to pass at a time and was sixty yards long. Beyond this causeway was the castle of Aughrim, into which St. Ruth put on that day Colonel Walter Bourk and two hundred men.

" He marshalled his army in two lines. The cavalry on his right were the regiments of the Duke of Tyrconnell, of the Earl of Abercorn, of Colonel Edmund Prendergast (previously that of Sutherland), besides dragoons. This wing was to see that the enemy's horse did not break in on the right of the wing through the pass of the ford and through the narrow ground lying between two morasses after passing the ford; for the English had double the number in cavalry, though the Irish had some advantage in the infantry. 'Twas here Lieutenant-General de Tessé and Major-General Sarsfield, now Earl of Lucan, were posted. On the left St. Ruth placed the Earl of Lucan's regiment of horse, and those of Colonel Henry Luttrell, of Colonel John Parker, and Colonel Nicholas Purcell with a body of dragoons. The Lord of Galmoye with his regiment was put behind the second line of the foot in the nature of a reserve to answer occasions. The conduct of this left wing was given to Major-General Sheldon, the first line of which Brigadier Henry Luttrell commanded. Their business was to defend the pass of the causeway, near to which, for more security, there were set two regiments of foot.

" Close before the first line of the Irish infantry there were a few old ditches which were serviceable to them at the first charge of the enemy. The management of the infantry was assigned to Major-General Dorington and to Major-General John Hamilton.

" No doubt St. Ruth showed good skill in choosing his ground, and in ranging his host for this fight where his all and the all of the nation lay at stake. The day before the combat he pronounced some words wherein he manifested his desire that all men would withdraw and reserve themselves for garrisons who were sickly or unable to fight as they should do.

" On July 11 the English army came to Ballinasloe, three miles from Aughrim. The next day being Sunday it arrived at Aughrim a little after six in the morning, where, having rested a little while, the whole army was drawn up in two lines of battle. The Irish were at that juncture assisting at the sacrifice of Mass, and a little after prepared for meridian repast; but General St. Ruth, observing the enemy arranging in order for fighting, commanded his men to be marshalled according as we have mentioned.

" Both sides being fully prepared, action began a little after eleven, which mostly consisted in the playing of the artillery and in skirmishes for gaining and defending some advanced posts and little passes towards the right of the Irish. The English were first repulsed and afterwards acquired those outward places. Both parties, to give them their due, contended with extraordinary valour, insomuch that their combat was comely amidst death and wounds because fought with military skill.

" But General Ginkel, not satisfied with the obtention of these little advanced posts, resolved to come closer to the matter and make himself master of the ford on the right of the enemy that he might get in that way with his cavalry amongst the Irish foot, which he perceived was somewhat superior, at least upon account of the ground, and which he seemed to fear most that day. Upon this he ordered down at two o'clock a great body of horse from his left to attack the pass of the ford. Here the dispute was such wherein the English were first repulsed until the Earl of Portland's regiment of horse joined them, and thereby they pushed the Irish from the ford to the body of their cavalry which was hard by, where they stood firm their ground all the day in spite of several attempts made on them, because the English horse, even after passing the ford, could not spread being enclosed on the right and left by the said morasses.

" General Ginkel did not like, hitherto, the countenance of the contention, because he saw no way to weaken the Irish infantry with his horse if he should generally engage. This consideration put him in a doubt whether he should continue and come to a close fight that day. But it was soon resolved that it was so best. Whereupon he commands his left wing to charge again violently the right of the Irish horse through the ford at five in the afternoon, which they did with great bravery, and as well they were resisted. Between these wings the conflict was fierce. But at the end the English were forced to recoil, not being able to compass their aim.

" 'Twas at this period of the action and about six o'clock the main bodies of foot on both sides came to close fight, and sharp it was. The English charged, and in their advancing the Irish slew numbers from their little old ditches; the English gained them and flew in boldly among the enemies. The Irish returned the charge and broke and pursued them with much slaughter. Fresh bodies of English came on again and held the strife a good while in balance. General Dorington being herein pressed sent for the two regiments of foot which were placed in the beginning of the day to guard the pass on the left. At the same time General Ginkel ordered down four fresh regiments of foot to reinforce his combatants, which made the contention very sanguinary till at last the English gave ground and the Irish advanced near the enemy's field of battle.

" This repulse was no sooner given than a grand corps comes pouring down on the Irish for the third time. 'Twas now the combat seemed more violent than before and as it were the last effort. After an obstinate storm the English were constrained to retreat. The Irish followed, making use of club musket whereby the foreigners suffered much. The regiment of Guards and the whole royal brigade were particularly noted by the field to have performed uncommon execution. The Irish pursued so far that they gained the enemy's ground and maintained themselves thereon. Colonel Gordon O'Neil with his regiment took some of their cannon.

" At this General Ginkel, seeing his centre wholly broken, his left wing to have had no small losses without being able to gain their point, that his right wing could not with any safety get over to the left of the Irish, and that the foe was on his field of battle, he became so disturbed in his thought that he could not well resolve what to do unless to take his flight, of which some marks appeared immediately.

" On the other side General St. Ruth remarking the

condition of the enemy and his own success cried out in his language with joy, ' Le jour est à nous, mes enfants ! ' (' the day is ours, my boys ! ').

" Amidst that confusion of General Ginkel some of his great officers advised him for his last remedium to attempt once the sending his right wing of horse over the pass of Aughrim castle, notwithstanding the danger thereof. The general took this desperate advice and so ordered it to be executed ; upon which the cavalry marched, Ruvigny's regiment being the first.

" The Marquis of St. Ruth observing the enemy coming towards the pass, he gave orders to the left wing of his horse that had been idle all the day to go and oppose him, which he knew was easily done and therefore he continued his joy as being sure of his point. Here we are to take notice that this long bloody contention is just a-ending, that the victory is so certainly in the hands of the Irish that nothing can take it away but the gaining of that most perilous pass by the castle of Aughrim ; that the defending of it is so easy that a regiment may perform the task. At least four regiments of horse and four of dragoons might make the passage impossible. . . . What excuse can the left of the King's cavalry make for themselves if they will not hinder the enemies gaining the said pass ? They have had all the day conspicuous examples of bravery before their eyes. . . .

" St. Ruth, having sent his command to the horse to march and oppose the enemy at the pass, must himself needs go along to see them perform this duty that there may be no failure in the last scene of this bloody tragedy. They march and the General followed with his guards. But as he was riding down a little hill a cannon ball from the other side directed by the cannoneer amongst the troops that were going to defend the pass struck him in the head, at which he fell and at the same time it laid the nation prostrate at his feet. As soon as the body was down one of the retinue carried it off, and brought the corpse to the town of Loughreagh and there interred it privately.

" His death was immediately made known by a deserter
to the enemy, who thereupon advanced in haste to the
pass. . . . As soon as St. Ruth was slain the guards withdrew from the field. Brigadier Henry Luttrell, who was at
the pass with the advanced troops, hearing of it did the like
after a small resistance given to the first arrived enemies.
Major-General Sheldon with the main body of the left wing
followed, making their way to Loughreagh and thence to
Limerick. At the same time the Irish infantry went on
thundering and their cavalry on the right stood firm to their
ground, being prepared at every moment to encounter
bravely as they had done several times that day, little
dreaming that their horse on the left would abandon
them. . . . The commanding officers of the left wing by
abandoning their station without compulsion, nay without
a stroke, were either traitors to their King and country, or
by exposing their foot to certain murder they showed a
barbarous indifference for the safety of their friends and
countrymen, or in fine were notorious cowards.

" But to proceed. By the time the King's horse went off
the field the enemy's whole right wing arrived at the pass, and
seeing no opposition beyond they confidently went through
notwithstanding the fire from the castle on the right, which
fire was insignificant for it slew but a few in the passage.
The reason of it was given because the men had French
pieces, the bore of which was small and had English ball
which was too large—a new miscarriage through heedless-
ness as bad as treachery.

" As soon as the hostile cavalry was got over they immediately enveloped the Irish foot, who were surprised at
their hard fate while they were mowing the field of honour.
They had no other remedy for their preservation than to
retreat as fast as they could, making their way to Portumna
and so forward to Limerick. Most of the horse on their
right made off likewise. Only the Earl of Lucan with some
troops thereof and the Lord of Galmoye with his regiment
did good service in covering their retreat as prosperously as

so small a body could do. This and the arriving night and some morasses brought them off indifferently well. 'Twas their officers respectively that suffered most. In the same evening late the castle of Aughrim was taken, and the commander Colonel Walter Bourk with his major, eleven officers and forty men were made prisoners. Thus you have seen a victory snatched out of the hands of the victorious."

The account of the battle given by James in his Memoirs may now be quoted as supplementing that of Plunkett. It was probably based on Dominic Sheldon's report supplied later, and does not materially differ from the Irish version. While seeking to explain how it was that " the extream good " cavalry did not charge and left the infantry in the lurch, the truth is not hidden that they " thought of nothing but saving themselves." There is also no reason for the disparagement of the Irish infantry. St. Ruth had under him some newly raised regiments and he was naturally anxious to accustom them to standing under fire, but the bulk of the foot consisted of the troops who had held the breach of Limerick, and there was no reason to be nervous about them. King James was also a little mixed as to the wings. It was the left not the right wing of the Irish army that was forced by the passage of Ruvigny's squadrons over the causeway and bog, and the right wing kept the enemy at bay throughout the whole of the day and did something to cover the retreat of the infantry while the left simply galloped away. Here King James speaks :—

" St. Ruth being a little piqued at the late disgrace, resolved to wait for the enemie at Acrim which he found an advantageous post, so encamped himself there in two lines upon a riseing ground with a bog before him on which there was but two passes, the one at the old Castle of Acrim on the left of the foot, the other about three hundred yards advanced from the right, and because he put his greatest trust in the horse drew the right wing of horse of the first line in rear of the right of the first line of foot. On Sunday July 12 the enemy advanced with their foot in columns to

the bog side, while their horse took a great round to flank
the right ; they had no positive design to come to a general
action, but to try the countenance of the King's army, and
to drive them if possible from that post with their cannon,
but being once engaged and encouraged by their former
successes soon brought it to a decisive point. On the other
hand, the Irish considering this was like to prove the last
effort for re-establishing the King's authority and secureing
the estates and liberties of an oppressed people, expected
them with great constancy, and convinced the English
troops they had to doe with men no less resolute than themselves ; so that never was assault made with greater fury
or sustained with greater obstinacy especially by the foot,
who not only maintained their posts and defended the
hedges with great valour, but repulsed the enemie several
times particularly in the centre and took some prisoners of
distinction ; in so much that they looked upon the victory
as in a manner certain, and St. Ruth was in a transport of
joy to see the foot, of which he had so mean an opinion,
behave themselves so well and performe action worthy of a
better fate.

"But it seems in the beginning of the day St. Ruth
(perceiving that the enemy who outnumbered him stretched
out their left so far that he feared being flanked) ordered
the second line of the left to march to the right ; but he
who was to execute that order caused a battalion of the first
line to file off with the rest supposing the bog in the front
would prevent the enemies advancing, but they who stood
in awe of that battalion while it faced them took courage
when it was gone, and by the help of hurdles made a shift to
get over the bog, and at the same time four squadrons of the
enemies horse passing a causey began to forme themselves on
the other side of the defile. As soon as the General was
informed of the fault that had been made he ordered all the
cavalry to march, putting himself at the head of it, which
being extream good would soon have dispersed those few
squadrons of the enemie, who as yet were but a formeing,

when by a cannon shot he was unfortunately killed just as he was saying to those about him : ' They are beaten, let us beat them to the purpose.' This accident caused a great confusion, and tho' endeavours were made to conceal his death, yet the first squadron of the Life Guards, who was next him, stopping upon it, the rest did the same and occasioned great delay, which the enemie took care to profit by, and passing in the interim a considerable body of horse through the defiles attacked and broke both the lines of the Irish foot, the horse advancing not in time to their assistance; but instead of that giving all for lost thought of nothing but saveing themselves, and so gave an entire victory to the English.

" The night, indeed, coming on prevented the pursute. However, the Irish lost near four thousand men, nor was that of the English much inferior."

Dumont gives the whole credit of the victory to Ruvigny and his regiment :

" The battle of Aghrim was obstinately contested, and the victory hung for some time in the balance. But M. de Ruvigny and his regiment fought so well that the contest turned in our favour. The enemy's cavalry fled and abandoned the infantry which suffered heavily. Only the intervention of night saved it from being cut to pieces."

The reports of the French officers on the battle have never been published. Here are some summaries of them.

Fumeron writes : " The battle began at 1 o'clock and continued till 8. The Irish fought well and would have won the day but for St. Ruth's death and Tessé's being wounded when no general was left." Fumeron concludes by asking for 7000 muskets to arm the troops in Limerick.

Tessé, despite his wound, wrote a little later : " The battle lasted from 11 to 7. Every attack was repulsed all along the line till at last the enemy's horse got over the causeway. The change in the conduct of the troops after St. Ruth's death was simply extraordinary." Finally

Q

Colonel La Tour wrote: "Ireland is not lost for this defeat if only arms and supplies are sent. There are plenty of men."

The details of a battle fought so long ago and ending in a scene of confusion are not clearly discoverable, and it would be almost idle to attempt to follow them. But it is not difficult to imagine what really occurred on the left wing. When the fight in the centre was at its height, Dorington, it will be remembered, withdrew the two foot regiments which had been assisting Sheldon's cavalry in guarding the causeway. That weakened the left wing materially. After the fight in the centre had gone in favour of the Irish, they advanced and took possession of some of the ground of their opponents. This forward movement not merely took the infantry further away from the left, but rendered it less easy to see what was happening there. It seems perfectly clear that the English, or rather the Huguenot cavalry, on traversing the causeway got in the rear of the centre, while the three cavalry regiments on the right, under Sarsfield and Tessé, were too far off and too concerned in guarding the ford to countermarch and arrest Ruvigny's progress in time. The culminating calamity was, however, the death of St. Ruth, and the delay that followed in bringing a reinforcement to the left.

But no excuse can be offered for the behaviour of the cavalry. Two of the Colonels, Henry Luttrell and Nicholas Purcell, were suspected of treason and their regiments simply right-about-faced and galloped off. Sarsfield's regiment, which was detached from its commander who was on the right, followed after, and the only excuse that was ever offered was that the cavalry horses were stiff from waiting throughout the long day, and that they were taken at a disadvantage and had not room enough to charge. But even if the fullest weight be allowed for all these circumstances, it leaves the flight of the cavalry in utter indifference to the plight of the infantry an unexplained enigma and an indelible shame.

Valentine Brown, Viscount Kenmare.
from the Portrait at Killarney House.

The full French report states that the heat of the battle lasted three hours, that the Irish infantry fought well, and inflicted as heavy a loss on the English as they suffered themselves. The losses of the Irish infantry were exceedingly heavy. Some regiments, those in particular of Lords Clanrickarde and Kenmare, were practically destroyed. The two Major-Generals, Dorington and John Hamilton, were taken prisoners. Lord Galway and Lord Dillon (Theobald) were killed. Lords Kenmare, Slane, Bophin (afterwards fifth Earl of Clanrickarde) and Duleek (Bellew) were taken prisoners and kept so till after the Limerick Convention. John Hamilton, the ablest soldier of all the Hamilton brothers, died of his wounds in Dublin three months later. Plunkett who, strangely enough, omits the name of Lord Dillon, writes :—

" In the long and bloody strife, both on the field of bravery and in the accidental retreat, there were slain of the Irish officers and soldiers about two thousand, and six hundred wounded. The wounded soon almost all recovered, and joined the army at Limerick within six weeks after. Amongst the slain was the great General St. Ruth, worthy of lasting memory. Next after him the noble youth the Lord Bourk (de Burgh), Viscount of Galway, son to the potent Earl of Clanrickarde. He was despatched by foreigners after quarter given as 'tis said. Brigadier Connel, Brigadier William Mansfield Barker, an English gentleman early killed by a cannon ball, Brigadier Henry MacJohn O'Neil, Colonel Charles Moore of Kildare with his Lieutenant-Colonel and Major, Colonel David Bourk, Colonel Ulick Bourk, Colonel Constantine Macguire, Colonel James Talbot of Templeogue, Colonel Arthur, Colonel Mahony, Lieutenant-Colonel Morgan an English gentleman, Major Purcell, Sir John Everard of Fethard, Colonel Felix O'Neil, and Dean Alexius Stafford of Wexford, an undaunted zealot and a most pious churchman, who fell in front of the royal regiment as he was encouraging them on the first charge. There were made prisoners the Lord of Duleek, the

Lord of Slane, the Lord of Bophin, son to the Earl of Clanrickarde, the Lord of Kenmare, Major-General Dorington, Major-General John Hamilton, who died at Dublin soon after of his wounds, Brigadier Tuite, Colonel Walter Bourk, Colonel Gordon O'Neil, Colonel Thomas Butler of Kilcash, Colonel O'Connel, Colonel Edmund Madden, and several others."

Creditable as it was to the men who fought there, the battle of Aughrim was really the fatal blow to the Irish cause. With the exception of St. Ruth and Tessé no French officers were present. It was an entirely Irish battle fought under a French general, who certainly displayed great tactical ability, but the death of this general left the Irish army without a leader. No. one seemed able to concoct a tactical plan, and all Tyrconnell could do was to prepare as well as he could to defend Limerick a second time whilst he sent urgent messengers to France to implore material assistance at once, to enable him to hold out through the winter, and a fresh army for the New Year. He sent the Earl of Abercorn and Dr. Doran on this mission in separate ships. Lord Abercorn's vessel was intercepted by a Dutch man-of-war, and he was killed in the fight. Dr. Doran, more fortunate, reached St. Germains, and told the story of Aughrim and how affairs stood in Ireland.

Chapter X

THE SECOND SIEGE OF LIMERICK

IN the final phase of the three years' struggle when the National or Jacobite cause is flickering to extinction, the Duke of Tyrconnell reappears in the ascendant. His enemies and detractors are silenced or themselves discredited. The French officers left are of no special rank or ability. Sarsfield, who might have taken the lead, is somewhat ashamed of himself for having aided traitors, and although the evidence is not yet conclusive, no one doubts that Henry Luttrell is guilty of high treason. Tyrconnell resumes the personal charge of affairs, and his advice and intentions are to prolong the defence of Limerick until the spring of 1692, by which time he declares aid must come from France. He has not lost his courage although his bulk has got immense, and he sets an example of fortitude to his despairing counsellors. Henry Luttrell and Nicholas Purcell, the laggards of Aughrim, do not conceal their opinion that further resistance is futile and that now is the time to come to terms. Tyrconnell has an old score to clear off with them. They are the same men who went to St. Germains to undermine his position, and who humiliated him in the camp at Athlone.

The defeat at Aughrim was speedily followed by another misfortune. D'Usson had been sent by St. Ruth to look after Galway while he was deciding what course he should take about his *lâches* at Athlone. The general-in-chief felt that there would arrive a better opportunity for a court martial than the eve of an important battle. The garrison at Galway did not exceed 2500 men, made up of several skeleton regiments. There were also six field-pieces in the place, but there does not seem to have been any good reason for supposing that it could hold out for any lengthy period if seriously attacked. The matter was soon put to the test, for four days after the battle at Aughrim, Ginkel marched to attack it.

The story may as well be given in Plunkett's words :—

" Ginkel marched towards Galway bringing along with him only his field-pieces, having left his heavy cannons at Athlone. It seems by this that he presumed on his good fortune that Galway would make little resistance. This town is maritime and chief of the province of Connaught. It is pretty strong by situation, but might have been made a noble fortress with an indifferent expense, which had been neglected during the war as other works of moment were. The houses within are built like castles for strength, so that a smart resistance may be given to the enemy even after entering the town, the governor whereof was then Lord Dillon (Henry), and to his assistance Lieutenant-General D'Usson entered.

" On the 16th Ginkel with his army came to Loughreagh, on the 17th to Athenry within eight miles of Galway. On the 18th Galway was invested, in which there were seven regiments of foot, not full nor well armed. Baldarg O'Donnell was expected there with a thousand men, but he came not and afterwards made conditions for himself and took the Prince of Orange's side at the end of the war. On July 19th Ginkel planted a battery against a little new fort which the Irish had made near the town. He took it that same day. Immediately after he raised his batteries against the town. On the 21st the Governor having considered the great declension of Irish affairs, thought it fit not to hold out the place any longer, and so the same day he called for parley. The treaty was concluded on July 24 whereby the garrison got their own demands, and the town also for en- joying their estates, the exercise of their religion, and other rights and privileges that are due to free-born subjects.

On 26th the Marquis D'Usson went to Limerick, so did the Lord Dillon with the garrison, being about two thousand three hundred men and six pieces of cannon."

Neither in Plunkett's version, nor in the Articles of Capitulation is there any evidence supporting James's attack on Lord Clanrickarde, who, he alleges, " considering with others nothing but their own security, made haste to surrender it." Probably James did not appreciate the facts of the situation. Lord Clanrickarde had just been deprived of his two sons—one slain, the other a prisoner although destined to survive the vicissitudes of prison—and the bulk of his followers at Aughrim. The garrison and resources of Galway did not admit of any protracted defence. To have attempted a futile resistance signified incurring the massacre of the garrison. An honourable surrender left it at liberty to join the troops at Limerick for the last rally. Among those who marched out of Galway with D'Usson and Dillon were Lady Iveagh, Lieut.-Colonel Luke Reilly and his brother Philip Reilly. The hostages for the due performance of the terms of capitulation were Lords Clanrickarde and Enniskillen, Dominic Browne and Thomas Dillon. Fumeron confines himself to stating that " Galway surrendered because the Irish were panic-stricken by Aughrim."

Tyrconnell had in the meantime ordered a *levée en masse* among the Irish of the counties left to him, and so far as numbers went the gaps of Aughrim were filled up, but the new levies were only raw troops and imperfectly armed. A French return shows how the Irish army after Aughrim had fallen to 8140 infantry (only 3910 armed), 2400 cavalry, and 2360 dragoons. Lord Kenmare's regiment had only 237 left out of 800 men. Some of the Duke's advisers wished him to risk a second battle, but, more cautious, he concentrated his efforts on defending Limerick. He had also to reckon with the disintegrating forces at work in his own camp. The circumstances did not, however, admit of his placing Henry Luttrell on his trial for cowardice at

Aughrim. Among other reasons for not doing so it would have been hard to explain how General Dominic Sheldon, chief commander of the cavalry of the left wing, should not be included in the charge. The Duke had to bide his time, but soon circumstances gave him his chance.

At the end of July (O.S.) news was brought of the approach of the Galway garrison under charge of an English escort, and Colonel Henry Luttrell was sent with his regiment to take over the men at Six Mile Bridge. Here he got into conversation with one of Ginkel's officers named Sebastian, and the subject not unnaturally turned up as to the possibility of terminating the war. Luttrell was only one of some fifty colonels in the Irish army, but he took it upon himself to say that he thought it would be an easy matter to arrange, provided General Ginkel had sufficient powers. That was the beginning of Luttrell's treason.

This proposal accorded so well with Ginkel's own wishes, for he knew that his master wanted the war in Ireland to be ended as speedily as possible, that he determined to follow up the matter. A trumpeter was sent a few days later to Limerick to enquire about the condition of some of the English wounded officers in the hands of the Irish, and at the same time he bore a letter to Colonel Henry Luttrell from Sebastian enquiring if there was any chance of the matter they had discussed at Six Mile Bridge coming off. The English commander had assumed Luttrell's presence in Limerick, whereas he was in the cavalry camp a few miles out of the town. The letter for him from the English camp was therefore taken to Lord Lucan, who at once broke the seal. The contents clearly revealed illicit communication with the enemy, and Lucan forthwith placed it in Tyrconnell's hands, although he and Luttrell had been friends.

Luttrell was thereupon arrested, tried by court martial, and received the benefit of the doubt, for the Court decided that he did not deserve death. This was proof that he had many friends, and Tyrconnell had perforce to content himself with keeping him a close prisoner and reporting the matter to James for his decision. There seems no doubt that despite the verdict of the Court Tyrconnell would have had him shot, but that Ginkel sent in a message to the effect that he would hang every Irish officer in his power if he were touched. But before any decision could arrive from the King in France much had happened, and after the peace was concluded Luttrell was released and received a pension of £500 a year from the English Government. Among the Irish he was always known as "false Luttrell," and in 1717, when the memory of his conduct might have been thought to have passed away, he was assassinated at the door of his house in Dublin by one who was never discovered.

This incident was almost the last act of authority in the Viceroyalty of the Duke of Tyrconnell. A few days after the Luttrell trial Tyrconnell thought it wise to call upon the army and the people to take an oath of loyalty binding themselves not to make peace until the following spring. This oath was administered with all the formalities of the Roman Catholic Church, and its breach would have entailed excommunication. A few days later Tyrconnell dined with the French general D'Usson. The party was described as a merry one and broke up late. On returning to his house the Duke suddenly complained of being ill, and was put to bed. Four days later, August 24, 1691, he was dead, and it was more than suspected that he had been poisoned. Before he became unconscious he signed the papers appointing three Lord Justices to administer the realm, or what was left of it, in the name of King James. They were the Chancellor, Alexander Fitton, Lord Gosworth, Sir Richard Nagle, and Mr. Plowden. These appointments were not popular with the Irish, because Fitton and Plowden were Englishmen. Tyrconnell was buried on August 26 (N.S.) in the Cathedral of Limerick, and Plunkett supplies his best epitaph : " Thus this great man fell, who in his fall pulled down a mighty edifice, videlicet a considerable Catholic nation, for there was no other subject left able to support the national cause."

Berwick, who inherited much of his father's inclination to ill-natured criticism, described him as " a man of very good sense, very obliging, but immoderately vain and full of cunning. He had not a military genius, but much courage. From the time of the Battle of the Boyne he sank prodigiously, being become as irresolute in his mind as unwieldy in his person." Juster than the Stuart family, the French who knew him styled him a *" fort honnête homme,"* and Father Anselm in his funeral oration in the Church of the English Sisters in the Faubourg St. Antoine on August 22, 1692, extolled him as the type of the faithful man " who feared God and honoured his King."

Finding that the negotiations with those who took a black view of the state of the Irish cause, and who were called by some " the desponders," were not likely to lead to any immediate result, Ginkel summoned his heavy artillery from Athlone and proceeded to attack Limerick, but he was also waiting for something else, namely, the arrival of the powerful Anglo-Dutch fleet, which had been ordered to the Shannon to co-operate in its siege. In 1690 William's attack had been made exclusively from the land. The French were for the moment masters of the sea in a qualified sense, and had at least a few vessels in the river. But Marlborough's successful expedition to Cork had opened the eyes of the authorities in London to the advantages of a combined attack, and in 1691 William, on hearing of the victory at Aughrim, sent a strong naval force to blockade the river and to lend a helping hand to the land troops. It was the addition of the fleet to Ginkel's army that baffled the Irish defence, and the reader of Colonel Richards's diary that follows will have no doubt on the subject. It was this attack from an unexpected side that more than neutralised the great improvement that had been made in the defences of Limerick during the twelve months which intervened between the two sieges. Our description of the second siege cannot commence better than with the narrative of the English Colonel :—

THE SECOND SIEGE SUMMARISED FROM THE DIARY OF COLONEL RICHARDS (WITH GENERAL GINKEL'S ARMY)

"*Tuesday*, 25 *August* (O.S.), 1691. After my tedious journey unto Brigadier O'Donel I arrived at Carrickonlish just as our army was decamping to invest Limerick. Here I found the heavy cannon and the three mortars from Athlone, where we were forced to leave one 18-pr. and a mortar for want of draught horses. We found the enemy posted in the old forts made in Cromwell's time. Their horse they passed immediately on the other side of the river. A party of foot, horse, and dragoons commanded by Sir John Hanmer attacked the forts and carried them, with the loss of three or four men. The river below the town is about eight or nine hundred paces.

"*Wednesday*, 26*th*. Two hundred horses this morning were sent to Carrickonlish for the heavy cannon there, which all arrived safe in our camp about two o'clock.

"*Thursday*, 27*th*. Early this morning the General went to the left to the water-side, where we had begun a sort of a trench. The enemies brought down two pieces of cannon to a house on the other side of the river, so that two or three of our regiments were obliged to change their ground, being incommoded by their shot. This morning went away a detachment with three 12-prs. under the command of the Prince of Hesse to Castle Connel, with orders to hang all the officers and to put the soldiers to the sword when reduced. The Prince of Hesse sent to acquaint the General that Castle Connel was of that strength as not to be forced, upon which the General sent me to his assistance. I took with me more powder and ball, a petard and petardier.

"*Friday*, 28*th*. About six o'clock we began to batter the envelope with two cannon only, one being split. At eight arrived the other two pieces, so now we have four. At this time about four or five hundred horse and dragoons of the enemy drew up on the other side, made signals to the castle, and told them they should be relieved immediately. I ordered the broken gun to be drawn on the top of a hill, with which we beat the horse from their ground. . . . The petardier, with two grenadiers, fixed the petard to the gate with very good success, upon which the enemies beat a parley, but their demands being extravagant the prince did not hearken to them. The news of the enemie's coming over was again confirmed, so that the prince thought it not prudent to play a hazardous game; therefore granted them to march out without their arms, and according to their capitulations they are to be subsisted till sent into Hungary to fight against the Turks in the Emperor's service. In the place we found fifty barrels of barley and meal, a stack of hay and about thirty cows, two casks of brandy and one of claret, with several barrels of powdered beef, and but little ammunition. The ships now lie within two miles of the town (Limerick); orders have been given for the unloading first of what is most necessary, as 24-pr. balls, powder, etc.

" 29 *August*. The General having ordered that the batteries for cannon should be begun, five hundred men are ordered for the same work. The line of communication, forts and retrenchments are continued against the town.

" 30 *August*. The 'Maid of Dort,' loaded with planks and timbers for our batteries, was taken out of Kingsale by a French privateer. This loss incommodes us very much. Last night a battery of nine 24-prs. was very much advanced. Our lodgment for nine mortar pieces was completed, and this night began to play bombs and carquasses, which put fire in several places in the town.

" 31 *August*. The battery of nine 24-prs. is now augmented to fourteen. The five new 24-prs. sent from the Tower of London, and the two great mortars of 18 inches are ordered to be landed to-night. We endeavoured to shoot at the great bridge, but the distance was too great to effect any good, and it was not thought convenient to approach nigher, so as to engage in a siege, but only to cannonade and ruin the houses.

" 1 *September*. The General sent very early for Colonel Goar, and ordered him to re-embark all our heavy cannon, etc., keeping only ashore the field-pieces with a proportion of powder and ball for a battle. Towards night the General sent orders that six mortars and nine twenty-four-prs. should be left in battery till further orders.

" 2 *September*. This morning the General went to see the ground where Cromwell (Ireton) made his bridge. The river hereabouts is very narrow, which I believe gives room for some new design, for the embarkation of our cannon is now countermanded. The cannon and mortars in battery continue playing. In the evening came a messenger from Brigadier Levison to acquaint the General that he had wholly routed a great party of the enemie's men to Newcastle, and had taken my Lord (Castle Connell) and his lady prisoners.

" 3 *September*. The enemie's horse now makes a motion, and have camped on the side of a hill three miles above the town over against Foxon's House. A design was immediately on foot to cut between the town and them, but, this changing, orders were given for the further bombarding the town by transporting the cannon and mortars from the right to the left of last year's attack.

" 4 *September*. This night we began our new batteries with about seven hundred workmen. Some little disasters happened this night by a false alarm, the regiments of Verner and Meath not being at their post to cover the pioneers which the General took very ill.

" 5 *September*. One hundred and fifty dragoons were sent to make the ways for our cannon from the camp to their new batteries. Four hundred workmen were also ordered to relieve the seven hundred employed last night, and to continue the same works by day being now under cover.

" 6 *September*. The English and Dutch men-of-war sent on shore about forty gunners to assist at our batteries, and the Danish regiments sent several officers skilled in fireworks to help our bombarding, the batteries for our mortars being now ready, as also a battery of sixteen 24-prs., besides another of six. The General ordered Colonel Goar to keep in readiness eight field-pieces and all the pontoons, that in the night we might fling a bridge over the river.

" 7 *September*. The mortars and cannon are now in battery. Three hundred men are ordered to make a battery for ten 3-prs. to shoot red-hot bullets. Eight 12-prs. and the two mortars from the "Salamander" are to be in battery on Cromwell's fort.

" 8 *September*. About six in the morning the General and Duke of Wirtemberg came upon the batteries and ordered the cannon to play on the side of the English town in the island, to see if a breach could be made. Towards night a great part of the wall was ruined, upon which it was thought we should attempt the passing into the island and attack the town this way. But men of experience thought this impracticable.

" 9 *September*. By break of day all our batteries played, and the breach on the wall augmented very much. We endeavoured to ruin an earthwork of the enemie's, on which were planted three pieces of cannon, but the distance was so great, and our not shooting in front with it could not hinder their annoying us. They also brought three pieces of cannon to the right of the town which flanked the breach and river. A kind of council of war was held about the passing this part of the river into the island, which met with so many difficulties that it is believed it will not be attempted, but rather keep to our first resolutions of cannonading and bombarding the town, and after that pass into the county of Clare.

" 10 *September*. Our mortars and cannon continue playing, and this last night were successful in putting fire into several parts of the town, but by four o'clock this morning they were put out.

" 11 *September*. The General ordered all our pontoons to be ready this night, as also four 12-prs., 2 long 6-prs., and 10 3-prs., with fifty rounds each. To cover this new-designed bridge a battery for six pieces was ordered to be made to the right of all, looking to the caussé on the other side the river over which the enemies continually pass, and it is thought the battery will oblige them to go about eight miles round to have communication with the town.

"12 *September*. A Danish swimmer was sent over the water in the night, with a rope to measure the breadth of the river where we design our bridge. It proved so rocky that he could not haul the said rope, from which we conclude we have not enough boats nor that our anchors will hold.

"13 *September*. Captain Van Esp was sent up the river as high as Brian's Bridge to find a narrower place for our bridge. He returned and made report that there was no place fit for the same, they being all marshy on the other side, or kept by entrenchments of the enemy.

"14 *September*. At eight this night we fired all our cannon three times for the victory obtained against the Turks on the Danube.

"15 *September*. Major-General Tettau went to the right of all our camp to the river-side, where it divides itself into four streams by three islands. The two first and last streams were fordable, the third not, which will take up twenty-five pontoons. The ground on the other side seemed very good; a little lower down the river came the road from Brian's Bridge to Limerick, on which the enemy were encamped on the side of a hill with the whole of their cavalry. Orders came to have all again in readiness to march at night, and the better to cover the making of the bridge, six pieces of cannon were put into battery to shoot on the caussé coming from Limerick. Six 12-prs. and six 3 prs. were placed on a rising ground to the left of the bridge, to annoy any horse that should come down on the other side, and four 3-prs. were placed at the beginning of the bridge to defend the same. As the night fell the pontoons, etc., marched, and, although we had not above two miles to go, yet the several accidents that attended us caused delay. At one o'clock past midnight all our artillery was placed as designed.

"16 *September*. About six this morning the bridge was finished, and we began to pass the bridge with a detachment of twenty men of a troop of the horse and dragoons. Six hundred foot detached followed, backed by three hundred others, and a little time after were followed by two hundred more. The enemy now having the alarm marched three regiments of foot, as also several squadrons of horse and dragoons. These latter, with their foot, they immediately posted within musket-shot of us by favour of some hedges. We marched straight to them, and drove them from their advantages, till we gained a high ground of them, and then they entirely broke. None were killed on our side, and but few on theirs. A gentleman that came this night out of the town says all the inhabitants are retired from it; that there is not a whole house in the town; that we have burnt two magazines of biscuit of above three thousand barrels, with a great magazine of brandy; and that by what he could understand there was not above three weeks' more provisions in the town for the garrison.

"18 *September.* The bridge is ordered to be removed a musket-shot higher up the river.

"19 *September.* We worked hard at this new bridge, as also at a horn-work on the other side to cover the same. The rest of the heavy cannon should have been drawn off this night, and the horses were ready for it; but at eight at night the General ordered our continuing to fire all night.

"20 *September.* Early this morning our bridge was finished. The enemies' horse marched early this morning towards Six Mile Bridge, and a deserter says they took six days' bread with them. It was observed that about a thousand foot marched with them.

"21 *September.* The line of contravallation is traced anew nigher the town, and we continue to finish our horn-work that covers the bridge.

"22 *September.* A disposition being made yesterday for the passing the greatest part of our horse and dragoons with about seventeen regiments of foot with the artillery before mentioned, early this morning the artillery passed. The General continued his march at the foot of the hills on the road going to Six Mile Bridge. At the same time several bodies of men drew out of the town and posted themselves in an old fort at the head of the bridge. The General halted, and thought it best to attack them before they were too much increased. Two regiments of foot and about two hundred dragoons were immediately ordered to perform this service. It was a dispute of about two hours, in which time the enemies were very liberal of their cannon from their walls and small shot; but being so opinionatively pressed by us, they gave way. We followed them to the bridge, over which about eighty got; but the garrison, apprehending our entering pell-mell with them, ordered the bridge to be drawn up. Two or three hundred of the Irish took the water, most of whom were drowned; the rest, being about 500, fell a sacrifice to the fury of our men at the end of the bridge and under the whole fire of the town. We lost in this action three officers and about two hundred men killed and wounded. We took prisoners one colonel, three lieut.-colonels, nine captains, six lieutenants, and three ensigns, with about sixty privates,

" 23 *September*. Last night we had some whispering as if the town would parley, which this morning did confirm, for Lieut.-General Scravenmore and Major-General Ruvigny were desired to meet Major-General Sarsfield and another at the river-side. They owned a mutiny in the town by the resentment of the garrison for the French general shutting the gates and letting so many of them to be cut off, and were for flinging all the French over the walls. Last night a lodgment was made just at the bridge, so that now the town is entirely blocked up."

Plunkett's version of the siege shows no great discrepancy in essential facts. The main portion reads as follows :—

" General de Ginkel, in a few days after Tyrconnell's death, having at last received his weighty artillery decamps from Carrickinlish and marches to Limerick, which he invests on August 25. At that juncture the Sieur Donep, Colonel of Danish horse, was killed by a cannon-ball from the town. General Ginkel having finished his lines before the town, he plants his grand battery of cannon on the south side of the city and that of his mortars on the east at the place called Ireton's Fort. The first thing the besiegers did was to try if, with that great battery of cannon, they could destroy Thomond Bridge to cut off communications with the County Clare. But the besiegers could not compass their aim after eight days' trial, in which space they cast into the town plenty of bombs night and day.

" The General seeing no success of moment hitherto, he resolved to remove his main battery to the north side of the town, or to that part of the city which is called the English town, where he understood the wall to be very weak. The battery did furiously play until it made a breach of forty yards wide. In opposition to this the besieged made a strong entrenchment within to stand the attack without fear of being overpowered.

" General Ginkel prepares for his attack. He gets ready his floating bridges in order to pass a branch of the Shannon before the breach. But before attempting the assault he thought it necessary to dismount a small battery on his left flank. He endeavoured to do so for three or four days, but could not prevail ; upon which he ceased for two or three days from all kinds of firing, so that there was a general silence. In the interim but few persons lost their lives. Of the besieged there was killed a hopeful young gentleman, a nephew of Monsieur La Tour, the governor, by a bomb, being at that time in the same chamber as his uncle. In like manner a gentlewoman (Lady Dillon ?) was slain before the door of her lodging after coming downstairs to shun the bomb. Upon a small sally or two there were lost Captain Walter Hore, of Harperstown, etc.

" General Ginkel then fixed to cross the Shannon in order to begirt the town on the other side in hopes to force it to a speedy surrender. On September 16 he gives orders to carry floats and pontoons to the ford where he intends to pass the river. He commands six hundred workmen to lay the bridge in that place and a hundred grenadiers to cover them while those men are working. The grenadiers were brought in boats into an island, where they remained undiscovered till it was almost morning. They were then discovered by an Irish dragoon patrolling. He gave notice of it to Brigadier Clifford, who seemed not to give credit to any such account. The alarm spreading, one of the colonels of dragoons, by name Dudley Colclough, brought down his regiment to the Brigadier's tent in such haste as some of his men did not stay to saddle their horses. The Brigadier neglected to decide so long that the bridge was finished and a great body of English came over. At which the Irish guards, seeing themselves too weak to beat them back over the said river, took a sudden resolution to save themselves by flight, which they hardly effected. The Irish cavalry, under the command of their General, Dominic Sheldon, hearing of this misfortune decamped suddenly and marched towards the town of Ennis, by which the horse lost communication with Limerick. At the same time the Irish Lords Justices and the ladies and such as were with them (who had a camp of their own in County Clare) had to run into the town with all speed. Here rises a question

R

whether the Irish cavalry should have come down and fought the enemy that was come over? This was a brave occasion for the Irish cavalry to show themselves, for from the beginning of the war to that day they were not brought to a trial as to the whole body of them. Here they would make recompense for all their past inaction, though the fault had not been in the men but in the great officers. But what Brigadier Clifford can say for himself by the way of vindication I do not understand. I suppose his comfort is that he believes he will never be brought to an account of this behaviour by the King.

" The bridge being perfectly finished and commodiously placed on the river, General Ginkel passed over on September 22 with the Duke of Wirtemberg and Lt.-General. Scravenmoer, bringing with him ten regiments of foot, fourteen small pieces of cannon and the bulk of the horse and dragoons.

" As the forces approached the city the Governor of Limerick sent out a small detachment of foot to the number of 200 men, under Colonel Stapleton, deputy governor, to skirmish. This was a foolish management for what end could it have? After fighting awhile Colonel Stapleton was overcharged with numbers and had to retire. Some of his men got into the gate that was on Thomond Bridge. He himself with the rear was also hastening thither, but a party pursued him so close that a French town-major who commanded the gate pretending to fear that the enemies would pour in with the Irish, shut the said gate against friends and foes, by which it happened that Colonel Stapleton, Major Purcell, some inferior officers with about eighty private soldiers were killed on the bridge."

There is a discrepancy in the figures, but the whole narrative is very much in accord with that of Colonel Richards. In one of the French reports Colonel La Tour admits that the gate on the drawbridge was shut too precipitately. But the fatal blow to the defence was the treachery of Colonel Clifford in not holding the pass over the river.

Although the Irish had not lost more than 600 or 700 men during the siege, the general feeling among them after Tyrconnell's death was to come to terms with the enemy and terminate the war. All the Irish leaders held this view, and men like Sarsfield and Wauchope considered that better terms would have been obtained by an earlier surrender. The oath taken to Tyrconnell stood in the path of direct overtures to the enemy, but there are ways known to casuists of evading a promise the literal fulfilment of which has become inconvenient. The first step taken was to shake the public faith in Tyrconnell by publishing and distributing the text of what purported to be the Duke's will, in which it was stated that he (Tyrconnell) knew " that the King of France would send no more help, and that therefore the Irish had no alternative to making the best terms they could with the Prince of Orange."

The French officers were all for resisting to the bitter end, and had no difficulty in showing that the place could hold out for a long period. They also declared that assistance was certain to arrive before long from France, and that as soon as a French fleet had cleared the river the chief peril to the place would be removed ; but they could give no positive answer to the question, " Are French troops coming ? " In their hearts they must have known, too, that they were not.

But what the Irish leaders asked was what would be their fate if no help after all did come from France? To hold out vainly meant absolute surrender, perhaps without quarter in the end ; to come to terms now signified honourable conditions with probably leave to seek a new career in France. The Irish view was indeed more reasonable than that of the French officers, who, moreover, had been only a few months in the country. Three years had the Irish been fighting for a shadowy cause, and now they were driven into a corner with no prospect of succour save the vague and uncertain promises of the French King. They, at least, were entitled to have the final word in deciding what course they should pursue in this supreme crisis of their fate. It was not that they were irresolute, as the French officers thought, when they proposed to give up a town which in the strictly military sense was in no danger of falling at the moment, but that they had braced themselves to face the fate most appalling to the human mind, to go forth into a foreign land as exiles, where the language was unknown, and leave for ever the country of their birth.

There was one obstacle, the oath exacted by Tyrconnell.

In this dilemma the only course open to those who had taken it was to apply to the representatives of the Church which had been a party to the contract. The view of the Bishops and other dignitaries of the Church in Limerick was as follows, to use the words of King James himself :—

" That being blocked up on all sides it was impossible to hear from the King should any answer come, which, being the thing their oath obliged them to, there was no possibility of keeping to the letter of it ; but that the King's permission to treat, considering the extream want they were in, might reasonably be presumed, since it could not be known." In plain English the Irish were relieved of the oath they had taken only a few weeks before to hold out till the spring, and at once made overtures to capitulate to General Ginkel on honourable terms.

We shall deal with the conditions of the Limerick Convention in the next chapter ; but on October 4 a suspension of arms was arranged. A fortnight later there sailed up the Shannon a fine French fleet under Château Renaud, before which the English fleet scattered and fled, losing two frigates in the operation. On board the fleet was the largest quantity of stores and supplies that Louis ever sent to Ireland, including 30,000 stand of arms. The capitulation rendered the succours useless and Renaud restored the two frigates captured, not to compromise the situation.

The whole incident of the broken oath because no aid

could be expected, and the arrival of adequate aid immediately after the formal repudiation of that oath, furnishes fruit for reflection. At the very moment that Louis had braced himself up to the task of making a real effort in Ireland in support of James, for Château Renaud's fleet was intended to be the precursor of a fresh land expedition, the Irish lost heart and threw up the game. The only fighting force left in the country had agreed to surrender the last foothold it possessed in the island.

To Louis the disappointment was intense, for he had personally directed all the arrangements himself for the Château Renaud expedition and the despatch of a fresh army. A few months earlier (July, 1691) the great statesman Louvois had died, leaving Louis to be his own Minister, for his successors were mere officials or courtiers. Clever and capable as Louvois was, he was no admirer of James, and he had not much faith in the Irish adventure. His support had never been lavish or even adequate. The French Court testified its sense of his worth in the following quatrain :—

> "Ici gît, sous qui tout pliait
> Et qui de tout avait connaissance parfaite,
> Louvois, que personne n'aimait
> Et que tout le monde regrette."

When James condoled with Louis on the loss of his Minister, Louis replied : "Tell the King of England that I have lost a good Minister, but that his affairs and mine will not go the worse for that." Château Renaud's expedition was the result of Louis's personal intervention, and he felt its abortive ending all the more as a rebuff. In the first heat of his resentment and disappointment Louis was disposed to punish his own officers, D'Usson, Tessé and La Tour, for surrendering a place entrusted to their charge without need. But the examination not merely of their reports after the surrender, but of their correspondence before it, showed conclusively that they had been no parties to the tame conclusion. They opposed coming to terms, and declared it to be unnecessary—even parting with their own private money to distribute it among the soldiers to keep them in good heart. Nor does it appear from their reports that there was any unwillingness among the private soldiers to go on fighting.

But among the officers there was general discouragement, and no one was sanguine enough to think that even if Limerick could be held the rest of Ireland could be recovered. The stage of exhaustion had been reached, and as William's policy had always been not to drive brave men to desperation, the terms he offered through his general, Ginkel, were fair and indulgent. Both sides being prepared to end the war it followed that even the arrival of the French fleet did not incline the Irish to change their minds. Relief was displayed at the conclusion of a long and, so far as Ireland was concerned, useless struggle. The Irish leaders were contemplating a new and more promising career in the service of France, and William, anxious above everything to get his own troops out of Ireland, was not indisposed to concur in and assist the departure of the bulk of the fighting-men who had kept them well employed during three campaigns.

Chapter XI

THE CONVENTION OF LIMERICK

THE responsible authorities in Limerick having decided on a capitulation, the arrangement of the preliminaries was taken in hand. The news was sent to the cavalry leaders, who on October 5 rode over to Ginkel's camp and then passed through to Limerick. Ginkel entertained them to dinner, and among his guests were the Archbishop of Cashell (Catholic Primate), the Earl of Westmeath, Lords Dillon and Galmoye, General Sheldon, and others. The next day Sarsfield, Wauchope, and two brigadiers visited Ginkel, the general terms were agreed to, and hostages given on either side. Those for the besieged were Lords Westmeath, Iveagh, Louth, and Trimlestown. Those for the Anglo-Dutch force were Lord Cutts, Sir David Collier, Colonel Tiffin, and Colonel Piper. The social position and reputation of the hostages were in themselves proof that the negotiations were taken up in a serious spirit and with a desire to carry them through.

It is correct to say with Plunkett that the terms for the surrender of Limerick involved a very much larger question than the capitulation of a town. The Irish leaders were negotiating for a definite peace on behalf of the Catholic inhabitants of Ireland, and for the drafting of a convention that should uphold their rights in religion, property, and personal freedom. The following persons acted as the Commissioners for the Irish party, namely, Sarsfield, Earl of Lucan, Lord Galmoye, Colonel Nicholas Purcell, Colonel Nicholas Cusack, Sir Toby Butler, Colonel Garrett Dillon, and Colonel John Browne. They opened discussions with a request which Ginkel at once refused. They asked that the Catholic owners in Leinster, who had been dispossessed of their estates by William in 1690, after the Boyne, should be reinstated. Ginkel declared that he had no power to reverse what his Sovereign had done, and his reply was endorsed by William's two regents, Sir Charles Porter and Mr. Coningsby, who arrived a few days later from Dublin to take part in the discussions.

General Ginkel acted as his own commissioner, but he called in to aid him all his officers of and above the grade of Brigadier-General. The principal discussion took place on October 8; much of the argument was rather heated, but finally it ended in a general agreement on all the essential points. Certain of these were reserved for final settlement after the arrival of the Regents on October 11. On the 12th complete agreement was attained, and the Treaty was signed and exchanged the following day (October 13, N.S., October 3, O.S., 1691).

The Treaty was divided into two separate sections, the Civil Articles numbering thirteen and the Military Articles numbering twenty-nine. The Civil Articles were those affecting the Catholic people of Ireland, and might be termed the Treaty. The Military Articles were those relating to the surrender of the troops in arms and their free conveyance to France. The importance of the former arrangement was permanent; of the latter transitory, expiring with the accomplishment of the conditions. It will clear the ground in a matter that has been the cause of bitter controversy to say at once that the Military Articles were faithfully and scrupulously carried out. We shall deal with the subsequent breaches of the Civil Articles a little further on, but in regard to them it is only just to say that Ginkel, who was an honourable man as well as an excellent general, had no share or part in the deviations from the text, which did not, as a matter of fact, occur till some time afterwards.

For this reason a summary of the Military Articles will be sufficient for all practical purposes. The first condition was

Colonel John Browne of Kinturk and Westport.
from the Portrait at Westport House in the possession of the Marquis of Sligo.

that all persons, without any exception, were to be free
to leave Ireland for any country beyond the seas excepting
England and Scotland, and that they might take with them
" their families, household stuff, plate and jewels." General
Ginkel also undertook to provide at Cork fifty ships of 200
tons burthen each for their conveyance, and if that number
was insufficient twenty more ships besides two men-of-war
to embark the principal officers and serve as a convoy.
General D'Usson entered into a personal bond for the safe
restitution of these ships after they had discharged their
passengers, promising to return and constitute himself a
prisoner if the French authorities attempted to detain
them. The troops and civilians taking their departure
were also to have leave to embark on any French ships, and
no doubt this clause was added in consequence of the expected arrival of Château Renaud's squadron in the
Shannon.

The right to quit the country was extended to all
garrisons, including the force at Sligo, which had surrendered shortly before Limerick. It was also stipulated
that 900 horses, including those belonging to officers,
might be taken out of the country. Finally, all the Irish
troops on leaving to join the ships at Cork or the other
ports of departure appointed were to march out of Limerick
with all the honours of war, " with their baggage, their
arms, drums beating, ball in mouth, match lighted at both
ends and colours flying."

The only difficulty that arose in connection with the
fulfilment of these articles was about the departure of the
women and children belonging to the soldiers. Count
Nassau seemed to think that shipping had only to be provided for the men, but on Lord Lucan's writing a letter of
protest to General Ginkel the difficulty was promptly
removed. The misunderstanding arose from the copying
clerk's mistake in omitting from the final draft of Article 2
the words, " and all such as are under their protection in
those counties." The best proof that all the conditions

were faithfully fulfilled is furnished in the following letter of release sent by Lord Lucan to General Ginkel in December :—

"Whereas by the articles of Limerick, Lieut.-General Ginkel, Commander-in-Chief of the English army, did engage himself to furnish ten thousand ton of shipping for the transporting of such of the Irish forces to France as were willing to go thither, and to facilitate their passage to add four thousand ton more, in case the French fleet did not come to this kingdom to take off part of those forces ; and whereas the French fleet has been on these coasts and carried away some of the said forces, and the Lieutenant-General has provided ships for as many of the rest as are willing to go as aforesaid : I do hereby declare that the said Lieutenant-General is released from any obligation he lay under from the said articles to provide vessels for that purpose, and do quit and renounce all further claim and pretension on this account, as witness my hand this 8th day of December, 1691.

"LUCAN."

"Witness, MARK TALBOT."

While leave was given to the men of the Irish army to leave their country, Ginkel made an effort to induce some of them to take service in the Williamite forces. A bounty and good pay were offered as inducement, and several thousands succumbed to the temptation. Indeed, it was the only alternative to going into exile or staying at home to starve, for there was neither food nor work left in Ireland out of Ulster, and Ulster was banned to the men of Munster and Connaught. But it will be seen that the bulk of these seceders deserted in France and Spain, and eventually the English Government refused to employ Irishmen in the army at all. However, in the two months of November and December, 1691, about 5000 Irish troops, under the influence of Henry Luttrell, Nicholas Purcell, and Robert Clifford, enlisted in Ginkel's army, and on the other hand about 13,000 decided to go to France. We shall deal more specifically with the latter in the next chapter, but with regard to the former it may be stated, before passing on, that one of the plans favoured by William was to employ them not in his own but in the Emperor's service, and thus utilise them on the Continent as a kind of set-off to their compatriots in France. But this scheme was not very successful, and although one whole regiment, under Lord Iveagh, was shipped to Hamburg and reached Hungary with the view of being employed against the Turks, its fate was not calculated to encourage others to follow, for practically speaking the whole of them, including Lord Iveagh, died of the plague.

Besides the soldiers who took service under William, a large number of those who had estates agreed to stay. The recovery of their estates, the promise that they would be left undisturbed in their rights and privileges, and the lightness of the oath required (one of allegiance only) all contributed to make the decision easier. As a general principle it may be laid down that all those who had estates and who were not keen soldiers elected to remain in Ireland. On the other hand, soldiers like Lords Lucan, Galmoye, Kilmallock, Trimlestown, and Bellew went to France. It is also noteworthy that the more important of the prisoners taken at Aughrim and Cork, like Lords Kenmare, Clancarty, and Tyrone, decided to sacrifice their estates for their principles. Strict good faith was not observed towards these prisoners who should have been released when the Treaty was ratified in March, 1692. Lord Clancarty, for instance, was kept in the Tower till 1694, and then only escaped by the aid of his father-in-law, Sunderland. James's civil advisers, Fitton, Lord Gosworth, Sir Richard Nagle, and Mr. Plowden, went to France. William Talbot, the Duke's nephew, who had succeeded his uncle in the earldom of Tyrconnell, also left the country, taking with him his son Lord Baltinglass, who eventually married in 1702 the Duke's only daughter and child Lady Charlotte Talbot. Some of the higher dignitaries of the Church of Rome, like the Archbishop of Cashell (John Brenan), also went to France.

As the details of the embarcation of the Irish volunteers for France belong most appropriately to the next chapter, we may now take up the consideration of the Civil Articles, and point out briefly and temperately where they were broken or departed from, and thus show what and how great was the breach of faith. It is necessary, in the first place, to give the text of the Treaty, so that each reader may be able to judge the matter for himself, although much of the text is irrelevant, and the space allotted to the affairs of Colonel John Browne reveals the complete absence of any sense of proportion :—

THE TREATY OF LIMERICK

Article 1

The Roman Catholics of this Kingdom shall enjoy such privileges in the exercise of their religion as are consistent with the laws of Ireland, and as they did enjoy in the reign of King Charles II, and their Majesties as soon as their affairs will permit them to summon a Parliament in this Kingdom will endeavour to procure the said Roman Catholics such farther security in that particular, as may preserve them from any disturbance upon the account of their said religion.

Article 2

All the inhabitants or residents of Limerick or any other garrison now in the possession of the Irish and all officers and soldiers now in arms under any commission of King James or those authorized by him to grant the same in the several counties of Limerick, Clare, Kerry, Cork, and Mayo, or any of them (omitted words subsequently restored by Act of Parliament, " and all such as are under their protection in those counties ") ; and all the commissioned officers in their Majesties' quarters that belong to the Irish regiments now in being that are treated with, and who are not prisoners of war, or have taken protection, and who shall return and submit to their Majesties' obedience, and their and every of their heirs shall hold, possess, and enjoy all and every their estates of freehold and inheritance, and all the rights, titles, and interests, privileges and immunities, which they and every or any of them held, enjoyed, or were rightfully and lawfully entitled to in the reign of King Charles II or at any time since by the laws and statutes that were in force in the said reign of King Charles II, and shall be put in possession, by order of the Government, of such of them as are in the King's hands or the hands of his tenants without being put to any suit or trouble therein ; and all such estates shall be freed and discharged from all arrears of crown rents, quit rents, and other public charges incurred and become due since Michaelmas, 1688, to the day of the date hereof ; and all persons comprehended in this article shall have, hold and enjoy all their goods and chattels, real and personal, to them or any of them belonging or remaining either in their own hands or the hands of any persons whatsoever, in trust for or for the use of them or any of them ; and all and every the said persons of what profession, trade or calling soever they be, shall and may use, exercise, and practise their several and respective professions, trades and callings as freely as they did use, exercise, and enjoy the same in the reign of King Charles II provided that nothing in this article contained be construed to extend to or restore any forfeiting person now out of the kingdom except what are hereafter comprised ; provided also that no person whatsoever shall have or enjoy the benefit of this article that shall neglect or refuse to take the oath of allegiance made by Act of Parliament in England in the first year of the reign of their present Majesties, when thereunto required.

Article 3

All merchants or reputed merchants of the City of Limerick or of any other garrison now possessed by the Irish or of any town or place in the counties of Clare or Kerry who are absent beyond the seas, that have not borne arms since their Majesties' declaration in February, 1689, shall have the benefit of the second article in the same manner as if they were present, provided such merchants and reputed merchants do repair into this kingdom within the space of eight months from the date hereof.

Article 4

The following officers, viz. : Colonel Simon Luttrell, Captain Rowland White, Maurice Eustace of Yeomanstown, Chilvers of Maystown, commonly called Mount Leinster, now belonging to the regiments in the aforesaid garrisons and quarters of the Irish army who were beyond the seas and sent thither upon affairs of their respective regiments or the army in general shall have the benefit and advantage of the second article, provided they return hither within the space of eight months from the date of these presents and submit to their Majesties' Government and take the above-mentioned oath.

Article 5

That all and singular the said persons comprized in the second and third articles shall have a general pardon of all attainders, outlawries, treasons, misprisions of treasons, premunires, felonies, trespasses, and other crimes and misdemeanours whatsoever by them or any of them committed since the beginning of the reign of King James II ; and if any of them are attainted by Parliament the Lords Justices and General will use their best endeavours to get the same repealed by Parliament, and the outlawries to be reversed gratis, all but writing clerks' fees.

Article 6

And whereas these present wars have drawn on great violences on both parts, and that if leave were given to the bringing all sorts of private actions the animosities would probably continue that have been too long on foot and the public disturbances last ; for the quieting and settling therefore of this kingdom, and avoiding those inconveniences which would be the necessary consequence of the contrary, no person or persons whatsoever comprised in the foregoing articles shall be sued, molested or impleaded at the suit of any party or parties whatsoever for any trespasses by them committed, or for any arms, horses, money, goods, chattels, merchandizes, provisions whatsoever by them seized or taken during the time of war. And no person or persons whatsoever in the second or third articles comprised shall be sued, impleaded or made accountable for the rents or mean rates of any lands, tenements, or houses by him or them received or enjoyed in this kingdom since the beginning of the present war to the day of the date hereof, nor for any waste or trespass by him or them committed in any such lands, tenements or houses, and it is also agreed that this article shall be mutual and reciprocal on both sides.

Article 7

Every nobleman and gentleman comprised in the said second and third articles shall have liberty to ride with a sword and a case of pistols if they think fit and keep a gun in their houses for the defence of the same or for fowling.

Article 8

The inhabitants and residents in the city of Limerick and other garrisons shall be permitted to remove their goods, chattels, and provisions out of the same without being viewed and searched or paying any manner of duties, and shall not be compelled to leave houses or lodgings they now have for the space of six weeks next ensuing the date hereof.

Article 9

The oath to be administered to such Roman Catholics as submit to their Majesties' Government shall be the oath above-said and no other.

Article 10

No person or persons who shall at any time hereafter break these articles or any of them shall thereby make or cause any other person or persons to forfeit or lose the benefit of the same.

Article 11

The Lords Justices and General do promise to use their utmost endeavours that all the persons comprehended in the above-mentioned articles shall be protected and defended from all arrests and executions for debt or damage for the space of eight months next ensuing the date hereof.

Article 12

Lastly the Lords Justices and General do undertake that their Majesties will ratify these articles within the space of eight months or sooner, and use their utmost endeavours that the same shall be ratified and confirmed in Parliament.

Article 13

And whereas Colonel John Brown stood indebted to several Protestants by judgments of record, which appearing to the late Government, the Lord Tyrconnell and the Lord Lucan took away the effects, the said John Brown had to answer the said debts and promised to clear the said John Brown of the said debts, which effects were taken for the public use of the Irish and their army; for freeing the said Lord Lucan of his said engagement, past on their public account for payment of the said Protestants, and for preventing the ruin of the said John Brown and for satisfaction of his creditors at the instance of the Lord Lucan and the rest of the persons aforesaid, it is agreed that the said Lords Justices and the said Baron de Ginkel shall intercede with the King and Parliament to have the estates secured to Roman Catholics by articles and capitulation in this kingdom charged with and equally liable to the payment of so much of the said debts as the said Lord Lucan, upon stating accounts with the said John Brown, shall certify under his hand that the effects taken from the said Brown amount unto; which account is to be stated, and the balance certified by the said Lord Lucan in one-and-twenty days after the date hereof.

For the true performance hereof we have hereunto set our hands: Charles Porter, Thomas Coningsby, Baron de Ginkel, Present, Scravenmore, H. Mackay, T. Talmach.

The Articles of this Treaty which were broken or materially deviated from are those numbered 1, 2, 5, 7 and 9. It is unnecessary to refer to the eight others. Of all these articles the language is clear and unambiguous with the exception of Article 2, which is involved, cumbrous, and bristling with qualifications and provisos. The Jacobite Commissioners, of whom Sir

Toby Butler seems to have taken the leading part in the drafting, were not very successful in putting into clear English the exact rights conceded by that article, and the exact classes of the Irish community which were to benefit by them. The exclusion from its benefits of those who were " prisoners of war," or " who have taken protection " was a flagrant error, and opened the door for subsequent exclusions and a general whittling away of the benefits themselves.

We may now take the points seriatim. With regard to Article 1 its purport relates to the religion of the mass of the Irish people, which in the seventeenth as in the twentieth century was and is that of the Church of Rome. This article pledged the English Government to allow " the Roman Catholics of this Kingdom " to " enjoy such privileges in the exercise of their religion as are consistent with the laws of Ireland, or as they did enjoy in the reign of King Charles the Second." The qualification, " as are consistent with the laws of Ireland," was a perilous term to introduce, for it subjected the privilege to the risk of hindrance or curtailment by future legislation, and the danger was only partially obviated by the addition of the promise on behalf of King William and Queen Mary to " summon a parliament in this kingdom," and " endeavour to procure the said Roman Catholics such further security in that particular as may preserve them from any disturbance upon the account of their said religion."

The first article, then, ensured for the Roman Catholics what was supposed to be complete liberty for the exercise of their religion. They were to revert to the position in 1688, before the outbreak of the war. Complete liberty in the exercise of one's religion naturally carries with it the maintenance of the hierarchy of the Church to which one belongs. Religious liberty cannot be said to be perfect because laymen can go to Church, if the bishops and clergy of that Church are at the same time driven out of the country.

One of the points raised by those who deny that the

Articles of Limerick were violated is as to the ratification of the Treaty, which by Article 12 was to be done within the space of eight months. One writer in 1825 went so far as to declare that the Treaty was " never ratified." It is only necessary to state that William and Mary ratified it on April 5, 1692, and the ratification is noteworthy because the introduction of the following sentence (" as words casually omitted by the writer "), " and all such as are under their protection in the said counties " was sanctioned by sign manual. In April nothing whatever had happened to ruffle William's temper about the Irish, or to make him think that his position was threatened by the Irishmen who had been in Limerick. But during the following summer the Irish army was assembled in Normandy for the invasion of England, and the greatest peril that had ever confronted him was only averted by the fortunate naval victory off Cape La Hogue. At Steinkerk, two months later, he saw the Irish contingent opposed to him.

When his first Irish Parliament assembled in the autumn of 1692, William was less anxious for these reasons to abide by the terms of the Treaty, and more disposed to leave his Irish legislature a free hand in establishing Protestant ascendancy. The Dublin Parliament knew very well what to do. The Articles of the Treaty had necessarily to be incorporated in the Statute Book to make them the valid law of the land. They concluded their deliberations by enacting only Articles 2 (radically altered), 3, 4, 5 and 6, ignoring and suppressing the eight others.

William's resentment towards the Irish Catholics continued to grow throughout the campaigns of 1692–5 in Flanders, where he received personal proof that they had become a valuable auxiliary to an enemy who was already too strong for him. The successive Irish Parliaments between 1692 and 1697 continued to display a desire not merely to disregard the terms of the Treaty, but even to extirpate the Roman Catholic religion. But it was only when the peace negotiations which led to the Treaty of

s

Ryswyck were set on foot that William found time to give personal attention to the affairs of that country. In the meantime his animosity towards the Irish, or to put it in another form, his conviction as to their being a hostile nation, had become intensified by his later experiences. The bulk of the Irish troops in his own army had deserted to the enemy in France and Spain, until at last in self-defence he had framed an order dismissing all Irishmen from his army and forbidding their being recruited at all. At the same time the Irish exiles had become a notable part of the French armies which were defeating his forces and those of his allies in Flanders and Italy, on the Rhine and in the Pyrenees. Instead of being anxious to enlarge the privileges conferred in Article 1 of the Treaty in accordance with its concluding passage, William not unintelligibly was more inclined to avail himself of any loophole to curtail them.

When men or governments decide to break their words they discover some excuse in the language of the promise or oath which bound them. At the time it was made it was simply an engagement to do a certain thing, and there was no intention not to do it. But reflection, or the introduction of new views and conditions, alters the standpoint, and the concession becomes repugnant. That was William's case. In 1691 he wanted to get his own troops out of Ireland. To that everything else was subordinate. He would have consented to almost any terms that ensured that object. He let the Irish troops leave to swell the French armies. He promised the Irish Catholics the free exercise of their religion.

But by 1697 it had been brought home to him very forcibly that the Irish were his opponents, and when he asked himself why they were his opponents he could only reply : " Because they are Catholics." He approached the solution of Irish questions in 1697-8, therefore, in a very different spirit from what had been the case in 1691. He was no longer even indifferent, the state of his mind was vindictive. What he forgot was that England, in his name, had passed her word to the Sister Island that she should have religious liberty, and in his vindictive mood he not merely broke that word, but revived that racial and religious antipathy which, if faith had only been kept, would have died out instead of being aggravated and fanned to a flame in the eighteenth century. William of Orange, a mere passing figure on the stage of English History, cast not merely a stigma on English honour, but also embroiled and embittered the relations between Englishmen and Irishmen for two hundred years. As an alien he knew nothing about our insular relationships, and his intervention in the Irish question might be styled a most disastrous instance of foreign interference with them. The Dutch are perhaps, of all continental peoples, the closest in resemblance to the English, but the gulf between them is still wide, whereas the English and Irish races are and have always been in all essential features the same people.

The first article provided that the Catholics should have the free exercise of their religion " as they did enjoy in the reign of King Charles II." Charles II reigned twenty-five years, and during the greater part of that period the Catholics were free in all senses and respects to follow their religion ; but there was a brief interval when this was not the case. During the period of the " No Popery " craze and the spurious Titus Oates plot there was repression in Ireland. Bishops, heads of orders, Jesuits, were expelled from the country, or, if they remained, arrested and thrown into prison. Catholics were also debarred from holding office, no Catholic was allowed to sit in Council, no Catholic was permitted to be armed, and this was the general position of affairs between 1678 and 1685, when James sent over Tyrconnell to rectify them. This period of repression occurred " in the reign of King Charles II." To have provided against the possibility of an infraction the drafters of the Treaty on behalf of the Irish party should have used the words " in the reign of King Charles II prior to the

year 1678." But to have done so would have been to cast
an uncalled-for reproach on the honour of English plenipotentiaries. No one who reads the text of the article will
have any doubt that what was conceded by it was complete
religious toleration.

But when the question was taken up in 1697 by a Protestant House of Commons in Dublin and a resentful King
in London, the dominant feeling was not to respect the
promise, but to read some restrictions and diminutions
into the conditions. It was decided in an arbitrary and
high-handed manner that " as in the reign of King Charles
II " meant " as in 1678-9 " when penal laws were in force
and no Catholic prelate was permitted to remain in the
country. The Catholics were not allowed a hearing. The
plenipotentiaries who had given up Limerick were, with the
exception of Lord Lucan, all living, and could have been
called in to testify to the conversations and discussions as to
what was meant ; but no reference would have been entertained. The Dublin Parliament passed a law banishing for
ever the hierarchy of the Roman Catholic Church. This
was intended as the first step towards uprooting the Roman
Catholic religion, which the Treaty promised to leave
unhindered and tolerated. But the history of the world
shows that religious convictions, when firmly held, are not
to be uprooted by persecution. Ireland remained, so far as
the native Irish were concerned, not less Catholic for the
loss of its Church leaders. What remained still more fixed
in the national mind was that England had played false
and broken her word; and this was unfortunately true and
deplorable.

It is to the credit of the Irish House of Lords that they
refused to be a party to the transaction. In some way that
has never been explained they stood aside, but the protest
of the dissenting peers remains on record. In their opinion
" not one of the Articles in the Treaty of Limerick is fully
confirmed." They declared that those who were nominally
intended to benefit by the Treaty were " put in a worse

position than they were in before." It is impossible to doubt that this statement was literally true.

We may pass now to the second article which, with all its cumbrous and involved terms and phrases, seems to have been drafted for the special purpose of creating disputes and differences of opinion. The restoration of estates and rights and the permission to exercise certain specified professions were restricted in a sense that the framers of the article never contemplated. In the first place, all prisoners of war were excluded from its benefit. This was an extraordinary blunder on the part of the Irish negotiators. To give only one instance, Lord Kenmare, who had done so much for the Jacobite cause, was excluded from the benefit of this article because he was one of the Aughrim prisoners in Dublin. A still larger number of persons were affected by the limitation of the right to practise the specified professions to the five counties of Limerick, Clare, Kerry, Cork, and Mayo. Throughout the rest of Ireland the Catholics were debarred from the liberal professions. In this matter the drafting of the article was faulty, and the Irish Commissioners showed incompetency. On the other hand, it is dubious whether the greatest competency and clearness would have availed to prevent an intentional breach of faith.

The fifth article, which was an amplification of the second, was broken by the refusal to surrender Lord Clancarty and others who were kept several years in prison, some, indeed, till the Peace of Ryswyck.

The seventh article, allowing the Catholic gentry to carry arms, was broken the very next year by the Irish Parliament, which simply ignored it and ordered the disarmament of all Catholics. The excuse given for this order was the assembly of James's Irish army in Normandy for the invasion of England. But when that danger passed away the disarmament edict was still rigorously enforced; the only concession made was in the case of a few particularly favoured persons who had the right given them to carry a sword by special license.

The breach of the ninth article was still more flagrant. This article reiterates the stipulation in Article 2 that the only oath to be required from the persons accepting the benefits of the Convention was to be that of allegiance " made by Act of Parliament in England in the first year of William and Mary." There was nothing in this oath incompatible with the religious views of the Catholics. It was a simple recognition of the *de facto* Government. There was nothing in it against the Pope or James II.

Many instances occurred in the Parliaments of 1692, 1695, and 1696 of persons (peers and commoners) refusing to take the additional oath required of them. There is not a case of any one refusing to take the oath of allegiance. But at the conclusion the officials of both Houses called upon the member to take " the new oath," and this was invariably refused by all the Catholics, whereupon their titles or seats were declared forfeited or vacant. The new oath was the Declaration of the English Parliament in favour of William and Mary, and the upholding of the Protestant religion with its minatory clauses against the Church of Rome. Considering that the simple oath of allegiance had been stipulated for in the Treaty of Limerick for the express purpose of avoiding the new English oath (already in force in England), it is impossible to see in the procedure anything but a flagrant breach of the Treaty of Peace which ended the war in Ireland.

An attempt was made in 1698 to pass a new oath calling upon the taker to denounce the Pope's spiritual power. This was found, however, to be going too far and was withdrawn, but the reason for doing so had nothing to do with Ireland. It was due to the curious anomaly that the Pope of the day was on the side of the Emperor of Germany and against the King of France, and thus indirectly an ally of William of Orange.

In 1703 a new oath was introduced, that of abjuration, by which the taker swore that " James Stuart, now residing at St. Germains in France, hath not any title whatsoever to the Crown of Great Britain." The taking of this oath was declared to be obligatory on all those persons practising a profession, who by the Limerick Convention would have escaped with the simple oath of allegiance. The refusal to take the oath was a permanent disqualification, and probably entailed serious after-consequences, of which banishment would have been the least irksome. The imposition of oaths, which could not possibly be taken by Catholics, was the method adopted as the easiest for expelling Catholics from all dignities, offices and the learned professions.

Among the minor provisions of the No Popery Bill may be mentioned the following :—

It was made a penal offence to send Catholic children out of the country to be educated ; at the same time no schools were allowed in the country. The children had to be taught in the open air, whence the origin of hedge schools. The law of inheritance by primogeniture was abolished among Catholics. No Catholic could vote till he had taken the oath of abjuration, which his religion forbade him to take. No priest was to come into the country. The parish priests were to be registered. Papist Archbishops, Vicar-Generals, Deans, Jesuits, Monks, and Friars were to be transported. Finally, Catholics were debarred from settling in either Limerick or Galway.

Enough has been said to show, without exciting controversy or accentuating bitter feelings, that the Limerick Treaty was broken, and without excuse so far as its unoffending beneficiaries were concerned. They had done nothing to deserve the treatment they received. Love of country had kept them at home, when so many of their fellow-countrymen, moved by the love of arms, went into exile to fight under foreign flags. Yet the following statement made by Count Gerald O'Connor, a general in the French army, after a visit to Ireland in 1720, may be deemed of interest as confirming the views that have been expressed :—

" The Treaty of Limerick, I have said, had been shamefully broken. Catholics had not only been cheated out of their estates by hundreds; they had universally been deprived, which was far worse, of the rights and privileges which had been guaranteed to them. The Colonial Parliament, with the full consent of the men in power in England, made a series of laws which placed the Irish Catholic in a position of permanent and degrading bondage, in some respects worse than when he was under the iron rule of Cromwell. The Irish Catholic was forbidden to buy land or even to have an encumbrance on it; he could not acquire a house or an acre in his own country. The Catholic who happened to be still an owner of land was subjected to a kind of social torture; his estate was made to descend in such a manner as to crumble away; his family was barbarously tempted to become his foe; the law watched at his hearth to make him wretched. The Catholic community of all classes was prohibited from rising in most walks of life; they were shut out from nearly all professions and callings; in some towns they could not even appear as traders. These laws, in a word, were passed to make the Irish Catholic a slave, to brutalise him and to debase his being; in many of the relations of life he was a mere outcast, he was, indeed, usually described as 'the Papist, the dangerous and common enemy.'

" And as it was with our people so was it with our Church. Our priesthood were not slain or banished as in the days of Cromwell, but they were persecuted in a variety of ways; they were compelled to give an account of themselves to the Government, and their hierarchy was not permitted to set foot in Ireland. The few Catholic owners of land who remained at home obscurely vegetated on their estates, and ceased to be the national leaders and guides of their people. The great mass of our race, excluded from the pursuits of industry and unable to better itself in the affairs of life, sank back on the land in abject thraldom and formed a poor and down-trodden peasantry repeatedly on the very brink of starvation. . . .

" As for our priesthood, persecuted and jealously watched as they were, they did the offices of Holy Church, sometimes in miserable hovels and sometimes in the open air, but they kept the Lamp of Life shining amidst the darkness around, and they saved our race from sinking into the depths of savage human nature."

There was one other person whose opinion about the Limerick Convention deserves to be quoted. But for James II there need not have been any such Convention at all. It was the taking up of the Stuart cause by the Irish nation that led to the war and the peace. But for that the picked manhood of Ireland might have stayed at home, with great advantage to their own country, and in the end to England and the Empire. If they had remained at home the Protestant tyranny could not have been attempted. It was only possible because the best manhood of the country had left it. James did not think of these things. His comments on the event show that he only rejoiced because the arrival of so large an army, which was to be under his own direct orders, would enable him to pose more as the ally than as the mere pensioner and dependent of the King of France. Here are his own words :—

" . . . Yet they had the courage to insist upon, and the dexterity to obtain, articles not only for their own security, but which had a respect to the whole kingdom ; consulting in the first place the King's honour and advantage in getting permission to go and even ships to transport them and all others into France who were desirous to follow their Prince's fortune and adhere to his service ; which, with what went before, brought into that kingdom first and last near 30,000 men. In the next place they articled for as free an exercise of the Catholic religion as in King Charles the Second's time, and a promise to procure a further security from any disturbance on that account ; that all the inhabitants of Limerick, all officers and soldiers in the Army, garrisons, or Countys of Limerick, Clare, Kerry, Corke and Mayo should upon submission be restored to their Estates they were in possession of in King Charles the Second's time; all persons to exercise their trades and follow their professions, possess their goods, cattles (chattels ?), etc., as before the war, and in fine a general indempnity for all such as had been concerned in it; which had the English kept as religiously as such agreements ought to be observed, the world had not seen so many crying examples of antient and noble famelys reduced to the last degree of indigence only for adhering to their Prince in just defence of his rights, when he came in person to demand their succour, which all Laws both human and divine obliged them to; for even that senceless cant word of Abdication, which was the poor and only excuse for their unnatural rebellion in England, had not the least shaddow of pretext in Ireland unless the King's comeing into a country he had never been in before, and governing a kingdom in person he had hitherto governed by a deputy, must be accounted an abandoning of it by the parliamentary logic of our days.

"Thus was Ireland, after an obstinate resistance in three years' campaigns, by the power and riches of England and the revolt of almost all its own Protestant subjects, torn from its natural Sovereign, who though he was divested of the country, he was not wholly deprived of the profits, for the greatest part of those who were then in arms for defence of his right, not content with the service already rendered, got leave (as was sayd) to come and loos their lives after having lost their estates in defence of his title, and brought by that means such a body of men into France as by their generous comportment in accepting the pay of the country, instead of that which is usually allowed there to strangers, and their inimitable valour and service during the whole cours of the war, might justly make their Prince pass for an Ally rather than a Pentioner or burthen to his Most Christian Majesty, whose pay indeed they received, but acted by the King their Master's Commission."

Chapter XII

THE IRISH ARRIVE IN FRANCE

THE French squadron, under the command of the Count de Château Renaud, which reached the Shannon on October 30, 1691, included twenty merchantmen, and thus the task of conveying the Irish troops to France was simplified and hastened. But anxious as the French admiral was to depart, he was dependent on a favourable wind to get out of the river and round the dangerous headlands of Kerry. Several times the poor Irish troops were placed on board and then disembarked because the passage could not be attempted, and it was not till the month of November was almost ended that the favourable opportunity arrived. Once out of the river the ships made a good passage, and all reached Brest without loss or accident between December 5 and 7.

According to one account, there were on board the French ships 4750 Irish troops, including officers, and these were divided into 3100 infantry, 1350 cavalry, and 300 dragoons. Practically speaking, all the Irish cavalry that emigrated sailed with Château Renaud, and although no specific mention is made of them it may be concluded that the 900 horses allowed to leave the country under the terms of the treaty were also on board. As the cavalry camp was south-west of Limerick and nearer Scattery, the highest point the French ships got to, than the city itself, it was natural that the mounted men should leave by them. Besides, this arrangement saved Ginkel the responsibility and trouble of providing forage, as he would have had to do if the cavalry had marched by road to Cork.

There is a fuller report of the Irish troops that came with Château Renaud among the French records than any yet published. The following details are interesting :—

Colonels	23	
Lt.-Colonels	21	
Majors	45	Total of Officers 792
Captains	230	
Lieutenants	227	
Ensigns	246	
Private Persons		29
Soldiers		4726
Servants (including 130 with French officers)		234
		———
		5781

In addition to the men were 552 women and 266 children. Among the private persons were Sir Richard Nagle, Mr. Plowden, and the other civil members of what was James's Government in Ireland. Immediately on arrival Lord Trimlestown, whom the French liked and who was declared by them to be a man of merit, was sent to St. Germains to announce to King James the arrival of the first part of his army. With a view to facilitating the handling of the force, and also no doubt to simplify the rationing of so many new arrivals, the troops were disposed in small garrisons throughout Brittany. Here is a first list as they were quartered on December 12 :—

Rennes	1100	St. Brieux	400
Malstout	300	Château Landin	200
Ploërmel	400	Pintrieux	200
La Trinité	200	Goungarille	200
Monmoutier	300	Redon	800
Pambast	400	Vannes	1000

Total, 5500 men (officers included).

There is consequently practical agreement between the different French reports as to the number of Irish that came over with Château Renaud. The belief in France at the time was that Sarsfield would bring four or five thousand more. As a matter of fact he brought nearly 7000 men.

A few days after Château Renaud sailed from Scattery, Sarsfield set out on the march for Cork, where he found thirty-eight merchantmen assembled for the conveyance of his force. Having got his men on board he signed the release for General Ginkel, already mentioned. He sailed on December 19 and reached Brest on the 27th, nearly three weeks after the arrival of the first division.

Unlike his predecessor, he had a very stormy passage, and the fleet scattered in the gale had to make for the most convenient port, some ships reaching St. Malo and others Brest. The troops, unaccustomed to the sea, suffered great hardships, but as nothing is said in the various reports of any losses, it may be concluded that there were none of any account. Whatever other good qualities the Irish emigrants possessed, they were not good in placing their own thoughts on paper, and it is a very remarkable fact that not a single Irish officer has left us any record of the events of the war in Ireland or of the formation of the Irish Brigade. Lord Clare's letter after Ramillies is the only piece of writing by an Irish author in the twenty odd years that closed with the Peace of Utrecht. It is true that some years ago the late Mr. O'Connor Morris gave us what he called the Memoirs of his remote kinsman, Count Gerald O'Connor, but their value, owing to the method adopted by the editor, is very uncertain. Here follows, however, what purports to be the only report left by an eye-witness of the scene at Cork :—

" Hundreds of the soldiers were in rags and unshod, but all bore themselves well and had a dauntless aspect. It had been agreed that the men who were to take service in France were to defile beyond an appointed spot ; those who were willing to remain were to turn away. The choice of the immense majority was soon seen ; some 11,000 passed beyond the selected point ; some 2000 went quietly to their homes. Scarcely 1000 threw in their lot with Ginkel. Sarsfield looked on with pride at the spectacle exhibiting the noble spirit of our race. ' These men,' he said, ' are leaving all that is most dear in life for a strange land in which they will have to endure much, to serve in an army that hardly knows our people ; but they are true to Ireland and have still hopes for her cause ; we will make another Ireland in the armies of the great King of France.' The transports from Limerick were soon under way ; loud wailing was heard from the adjoining shores as the departing sails glided down the Shannon ; a few of the soldiery on board escaped by swimming, but nearly all remained faithful to their heroic choice. Some regiments, however, had to march a long distance to Cork ; I was in the company of Sarsfield with these ; the temptation was too strong for some failing hearts ; hundreds deserted and were never seen again. A woeful sight was seen on the Lee when the transports set sail ; Sarsfield had promised the exiles who had embarked that their families were to go with them to France. There was no room in the ships to enable the pledge to be fulfilled. Loud cries and lamentation broke from the wives and children who had been left behind ; some dashed into the stream and perished in its depths ; some clung to the boats that were making off from the shore ; many of the men, husbands or fathers, plunged into the waters ; not a few lost their lives in their efforts to reach the dry ground. Nevertheless, the mass of our army arrived in France in safety."

On December 8 Louis XIV appointed Sir Andrew Lee his Inspector-General of the Irish troops, and sent him express to Brittany to report on the new arrivals. But he had another and more pressing mission. He was to pick out 600 of the best Irish troops and to send them off at once to join the Irish regiments in Savoy. The French authorities considered that they had been owed on balance 600 recruits for the Mountcashell Brigade from the time of St. Ruth's being sent to Ireland, and having now got the opportunity they proceeded to pay themselves. Of course, King James was a party to this transaction and issued his commission for the purpose.

By way of compensation for this abstraction from the force, all English, Irish and Scottish troops unattached in France were ordered to join the Irish troops in Brittany. Among these were about 100 Scottish officers—the survivors of Dundee's army—under Colonel Cannon, who were temporarily quartered at Calais. A second and larger contingent was supplied by the garrison of Cork, which had surrendered to Marlborough in October, 1690, on the honourable conditio that they were to be conveyed to Flanders and exchanged for Prussian, Huguenot, and Danish prisoners held by France. Never were conditions of war more flagrantly broken than these were by William of Orange. It will be remembered that even while still at Cork the English were accused of leaving the wounded Irish to die and rot in a tower in the midst of the camp, so that they might spread pestilence amongst the force that had surrendered.

As I fail to find any corroboration of this popular belief in the available records, I do not accept the story, but there can be no doubt that there was great delay in furnishing the ships to convey the surrendered garrison to Ostend, that when they arrived they were few in number and badly supplied, and that the unfortunate Irish suffered much unfair and unnecessary hardship. When the fleet did sail it encountered a severe gale, and was dispersed, some ships beating into Milford Haven and others into Plymouth. The officers, more fortunate, had accompanied Marlborough and been duly interned in the Tower, where they were awaiting the orders of the British Government to join their men at Ostend.

It was April, 1691, before this reunion took place, and then the Irish troops were locked up there and in Bruges. No arrangements had been made for their reception, and the sufferings and hardships undergone defy description. So intolerable did these become that the Irish officers resorted to violence in an attempt to remedy them, whereupon they were placed in chains. The arrangement was that they were to be exchanged for foreign, that is to say non-Dutch, prisoners in the hands of the French, but the French authorities had not been a party to the arrangement, and William never informed them. His plan was to leave the starving soldiery no alternative save to enter the service of the Emperor and to proceed to Hungary to fight the Turks. The French report states that " although subjected to the harshest treatment they held out loyally."

At last Colonel John Barrett and another officer were allowed to go to France to see about arranging for the exchange, but afterwards the Dutch Commissioners complained of the delay of the French, and threatened to ship off all the Irish to America. While these negotiations were in progress a large number of the Irish officers escaped from Bruges and made their way to Lille. The names (among which I wish to take note of three Kavanaghs and one Boulger) are given in the French report of ninety-three officers as those who escaped from Bruges. They were divided in rank as follows : 3 majors, 29 captains, 25 lieutenants, 27 ensigns, and 9 cadets.

James intended sending these officers back to Ireland, and it is not improbable that some of them were on board the fleet with Château Renaud. But in any case they never landed in Ireland, and were back in France at the end of 1691 and thereupon incorporated in the Brigade. As to the Irish soldiers at Bruges and Ostend, it is not certain that all of them ever reached France, although the bulk of them no doubt did so sooner or later. Indeed, I have reason to think that one regiment, at least, found its way to Germany and eventually entered the service of the King of Poland and Saxony, but its adventures belong to another scene and another story.

If we add to the troops that came with Château Renaud those brought by Sarsfield and the portion of the Cork garrison that escaped from Belgium, we get a total of about 14,000 Irishmen for the French service, independent of the original Mountcashell Brigade. This total practically agrees with that given by the Duke of Berwick in his Memoirs, where he states that there were 20,000 Irish troops, or thereabouts, in the French service. We will now proceed to show what was done with them, and how the force was re-formed in order to make it accord with the system and organisation of the French army. But before entering into these details, it will be proper to give the text of the letter in which James welcomed the loyal Irish troops on their arrival in France.

" James, Rex. Having been informed of the capitulation and surrender of Limerick and of the other places which remained to us in our kingdom of Ireland, and of the necessity that forced the Lords Justices and General officers of our forces thereunto, we shall not defer to let you know and the rest of the officers that came along with you, that we are extremely satisfied with your and their conduct, and of the valour of the soldiers during the siege, and most particularly of your and their declaration and resolution to come and serve where we are. And we assure you and order you to assure both officers and soldiers that are come along with you that we shall never forget this act of loyalty, nor fail when in a capacity to give them above others a particular mark of our favour. In the meantime you are to inform them that they are to serve under our command and by our commissions. And if we find that a considerable number is come with the fleet it will induce us to go personally to see them and regiment them. Our brother the King of France hath already given orders to clothe them and furnish them with all necessaries, and to give them quarters for their refreshment. So we bid you heartily farewell.

" Given at our Court at St. Germains, November 27, 1691." (Evidently O.S.)

The Irish troops having arrived in sufficient numbers, James fulfilled his promise to come and see them. On December 15 he left for Brest, accompanied by the Duke of Berwick, for the purpose of inspecting the new force, and as

T

a special favour from the King of France he brought the news that the Irish were to have red coats instead of the grey in which they had fought at Aughrim and Limerick.

The Capitulations by which the Irish troops were to be paid by the French Government began with the statement that " the King of France is very well satisfied with the Irish troops already in his service," and then set forth the details of pay for the various ranks. The Irish received " *la petite solde*," that is to say the same as the French soldier, whereas the Swiss and German mercenaries were paid at a higher rate. From every point of view, then, the Irish contingent was a valuable addition to French resources ; the only limitation to its value being that it was for a time subject to the orders of James alone, and not to those of Louis.

The agreement sets forth that the force is to be subject only to the laws of discipline of the King of England, and the following order in the grades of commanding officers was formally recognised on the part of the King of France. They were to be General, Lieutenant-General, Maréchal de camp, Brigadier-General, Major-General, Quartermaster-General, and Adjutant-General. As a matter of fact, James never appointed any of his officers to the grade of full General, and several of the other ranks also were never filled.

The process of regimenting the force went through several stages, and James's own plan, as described by Dangeau under date January 5, 1692, was not carried out. Here we read that: " King James has formed seven regiments of 1400 men each in two battalions and one regiment of cavalry of 600 men, giving a total of 10,400 men. It is believed that Sarsfield has brought 4000 or 5000 more troops with him."

This arrangement did not accord with the French system, and finally the views of the French authorities prevailed. It was decided that each battalion should be composed of sixteen companies of 50 men apiece, with 3 officers, 8 non-commissioned officers, 1 trumpeter, and 1 drummer—so that a battalion contained 48 officers, 128 non-commissioned officers, 32 for the band (who were also to be tailors and shoemakers), and 800 privates, or about 1000 men in all. The nine regiments of Berwick's list and the eight of Mr. O'Callaghan's were finally reduced to six. Their names and those of their first Colonels-in-chief were :—

Regiment	Colonel
The Guards	William Dorington
The Queen's	John Wauchope
The Marine	Henry FitzJames (The Lord Prior)
Dublin	Simon Luttrell
Limerick	Richard Talbot
Charlemont	Gordon O'Neil

This gave an infantry force of 12,000 men.

With regard to the cavalry two troops of Horse Guards were first formed of 100 men each, as the personal body-guard of King James at St. Germains, or when he took the field. As a matter of fact, they took part in the campaigns of 1692–3 without him. The first troop was commanded by the Duke of Berwick and the second by Sarsfield, Earl of Lucan. Both Berwick and Lee reported that these troops were as fine as any in the French service, and when they reached St. Germains, later on in the year 1692, Louis nominated three officers of the Maison du Roi to train them after the fashion of his own corps.

The following are the names of the officers in the first list :—

THE FIRST TROOP
Commander, Duke of Berwick

Officers under him

Major-General Sutherland
Colonel Christopher Nugent
Lord Trimlestown
Francis La Rue
Matthew Cook

Corporals or Brigadiers

Robert Preston
Maurice Dillon
Brian Carroll
Thomas Bietagh
George Rienan

THE SECOND TROOP
Commander, Patrick Sarsfield, Earl of Lucan

Officers under him

Charles O'Brien

Nicholas Cusack

John Gaydon

Robert Arthur

Corporals or Brigadiers

Edward Broghall

Edward Plunkett

Edward O'Brien

George White

Francis Bada

Besides the Household troops two cavalry regiments were formed, each containing two squadrons of 186 officers and men, or 372 men per regiment. They were called the King's and Queen's regiments respectively. Dominic Sheldon (Lieutenant-General) was the Colonel of the former, and Piers Butler, Lord Galmoye, of the latter. Among these and the bodyguard the 900 horses brought from Ireland were distributed.

Finally two regiments of dismounted dragoons were formed. The first called the Royal regiment was commanded by Lieutenant-General Thomas Maxwell, and the second named the Queen's was placed under the orders of Major-General Francis Carroll. Each of these numbered 558 officers and men.

The total strength of King James's Irish army after it was re-formed and regimented in Brittany was then as follows :—

Two troops of Horse Guards	=	200
Two regiments of Cavalry	=	744
Total of Mounted Troops		944
Two regiments of Foot Dragoons	=	1116
Six regiments (twelve battalions) of infantry	=	12,000
Grand Total		14,060

There were also three so-called Independent Companies

with a total of 201 men, but these were gradually merged in the main body, and disappeared from the roster.

After this force had been organised it was discovered that there were about 1000 Irish troops over, and with these and others already sent to Savoy the three regiments of the Mountcashell Brigade were given an extra battalion apiece, raising each of these regiments to a total of 2013 men besides officers.   Over and above these figures the French fleet secured nearly a thousand Irishmen as sailors, and a few of the Irish colonels complained that some of their best men were being taken away from them for sea service.   Nine Irish officers, whose names appear in the list printed by William Weston, King James's printer at St. Germains, were also appointed to command privateers operating from St. Malo.

The voluminous reports of the French intendants sent from Paris to superintend the clothing and arming of the Irish troops contain much of interest, and although they are not in accord on all points, they agree in one, and that is as to the fine physique of the men themselves. The phrase occurs frequently " *ils sont des gars très beaux*." Of the officers they had not such a high opinion as of the men, for " many of them were old and slow "—adding, with a cheerful note—" but these can be soon weeded out." They also showed their good sense and their desire that the experiment should succeed by removing a cause of friction.

A certain number of Frenchmen had continued to serve in Ireland down to the end of the war, and it came out that many of them had lent their Irish comrades money. As there was no possibility of these sums ever being repaid the French officers were removed as quickly as possible to garrisons where there were no Irish troops. It cannot be disputed that the French authorities did everything in their power to ensure the success of the experiment, and to remedy without too much interference the defects due to the very imperfect discipline of the Irish army. Thanks to the efforts of Lee and the Duke of Berwick, who aided the

French in their difficult task, order was evolved out of the confusion inseparable from the task of dealing with foreigners, who did not know the language of the country in which they had arrived.

Having got control of a considerable Irish army the uppermost question with the French Government was how to make use of it, and to secure some equivalent for the great expense to which it had gone in equipping it. It is possible that the dual control to which it was subjected embarrassed the French authorities, but certainly the steps taken did not reveal any great intelligence in the French Cabinet. The perfectly obvious course to anyone who understood the circumstances of the case and also the Irish character was to have marched the whole corps into Flanders to join the army of Luxemburg, with the assurance that there they would have the chance of settling their score with William of Orange. If the Marshal had had the disposal of these 14,000 men the campaign of 1692 should not have seen only the barren victory of Steinkerk, but the expulsion of the Dutch from the greater part of what is modern Belgium.

But the French idea was to break up the force into separate detachments, some for Savoy, others for Roussillon, the Rhine and local garrisons, of which Metz was the most important. As a matter of fact, the two regiments of dismounted dragoons, under Maxwell and Carroll, were sent off at once to Savoy, where it was considered that they would be specially valuable in dealing with the Barbets. But before any further dislocation of the force took place there was a remarkable change of plans at Paris.

It is only natural to suppose that James felt his hopes revive when he reviewed his Irish soldiers in the full bravery of their new scarlet uniforms. He saw before him the force with which England might be recovered, and it was his own force entirely, amenable, as Louis informed him, to himself alone. Providence had furnished him with the means of making one more bid for his lost Crown. James was back at St. Germains in February, 1692, and Louis was busily occupied with his plans for the coming campaign. Louis proposed to take the field himself in Flanders, and to conduct in person the siege of Namur. All the appointments had been duly made, to each of the prominent actors a rôle had been assigned, and as for the Irish troops, out of Savoy and Roussillon, they were to be given a passive and secondary part. At this moment James returned from Brittany.

He was full of hope and confidence about his prospects of recovering the English throne with the fine army he had received out of Ireland, and after a few consultations Louis, who since the death of Louvois was his own chief Minister, became infected with his guest's enthusiasm and assented to his proposals. To tell the truth, Louis was in a somewhat awkward position in regard to his guest in this matter. He had told James that the Irish army was his own, and all the arrangements had been on that basis. How could he oppose James when he proposed to use his own troops for his own service ? There was no choice but to acquiesce.

But James did not base his hopes entirely, or perhaps even mainly, on the Irish soldiers. His agents in England assured him that there was great discontent in the country. They also got up an intrigue with two of the English admirals, Admiral Russell and Vice-Admiral Richard Carter, and James, who had known them both in earlier days, felt satisfied that they would come over and bring with them half the fleet. So confident was the King of their adhesion, that he entirely ignored their own reservation, which was that " there should be no fighting," and that " on no account was the French fleet to be present " when they and those who followed them should throw off their allegiance to King William and attach themselves to the side of King James. Russell was a brave and capable seaman, but the condition he attached to his coming over shows him to have been either a most astute person or a

fool. He was astute if he qualified his second act of disloyalty with an impossible condition ; he was a fool if he
thought that the part of the English fleet he hoped to
detach from William could hold its own against the Dutch
without the aid of the French. James's confidence had
been abused so often that it is surprising to find him once
more childishly credulous about these assurances. Among the
public men of England at that moment there was not one
whose word could be implicitly relied on, and Carter,
before the hour of defection arrived, informed the Queen,
who was acting as sole ruler while her husband was in
Flanders, of the whole transaction. James was nursing the
hope that the better half of the English fleet would come
over to his side at the very moment that the conspirators
had repented and given the existing Government full
assurance that they would fight to the death.

The defection of the Navy was only part of a general
plot for the restoration of James, which looked so promising
about this time. It had been engineered by Lord
Preston (James's accredited agent), Mr. John Ashton, and
Mr. Cross. The Marlboroughs were deeply implicated in
it, and the Princess Anne had promised to return to her
obedience to her father. But at the end of 1691 it had become
known in London that there was a Jacobite movement of
more than usual importance afoot. Preston was arrested,
and to save his life confessed all that he knew and rather
more. Ashton and Cross were also arrested and promptly
executed. The more important conspirators were warned
by their friends to destroy their papers and show great
circumspection. James continued to regard the plot as in
full activity at a time when the intended participators had
abandoned all interest in it and were thinking only of saving
their own necks.

Having induced Louis to fall in with his plans and to
promise him the naval and military support he needed,
James drew up, with the assistance of his Lord Chancellor
Herbert, a Declaration intended to convince his English

subjects that there would be no interference with their religion, and that all the foreign troops he brought with him should be sent back to their own country as soon as he, their lawful King, had been restored to the throne of his ancestors. A free pardon was promised to the nation at large, with a reservation as to certain persons whose names filled a long list. Amongst these were persons of great account like Sunderland and Ormonde, and of little account like the common people of Faversham, who had offered James personal indignities, and the jurymen who had taken part in "the barbarous murder of Mr. John Ashton and Mr. Cross." The Declaration did James a great deal of harm. The public fastened not on the pledges, but on the reservations.

Louis, having assented to the expedition, did everything in his power to ensure its success. He appointed Marshal Bellefonds to the command-in-chief, and de Tessé to assist him as Lieutenant-General on account of his knowledge of the Irish. He sanctioned the employment of as many French troops as could be spared out of the garrison of Normandy to raise King James's own forces to a total of about 20,000 men. By the end of April, 1692, this army was encamped on the heights above the Channel between Havre de Grâce and Cape La Hogue. It was composed of 12,000 Irish infantry, 1000 Irish cavalry, 3000 French cavalry, and 4000 French infantry and artillery. King James and all his councillors, including Melfort, were at head-quarters. Richard Hamilton, released from the Tower in exchange for Mountjoy, and Sarsfield, were the Lieutenant-Generals under James in person; Sheldon, Galmoye, and Wauchope the Brigadiers. The utmost confidence prevailed in the Jacobite camp. It was generally believed that the hour of restoration had arrived.

The army of invasion having been collected, it only remained to get it over the Channel into England. The combined Anglo-Dutch fleet of over eighty sail lay at Spithead watching and waiting for the moment to issue forth. It was clear that the passage could not be attempted until a victory at sea had cleared the way. A French squadron of forty-four ships was anchored in the roadstead of Cherbourg under the command of Tourville, the principal French Admiral, and perhaps the ablest seaman of his day. Louis had ordered the Chevalier D'Estrées to bring his squadron of thirty-five ships from the Mediterranean, to join Tourville and to co-operate with him in clearing the Channel. It is to be noted that none of the French authorities entertained the smallest doubt that Tourville and D'Estrées combined would be more than a match for the Anglo-Dutch force. If the plan had been carried out as arranged the balance of probability favoured the French scheme, and James might have recovered his throne. But the strong westerly gales that blew through the Straits of Gibraltar kept D'Estrées shut up in the Mediterranean and led the three chief directors of the enterprise, Louis, James and Tourville, to commit a stupendous act of folly. All were in their several degrees to blame, but whereas the French diarists throw the chief responsibility on James, a more dispassionate enquiry would place it on the shoulders of Louis himself.

It was not easy to feed an army in those days, and the strain of providing for 20,000 troops for several months, including provender for 4000 horses, was felt even in so productive a province as Normandy. Week followed week in enforced inaction. Several times the cavalry were embarked in their flotilla at the mouth of the Seine, and as often they had to be landed again, as D'Estrées had not arrived and the Channel was not clear. May was drawing to a close, the ardour displayed in April was cooling, and there seemed no alternative to abandoning the undertaking except by Tourville risking an engagement with a fleet twice his superior in strength. Left to himself Tourville would not have done anything so foolish, but at the end of May he received the formal orders of his Sovereign to engage the enemy at all hazards.

Why did Louis give this unwise order ? The principal

cause of his later misfortunes was, as we shall show when we come to deal with them, his interference with the man on the spot, his arbitrary order that a battle was to be fought whatever prudence said to the contrary. But in 1692 he had not reached this stage of haughty arrogance, and besides he generally left a little more discretion to his naval commanders than to those on land. It is impossible to avoid the conclusion that Louis ordered Tourville to fight because he relied on James's assurances that at least some part of the English fleet would not participate in the contest. It had not fought at Beachy Head under Torrington ; why should it fight off La Hogue under Russell, who was dubbed James's man ?

We must make allowance for James's feelings. He saw one more chance—what he conceived to be his best chance —slipping away. To the French Government it meant comparatively little that the camp in Normandy should be broken up and the expedition abandoned. To James it meant the destruction of all his hopes, and it is not surprising that he did everything possible, whether prudent or not, to avert such a decision. As the arrival of D'Estrées's squadron became more and more deferred, so did James's assurances that Russell and Carter would not fight become more positive. Despite all his experiences he continued to believe in the loyalty of his English sailors. Besides, had he not Admiral Russell's assurances conveyed through his agent Mr. Lloyd in his pocket ? James, having convinced himself of the imminent defection of the English fleet, succeeded in infecting Louis with his own optimism. Tourville was not strong enough to deal with the Anglo-Dutch fleet combined, but if it was only to prove an affair with the Dutch he was able to count on victory.

Thus influenced by the Stuart King, Louis, relying on his luck, for he had not at that moment tasted the bitterness of defeat either on sea or land, wrote the fatal order to Tourville to sail and attack at all costs the enemy's fleet. Among all Louis's commanders Catinat was the only one to disobey the King's orders when he did not approve of them. Tourville had some sense of responsibility to his men, and was not without a certain natural obstinacy of his own, but unfortunately he was at the moment suffering from some idle gossip at Court, where the heroes of the boudoir had pronounced Tourville a sluggard in action. One Minister even went so far as to accuse him of cowardice, and subsequently had to explain his words by dividing cowardice into two separate compartments. There was, he explained, the physical cowardice known to everybody, but with which he had never thought to couple the name of the brave Tourville; there was another kind of mental or spiritual cowardice which prevented a man taking decided action, and that was what he meant to imply. The distinction was not very clear, but it sufficed to avert a duel.

Tourville then received his Sovereign's order at a bad moment. His blood was up and his judgment suffered. He gave his orders to weigh anchor and to go in search of the enemy. At that moment James had a letter in his pocket stating that " Russell entreated him to prevent the two fleets from meeting, and gave him warning that as he was an officer and an Englishman it behoved him to fire on the first French ship that he met although he saw James himself on the quarter-deck." In face of this plain speaking there could be no justification at all for the opinion that the French would have to deal only with the Dutch fleet. When St. Simon and other French chroniclers accuse James of having been responsible for the defeat at La Hogue, we must state with some precision the degree of his responsibility. He allowed his hopes to carry him away as to the intentions of the English commanders, even to the extent of ignoring the written evidence in his pocket. But the French writers affirm what is manifestly absurd when they say that James expressed his pride and pleasure at seeing the English fleet beat the French. That defeat meant the destruction of his fondest hopes, and James could not be conceived by any possibility as in a rejoicing mood; but perhaps the most conclusive proof to the contrary would be the simple fact that James saw nothing of the battle, as is made clear by the Duke of Berwick's narrative which reads as follows :—

" This winter the Most Christian King, convinced that the speediest method of putting an end to the war would be to re-establish the King on the throne of England, and excited, moreover, to this generous undertaking by the friendship he naturally entertained for that prince, gave orders for equipping a great fleet, forty-four ships of which were fitting out at Brest and thirty-five at Toulon. All the Irish troops with some battalions and some squadrons of French were cantoned in the neighbourhood of La Hogue and Havre de Grace, where the embarkation was to take place, and the King repaired to a small distance from La Hogue at the latter end of April.

" The fleet was ordered to rendezvous off Ushant in the month of May, but the Count D'Estrées with the ships from Toulon was detained six weeks in the Mediterranean by contrary winds. The Most Christian King, impatient to execute his plan, sent orders to the Chevalier de Tourville, Admiral of the Fleet, to enter the Channel with the ships from Brest, without waiting for the squadron under the Count D'Estrées, and to fight the enemy at all events if he met with them.

" The Admiral, who was the most able seaman in France and perhaps in the world, was piqued that in the last campaign some persons had endeavoured to do him ill offices at Court, and even accused him of not being fond of engagements. He therefore without hesitation executed the order he had received. He entered the Channel with his forty-four ships of the line, and having learned that the combined fleets of England and Holland, to the number of eighty-five ships of the line, were at Spithead, he steered for that place. The Dutch, seeing him advance with all his sails set and so inferior a force, at first suspected some treachery and kept their wind ; but they soon found their fears were false. Tourville attacked the English with great spirit; the action continued till night, and never was any engagement more brilliant, bolder or more glorious for the French Navy. Tourville, though surrounded by enemies, fought like a lion. The enemy did not take a single ship, nor even ventured to force his line. However, as he saw that he could not maintain so unequal a combat, and had already lost a great number of men, he thought prudence required of him to retreat in the night to the coast of France, which he did, and was followed by the enemy's fleet.

"We had heard the sound of the guns very distinctly, and the next morning we descried a number of ships advancing to our coasts. At first we distinguished only the French colours and thought that our victorious fleet was come to transport us to England, but our joy was of short duration, for soon after we discovered the English flag, which convinced us but too fully that the allies were in pursuit of our ships. . . . Four of Tourville's ships that were most damaged put into Cherbourg, where the enemy burned them a few days later, and he with thirteen ships entered the bay of La Hogue. He immediately anchored in line as near land as he could and came on shore to wait upon the King of England, who lodged near the coast, to receive his orders and consult upon what was proper to be done.

"The Marshal de Bellefonds, who was to command the land forces, and all the general officers, as well of sea as land, were summoned to the Council. Tourville proposed all the different courses that remained to be taken, but at the same time showed that according to all appearances *there was not one by which the ships could be saved,* and in case it should be determined to defend them, every soul in them must inevitably perish if the enemy should set fire to them. It was resolved, therefore, to run them aground after having taken out of them everything we could and to employ the sloops, of which we had a great number destined for the disembarkation, to prevent them from being set on fire.

" The enemy who were in line of battle at the entrance of the bay sent some ships of war to cannonade the fort of La Hogue, and to support their sloops which were advancing in good order with some fire ships ; ours put forward to meet them, but as soon as they came within musket shot the enemy, more accustomed and better skilled in manœuvres of that sort than our people, drove them back to land ; after which they took possession of the ships, but not being able to get them off burned them.

" After this unfortunate expedition, we continued some time longer on the coast ; till by order from the French Court, the troops marched to reinforce the army on the frontiers. Then the King returned to St. Germains."

St. Simon, not content with accusing James of having lost the battle by raising false hopes as to the defection of part of the English fleet, goes on to make him responsible for the burning of the ships, which took place under the eyes of James and Bellefonds, and he roundly accuses James of being the chief culprit through his " *fatalisme inerte.*" This does not accord with Berwick's story, or with his assertion that according to Tourville himself, " there was not one way by which the ships could be saved." However, it justifies the quotation of James's own narrative of the event. This differs in some material details from Berwick's, but unfortunately the feeling cannot be repressed in dealing with anything put forward by James that he is placing his apology before the judgment of posterity. Here is his story :—

" He (James) began to embark his men the day after he came to the sea coast, but the transport ships were so long in getting together, and those which came from Havre de Grace so cruelly battered by a storm, that they were not in a condition to sail till they had notice of the English and Dutch fleets being joined ; upon which corvettes were sent to acquaint M. Tourville, but he having orders to seek out the English (then supposed to be alone) came in presence of the enemie before that intelligence rought him, and being piqued at those reflections mentioned before of his not pursuing the victory at Bechy Bay, thought fit to observe his orders to the letter though the Dutch were joined : so, notwithstanding the great inequality, bore down upon them on May 29 in the morning S.W. of Cape Barfleur, and maintained the fight with equality enough till about four in the afternoon, and then the wether coming calm the French thought fit to tow away with their boats considering how much they were out-numbered and that no defection appeared on the English side. Whether Admiral Carter had any real design for the King's service (as was reported), he being killed at the beginning of the engagement, left that matter in doubt as well as by what hand he dyed. However, the damage the French had undergone hitherto was not considerable, but the wind springing up a fresh gale about six the English renewed the engagement, which the un-seasonable bravour of Admiral Tourville prevented the French from declining, and was the occasion of a mighty loss soon after ; for he counting it too great a dishonour to shew his stern to an enemie and trusting to the strength of his own ship ' The Royal Sun,' a mighty vessel of 120 guns, resolved to stand the brunt and lay like a Castle in the sea, tho' attacked on all sides, being too well manned to be boarded by the enemie ; but by this means both he and those who thought it their duty not to abandon their Admiral could never after get cleer of the English, but were forced to that scurvy alternative either to be taken or to run ashore. Part, indeed, of the French fleet got into the race of Aldernee betwixt the promontory and the Isle of Guernsey and so saved themselves at St. Malos, but Tour-ville with sixteen great vessels was necessitated to run aground, and yet even then it had not been impracticable to save them *if the King's Council had been followed*, for the frigates and fire ships which Russel sent to destroy them could not come near enough to doe them any mischief, upon

which the King proposed to put land men on board who
would undertake their defence against the Enemie's armed
boats, which was the only way they had to attack them in the
shallow water where they lay. But the Admiral thought it
a dishonour to commit the care and defence of his ships to
any but the seamen themselves, who, being disheartened by
the late defeat, soon abandoned their posts, at the first
approach of the English (though but in chalops), who,
notwithstanding the continual fire of several batteries
raised on the shore, burnt all these men-of-war that had
run upon it. . . .

" This defeat was too considerable to be redressed and too
afflicting to be looked upon, nor was it even safe to do it
long, for as if everything conspired to encreas the King's
misfortune and hazard, his own ships, as if it were with
their dying groans, would have endangered his life had he
not been timely advertised to remove from the place where
he fortuned to stand ; for as soon as they were burnt to the
guns, which were most of them loaden, they fired on all
hand, which raked the very place where the King had been
and did some small damage on shore, so little was such an
accident foreseen."

Whether we accept Berwick's or James's version as the
truth, there is no reason to fasten greater responsibility on
James for the disaster than that he allowed his hopes to bias
his judgment as to the feelings of his English sailors
towards him. France lost on this occasion the naval
equality which she had long maintained against two powerful rivals combined, but Tourville was covered with glory.
His desperate battle with a fleet twice his strength in
numbers was compared with the most heart-stirring feats of
chivalry, and the English Admiral sent a special envoy on
shore to add his tribute to his glory for the most gallant
fight he had ever witnessed. Louis received Tourville at
Versailles before the whole Court, and personally complimented him on his valour. But the days had passed
when the gallantry of the individuals concerned atoned for

U

a national reverse. During the remainder of the war the French coast continued to be exposed to the raids and insults of the English. A new barrier had been placed in the path of Stuart enterprises against England. The English fleet commanded the Channel.

The means of conveyance destroyed there was no further use in keeping the army intended for the invasion of England idle on the Norman coast. The French troops returned to their garrisons. The Irish received marching orders in various directions. King James hastened back to St. Germains, where a week later his daughter the Princess Louise Mary was born on June 28, 1692. In this princess, to whom Louis stood as godfather, the highest courage and the most attractive qualities of the Stuarts were combined. If she and her brother, the Old Pretender, could have exchanged parts, history might well have taken a different course.

However great his disappointment at the failure of the expedition for the recovery of England by his guest, however deep his anxiety at being placed in a position of naval inferiority in the Channel, Louis still preserved in his attitude towards James all the cordiality and courtesy of the genial host. He allowed neither defeat nor disappointment to ruffle his temper or demeanour. The relations between Versailles and St. Germains remained without a cloud. Madame de Maintenon declared that Heaven had inflicted these troubles on their poor English Majesties, because it wished to qualify them to become Saints.

But there was another consequence of the Hogue defeat, which was not altogether disadvantageous to France. It left the Irish troops free to be employed against her foes. The English expedition, if it had succeeded, would have deprived her of the new auxiliaries upon which she was counting so much. When they had first been brigaded in Brittany it was proposed to employ them on the southern frontier, and in garrison work generally, but when the camp broke up at La Hogue it was too late in the summer to march troops across France. Certain detachments were sent to reinforce the troops in Savoy and Roussillon ; and specific mention is made of forty-seven Irish officers, under Colonel Reynolds, proceeding to Savoy to join the Talbot regiment. These were to form the third battalion of the regiment, which was really the O'Brien or Clare regiment, of which Colonel Richard Talbot had the temporary command. The French practice of the time was to name a regiment after its colonel, which led to much confusion in distinguishing between the Irish corps. Colonel La Rue was also sent with eighty of the Foot Guards to Roussillon to join Mountcashell, who was still serving with Noailles.

But the bulk of the troops marched into Flanders to join the army of Luxemburg, which was opposed by the main Anglo-Dutch army under William in person. The Duke of Berwick had not waited long after the naval fight to proceed to the scene of action. He had served as a volunteer on Luxemburg's staff in 1691, and had distinguished himself at the siege of Mons. He was sure of a hearty welcome, for he had gained Luxemburg's esteem by his attention to his duties as much as by his good looks. Berwick probably suggested that it would not be a bad thing to bring the Irish troops from Normandy and thus secure a numerical preponderance over William. In the course of July the main body of James's own army in name had joined the French operating in the valley of the Scheldt. Sarsfield, Earl of Lucan, was given the rank of Maréchal de Camp, and Sheldon and Galmoye that of Brigadier. Part of the force was diverted from Flanders to join the French army on the Moselle, where we will describe some of their deeds a little later on. Before the summer of 1692 closed, Irish troops were before the enemies of France at the three most menaced points.

Chapter XIII

THE FIRST ACHIEVEMENTS
OF THE BRIGADE

ABOUT the time that James left St. Germains for Normandy King Louis was making his own arrangements to take the field in Flanders in person, which meant, on this occasion at least, that the ladies of the Court were to go with him. These preparations required time, for when the King took the field all the household troops and all the privileged regiments had to accompany him. The ensuing campaign, which was signalised by the capture of Namur, was commonly spoken of as the " campaign of the ladies."

At that moment Louis had the largest force he had ever assembled together in one place in Flanders, and with the troops he brought with him it did not fall short of 150,000 men. Marshal Luxemburg was in command of the army of Flanders assembled round Mons, and Marshal Boufflers of a second army, with its head-quarters at Enghien. The question was what was to be done with this considerable force, double the strength of the hostile army lying round Lambecq, near Brussels, under William of Orange ?

But if there was some doubt as to the practical course to follow there was none as to the parade. Louis left for the seat of war on May 10, and with him went Madame de Maintenon and the Princesses. Their first camp in the Netherlands was fixed at Mons, and as the left wing of Boufflers' army almost touched the right wing of Luxemburg's, it was decided to pass them both in review at the same time. The King and his Court drove one fine morning along the front of the two armies, drawn up for the occasion, and covering a space of nine miles. The review lasted several hours, and it was said with reason that the spectacle was magnificent. It only remained for Louis to render the event memorable in history by undertaking some enterprise that should give a decisive turn to the war. At the least, he ought to have expelled William of Orange from the southern or Spanish Netherlands. But Louis was content to assign it a more modest rôle. For a Court under canvas, what could be more interesting than a siege ? He decided that the capture of Namur would be a sufficient return for all his effort and outlay.

This was the turning period when, as Marshal Villars puts it in his Memoirs, Louis, abandoning the ideas of conquest which had inspired him throughout what might be called the grand era, confined his efforts thenceforth to the preservation of his own frontiers. He was content if he beat those hostile armies which ventured close enough to be reached without too fatiguing an effort, and having beaten them he and his generals uniformly returned to the pleasures of the table, the theatre, and games of chance. The only exception to this general rule was hard-working and neglected Catinat, in the south-east of the realm. The worst offender was Luxemburg, who, on the other hand, was the greatest tactician on the field of battle in the French army.

Louis and the army subject to his immediate orders, with Boufflers as adviser, marched to Namur and sat down to besiege it, while Luxemburg drew up his forces round Gembloux to cover its operations. As there was not sufficient accommodation nearer the ladies were sent to Dinant, where they had to climb four hundred steps to reach their quarters in the old citadel above the town. With them the campaign soon ceased to be popular ; but Louis had thrown himself into the siege of Namur with full ardour, and under the eyes of their King the French troops surpassed themselves. He had at his side one of his wisest counsellors in Vauban, a man of clear vision, free of prejudice, and full of resource.

While the Maison du Roi talked of storming the citadel in their shirt sleeves, Vauban would not allow the fortress to be attacked until he had first captured the town, and having captured the town he proceeded to assail the fortress by all the rules of sap and mine.

After twenty-seven days of open trenches the citadel surrendered on June 30, 1692, and the following day the garrison, two thousand strong, marched out under the command of the Prince Barbançon (Duke d'Arenberg), who commanded the defence. On the same day Berwick arrived in the French camp from Normandy. Having captured Namur, a place which had the reputation of never having been taken, Louis returned to France. He was visited at Versailles on his return by James, on July 16, which fixes the date of his arrival. The King's achievement in capturing the virgin fortress at the junction of the Sambre and Meuse was celebrated in a poor ode by the Court poet Boileau.

William of Orange was greatly irritated by the loss of Namur, and drew his army to a head in a strongly situated camp at Tubize, near Hal. Luxemburg concentrated his forces at Steinkerk, near Enghien. The country intervening between the two camps was very undulating, thickly set with hedgerows and not at all favourable for the style of fighting general in that age, which was one of set formations. The opinion in the French camp was therefore that there would be no encounter, and probably there would not have been any if William had not been so exasperated by the loss of Namur, and if an accident had not thrown what seemed a good chance in his way of surprising the French army.

Luxemburg had a well-placed spy in the camp of the Allies. The secretary and head musician of the Elector of Bavaria was in his pay, and sent him notes regularly at short intervals. He was an excellent spy, but he had the bad habit of writing too often, and on a certain day one of his letters miscarried and came into the Elector's hands. While some were for stringing up the traitor without more ado, William thought it wiser to make a final use of him before consigning him to his fate. He was compelled to write a letter to Luxemburg informing him that on the following morning William intended to lead out a foraging party in the direction of the French camp, but that it would be nothing more than a foraging party. Luxemburg received the letter and accepted the statement without hesitation, and when early in the morning the news came that the enemy was visible in the neighbourhood of his camp he vowed that he had a most excellent spy and turned over in his bed to sleep again.

But not many minutes elapsed before other messengers arrived with the intelligence that the enemy—horse, foot, and guns—were coming on, and finally all room for doubt was removed by the information that the Bourbonnais Brigade, holding an advanced position, had been overwhelmed by superior numbers and was retiring with the loss of its seven guns. By this time the Marshal was not merely wide awake, but fully alive to the situation. It was said that his genius only revealed itself when he was in a serious difficulty, and certainly he had never been in a worse difficulty in his life. The crisis required a desperate move, and he made it.

The Household troops of France, including the Maison du Roi and the Palace Guards of the Louvre, had remained, after Louis's return to Paris, with the idea of seeing the end of the campaign. The celebrated mousquetaires were there under the leading of the young Duc de Chartres, famous long afterwards as the Regent Orléans. They turned out at the final alarm, half dressed, with lace collars unfastened, but armed and mounted. The ancient chivalry of France, the noblest names in the French *livre d'or*, were there ready for the fray and keen to be led at once against the presumptuous foe who had broken in upon them, and at their head was the King's nephew. Luxemburg was in a dilemma, but at his elbow he saw the means to extricate himself, and he never hesitated, although he knew that many great people at Court would have to wear mourning for that day's work. To that peerless cavalry, with horses straining at the bit, he merely waved his sword and shouted : "¡Go ! " (*En avant !*)

William's troops, emboldened by their success over the Bourbonnais Brigade, were coming on in full confidence of an easy success when this whirlwind of French horsemen burst in amongst them. Many bit the dust, but the majority simply turned about and fled. The guns were recovered, the camp restored, and an hour after Luxemburg awoke to the situation the two armies had reoccupied their first positions. But the battle was far from over, it was only entering upon its second phase. The Duke of Wurtemberg was at the front in command of twenty-two English and Danish battalions of infantry. With him were the best of William's English officers, Lanier and Mackay, Tollemache and Mountjoy. They were in full belief that the Dutch close behind them under Count Solmes would come forward to their support, and that behind him in turn was William, who would not fail them. Whatever the explanation, the Dutch failed to join in. Solmes did not advance, and the comment attributed to him—" Let us see how the bulldogs fight to the death "—was in harmony with his character. William sent orders to the hotly engaged force to retire. The Dutch Prince had enjoyed some popularity with his English soldiers before the battle ; after Steinkerk none spoke well of him.

The following description of the fight by the young Count de Mérode-Westerloo, subsequently Field-Marshal— of which family the Colonel Mérode, in Lauzun's Brigade, was a scion—gives a very good idea of what took place :—

" Nous étions dans le camp ennemi avec un corps d'Armée considérable, et faute d'être soutenus comme on en avait le temps et les moyens nous nous laissions repoussés et nous nous retirâmes. Le feu fut terrible, la cavalerie n'agit pas de tout et celui qui essuya tout le feu fut le Duc de Wurtemberg qui, commandant les 22 bataillons d'infanterie qui donnent, souffrait beaucoup, et fait des miracles. Ce fut toute l'infanterie anglaise et danoise que ce Duc commandait qui eut à mordre. Je fus envoyé au Duc de Wurtemberg par le roi Guillaume pour le faire retirer. Il enrageait et moi aussi, tout jeune que j'étais, de voir que l'on avait perdu le temps si mal à propos."

As a matter of fact, William's attack failed because he did not know how to turn the opportunity to the best account ; but perhaps his greatest fault was in stationing himself too far from the front. So much time was wasted in taking him the news and bringing back his orders that the opportunity of doing something decisive was never forthcoming. His best course, under the circumstances, was to recall, as he tried to do, the Duke of Wurtemberg ; but that was no excuse for his not covering the retirement of the English regiments by advancing with the Dutch infantry. He seems to have excused himself by alleging that the delayed arrival of his right, which was to have attacked the French left at daybreak, had upset all his plans. This admission tends to corroborate the Duke of Berwick's view of the battle, as expressed in the following extract from his Memoirs :—

" The Prince of Orange committed two great faults that day. The first was not attacking our left at the same time as our right, for he could not expect to beat a whole army in one point. The second was in not having fresh troops ready to support those that began the attack. If he had done this I do not know what might have been the consequence, but I have been assured that during the action the Prince remained at a great distance without making any motion or giving any order, though the general officers were every moment sending to him for assistance."

It was fortunate for William that the country north of Steinkerk was so unsuitable for operations, because Marshal Boufflers, hearing the heavy firing, hastened to his colleague's aid, and before the combat closed came into contact with the left of the Allies. Feuquières, in criticising this action, admits that Luxemburg could not follow up his success, which was not the view generally held in Paris, and as Feuquières was a captious critic the obstacles in the path of the French Marshal must have been great.

The most remarkable circumstance in connection with the defeat at Steinkerk was the increase it brought to the reputation of English troops for valour and steadiness. It was the first pitched battle in which they had taken part on the Continent since the battle of the Spurs, in the reign of Henry VIII. Detachments had done very well in the days of Elizabeth and Cromwell, but Wurtemberg's English force might be described without exaggeration as an army. The valour and resolution it displayed when practically abandoned by all its allies except the Danes, and attacked by the choicest French troops in far superior numbers, formed an appropriate opening to the reappearance of English troops on the Continent in a victorious rôle. Victory was not to come till a still remote future, but Steinkerk was a good forewarning of Blenheim.

The French reports state that the English and Danish Guards were practically annihilated. Mackay was killed, Mountjoy, only a few months out of the Bastille, was killed ; Lanier, severely wounded, died of his wounds. Three thousand English and Danish troops were killed, as many more were wounded, while about two thousand of the other Allies were placed *hors de combat*. The French, on their side, admitted a loss of 6500 men in killed and wounded.

The Irish troops present at Steinkerk were in the left wing of Luxemburg's army, but the cavalry was in the centre, and some part of it at least took part in the charge of the Household troops. There is no specific reference to the Irish in Luxemburg's report, and, indeed, it was not until a later period that French commanders (Catinat and Noailles always excepted) got in the habit of rendering justice to the Irish troops. This was due not to jealousy, but to ignorance of the English language and names, and also to the fact that in these great battles the Irish contingent, owing to its being so dispersed by the French authorities, formed only a small part of the forces under the French Marshals. But the chief reason for silence about the Irish troops at Steinkerk was that, being stationed on the left of the army, they were not closely engaged.

But if Luxemburg was silent about the Irish troops he spoke out loudly in praise of two of their commanders, Berwick and Sarsfield, and the praise of Sarsfield is all the more remarkable and generous because he had only known him a few weeks before the battle.

Of Berwick, who had served through the campaign of 1691, he wrote: "The Duke of Berwick was with me throughout the action, and behaved as bravely as in the last campaign, of which I informed your Majesty at the time."

Of Sarsfield he wrote: "The Earl of Lucan was also with me, and his courage and intrepidity, of which he had given proof in Ireland, were very noteworthy. I can assure your Majesty that he is a very good and capable officer." Luxemburg's appreciation of Sarsfield's capacity is perhaps the surest test of his real merit.

In accordance with the usages of war on the grand scale at that epoch, Luxemburg having thrashed his enemy in a good stand-up fight, thought he had done enough for that year, and kept to his camp. It was said of him that he generally pitched it in a locality where poultry was plentiful and the veal known to be tender, and if there were also agreeable ladies at the place so much the better. But although nothing was to be attempted against William, there were rumours of a German diversion from Luxemburg into the Ardennes, of which Marshal Lorges, operating on the Rhine, had sent him warning. The following incident is specially interesting, as it gave the Irish cavalry an opportunity of distinguishing itself.

The Marquis d'Harcourt was accordingly detached by

Luxemburg in September, with a flying camp beyond Namur, with orders to watch the enemy if he advanced west of the Ourthe. Harcourt, making his head-quarters at Marche, threw out his picquets as far as La Roche and Tenneville. The enemy determined to surprise his outposts, and with that view a cavalry force of 4000 men, representing thirty squadrons, suddenly appeared in the Ourthe valley. Harcourt, a man of resource as well as courage, got his troops in hand very quickly and opposed the enemy with twenty-six squadrons. Among these were the two troops of Irish Horse Guards, the two Irish cavalry regiments known as the King's and the Queen's, and at least the two French Dragoon regiments of Asfeld and De Rannes. With this force he crossed the Ourthe near Raumont à Pic and at once charged the enemy, who was unprepared for such vigorous measures.

Harcourt led the charge himself at the head of Berwick's troop, and Lord Lucan's troop was led by his lieutenant, Major-General de St. Frémont, and the other regiments followed in support. The Germans were routed and pursued for six miles, losing nearly 500 killed and 200 prisoners. The report of the encounter states that "the King of England's Guards, and the Irish regiments greatly distinguished themselves." The French loss was not heavy. The only officer killed was Matthias Barnewall, Lord Trimlestown. There still exists in the little churchyard of Tenneville a scarcely legible stone to his memory, but it is curious to note that it is always spoken of in the neighbourhood as that of an English officer killed fighting the French ! Lord Trimlestown was only a little over twenty-one at the time of his death, and both in Ireland and in France the French authorities always spoke of him as a man of promise.

A certain number of the Irish troops—all infantry—were sent from Normandy to join the French army operating round Spires under Marshal Lorges, one of the three Duras brothers. A supporting force was stationed on the Moselle under Marquis d'Huxelles, and the Irish were sent in the first place to reinforce him. Soon after their arrival General Feuquières succeeded to the command, and under his orders the Irish took a prominent part in the capture of Thionville or Diedenhoven. From Thionville they marched to take part in the siege of Spires, where they specially distinguished themselves, losing two officers in the final attack on the place.

In Italy the French army under Catinat had to evacuate Piedmont owing to the great increase in the number of the Imperial troops sent to assist the Duke of Savoy. These were not merely brought from Hungary, where the pressure from the Turks had been much relieved, but included a strong contingent of Huguenot regiments in the Prussian service; and an English regiment or two under the command of Charles, Duke of Schomberg, came later on. Catinat retired as slowly as possible, with the view of losing but little ground before winter should end the campaign. With him it was a matter of vital necessity, therefore, that all the passes into Upper Savoy should be held to the very last moment. He relied for this on the Irish contingent and local levies, while he kept his French troops concentrated under his own command.

Catinat had repeatedly asked for reinforcements, but Louis had none to send him except the Irish. In 1692 he got Maxwell's and Carroll's foot dragoons. He received the 3rd battalions of the Clare and Dillon regiments, freshly created. Finally, he got the Athlone regiment from Normandy. He had also some of the best Irish officers, Lords Kilmallock and Clare, Maxwell, Wauchope, Talbot, Carroll, Charles O'Brien, and Edward Scott. But for these men Catinat would have been swept out of Savoy as well as Piedmont in 1692.

Prince Eugene led the force that was to get into Savoy before Catinat and cut him off. He was in a desperate hurry and not in a mood to put up with obstacles. He reached Guillestre, a miserable little place with no pretension to a fortress—" qui ne vaut rien," as Catinat wrote—

but held by two companies of the Clare regiment and 600 militia of Dauphiné, under Chalandières. Prince Eugene demanded its immediate surrender, threatening to hang every man in the place if they attempted a futile resistance. He was told to do his worst, and his first attack was repulsed. Schomberg seems to have led the assaulting party which failed, but Guillestre was surrounded by houses which commanded the interior of the place and was quite untenable. After holding out for three days the garrison capitulated on honourable terms, being interned in Piedmont.

The Irish were not present in the defence of the pass of Cabre, between Valence and Sisteron, by the heroic Mdlle. de la Charce, who was rewarded by Louis with a colonel's pension in the following year. But they took the most prominent part in the defence of St. Clément and Embrun, which so retarded the enemy's advance that he was unable to accomplish anything more in 1692.

The defence of Embrun by Catinat's best lieutenant, the Marquis de Larray, was the most important of these minor incidents. The bulk of the garrison under him consisted of six companies of the Clare regiment, and he held the place for three weeks against all Eugene's attacks. Before he could attack Embrun Eugene had to carry the bridge of St. Clément, which was defended by two companies of the same regiment. They delayed the Imperialists long enough to enable Larray to complete his defences at Embrun. Embrun itself held out for three weeks, to the great delight and relief of Catinat at so much valuable time being gained. It may be mentioned that among the French officers killed in Embrun was the Marquis d'Amanzé, who had fought in Ireland. It then surrendered on honourable terms, the garrison being allowed to retire to Grenoble, on the condition that it was not to serve again during that year's campaign. Larray himself, and four aides-de-camp, were to be considered exempted from this condition.

In his report to Catinat Larray gives their full due to the Irish troops, and singles out Sir Edward Scott, who had defended Kingsale so well in 1690, for special praise. " M. Scott, Lieut.-Colonel du régiment irlandais de Clancarty (really Clare) m'a été d'un très grand secours tant par sa capacité que par sa vigilance continuelle. Le capitaine des grenadiers de ce régiment-là s'est aussi extrêmement distingué ! "

The captain referred to killed seven of the enemy with his own hand. Louis's recognition of these deeds was of a material character. In compliance with Catinat's request he wrote giving orders that " the Irish troops in Savoy were to be provided with shoes free, as they received only *la petite solde*." Before the campaign of 1692 ended Catinat was further reinforced by the two battalions of the Limerick regiment under Colonel Richard Talbot. Owing to the comparatively small French army employed in this quarter and the proportionally large Irish contingent, the Irish Brigade had a far better chance of gaining distinction and recognition in the Italian campaign than in Flanders.

There is no doubt that the French authorities were very disappointed that the campaign of 1692 waged in four separate fields had not given more tangible results. In the Netherlands, with no inconsiderable loss to the victors, a fortress had been captured and a barren victory gained. In Catalonia Noailles was marking time ; in Germany Lorges had advanced a little further from his base into a country too poor at that time to feed his army ; and in Italy Catinat was fighting a retreating battle. These were but poor results for the enormous outlay in men and money to which the King of France stood committed. Louis was not blind to the situation. His Ministers, even Barbezieux, Louvois' son, who was not seventeen, as Macaulay states, but twenty-four when he succeeded his father as Minister in attendance, were not blind to the facts. It was admitted on all sides that France must make a supreme effort, in 1693, to crush finally one or other of her antagonists and to pierce the ring by which she was encircled.

In the prescribed manner the month of March, 1693, saw

the nominations to the different high commands in the army for the coming campaign, and from the imposing list of names we need only take those of the Duke of Berwick as Lieut.-General, Sarsfield, Earl of Lucan, as Maréchal de Camp, Dominic Sheldon as Brigadier of Cavalry, and John Wauchope as Brigadier of Infantry. The first three were to serve with Luxemburg; the last-named with Catinat. Very shortly after these nominations it became known that Louis intended to take the field again in person, but as he was set on sterner work than a siege he left the ladies of his Court behind him. Perhaps also the tiring ascent to the Citadel of Dinant had satisfied their love for active campaigning. The Maison du Roi and all the privileged troops, however, went with him.

Of all the armies in the field it was decided that that under Noailles might be weakened with the least amount of evil consequences, and he was ordered to send his Irish regiments to Savoy. With these and the others—the Limerick regiment among them—which had reached him too late in 1692 for active participation in the war, it was believed that Catinat would be able to hold his own. He had too few friends at Court to expect a generous response to his own demands, and he of all the commanders was the one always required to give the greatest results with the very smallest resources and the most grudging aid. There was no intention in the first place to swell the army on the Rhine. Lorges and his lieutenants were to do the best they could. The plan for the year was to throw an overwhelming force into the Netherlands, to raise the two armies of Luxemburg and Boufflers to the greatest possible strength, and to finish once and for all with William of Orange. It was an excellent plan, and the means of carrying it out were available. All that had to be done was to adhere to the plan and not to change one's mind.

It was on this understanding that Louis went to Belgium, pitching his own royal camp with that of the right army commanded by Boufflers, whose head-quarters were at Namur.

Each of the French armies numbered between 70,000 and 80,000 men, while William of Orange had only 50,000 under his orders. He occupied, however, a very strong position at Parc, near Louvain, which he had carefully fortified. Strong as it was, he would have had no choice except retreat if the two French armies had advanced to attack him. He admitted this to his friends ; he made his preparations to retire behind the Moerdyck.

Louis had suffered a good deal from gout during the previous campaign, and in order that he might be sure of fine weather, he did not leave Paris till the end of May. On arriving in the camp he held a review of his army near Gembloux, and then gave himself up to deliberate discussions with his two generals as to what should be done, for Luxemburg rode over whenever he was summoned. Discussions with the Great King meant acquiescing in his pleasure, and Luxemburg was notoriously easy-going and courtier-like. Besides, the accepted dogmas were that the King was omnipotent, his arms invincible. The minor arrangements appeared of little moment when the final result was assured.

It was written of an earlier King of France that he marched a large army up a hill and down again. Louis did very much the same thing in 1693. Having got together an enormous force for the purpose, having brought it within forty miles of his enemy, Louis did not proceed to overwhelm him. He suddenly changed his mind and altered the whole plan of the war. He decided to distribute his forces, to detach the army of Boufflers, or the bulk of it, from that of Luxemburg, and to send it under a new commander-in-chief in the person of the Dauphin (Monseigneur) to the Rhine. At least 60,000 French troops marched out of the Netherlands on this errand, and Louis himself returned to Versailles.

This sudden departure from all the arrangements that had been made produced an immense sensation, and at once the gossips began to whisper that for so extraordinary a

x

decision there must be a motive quite out of the common. That meretricious and malicious chronicler Saint Simon, whose rôle was to know more than every one else by reckless invention, throws the whole blame on Madame de Maintenon, who wanted the King back at Versailles. The story has been reduced to fragments by the authoritative biographer (Noailles) of Madame de Maintenon and later commentators. But it was perfectly obvious to every one, except the ill-natured inventor of the story, that in order to get the King back to Paris it was not necessary to commit an act of folly with regard to the conduct of the war. If the uncrowned Queen was inconsolable at the absence of her lord, she could have found some other lure to call him back, or she could have joined him in his camp. She alone of all the Court ladies in 1692 had found the daily ascent to Dinant citadel, as she tells her correspondent at St. Cyr, rather amusing.

Berwick, equally at a loss with the rest to explain this sudden break-up of the overwhelming French army, states, philosophically, that it could only be accounted for by the mysterious and inexplicable decree of Providence.

It is possible, however, to give some intelligible reasons for Louis's action if full allowance be made for the atmosphere in which he lived and controlled the destinies of France. The conduct of the campaigns which signalised his reign passed through three distinct phases. In the first phase his armies were led by generals, who, although they might be princes and nobles, were still trained soldiers ; in the second phase courtiers were thought competent enough to lead his armies; and in the third phase Louis bethought him of the members of his own family. He conceived that it would strengthen the Royal House that the victorious bulletins should bear the signature of one of his descendants. A first step had been taken in this direction when he sent his son, the Dauphin, to the Rhine, in 1690. Its more important sequel was the despatch of the same personage to the same scene in 1693.

An easy campaign was sketched out for him on paper, culminating in a signal triumph at Heidelberg, and the competent Boufflers was sent with him to see that the Son of France did not come to much harm.

A final and always the irresistible motive was behind this decision in that curse of human nature called jealousy, which deposes reason and renders the mind oblivious to all other considerations. Louis wished to augment the glory of his own family, but he did not include the House of Orleans. He had shown this when he refused to allow his brother, the Duc d'Orléans (Monsieur), to take any further part in the wars after 1677, because of the distinction he gained by defeating William of Orange during that campaign. And now, after an interval of fifteen years, his nephew, the Duc de Chartres—the same brother's son— had also covered himself with glory at Steinkerk. He was, for the moment, the hero of France, and, besides, he was undoubtedly a young man of the most brilliant promise. This elevation of the Orléans branch was not in accordance with Louis's idea of the fitness of things. The balance was to be adjusted by a son of his own setting France a-talking, and to enable this dream to be realised he drew up and sanctioned the programme, for the summer of 1693, of a promenade of triumph beyond the Rhine.

The King and Boufflers gone, Luxemburg moves his army eastwards, and takes up a position to cover the siege of Huy, on the Meuse, half-way between Namur and Liége. The conduct of the siege itself is entrusted to Villeroi, the most incompetent of all Louis's courtier generals; but the siege of Huy is a trivial task not disproportionate to his intelligence. Luxemburg is still far superior in strength to William of Orange. He has 96 battalions and 210 squadrons to the Dutch Prince's 55 battalions and 150 squadrons. Huy surrenders and a considerable part of the French army is left there under the Marquis d'Harcourt. Luxemburg moves on to examine the enemy's position near Louvain, and decides that notwithstanding his numerical superiority it is too strong to be attacked. He then marches eastwards and manœuvres as if he intended to attack Maestricht. William quits his fortified camp at Parc, and following on a parallel line the movements of the French Marshal, reaches Landen. Luxemburg, having achieved what he wanted, retraces his steps, and draws up his army in front of the Anglo-Dutch army on July 28, 1693.

William had ample time to retreat, and if he had been well advised he would have done so. But his blood is up. He has felt the taunts cast at him for his cowardice or over-caution at Steinkerk. He occupies an admirable position for a defensive battle, and he decides to fight where he stands. The battle began about seven in the morning of July 29, and was not decided till late in the afternoon. Steinkerk was a foiled surprise. The battle of Landen, or Neerwinden, was the fiercest stand-up fight in the whole war. Men who were present at all the great battles of the long wars from 1689 to 1712, including Blenheim, declared that there was no struggle to compare with that at Landen until the day of Malplaquet.

The Irish troops present at this battle were the cavalry, who had served the previous year, the Guard regiment under Dorington, and the Dublin regiment under Simon Lutt-rell. Sarsfield was Maréchal de Camp under Lieut.-General Rubantel, and Dorington's regiment was included in his force. This was the regiment which did so well at the Boyne and again at Aughrim. It was now in front of the same enemies, for to it was confided the honour of leading the attack on the strongly fortified village of Neerwinden. With Dorington was Colonel John Barrett, one of the un-fortunate prisoners of Cork and Bruges. He led one of the Guard battalions into action and was killed as he entered Neerwinden at its head. As the Duke of Berwick was one of the three generals who directed this initial movement, and as he was taken prisoner, it may be as well to quote his account in the first place :—

James, Duke of Berwick.
from the Portrait, in the possession of the Duc D'Alba.

" Lieut.-Generals de Rubantel, Montchevreuil, and myself were ordered to begin the attack : Rubantel on the entrenchment to the right of Neerwinden with two brigades ; Montchevreuil on the left, with the same number, and I on the village with two other brigades.

" The village projected out into the plain, so that we all three marched abreast of each other. I, who was in the centre, attacked first. I forced the enemy to give way and drove them from hedge to hedge as far as the plain, at the entrance of which I formed again in order of battle. The troops which were destined to attack on the right and left of me, instead of following their orders thought they would be less exposed to the enemy's fire by throwing themselves into the village, by which means they got at once into my rear. The enemy, perceiving this ill-conducted manœuvre, re-entered the village by the right and left ; upon which a terrible fire commenced ; the four brigades under Rubantel and Montchevreuil were thrown into confusion and driven out of the village, and in consequence I found myself attacked on all sides. After having lost a prodigious number of men my troops likewise abandoned the front of the village, and while I was endeavouring to maintain my ground, in hopes that M. de Luxemburg, to whom I had sent, would advance to relieve me, I found myself at last completely cut off. Seeing this, I resolved to escape if possible by the plain, and having taken out my white cockade, passed for an officer of the enemy.

" Unfortunately Brigadier Churchill, brother to Lord Churchill, now Duke of Marlborough, and my uncle came up, and recollecting the only aide-de-camp I had with me suspected immediately that I might be there, and advancing to me made me his prisoner. After mutual salutations he told me he must conduct me to the Prince of Orange. We galloped a considerable time without meeting with him. At last we found him at a great distance from the place of action, in a bottom, whence neither friends nor enemies were to be seen. The Prince made me a very polite compliment, to which I only replied by a low bow. . . .

"After I was taken Marshal Luxemburg made another attack and got possession of the greater part of the village, but was very near being dislodged again ; at last, however, by pouring in fresh troops, he drove the enemy quite out, and then, assisted by the fire of our infantry, caused his cavalry to enter the entrenchments. After repeated charges the enemy were entirely beaten and put to flight. . . . The enemy lost in this battle near twenty thousand men, and we at least eight thousand."

The fight for the possession of the village was far more protracted and bitter than might be gathered from Berwick's narrative. Several times taken by the French and Irish troops, it was as often retaken by the English and the Dutch, and after five hours' fighting it was still held by William's forces. Luxemburg advanced his cavalry up to the entrenchments in the hope of unnerving the defenders by so imposing a display of horsemen, but the demonstration failed, and the cavalry, having suffered heavily, had to be brought back to wait for their opportunity later on. It was in the closing stage of the battle that Sarsfield received his death wound. His chief, Rubantel, was already severely wounded, Montchevreuil was killed, Berwick a prisoner, and thus Sarsfield had his chance of coming to the front, for the direction of the attack passed into his hands. It was just as the French reinforcements had finally made their way into and through the village, and the supporting cavalry following in their track had reached the plain, stretching northwards of it, that Sarsfield was struck by a bullet in the breast. He was conveyed to Huy, where he died a few days later.

Of Dorington and his regiment, led by himself and Lieut.-Colonel Michael Roth, after Barrett's death, it was said by a historian many years later : " At Landen the Irish Guards avenged the affront of the Boyne." Many of the officers and men were killed. Christopher Nugent was severely wounded in four places, but more fortunate than his leader, Sarsfield, recovered from them.

There was one incident connected with this battle, which raged from seven in the morning till four in the afternoon, that deserves mention. The Marquis d'Harcourt at Huy, fifteen miles from Landen, hearing the firing soon after sunrise, decided at once to move in its direction, and set off with all his cavalry, amounting to twenty-six squadrons. It is probable that some of his horsemen were the Irish cavalry which had taken part in the Ardennes the year before. Harcourt arrived at a critical moment of the battle, and his cavalry took part in the final charges beyond Neerwinden, which completed the overthrow of William's army. The French triumph was incontestable after the capture of the village. The Allies lost, by the French computation, 20,000 killed and wounded, and by their own admission 12,000. William lost over a hundred cannon, and eighty standards and flags. Luxemburg sent the latter to Paris by Brigadier-General d'Artagnan (afterwards Marshal Montesquiou), and they were hung up in Notre Dame. Luxemburg had sent so many trophies of the kind to Paris that he was called " le tapissier de Notre Dame."

Two incidents connected with the battle just described claim our notice. The first is the death of Sarsfield, who, whether he altogether deserves the pre-eminence or not, is considered by his countrymen Ireland's greatest hero. The reader will not have forgotten that in 1689 D'Avaux had written of him that he had more influence with the Irish people than all the others put together. Yet at that moment he was not the hero of Ballineedy. Some critics have attempted to show that he was not an Irishman in blood, but this charge is so easily refutable that the only marvel is that it should ever have been made. His mother, Anne O'Mor (or Moore), was the daughter of Rory O'Mor of the Hills, and died at St. Germains many years after her famous son was killed.

With regard to his military merit it is necessary to speak

in measured terms, for he never led an army in the field.
But there need be no hesitation in saying that he was a good
soldier, and Luxemburg's praise of him as a capable officer
after but a brief acquaintance is a completely convincing
tribute to his merit. Berwick's declaration that he was not
a general is merely ill-natured and reposes on nothing.
Military science in his day consisted of set rules and set
formations. The order of battle was the *sine quâ non* of the
French martinet, and required several hours to put in effect.
There were many authorities who refused to recognise
Steinkerk as a battle because there was no time to set the
troops in proper array. In that sense, indeed, Sarsfield was
not a general; none of the Irish officers were generals, for
they had no such training. But if we turn to the less professional side of war, we have no reason for diffidence. In
the display of personal courage, in the capacity to raise
courage and enthusiasm in others, Sarsfield shone in the
first rank. Not merely a regiment or an army, but an entire people saw in him the champion of its cause, the em-
bodiment of its national qualities and its most passionate
regrets. Sarsfield was the exponent of Irish aspirations in
one of the most bitter epochs of Anglo-Irish history, but
after Steinkerk he appeared among the English wounded
and prisoners as an alleviator and friend. It was one of the
most touching incidents in a feud due to an unfortunate
misunderstanding.

The disappearance of the Irish leaders in the Jacobite
movement, which was more or less complete by the end of
the war of the Spanish Succession, may be said to have
commenced on the field of Landen, where Sarsfield and
Barrett shed their blood under the French lilies. They had
not made, they never could have made, the new Ireland of
their dreams; but they had died as became their race and
their reputation, on the field of honour for a great King
and a gallant nation. Frenchmen, then the proudest and
most exclusive military caste on the Continent, took the Irish
into their brotherhood of the sword, and they did so only be-

cause Sarsfield and the men who went into exile with him established their claim to be so admitted in face of their foes. The Irish mourned the death of Sarsfield in a dirge that has become known all over the world :—

> "Oh! Patrick Sarsfield, Ireland's Wonder,
>   Who fought in the fields like Heaven's thunder!
>   One of King James's chief Commanders
>   Now lies the food of crows in Flanders.
>   Oh Hone!   Oh Hone!"

The second incident was the Duke of Berwick's capture. We have quoted his interview with William ; but the Dutch Prince was in a sour mood, and it was not improved by the later stages of the battle. He ordered his officers to convey Berwick to Antwerp, where he was shut up in the citadel, and he talked of sending him over to the Tower to be tried for high treason. He affected to regard the Duke as his rebellious subject ! William had never been a very scrupulous observer of the cartel, his treatment of the Cork prisoners was abominable, but he was exceeding his power in his proposed method of dealing with Berwick, and he had to be brought sharply to his senses.

Berwick was a Lieutenant-General in the French army. Among the prisoners taken by the French was the Duke of Ormonde. By the cartel Ormonde would have been sent back after the battle, but as Berwick was not returned the Duke was kept as a hostage. When rumours came as to William's design on Berwick he was warned that if he were harmed reprisals would be made on the person of Ormonde. Moreover, as William chose to break the cartel he must surrender General Scravenmore, another prisoner at Landen who had been released before the retention of Berwick was known. William had gone too far ; he bit his lip in characteristic fashion, and Berwick was allowed to return to the French army. This experience may have helped to confirm Berwick's inclination to become a French subject by a formal naturalisation, which he did a few years later.

Notwithstanding the completeness of this victory, its

fruits were practically *nil*. Luxemburg was unable to
follow it up, and for this inaction he was much criticised.
But he represented that he had no provisions and no horses,
and that his army was in peril of starvation. As a matter of
fact, the scene of war had been shifted to one of the least
productive regions, at that period, in Belgium, where so
considerable an army as that under Luxemburg could not
be fed out of the local supplies. It was entirely different
from the rich and well-cultivated fields of Flanders and
Hainaut. Luxemburg very wisely determined to quit
Limburg and to return to his original positions round
Namur.

His decision was no doubt influenced by the fact that
William had summoned all the troops that he could get
together to his aid, including a considerable corps commanded by the Duke of Wurtemberg, so that three weeks
after the battle he found himself at the head of a larger
army than the one he had fought with. Luxemburg, resolved to give Louis some definite result of the fighting
before the year closed, undertook the siege of Charleroi,
which surrendered on October 13, after twenty-seven days
of open trenches. Boisseleau, the defender of Limerick in
1690, was appointed its commandant.

If the campaign in the Netherlands was not an absolute
triumph, which it might well have been but for Louis's decision to divide his forces, that under the Dauphin beyond
the Rhine might be described as a fiasco. The only result
was the plundering of Heidelberg, which had been pillaged
by a French army four years before. None of the anticipated combinations came off, and the Dauphin returned to
France without the laurels that had been predicted for
him. Boufflers was ordered back to Flanders; the ill-
health and advancing years of Luxemburg seemed to call
for the presence of a younger and more energetic commander.

The year 1693 was not to close, however, without a more
striking military success for French arms than that of

Landen, and a further exhibition of the courage and devotion of the Irish Brigade to its new country.

In 1690 the arrival of the Mountcashell Brigade in Savoy had enabled Catinat to call up Larray and win the battle of Staffarde. In 1692, after fighting a retreating battle throughout the autumn, Catinat found himself reinforced by a strong Irish contingent, which did not total less than 5600 infantry and 1000 unmounted dragoons. The Dragoons were the King and Queen of England's; the infantry were the Queen's regiment, the Limerick, and the O'Brien of Clare. When the season became fit for campaigning, and the snow had melted in the passes, the Duke of Savoy resumed his forward movement interrupted at the close of the previous year. He was in superior force, but Catinat cantoned round Grenoble was calling up levies from all sides, and as a last resource had summoned La Hoguette to join him with the garrison of Lower Savoy. He was also getting together mules and other means of transport from Dauphiné. Thanks to his having withdrawn some distance from the Piedmontese frontier, his movements were well screened, and the Duke of Savoy had no suspicion that his old antagonist was making every effort to resume the offensive.

The course that the campaign would take turned very much on whether the French could successfully hold the advanced posts that guarded the entrances to Savoy. If these were carried Catinat's whole position would be compromised, and his complete concentration would be rendered impossible. The most important of these places, the pivot, as it were, of the whole frontier defence, was Pignerol, the charge of which was entrusted to Larray, with an adequate Franco-Irish garrison. In advance of Pignerol was the Fort of St. Brigette. This was held by four companies of the Clare regiment under Colonel Scott, and an equal number of the French regiment of Maine.

At the end of July the Duke of Savoy began his forward movement. He attempted to carry St. Brigette by storm, but was repulsed. He had then to wait some days for his heavy guns, and just as he had got them into position the garrison quietly slipped out and made its way, without loss, into Pignerol. When the Duke of Savoy came in sight of this place he realised that its natural strength had been increased by artificial defences, and that the advantages of a difficult position had been turned to the best possible account. Still, if he was to transfer the war from Italy to France, and to recover his ducal estates, it was necessary to get possession of Pignerol and pass on.

Pignerol was besieged in form, but the difficulties were immense. The rock was too hard for sapping and mining. The batteries had to be placed with little or no cover. The fire of the guns from the town proved surprisingly accurate and vigorous. After a few weeks the Duke, seeing that he was not likely to make any impression in a reasonable time, broke up his camp and retreated into Piedmont. He established his camp on the banks of the small stream called the Marsaglia, or the Marsaille. As he was still far superior in numbers to any force that Catinat was likely to be able to get together, he waited in the hope that the French army would have the temerity to advance and give him the opportunity of dealing it a heavy blow. There was one detail that the Savoyard had overlooked. His own movements in the plain were clearly visible to the French general from his outposts, whereas those of the French general himself had been and remained screened from the Duke.

Unknown to the Duke, Catinat, who was now joined by La Hoguette, had got together a larger army than his own. Such a contingency had never been conceived to be possible, and the last man to suspect it was the leader of the allied forces. Neither the Duke nor Prince Eugene imagined that Catinat would succeed in arraying against them in the field 50,000 men to their 40,000. They did not believe that he could get the men, but even if they had thought such an unlikely thing possible they would have felt quite certain that he could never provide the transport to enable it to descend into the plains of Italy. They were therefore quite easy in their minds about the matter, and they pitched their camp on the plain, through which the little stream of the Marsaglia flows not far from the Alpine passes, so that the French should not have to go too long a journey to find them. And at last it was reported from the outposts that the French columns were advancing down the mountain slopes. There was rejoicing in the allied camp at the sight, but it was only for a brief space.

Owing to the care with which the French authorities preserved the unit of measurement in the intact battalion and squadron it was quite easy for the expert to tell within a few hundreds the strength of a French army on its going into battle. As the Duke and Prince Eugene watched the French army descending to the plain they exclaimed together : " They have 10,000 more men than we have ! " Prince Eugene counselled retreat, and there was time, for the battle was not fought till the day after the first appearance of the French army. But the Duke displayed more of the recklessness than the caution of his family, and decided to make a stand, although both knew quite well that there was little or no chance of a victory for them. The belief that " God fights with the big battalions," is of older date than the Emperor Napoleon.

When Catinat saw that the enemy did not contemplate retreat he made his arrangements for the attack with greater deliberation, and his order of battle was prepared with much care. Whether it was at their own request, as some say, or because they happened to be in the van, the Irish infantry were selected to head the centre attack. The advance was made over one mile of open ground exposed to the fire from the enemy's entrenchments. The Irish are reported to have made very little reply by firing, and to have charged home with fixed bayonets and clubbed muskets. In the space of half a league they despatched a thousand of the enemy in this way, but their own losses, especially in officers, were heavy. John Wauchope was killed at the head of his brigade. Lord Clare was mortally wounded. His brother, Charles O'Brien, was seriously wounded. James de Lacy, father of the Russian Marshal Peter, was killed.

But if the Irish infantry distinguished itself the two Dragoon regiments surpassed themselves. From Catinat's own account it appears that on this occasion they were mounted—a dragoon being supposed to be equally at home on foot or on horseback—for he writes :—

" Ces deux régiments de dragons qui étaient dans le centre de la ligne ont fait des choses surprenantes de valeur et de bon ordre dans le combat. Ils ont renversé des escadrons l'épée à la main les chargeant tête par tête et les ont renversés."

In this charge Maxwell and Francis Carroll, the two commanders, were both killed. Dicconson, the Lieutenant-Colonel of Carroll's regiment, was also killed. Lord Kilmallock, who succeeded to the command of Maxwell's regiment, was especially distinguished. It was said of Dorington at Landen that he avenged the Boyne. Of the Marsaglia it might be said that the Irish Catholics avenged themselves on the Huguenots, who had done so much against them in Ireland. The Huguenot regiments in the Prussian service were practically annihilated, and they and the Irish bore, in their respective armies, the brunt of the fighting between them. La Hoguette had an opportunity of revising his judgment on Irish troops ; he had also that of showing himself in a better light than at the Boyne. He received a mortal wound in the heat of the fray and died some hours later in his tent, after an affecting interview with Catinat.

De Sourches more than corroborates Dangeau's verdict that " the Irish did very well at Marsaglia, and that King Louis is much pleased with all he hears and is told of them," when he writes :—

" On ne saurait assez donner de louanges à toutes les troupes du Roi et de la Reine d'Angleterre qui ont fait des miracles."

" Too high praise could not be given to all the troops of the King and Queen of England, who did wonders."

Among the officers who especially distinguished themselves, and who were fortunate to come out unscathed, were Edward Scott, Richard Talbot, Andrew Lee, and Lord Kilmallock. Edward Scott got Wauchope's Brigade, Andrew Lee succeeded Lord Clare as full Colonel of the O'Brien regiment, Lord Kilmallock got the command of one Dragoon regiment, and Charles O'Brien, soon to be Viscount Clare by his brother's death, got that of the other. The Queen's Dragoons were the nucleus from which sprang the famous Clare Dragoons of the later wars.

The allied army suffered very heavily. An English regiment was said to have been wiped out, and the general in command of this contingent, Charles, second Duke of Schomberg, was killed. The Earl of Warwick was among the prisoners. In those cases where the Huguenot prisoners were found to have served formerly in the French army they were hanged as deserters. The battle of the Marsaglia added immensely to Catinat's reputation, and freed France from the danger of invasion through Savoy. This relief was not inappreciable, because if the enemy had once effected a firm lodgment in that quarter he might have fomented the Protestant agitation in the Cevennes, which was about to cause the French Government a great deal of trouble.

The year 1693 was therefore memorable for establishing the reputation of the Irish Brigade as an integral part of the regular army of France. What had been only an experiment in the first place was then proved to be a success by the conspicuous valour and remarkable achievements of the Irish soldiers, not in minor engagements, as in 1691 and 1692, but in pitched battles with the most formidable opponents of the French monarch. It was no wonder that he was pleased and satisfied with the men who shed their blood so freely in his cause, or that he provided them with new shoes gratis, and declared that he regarded the Irish

Catholics as being on an equality with his own subjects. That expression of the Royal will served as a grand act of naturalisation down to the date of the French Revolution, when the *sans-culottes* repudiated the understanding, and left the descendants of the poor Irish exiles—a sadly reduced band—no choice save to flock back to England and to form there the nucleus from which Wellington's Irish troops in the Peninsula were drawn. But that is looking far ahead of the period with which we are dealing. In 1693, Louis and his Court are only glad that, girt in by foes on all sides, they have found at least some loyal auxiliaries, " a legion of the lost," who will give their lives for small pay and few honours. It is not an aid to be despised at such a juncture.

Chapter XIV

THE PEACE OF RYSWYCK

NOTWITHSTANDING the victories gained by Luxemburg and Catinat, which were augmented before the year 1693 closed by Tourville's capture of the rich Smyrna fleet in Lagos Bay, the French Government desired peace, and Louis made overtures through the Danish Court for an accommodation on terms very favourable to the Allies. His proposals were rejected and interpreted as a confession of weakness. William especially was opposed to peace because he wanted to secure the reversion of Flanders for himself, whereas Louis's proposals implied that if the King of Spain died without direct heir, it would pass to the Empire. In the winter of 1693–4 Louis then was alone sincere in his desire for peace. His enemies counted on some military successes to secure better terms, and William at least felt with some confidence that he might in the coming year obtain them. As a matter of fact, the campaign of 1694 proved exceedingly uneventful, and although William commanded a larger army than the French, he did nothing with it. Luxemburg was sick and ailing all the year, although he retained the nominal command, and Villeroi was the most active of his lieutenants—active only in the sense of moving about, for he accomplished nothing.

If there was inactivity in the camps there was a good deal of intriguing at the Courts, and James in particular had been very busy. In the spring of 1693 an old friend and councillor rejoined him in the person of Charles, second Earl of Middleton. After passing over four years in England, sometimes in the Tower and always more or less as a state prisoner, Lord Middleton escaped in disguise, making his way to France through Holland. He was a man of considerable ability and discernment, and if any one could recover James's crown by giving good advice, he was the man to do it. There is no doubt that after his arrival an improvement was perceptible in the methods pursued by the State Council at St. Germains. Melfort was got rid of and sent to Rouen, and Middleton took his place. Of Melfort at this juncture, James wrote in his Memoirs : " He is not liked by the English, or by the Irish, or by the French, but perhaps he is not so much the worse for all that." Lord Middleton, fresh from England, knew that James would have to yield much in order to get back, and, indeed, he came to a certain extent as the accredited envoy of the more important Jacobites or quasi-Jacobites like Marlborough. On the other hand, Lord Melfort claimed the free exercise of the royal prerogative and would yield little or nothing. Middleton's party became known as the Compounders ; Melfort's as the non-Compounders.

As the consequence of Middleton's taking over the direction of James's affairs, there was a revival of the efforts made in 1692 to rally the Jacobite party in England, and to prepare a popular rising on behalf of King James. James even renewed his correspondence with Admiral Russell through the intermediary Lloyd, but there is no doubt that Russell reported everything to William, and besides, his promises were so vague and so conditional that it is impossible to imagine how they could have taken any one in.

Among those who still protested their loyalty to King James and their desire to serve him was Churchill, Earl of Marlborough. He had passed a few weeks in the Tower for his treasonable transactions in 1692, but the little contretemps seems only to have whetted his Jacobite ardour. Marlborough had certainly no sympathy for William, and was probably quite willing to help James if he found it profitable to his own interests. It was also a doubtful point

Charles. Earl of. Middleton.
from the Portrait in the possession of James Paton. Esq.

with him and with others whether a Jacobite restoration
was at all possible, and he did not see how it would benefit
himself to be associated with a dismal failure. James's
restoration depended on the successful combination of a
double movement, a vigorous rising in the country, and the
landing of a considerable force in it from outside; and the
conjunction of two totally distinct bodies set in motion
and moved by different influences is always difficult to
carry out. Marlborough gauged the situation accurately
and waited on events. Sympathy with his old Sovereign
conveyed in courtly terms cost nothing.

But in one letter he sent more than sympathy; he sent
priceless information of its kind. Writing on May 4, 1694,
he stated that he had learnt that " the bomb vessels and the
twelve regiments that are now encamped at Portsmouth,
together with the two marine regiments are to be commanded by Talmach, and are designed to burn the harbour
of Brest and to destroy the men-of-war that are there."
The English idea was not merely to destroy the arsenal, but
to seize and fortify one of the headlands, which would
render the harbour useless as a French base for the future.

On receiving this warning James hastened with the news
to Versailles, and Vauban was sent off at once to put Brest
in a state of defence and to give the invaders a warm
reception. His measures were so quietly taken that the
English authorities had no suspicion that their plans had
been divulged. They were so well taken that the expedition was repulsed with very heavy loss, and Talmach, the
most popular English officer of his day, was killed. It was
said that Marlborough was jealous of Talmach, and that his
chief motive in giving the information was to get rid of a
rival. But this Machiavellian design reposes on nothing
substantial, and credits Marlborough with a prophetic
power to which it would be absurd to attach serious
importance. He sent the best piece of information that he
possessed at the moment with the idea of proving his
attachment to James, but he could not have known on

May 4 when he wrote that the plan would be put in execution on June 22, with the dire results we all have read about. The sending the information at all was an act of treason, but we need not for that attach any weight to the petty motive which Macpherson assigns for it.

At the close of the year, which was marked by the Brest expedition, James's daughter, Queen Mary, in right of whom William shared the British throne, died, and it was hoped that this event would improve James's chance of regaining his crown. But James had in his turn become cautious, and he was loth to involve his friends in plots and undertakings which achieved nothing beyond placing the individuals implicated at the mercy of William. There were many indications that William had grown vindictive, and his wife's death removed a moderating influence. In 1692 James had at last issued letters of marque to a certain number of privateers flying his flag and operating from St. Malo. Their captains were for the most part Irishmen, and one was named Captain Golding. The object of this step was to provide James with a little independent revenue of his own, for he was to receive a share of the profits. The crews were mixed Bretons and Irish, and in no part of France are there to-day more descendants of Irishmen than in Brittany, although the surnames have undergone curious metamorphoses—the ancient Hiberno-Norman family of Bermingham, for instance, being represented there at the present time in the form of Brindijonc. For a time the adventurers did very well, and the privateers of St. Malo became famous for their daring raids. But in 1695 Golding was captured, and, despite the fact that his papers were in order, William hanged him as a pirate.

In this year, too, a very bitter feeling was aroused along the French coast by the descents made by the English fleet at different ports. Dunkirk was seriously damaged, and Villeroi declared that it was done by the use of " infernal machines." Dieppe was destroyed. These petty operations had no real effect on the fortunes of the war. They were undertaken as a sort of retaliation for the Brest failure. In their turn they led to reprisals by the French. Louis ordered Villeroi to bombard Brussels with red-hot bullets as a set-off for the burning of Dieppe, and when he was told of Golding's fate and of William's high-handed action generally, he threatened to exact a summary vengeance on the 10,000 prisoners in his power. When William discovered that Louis had the means of retaliating and intended to exercise it, he changed his programme and gave up the practice of useless but cruel provocations. William might have defied Louis, but he could not ignore the representations of his ally the Elector of Bavaria at the sufferings of Brussels.

The bombardment of Brussels by Villeroi at Louis's direction has been considered an inexcusable act of severity, but it is only right to state what does not seem to be generally known that Villeroi, before firing, called on the Elector to give a pledge for his ally that the bombardment of Dieppe should never be repeated. The Elector replied regretting his inability to do so, and it was only after that answer that Villeroi began the bombardment. This was witnessed by the Duke of Berwick, who in his Memoirs compares the scene to the burning of Troy.

The years 1694–5 saw some changes in the ranks of the foremost personages so far as our narrative is concerned. Lord Mountcashell after serving in Savoy and Catalonia, was appointed Lieutenant-General under Lorges for the campaign on the Rhine, in 1694. He had been frequently wounded, as we have seen, and several of his old wounds broke out afresh under the hardships of campaigning. In July, 1694, he was obliged to leave the camp for Barèges, in the Pyrenees, but instead of benefiting by the waters he died there. Andrew Lee was given the command of his regiment, and Richard Talbot was nominated Brigadier of infantry. At the end of the same year, Marshal Bellefonds died, and Luxemburg was stricken with his last illness. When Louis heard of this he sent Fagon, his own physician, to him with these instructions : " Do for M. de Luxemburg all you would do for me if I were in his state ; " and to those near him he remarked : " The Prince of Orange will be glad if he goes ! " A few days later Luxemburg was dead and France was all the poorer for losing the general who had won three great victories.

If Luxemburg had been living in 1695, William would never have scored the one success he ever achieved over France in the recapture of Namur. While the main army in the field was left under the command of Villeroi, the defence of Namur was entrusted to Boufflers and a garrison of 15,000 men. William appeared before the place at the commencement of July, and attacked the town with such vigour that it was only realised when too late that it was in danger. Villeroi was inexcusably remiss in his effort to intervene, and the only attempt he could be said to have made was the attack on Brussels, to which William remained absolutely indifferent. On August 4 Boufflers found himself compelled to surrender the town with 14,000 men, and three weeks later the citadel followed suit. This was the most serious reverse Louis had suffered up to that point of his career, and was quite the equivalent of Landen or Steinkerk. The loss of Namur and the inactivity that characterised the campaign of 1696 more than ever predisposed Louis to make peace on terms, which even his enemies could not represent as unfavourable to themselves. But before the peace negotiations were absolutely set on foot James made one final effort to recover England.

There can be no doubt that Louis's desire for peace caused considerable alarm at St. Germains, for peace could not be made without France recognising in some form or other the authority of William as de facto King of England. James must have felt that an embarrassing situation would then be created about his stay at St. Germains. The only solution that could at all meet the case from his point of view was a successful rising in England for the return of the Stuarts.

The winter of 1695-6 saw, therefore, a revival of Jacobite activity. Middleton and the second Secretary Carryll (an Englishman not to be confounded with the Irish Carrolls) were busy drafting proclamations and declarations. The goodwill of the French Court was ensured, and once more, as in 1692, it was agreed that James's Irish troops should be free to leave France and embark for England. In February Berwick was ordered to review all the Irish troops in the French service, at that moment estimated to number 16,000 men, and the official announcement was made that for the next campaign the Irish troops were to be principally employed in Italy and Germany. But this was only a blind, for the Irish troops were sent by forced marches to Calais, and Berwick left France in disguise for London.

The drafting of a fresh Declaration that should satisfy all parties and sects in England at a moment when sectarianism ruled everything was an impossible feat, and James was wise in his generation when he decided to hold back the Declaration until he had landed in England, and as he never landed it was never published. But with the view of sounding and encouraging Jacobite opinion, he sent over the Duke of Berwick to consult with the leaders, and Sir George Barclay, properly authorised thereto, to rally all available forces to his side and to prepare for a rising. The main question was, were the Jacobites strong enough to rise of their own accord in the first place and hold their ground for a little time until aid could come from France?

The Jacobites sent over a representative named Powell to St. Germains, and whether it was due to his desire to please or to a want of judgment he represented that the Jacobites were ready to rise at any moment. He made a statement to this effect for the information of the French Government, which was shown to Louis, who agreed to afford the aid necessary to support the English rising. But the assumption was that the rising in England was to precede the departure of the French expedition. The King of France and his advisers made this stipulation the indispensable condition of their co-operation. It was then that Berwick and a certain number of officers were sent over in detached parties to head the movement, and to lend the Jacobite insurgents the aid of their experience in war.

Berwick arrived in London and was placed in a secure retreat by his uncle Marlborough, and he seems to have been also sheltered by the young Duke of Richmond. He had several interviews with the leading men which satisfied him that there would be no rising until James had himself landed in sufficient force. But he saw others besides the leaders. He met some of the minor tools. He saw Sir George Barclay, and he learnt from him that there was a plot on foot for the assassination of William, and that in a weak moment Barclay had committed himself to approval of it. Berwick, fearful of his own reputation, hastily quitted London and arrived in France in safety. Considering his experience after Landen it was a brave thing to venture to London at all, but to leave himself open to the suspicion of being a party to a common murder plot was so shocking to his delicate and chivalrous mind that he took to flight as soon as he heard the first rumour of such a scheme.

On February 29, 1696, Berwick met his father a day out from Paris as he was posting to Calais to join his army. Having given him his news he hastened on, and was received the next day by Louis and Madame de Maintenon. After two interviews with them Berwick was ordered to Calais to inform James that Louis was fixed in his decision that no troops should leave France until a rising had actually taken place in England. For three months James remained on the coast, passing his time between Calais and Boulogne in expectancy of the rising which never came, and reviewing periodically the eighteen battalions of which the expedition was to consist. As generalissimo, the Marquis d'Harcourt, who had led Irish troops in the Ardennes, was lent to the English King, and later on the services of Marshal Joyeuse were added. But nothing came of all these preparations because of the occurrences in

England which seriously compromised James's position and chances, although there is not the least room to doubt that he never had anything to do with any of the so-called assassination plots.

But before those matters are dealt with there is one incident that more nearly affected the Irish troops which may be described. Among the Irish officers not one had more signally distinguished himself than Colonel Richard Talbot, the natural son of the Duke of Tyrconnell. As Brigadier he had rendered material assistance to Boisseleau in the first siege of Limerick. He had commanded the Clare regiment in Italy, and at Marsaglia had so distinguished himself as to be nominated Brigadier of Infantry among the next appointments. He and his regiment were at Calais in readiness to sail for England. It became known that Louis had vetoed the expedition unless there were first a rising in England. This decision was, naturally enough, not popular in the force, and there was some grumbling. Talbot was the loudest grumbler, and he criticised Louis in terms that could not be condoned or passed over, more especially as they were uttered in James's own presence. Tale-bearers carried the story to Versailles and St. Germains. The matter had made too much stir to be overlooked, and Talbot was ordered to leave his regiment at Calais and proceed to St. Germains to explain his conduct.

On arrival he was received by Mary of Modena, who had invited Madame de Maintenon to be present, and was then examined as to his language and conduct. He could not deny what he had said, which was tantamount to *lèse-majesté*, and he was at once deprived of his command and sent to the Bastille. This incident occurred on March 29, 1696. The information as to the length of his detention in the Bastille is of an uncertain nature, but in 1701 he was allowed to join his old regiment as " a volunteer " and was killed at Luzzara performing prodigies of valour. His regiment, with a revenue of 20,000 livres a year to the

Colonel, was given to Charles O'Brien, now become Lord Clare, and it cannot be denied that Talbot was very heavily punished for a few indiscreet remarks.

A few days after James's arrival at Calais news reached him of many arrests in London of persons connected with the Jacobite movement, who were accused of plotting the assassination of William. Sir George Barclay, in his official report of his mission, explains very clearly how this conspiracy had originated, and James records regretfully in his Memoirs that " it was a more than usual trouble to the King to see his projects broke, his hopes blasted, and his friends ruined by their pursuing methods contrary to his judgment and without his consent."

Barclay, accompanied by Major Holmes, reached London on January 6, 1696. A day or two later he met Charnock, who complained of James's refusing to approve a scheme that he and others had prepared for getting rid of William. Charnock brought Sir William Perkins, who shared his views, to see Barclay. They explained how easy the plan would be of execution and how resolute they were in their purpose. Barclay was favourably impressed, and producing his commission extended the phrase of " levying war " into " any open attack on the Prince of Orange surrounded by his guards." The definite project of Charnock and his associates was to attack William as he was returning from hunting in either Windsor or Richmond Parks. Other persons were brought in, mostly military men like Captains Knightly, Fisher, and Hungate, and all the preparations were made with great care and deliberation. Forty armed men were got together, horses were bought by Barclay, and the spot for the attack was carefully selected on Turnham Green.

Among forty adventurers chosen from unemployed officers, it is not very surprising that there should be a few traitors. Captains Fisher and Prendergast carried the information to Lord Portland. Another individual named La Rue went alone, and when the authorities thought they

could secure the whole band they struck their blow.
William left Kensington Palace to go hunting in Richmond
Park, and the conspirators hastened to the rendezvous at
Turnham Green to attack him on his return. But William
did not return that way, and a regiment of cavalry swooped
down on those of the conspirators who had arrived. Barclay
and Holmes had not arrived, and eventually escaped to
France ; but the others were brought to trial and executed
with as little delay as possible. It is said of Prendergast
that his conscience pricked him, but it had not pricked him
soon enough to prevent his joining the plotters and learning
their secrets.

The worst injury to the Jacobite cause from this conspiracy was in its consequences, for several of the parties to
the murder plot knew of the intended Jacobite rising, and
in the hope of saving their own necks were not backward in
incriminating others. Many arrests followed, and among
the most notable persons seized was Sir John Fenwick. He
was a fervent Jacobite prepared to fight for King James,
but had no part in the murder plot. It was, however,
easier to get from an English jury a death sentence for the
latter offence than for vague intriguing, and Fenwick was
tried and condemned. William owed him a grudge and
was set on his death. Fenwick's attempt to save his life by
revealing the treason of Marlborough and others in high
station did not help him, but it had the effect of frightening
all the Jacobite sympathisers, who conceived that there
had been indiscretion at St. Germains and that it was too
perilous to correspond with it any more.

So in every way James was a sufferer and loser by the
abortive movement of 1696 to recover his throne, which was
destined to be the last he was to make. Louis withdrew his
troops from the coast, and came to the conclusion that a
restoration of James was no longer possible, and this made
him more than ever set on closing the war. In England
James was discredited by the murder conspiracy with which
he had nothing to do, so it turned out that he suffered

through his friends.   In more than one quarter, too, the view was growing that the Stuart cause would be more likely to prosper if it were represented by the young Prince of Wales than the old King, but James had very strong views on the indefeasible rights of royalty and refused to waive them on any terms.   He was King of England *de jure*, and nothing would induce him to give up that position, not even the offer of another crown, which was made him in Poland.   This he rejected because it would entail the abdication of the one that was his by right.   The Polish throne was then placed at the disposal of the Prince of Conty, one of Louis's natural children, and for a brief period it was occupied by him.

Although peace was not to be attained for some time longer, Louis's efforts in that direction were not wholly fruitless.   After Marsaglia the Duke of Savoy had become less keen for the prolongation of the war, and seeing the chance of recovering his paternal estates growing more and more remote as the ally of the Emperor, he decided at last on coming to terms with Louis.   A truce was concluded between them in July, 1696, and this was followed by a formal treaty and alliance.   By its terms the Duke was appointed generalissimo of the French and Piedmontese forces in Italy, and in this capacity he undertook the siege of Milan.   A still more important part of the convention was that his daughter should be betrothed to the Duke of Burgundy, and as she was only eleven years of age it was arranged that she should be sent to France to receive her education under the supervision of Madame de Maintenon at St. Cyr.

Towards the end of 1696 Louis induced Charles XI, King of Sweden, to act as mediator between him and the other Powers, and although that King's death somewhat interfered with the negotiations, the *pourparlers* had commenced before it took place, and his son and successor, the warlike Charles XII, was able to employ his good offices for the first and only time in the cause of peace.   James, well aware of all that was proceeding and apprehending even that the consequences of peace would be worse for him than they proved, made many efforts to assert what he termed his rights, and represented his case in a special manner to the Emperor. He proposed to that potentate to make a separate and advantageous treaty with the King of France, who would then be able to take up his cause for the recovery of the English Crown in real earnest. These representations were vain, and were received in a slighting manner at Vienna. James's further proposal that he should send a Minister plenipotentiary to the peace negotiations was also not entertained.

The negotiations between France and the Allied Powers got so far as the selection of a place of meeting and the nomination of plenipotentiaries by the respective Governments. Ryswyck, a country house belonging to William, situated half-way between the Hague and Delft, was selected for the conference; and the plenipotentiaries were as follows: for France, Harlay, Comte Bonneuil, Verjus, Comte de Crécy, and M. Callières; for England, Earl of Pembroke, Viscount Villiers, and Mr. Williamson; for the Empire, Count Kaunitz, Count Stratmann, and Baron Seilern; and for the States, Messrs. Dichult and Burel.

The negotiations covered from beginning to end a period of ten months, and Louis made just as strenuous an effort for the campaign of 1697 as he had done for any of its predecessors, although there is no doubt that his instructions to his generals were not to force on engagements. Three armies were in the field in the Netherlands under the separate commands of Boufflers, Villeroi, and Catinat. Catinat had been transferred from Italy in order not to clash with his late opponent the Duke of Savoy, and he was the only one of the three to do anything in the field. He laid siege to and captured Ath on June 7. In Spain the French arms achieved a signal success when Vendôme captured, on August 18, Barcelona, considered by the Spaniards to be their chief fortress. These successes

showed that the fortune of war was still on the side of
France, and to the Jacobites they supplied an argument for
urging their friends at Versailles to make one more effort
for the recovery of James's throne. Why make peace, it was
said, in the midst of victory when your adversaries are
known to be divided among themselves and in grave financial embarrassment ? But this opinion could not be
expressed loudly. James could not utter it to Louis
himself, who, with the Spanish succession looming not far
ahead, was resolved to close the struggle in progress if he
could do so in honour.

At last William, who had been reluctant to make peace,
and who was the real hindrance to the rapid progress of the
negotiations at Ryswyck, came to the conclusion that peace
was just as necessary for himself as it seemed to Louis. The
English Parliament had become less generous in its supplies,
the relations between English and Dutchmen were strained,
and the support of the Empire was weakening. William
determined to hasten matters by taking an independent
course. At the end of June he instructed the Earl of
Portland to write to Marshal Boufflers and suggest an
interview. Boufflers had met Portland after the surrender
of Namur, and they had consequently a slight personal
acquaintance. Boufflers informed Louis of the proposal,
and awaited his orders. They soon came, with the royal
permission to have the interview. Boufflers, cautious and
honest, took the precaution of sending a report to the
King after each interview, and with one exception of not
having a second meeting until he had received a fresh
authority from the King his master.

The field conferences, as they were called, between
Boufflers and Portland were held with one exception at the
advanced posts between the two armies. A comparatively
small party accompanied the principals, who on meeting
stood apart or walked aside, no one being permitted to
overhear or take part in their conversations. It was therefore
Boufflers against Portland, the word of one man against the

other, and as there were seven meetings altogether and as there were many hypothetical situations discussed, it would not be surprising if, equal good faith granted on both sides, there were some discrepancies between the reports of the two negotiators in details. The meetings were held on July 8, 15, 17, 20, and 26, August 2 and September 11. The last of these took place in a country house at Tubize.

The subject of these conferences was exclusively the question of the Stuarts. As to the main conditions of the peace they were left to the plenipotentiaries at Ryswyck, and in themselves called for no prolonged discussion as they were based, so far as England and France were concerned, on a mutual surrender of all advantages gained or a return to the *status quo ante*. But William wanted very much to inflict a personal humiliation on James. He had taken away his Crown ; he wanted to deprive him of his place of exile, the sure retreat put at his disposal by the French King on the banks of the Seine. It was a design in perfect accord with the petty spitefulness of William's character, no longer modified by the broader views of his wife. He instructed Portland to say that the real obstacle to the conclusion of peace was the continued presence of the Stuart family in France, and that if they were sent out of the country, to Italy, or elsewhere, the treaty should be signed at once. To that proposal Boufflers gave, on behalf of Louis, an absolute refusal.

Portland then changed his ground. His Prince would be satisfied if James were sent to some other part of France— Avignon being named—and if the Court of St. Germains were broken up. But at the same time that he made this proposal he put forward a very specious suggestion which might tend to soften its effect. William, said Lord Portland, had no heir, and at that moment was not on speaking terms with his sister-in-law Anne. He would be willing to adopt the young Prince of Wales as his heir so far as England was concerned, if he were sent to that country to be brought up as a Protestant.

It may be fully admitted that this proposal represented the best chance the Stuart family ever had of recovering the English throne, but it would have been disgraceful if James had listened to the proposal for a moment. It is to his credit that he treated the offer with contemptuous scorn. William was the man who, more than any one else, had spread the story that the young Prince of Wales was no Stuart, but a child foisted on the English people. The slander had served his turn; he was now willing to make him his own heir so far as England was concerned. He squared his conscience by adding, " but it must ensure the Protestant succession." On this understanding he was even willing to allow Queen Mary of Modena to receive her dowry of £50,000 a year, although still insisting on the break-up of the Court of St. Germains. William's proposal was then that James should waive his rights in favour of his son, who should be sent to England, that the Court of St. Germains should be dissolved, and that in return he would recognise the Prince of Wales as his heir and get the English Parliament to pay his mother the £50,000 a year which was her due.

James simply rejected the proposal. He confined himself to the statement that his rights were indefeasible, and that he could be no party to their diminution or abrogation. It is impossible not to feel that in this instance James appears to greater advantage than his rival. Although there is no reference to the matter in the text of the treaty, it was assumed by the French, rightly or wrongly, that William had agreed to pay the Queen her dowry, but when Portland arrived in France as William's ambassador, and the point was brought before him, he replied that William would not pay it so long as the Stuarts remained at St. Germains. He even went so far as to declare that Boufflers had promised him that the Stuarts should be banished from St. Germains, but Boufflers was at hand to contradict him, and it is quite certain that Boufflers throughout had only re-echoed Louis's words, and that Louis always repelled the proposal and would never listen to it. Dangeau makes Louis's position clear in the following passage :—

" Ils avaient proposé que le Roi obligeât le roi et la reine d'Angleterre de sortir de France, et ensuite s'étaient réduits à demander qu'au moins ils ne demeurassent pas à Saint Germain, si près du Roi qui est d'ordinaire à Versailles. S. M. n'a voulu écouter aucunes propositions là-dessus, disant toujours que c'étaient des gens malheureux à qui il avait donné asile et des gens véritablement ses amis, et qu'il ne voulait point les éloigner de lui ; qu'ils étaient assez à plaindre sans augmenter encore leurs malheurs."

When Portland, not satisfied with Boufflers's dissent, brought the matter officially before the French Government, he received the following answer from the Marquis de Torcy :—

" This point was frequently raised during the Conferences with the Maréchal de Boufflers, and it was also discussed under different forms at Ryswyck. It was always and uniformly rejected. It is a matter absolutely finished with. I know that the King will not only never allow anything in the least degree bearing on the subject to be taken in hand, but that he will feel exceedingly wounded if he hears it spoken of any more. I can assure you of his good disposition to correspond in every way with the bond which has been established between him and your sovereign ; but a single word about St. Germains might spoil these good dispositions and render your embassy sterile and unpleasant. If it were permissible for me to give you a word of advice, it would be not to say a single word to the King, nor even to his ministers, on a question that has been settled, and about which the King has definitely made up his mind."

Language could not be clearer or more emphatic than this, and Louis took occasion to say that he entirely approved of what the Marquis de Torcy had stated.

As a matter of fact, Queen Mary of Modena did not get a penny of her dower for another eighteen years, or till after the Treaty of Utrecht. Mr. Secretary Vernon was quite

z

correct when he wrote of the events of 1698 that " he feared
the poor lady never received any payment on this account."
The resources of the Stuart family continued to be no more
than the amount of Louis's pension.

The treaty of peace was signed on September 20, 1697,
while James and Mary were paying their usual annual visit
to Fontainebleau, and Louis, to show his regard for his
guests, gave orders that no rejoicings for the welcome
event were to be made until after their departure. Only
after they had left were the bands allowed to play, the Te
Deum to be sung in the Royal Chapel, and the terrace to
be illuminated in celebration of the Peace of Ryswyck.

James had fully realised all the consequences of peace
when in 1696 he had striven to avert it.   The first consequence was that Louis had recognised William as King of
Great Britain, and as there could not be two holders of the
same style James ceased to be called the " roi d'Angleterre "
and became instead " le roi Jacques." The second consequence was that an end was put to Jacobite intriguing.
St. Germains remained a residence, a home, as it were, but
it ceased to be the head-quarters of a King striving to
recover his crown.

On the other hand, James had preserved his dignity and
his honour. He had not truckled to his old enemy, he had
spurned his specious offer. He even published his Protest
to the signing of any treaty with " the Usurper of our
Kingdoms," and declared it to be null and void. Of all
the prominent actors in the Stuart drama James was the
most consistent, and his conduct at this crisis was the exact
opposite of that of Henry of Navarre, who changed his
religion because, as he said : " Paris vaut bien une messe."
Even to recover the throne of his ancestors James would not
waive a tittle of his rights, or allow his son to be brought
up in another religion than his own. His firmness was all the
more remarkable and commendable, because it was no
secret that Louis was favourably inclined to the project.
Among Stuart failings must not be placed the moral

cowardice that dictates the dropping of one's principles for the sake of worldly advantages.

James, however, soon found definite reasons for appreciating the change in his position. As King of England, temporarily absent from his realm, he had possessed his own bodyguard in the two troops first commanded by the Duke of Berwick and Lord Lucan. He received a hint that such a bodyguard was no longer appropriate to his circumstances, and to leave him in no doubt on the subject the French authorities called in the horses they had lent for this corps. Moreover, the French Government was the paymaster, and had merely to notify that it could no longer recognise it for the bodyguard to cease to exist. This was the little corps that had done so well under Harcourt in the Ardennes, and again at Landen. Nor did the matter stop here.

If a deposed King had no right to a bodyguard, it was also quite clear that France, being at peace with England, could not continue to pay a regiment known as His Britannic Majesty's Guards. This regiment, despite its heroism at Landen and its good services generally, was therefore disbanded, and finally disappeared from the list of Irish regiments in France. Its Colonel was General William Dorington, and it was reformed into the Dorington regiment, of which we shall speak a little further on.

James was thus deprived of what might be called his military household. No interference was attempted with his civil establishment, and his chief advisers continued to be called Secretaries of State. But even for them times were changed, and they were no longer allowed the free access to French Ministers, which they had hitherto enjoyed. Lord Middleton went over to Versailles on an occasion in February, 1698, and Lord Portland, who got on very well with Louis and received from him his portrait set in diamonds, happened to be there at the same time. Some confusion and embarrassment arose, and Louis begged the gentlemen from St. Germains not to attend on those days that he received the British ambassador.

These were indications of the change that had taken place. A less embarrassing meeting of the opposing representatives of England occurred a little later when King James was present at a review of French troops at Grevillon near Poissy. Portland does not seem to have been there, but his son, Lord Woodstock, was, and his suite was largely represented, and they were all said to be greatly impressed by the good looks of the young Prince of Wales, who was now ten years of age. King James had a long talk with a Dutch gentleman, Mr. Wassenaer, in the confidence of King William, but his efforts to obtain some recognition from the English gentlemen present are stated to have failed.

Some of the great French nobles who knew James, not as a man of business and politician, but as a sportsman, sympathised with him in the days of his adversity, and one of them found an opportunity of showing this in administering a snub to Lord Portland. The Duc de Rochefoucauld was Grand Huntsman to the King of France, and King James found his only amusement in following the hounds. James was not merely a good rider, but an accomplished horseman. As such he was very much admired, and was generally in at the death. One of the hospitable acts of Louis had been to place the hunt at James's disposal, and to request Rochefoucauld to take his orders from the King of England. Lord Portland was also a keen sportsman, and one day he expressed his desire to attend a great meeting when the *meute* of sixty big dogs assembled. The Duc de Rochefoucauld replied in the most icy tone of formal politeness : " I have the honour, it is true, to be the Grand Veneur, but I do not arrange the hunts. It is from King James that I take my orders, and although he comes often to the meet, I do not know until almost the moment of setting out." It is said that Portland was very mortified and not sorry to quit Paris when he gave up the embassy to his successor, Lord Jersey.

The only person among the Jacobites to whom Louis extended a large measure of his goodwill was the Duke of Berwick. Berwick had done well in the army, and he had also shown that he possessed extraordinarily good judgment and tact. He had been tried in many situations and never found wanting. At the time of his marriage, in 1695, with Honora de Burgh, widow of Sarsfield, Earl of Lucan, Louis had assigned him a suite of rooms at Marly, and when peace was approaching, in the summer of 1697, he granted him a pension of 12,000 francs, to be enjoyed in addition to his pay as Lieutenant-General. His brother, the Duke of Albemarle, the Lord Grand Prior (generally called in France " le cadet de Berwick "), also benefited by his popularity, and got a pension of 2000 écus in addition to his pay as Chef d'Escadron in the French Navy.

If James suffered from the Peace of Ryswyck in his state, and in the deprivation of some of the attributes of royalty, the sufferings of his unfortunate Irish soldiers proved incomparably greater, and reduced with little or no warning the majority of an army of warriors to a condition of indigence and misery that defies description, and that those who have only thought it their mission to extol the glory of the Irish Brigade have consistently ignored.

Louis made peace primarily and above all things for financial reasons. His resources were strained, the taxes were producing less, no new sources of revenue could be found, and the commerce of the country had seriously declined since Tourville's defeat at La Hogue. Besides, wars had been discovered to be unprofitable. Victory brought no advantage. The successful generals were afraid to follow up their successes lest their armies should starve. Experience had shown that Germany was an exceedingly poor country, in which an invading army could not be fed. The Belgian provinces, always productive, had been drained and exhausted by the long wars. From every point of view peace was desirable, and there was urgent need also to secure a cessation of the immense outlay, and to allow of the recovery of exhausted nature.

Louis turned his attention to economies, and the first step he took was the reduction of his armies to a peace establishment. A peace establishment meant the reduction of the army by three-fifths. If we fix the total strength of all the French armies in 1697 at 250,000 men, the meaning of this reduction was that by January, 1698, 150,000 of them had been dismissed and sent to their homes. For the French soldier this was no hardship; it was rather the reverse of one. The fields needed tillage, the vineyards called for attention. Throughout France there was such a scarcity of labour due to the wars and the exile of the Huguenots that only women and children remained available. The reduction of the army was for the French soldier and people a positive blessing and advantage.

Nor was it a hardship for the Swiss, Flemish, or Walloon mercenaries fighting under the white cockade. Their homes were not far off. For many of them also was there work to do and a living to be gained in their own lands.

But these conditions did not apply to the poor Irish. They had no home to return to. They had given up all to follow a myth, urged thereto by a short-sighted and unreasoning antipathy to their brother people. Even if they had wished to do so they could not return to Ireland, for on the morrow of the Peace of Ryswyck, William had passed a law ordering none who had served the Stuarts to stay or be received in the three Kingdoms under penalty of being indicted for treason. Unlike the others, then, the Irish had no place of retreat or retirement.

When the capitulations were drawn up for the formation of the Mountcashell Brigade in 1690, and for the larger contingent in 1692, no conditions were made for the time when peace would supersede war. The Irish soldiers passed under the conditions of French law without realising exactly what they had done. Louis had said very charmingly and very hospitably that " he would always treat the

Irish Catholics who came to his Kingdom as his own subjects, and that he would see that they enjoyed the same rights as native-born Frenchmen without their being obliged to take out letters of naturalisation." But " the same rights " carry with them the same obligations and penalties, even when they weigh with peculiar hardship on the individual as in the case under consideration. In 1690 and 1692 it was not to be expected that Louis should look too far ahead and attempt to provide for all contingencies. He was satisfied that in the Irish contingent he was obtaining some return for his great sacrifices on behalf of the Stuarts. And as for the Irish they did not look ahead at all. The leaders were set on gaining military distinction in the French army, the men followed like sheep where they were led.

The Irish having become for all practical purposes French subjects, they could not expect to escape the common lot. A privileged position could not be created expressly for them. The French army could not be reduced to less than one-half its strength, and the two Irish contingents preserved in their integrity. The same edict applied to all, and its effect was as follows :—

The Mountcashell Brigade, with its three regiments of Lee (Mountcashell), Clare and Dillon, each of which had been increased to three battalions in 1692, as described, was reduced by the suppression of two battalions apiece. Each regiment was to be restricted to one battalion of fourteen companies of fifty men each, or a total of seven hundred men. In this corps alone 4000 Irishmen were turned adrift ; the total of 6000 with the colours being reduced to 2100.

The other Irish contingent, which was officially known down to the Peace as the King of England's army, was treated on the same principle. It had been divided in 1692 into the two household troops, two cavalry regiments, two dragoon regiments, and six infantry regiments of two battalions each. Its total strength had then been 14,000 men. The ravages of war had reduced this total by the end of 1697 to little more than 11,000 men, and that was the number with which the French authorities had to deal at the time of the reduction. As some of the battalions were very attenuated—notably the Guards, which after Landen mustered for its two battalions only the strength of one—the task of reducing this corps in the symmetrical form desired by the French disciplinarian was simplified, for it was deemed necessary in their case to suppress whole regiments and not merely battalions.

We have seen how the two household troops were abolished as being no longer in harmony with the altered circumstances. Of the two cavalry regiments one—Lord Galmoye's—was abolished. The other, called after General Sheldon, its commander, was preserved. The two regiments of Dragoons, called the Royal and the Queen's, were totally suppressed. The six regiments of infantry of two battalions each were reduced to four regiments of one battalion each. These four regiments received new names, taking those of their Colonels. They were the following : Dorington, Berwick, Albemarle, and Bourke. Each of these battalions was of the recognised strength of seven hundred men divided into fourteen companies of fifty men each.

The Irish contingent, titularly subject to King James, was thus reduced to a cavalry regiment of 300 men and 2800 infantry. If we take the effective strength of the corps at the declaration of peace to have been no more than 11,000 men, we find that from this force 8000 Irishmen were turned adrift in a foreign land. Joining the figures of the two contingents together, it follows that nearly 12,000 Irishmen in all were suddenly deprived of their only source of livelihood.

It would be most interesting to follow the peregrinations of some of these unfortunate exiles during the four years after Ryswyck, but there are no materials for the purpose. They suffered in silence, and we can only imagine what their hardships must have been in the nature of things and from the indirect evidence that has come down to us. Under any circumstances the situation thus created could not fail to be hard on the individual, but there were many aggravations of it in the case under consideration. The Irish did not know French, and for some reason or other the French authorities did not trouble themselves to provide facilities for their learning the language of their new country. It almost seems as if the French continued to regard them as guests rather than as fellow-subjects, and to think that a Stuart revival might recall them to England. Thus it has always appeared to me one of the most extraordinary phenomena in this topsy-turvydom of Anglo-Irish relations that the Irish exiles who went out of Ireland through hatred of England in the seventeenth century preserved the use of the English language as long as there was a brigade in existence, and that the men who charged the English column at Fontenoy under Lally were addressed by him in English and replied in English. So also did the prisoners of the regiment de Lally, taken in India after the battle of Wandewash, speak in our common tongue.

But the limitation of the linguistic attainments of the disbanded Irish soldiers after Ryswyck was a serious aggravation of their troubles. One of its direct consequences was that they flocked to the same place, and tended to herd together. St. Germains became full of Irish beggars, Montmartre was also crowded with them. They had no qualifications for civil life. They knew no trade, they had no industry, they were skilful at nothing. The explanation was not that they were dull or stupid, but simply that in Ireland there had been no opportunity to follow the pursuits of the ordinary citizen. One thing alone they had mastered, the profession of the soldier. They had learnt it in the hardest, but the most instructive, of all schools, that of dire necessity, and now just at the moment that they are reaching a stage of absolute excellence if not perfection in the art of war, the prop is struck from under them, and they are left bewildered and resourceless to face the frowns and the neglect of a hard world. It is not merely that their only resource in life has been taken from them. They are no longer of any use to the French people. They are only an encumbrance, taking away so much of the much-needed and desperately limited supply of the bread of France. In every sense of the word they are aliens, and behind them are locked and double barred the doors of their own country.

Poor King James pities them as they flock round the gates of his château at St. Germains, but what can he do for 12,000 men suddenly deprived of all their means of existence ? He has £2000 a month to provide for all his family, and all the members of his Court who have given up their worldly possessions for his cause. There is not one of them with any resources of his own. The King has to help in a larger or smaller degree all of them. He does all he can. He denies himself everything. He takes fourteen Irish Colonels, and sixteen Irish Lieutenant-Colonels on his pension list, and he allows the former thirty sols and the latter twenty-five sols a day. This mere pittance (the equivalent of 1s. 3d. and 1s. a day) could not go far, but it was marvellous what a man could live on in the France of old days without derogating from his gentility. These were the fortunate ones; the majority were not so happy, for they got nothing.

Many received their lodging, the hospitality at least of a roof, in the château of St. Germains, and thus began the practice of treating it as a sort of asylum for the poor Irish, which was not broken till the French Revolution. But these were only the minority. What the greater number did, God alone knew. Some of the higher-placed personages spared James's pockets by seeking charity elsewhere. Anthony Hamilton found a home with his sister, the Countess of Gramont, in the villa of Le Moulineau in the park of Versailles, given her by Louis XIV. Richard Hamilton was the constant guest of the Cardinal de Bouillon, who kept open house for the Irish officers. He visited other houses, like that of the Croissys, and wherever he went he gained the reputation of being an agreeable and amiable gentleman. No doubt the officers fortunate enough to be kept on the full establishment of the army, like Dorington, Lee, and Roth, did what they could to help their less fortunate brethren in arms, but it must have been very little, for the diminution in the strength of the regiments had materially reduced the Colonel's recompense, and no one could pretend that the pay of the lower grades among the officers was more than sufficient for their own needs.

As a matter of fact, too, the colonelcy of a regiment no longer brought in the £800 a year in poundage which it had done when Lord Mountcashell first received his commission in the French army. Even if the men had been mulcted the sol in the livre it would not have produced for the chief over £300 a year, and the deduction had become so unpopular with the men that, shortly after the Peace, Louis saw fit to abolish the custom, and to pay it to the colonels out of the sixteen deniers hitherto deducted from the soldier's nominal pay for his food. To compensate the Colonel for the difference between the sol (sou = twelve deniers) and the four deniers paid him under the new order, the Colonel's pay was raised from 2700 to 4700 livres a year. There was not much margin here for the support of others.

The principal relief for the poor Irish came from the Church. The Papal Nuncio made a grant of 25,000 livres for the purpose—an immense sum for that period. The Archbishop of Rheims was another benefactor; the Abbé Bailly devoted all his time and income to alleviate the sufferings of the Irish soldiery, and when he died a few years later he bequeathed all his fortune for the same purpose. Some relief, too, came from an unexpected quarter. By the Treaty of Ryswyck the Duke of Lorraine recovered his province, and he sent his trusty friend and brother in arms, Count Taaffe, to Nancy to take over the Government. Some of the Irish troops dismissed from the army of the Rhine came to him and were given employment in the Ducal service. Taaffe, both of whose brothers had been killed in Ireland in James's cause, was really Earl of Carlingford, and he was the only Irish Catholic nobleman whose estates were not escheated by William, and against whom the Act of Attainder was waived by that Prince. Count Taaffe was a friend in need to many of the Irish. On the other hand, he induced a certain number of them to exchange the French for the Emperor's service.

Other sympathisers included the doctors of the Sorbonne, who raised a subscription among themselves for the Irish sufferers. So unusual a course in the seventeenth century testifies in itself to the magnitude of the distress and to the publicity it had aroused. The poor Queen Mary of Modena, whose dowry, if it had only been paid by William, would have been received at a most opportune moment, did what she could to mitigate the troubles, and there are occasional references to raffles for the benefit of the sufferers. The situation of the Irish in France was aggravated by the arrival of the persons expelled from Ireland under the penal laws. These men brought no property with them, and their needs only swelled the sum total of the prevalent distress. On this point James wrote a paragraph which completes the picture by one who certainly did not look on unmoved at the misfortunes of his followers :—

"The Bill of Banishment which followed immediately upon the peace was a fresh subject of trouble and additional burthen to the King. The Parliament in England passed an act to make it high treason, not only for any to correspond with the King, but obliged all those who had been in his service since the Revolution, or even in France itself, except with a pass from the government, to quit the Dominions in a day prefixed, or be guilty of high treason *ex post facto* without a possibility of avoiding it, which was such a piece of cruelty and injustice as has not been equalled in any Government. This his Majesty sayd afflicted him more than all the rest. He was sensible what he had suffered himself was nothing comparatively to what his past disorders might justly deserve, but to see his Loyal subjects so used for their fidelity to him, was what made him stand in need of a more than ordinary grace to support. He had the like vexatious news from Ireland too, the Prince of Orange, notwithstanding all his fair pretences to the Confederate Princes, even during the Conference at Ryswyck, passed a new law in that Kingdom for the rooting out of Popery, which amongst other articles ordered the banishment of all Regular Priests which M. Ruvigny, who commanded there, failed not to put in execution ; so that they came flocking over into France, and above four hundred arrived there in some months after. The relief of these distressed persons, together with such numbers of other Catholics as these Bills of Banishment forced out of the Kingdoms, brought a new burthen as was said upon the King, who had the mortification, even after having distributed amongst them what was necessary for his own support, to see great numbers ready to perish for want without his being able to relieve them."

The Peace of Ryswyck with its accompanying consequences seemed to exercise a baneful influence on James's character. It meant the extinction of his hopes of recovering his throne, and left him no resource save the practice of the severer forms of his religion. He sank into a moody lethargy from which nothing could rouse him. The *fatalisme inerte* which had characterised his conduct in Ireland became more marked, and he showed by his conduct and his observations that he regarded his misfortunes as Heaven's punishment for his faults. It is said that he tortured himself by wearing a spiked belt next his skin, and certainly he observed all the fasts so strictly that he was often on the verge of starvation. But it must always seem strange that the man who spared no effort to show that he had cast aside all human considerations and submitted himself to a higher law, should have hung on to the title and position of King at the very time that he was ostentatiously declining to play the part appertaining thereto. He would not abdicate in set form, and yet he had abdicated in reality. So far as he was concerned the Stuart cause was dead, but he seemed resolved by his exhortations to his son to think more of a heavenly than an earthly crown, and to hold fast to his religion that it should never come to life again. He passed the years following Ryswyck in religious meditation, and every year for a certain period buried himself in the solitary seclusion of La Trappe.

For the majority of men the sad and silent Court of St. Germains seemed a sufficiently appropriate place of penance, and as James always paid his devotions twice a day in the adjoining chapel some one composed the following quatrain on the regularity with which he said his prayers :—

> "C'est ici que Jacques Second
> Sans ministre et sans maîtresse
> Le matin allait à la messe
> Et le soir allait au sermon."

The sight of the deposed monarch detaching himself more and more from the world and devoting himself more exclusively to his religion did not commend itself to all observers. The Archbishop of Rheims said before a large circle in the ante-chamber of St. Germains, after James had passed through on his return from chapel : "Voilà un bonhomme qui a quitté trois royaumes pour une messe." The Archbishop was the brother of the late minister Louvois, who certainly was no believer in James's capacity to keep or regain a crown. By this time the French Government had given up all hope of making use of James as a political ally. He was recognised to be hopelessly unpractical. His information had always been proved false and misleading. He was regarded as a man who brought ill-fortune to every undertaking with which he was connected. Indeed, he was given to proclaiming the same fact himself.

James's own admissions, then, may be regarded as the

final proof of the state of distress to which the Irish exiles were reduced by the peace. Indeed, it was a case about which there is not any need of evidence. Given the established facts, about which there can be no dispute, the inevitable consequences could be imagined without a single record in support.

The Irish suffered in enforced silence. There was no real remedy, but during the four years' peace their ranks were decimated as if in the most sanguinary of wars, and it was with a far weaker Irish contingent that the reconstruction of the Irish Brigade was carried out in 1701. But it was fortunate for them that the peace did not last longer than it did, or in place of the word " decimated " it might have been necessary to have penned the word " exterminated." We do not lay the blame for the neglect of the Irish on Louis's shoulders. It was a hardship created by the special situation that arose through the arrival of a large alien force in the country without any understanding or arrangement as to what should be done when the fighting ceased. Moreover, in fairness to the King of France, it must be remembered that there was an element of uncertainty and doubt as to the stay of the bulk of the force in France. They were King James's men. They could have been employed in the effort to recover his crown had such an effort been made. If La Hogue had not been lost, if the 1696 expedition had really landed in England, the Irish regiments (excepting the original Mountcashell Brigade) would have quitted France perhaps for ever. At least, the restoration of James, which was always hoped for in France, would have led to the departure of the great bulk of the Irish troops.

There was consequently an element of uncertainty as to their permanent stay in France, which has never been properly appreciated. Irish popular writers have always sought to represent that the Irish emigrants after Limerick went abroad to found a new Ireland in France. Something of the sort may have been uppermost in their own mind, but the facts are that on landing in France they became in form and in fact the soldiers of James, whose chief pride was to be King of England. They were twice brigaded to invade England for the purpose of regaining his English crown, and prior to Ryswyck they were always at his orders to make the attempt. Had any of these efforts succeeded they would no doubt have quitted France for ever.

If we bear these facts in mind, and principally the uncertainty of their stay in France, we shall not come to any other conclusion than that Louis behaved with considerable generosity in allowing the ordinary Irish regiments, subject to King James, to be retrenched in the same proportion as the regular French army and not abolished altogether. No doubt he had his eye on future contingencies, and foresaw the arrival of a time when the whole of the Brigade would be included in his own army. No doubt, also, he had been favourably impressed by the warlike capacity of the Irish soldiers. But prudent calculations are not to be considered destructive of all right to a claim for generosity. Generosity was the main element in Louis's treatment of the Stuarts, and of the Irish, and to represent that he had material motives as well is no detraction from his merit. He was a great ruler confronted by enormously great responsibilities. He could not be expected to ignore the fact that the Stuart succession and the Irish problem, as it presented itself at the end of the seventeenth century, were factors in Europe that might tell in his favour. He could not be indifferent to them because there were so few that did.

Let us leave the great ones of the earth to the judgment and rejudgment of history, ever changing in its verdicts by the light of new facts, the reception of fresh impressions and the removal of old prejudices, and endeavour to draw some useful lessons, some sound general deductions, from the lot and experiences of the poor Irish exiles in France. Of Louis and of James it is safe to say that they will receive, as their epoch passes into the true focus for faithful reproduction, a larger measure of justice and tolerant appreciation. But who will think of the sufferings of the Irish emigrants, who went away from their country in 1691, " out of pure devotion to his cause," said James, whilst Sarsfield declared it was " to found a new Ireland in France " ? And who will have the courage to declare that it was one of the most stupendous blunders that the Irish themselves ever committed, or that an English ruler ever allowed ? The person mainly responsible for that act of short-sighted policy was William of Orange—a foreigner who thought nothing of the common vital interests of the two sister islands, but only of his own immediate need to get his continental army out of Ireland.

We must assume that the Irish who marched past Limerick stone, who would not left-wheel or right-wheel as the case might be when they reached it, went out of their country because they would not submit to the English. The decision not to submit to any antagonist excites our admiration, and we can say whole-heartedly and unreservedly that the men who followed Sarsfield and their hereditary chiefs into exile did a fine thing, of which every Irishman may feel proud. But the question cannot be left there. Individuals may do a very fine thing, and yet when the whole question comes to be examined in a later generation, when each incident has to be fitted into its proper place so that a comprehensive view may be taken of the transaction or episode, the fine thing is seen to have been only a stupendous blunder, a permanent injury to the people concerned, and a useless waste of national forces.

Ireland was all the poorer for that emigration of the pick of her manhood, and it is not going too far to say that in some of her counties it entailed a permanent decline in the physical stature of the people which has never been arrested. As has been already pointed out, the departure of the great majority of the survivors of James's Irish army left those who remained at home entirely at the mercy of William's Parliaments. It is no exaggeration to say that the Irish Catholic peasantry, for a century after the Treaty of

2 A

Limerick, was reduced to the lowest state of serfdom verging on savagery. This policy of repression could not have been attempted if the 20,000 stalwarts, who sported the White Cockade, had only remained in Ireland to look after their own and their country's interests in a proper way.

There would have been at least one clear consequence. The English recruiting sergeant, who was forbidden for a whole century to recruit in Ireland, would have plied a busy trade in Ireland during Marlborough's wars, and the laurels which would have been gained in establishing the Imperial power of England instead of under the Fleurs-de-Lis would have contributed to heal the breach between the two brother nations, and to hasten the conclusion of the firm and indissoluble union which is so vital for them both. But instead of that natural and desirable working out of a racial and religious problem the Irish went away to the land which was then thought to be " England's hereditary enemy," and they were arrayed against their English brothers for the better part of half a century. In that time they gained much military glory, they became known among the bravest of the brave, and to a considerable extent they preserved the Irish reputation during the dark period of the eighteenth century when all Englishmen treated Ireland with scorn and contumely.

But it is impossible to avoid the conclusion that this was but a poor return for so much devotion, so much self-sacrifice, so much suffering. Never, it might be contended, was there such an unprofitable waste of national force. The sum total of the good that this ever-dwindling band of Irishmen, however heroic, were able to do in the interests of a rich and powerful country like France must have been small, whereas the direct and indirect injury to their own country by their going out of it may be affirmed to have been very considerable.

Nor did they do themselves any good in the land of their adoption. They obtained no definite status, they received no grant of lands, they were so many social pariahs until the call to arms resounded through the land, and then it was remembered that they were good at fighting. The Irish exiles were poor beggars ("pauvres gueux" when they were not merely "pauvres diables") until there was need to use them as "food for powder." Even if we take count only of the higher grades, the recognition was meagre. A higher rank than Lieutenant-General, which did not carry independent command, was never conferred on a soldier of Irish birth or descent for half a century after Limerick, and then only in the solitary case of the second Viscount Clare, who was known in the French army as Marshal Thomond. Yet we shall come across in the sequel many instances where it was deserved.

The explanation of this neglect, of this inequality of treatment, is not to be found in any petty jealousy among the heads of the French army. It was due exclusively to the fact that the highest army commands were always a reflection of Court life and Court favour. To be a Marshal of France was the prescriptive right of the noblest and most ancient families of the country. There was no room in such a system for outsiders, least of all was there room for the poor Irish leaders so cramped in their poverty. In the eighteenth century down to the Revolution only two foreigners besides Thomond attained the Marshalate. They were Berwick and Saxe, both, curiously enough, the natural sons of Kings. But although it is the somewhat loose practice to speak of Berwick as if he were an Irish general, because he led the Irish troops in the field, he was not one, and this half Stuart, half Churchill, was never very appreciative of his Irish colleagues. He was perhaps too cold, cautious, and self-restrained for their effusive temperament.

The point of these observations is that the Irish themselves did not obtain the personal satisfaction in the French army that they might have expected and that their services entitled them to receive. In other armies, in Austria, Russia, and Spain, Irish officers rose to the highest rank and led large armies in the field. In France this never happened, although she possessed an Irish Brigade for half a century and Irish regiments for twice as long. There was no breaking through the caste or custom of French procedure in such matters. The Irish officers were only held good enough for the subordinate positions, and the unfortunate Lally, probably the greatest military genius of them all, was only held good enough for the block.

By the force of things, by the insuperable barrier of ancient privilege, the Irish officers of any pretension to high command could not find contentment for their aspirations in the French service. But they had committed themselves to a course from which they could not turn back. They had to make the best of their position, and the long war that marked the close of Louis's reign gave them little leisure for grumbling.

Finally, it must be admitted that the departure of the Irish exiles who constituted the Brigade in France in no way benefited their country. It did not bring Irish problems nearer solution. It rather tended to make them more difficult, and to aggravate a sufficiently complicated and threatening situation. At the most, the only beneficial consequence that I can see from it is that it was no longer possible for prejudiced Englishmen to taunt the Irish race with cowardice. It is only as furnishing an opportunity for the vindication of national character that I can discover any material result from the going forth of the Irish after Limerick. It counts, no doubt, but it could have been attained in a much more practical and profitable manner if Englishmen and Irishmen had only come together after the Boyne instead of fixing upon that misjudged and ill-described event—a foreign victory on British soil—as a line of cleavage.

But hard as is always the exile's lot, it may be questioned whether any fugitives from their native land ever had a worse experience than the poor Irish after the conclusion of the Peace of Ryswyck. They must have been brought to the lowest depths of despair, and wished themselves back in their own country. If William had only known what was the wise course for the country upon which he had, half by good luck and half by the division of English political parties, forced his foreign rule, he would have sent his ships to Brest and St. Malo for the purpose of offering the Irish free passage back to their own land. There can be no doubt that the starving men would have greeted the offer with effusion. But instead of seizing the opportunity William fanned the flame of national discord, and intensfied the racial animosity by passing penal laws and decreeing wholesale banishments. These were the acts not of an Englishman but of a foreigner, who did not know England and knew still less of Ireland. The foreign conquest of England in 1688, for England was conquered for a brief space by the Prince of Orange with his collection of continental levies, stands as a warning to all time that when party strife reaches the acute stage of passion and prejudice, the door lies open to the invader.

We leave the Irish Brigade at the lowest stage in its fortunes, when it is threatened with slow death by inanition and starvation. The general peace, which has brought others pleasure and content, threatens the Irish exiles with ruin and extinction. But happily for them it is not to prove too long. The crisis in their fate will be surmounted. In four years the great King will once more "*fait battre le tambour*," and then he will bethink him of his brave and unfortunate Irish auxiliaries.

NOTE.—*The further history of the Irish in France by the same Author is in course of preparation, and the volume will be issued next year under the title of* "THE IRISH EXILES AT ST. GERMAINS."

INDEX

Abbeville, 47
Abercorn, Earl of (first), 67
Abercorn, Earl of (sixth), 244
Abercorn regiment, 176, 233
Agnes, Mother, 37
Albemarle, Duke of, 357
Albemarle regiment, 360
Albeville (Marquis), 176, 199
Albuquerque, 150
Almonde, Countess d', 10, 18, 23, 32
Amande, M. d', 163
Amanzé, General d', 93, 120, 318
Ambleteuse, 22
Amfreville, Admiral, 136
Anglure, M. d', 93
Anne, Princess, 203, 296
Annécy, 219
Anselm, Father, 63, 250
Antrim's regiment, 151, 159, 167
Antwerp, 329
"Apollon," the, 57
Archives, French, 216, 220
Ardee, 125, 144
Ardennes, 315
Argelles, 221
Arklow, 177
Armstrong, Captain, 138
Arthur, Colonel, 243
Arthur, Major, 160, 161
Arthur, Robert, 292
Artillery at the Boyne, 151
Art Macmurrogh, 60
Artagnan, Brigadier d', 327
Asfeld Dragoons, 316
Ashton, John, 296, 297
Ath, 349
Athenry, 246
Athlone, 145, 185; successful
    defence of, 186; 227, 228, 229;
    captured, 231
Athlone regiment, 317
Aughrim, 233; battle of, 233–44
Augsburg, League of, 11, 39, 56
Aumont, Duc d', 21
Austria, 60
Avaux, Count d', 51; his diplo-
    matic career, 52; his instruc-
    tions, 53; his opinion of James,

83; reports on Irish soldiers,
85; his plan to exchange troops,
86, 90–1; denounces Irish dila-
toriness, 87; opposes James,
88; joins Council, 89; writes
Louvois, 90; his view of Anglo-
Irish relations, 97; charged by
Macaulay with recommending
Irish St. Bartholomew, 99–103;
his criticism of the Hamiltons,
110; his opinion on Derry army,
111; and Melfort, 112–7; ac-
cuses James of wasting money,
113; reports improvement in
Irish army, 123; 128; prepar-
ing departure of Mountcashell
Brigade, 131; criticises young
FitzJames, 132; 140, 141, 146,
147; forbidden to select a
Hamilton, 208; opinion of
Mountcashell, *ibid.*; considers
eligible officers, 213
Avignon, 351
Aylmer, Sir Garret, 103
Bada, Francis, 292
Badges at the Boyne, distinctive, 150
Bagenal regiment, 106
Bagot, Mark, 129
Ballinasloe, 234
Ballineedy, 189, 190
Ballymore, 227, 228
Baltinglass, Lord, 267
Banagher, 190
Bangor, 124
Bann, the, 90
Barbançon, Prince, 310
Barbets, the, 218, 219, 293
Barbezieux, 319
Barcelona, 349
Barclay, Sir George, 343, 344, 346,
    347
Barèges, 341
Barker, Brigadier, 243
Barnewal, Captain, 105
Barnewal, Captain Patrick, 105
Barrett, Colonel John, 205, 288,
    324, 325, 326, 328
Barrett regiment, 185, 204

Base money, 130
Bass Rock, 58
Bastille, the, 15, 45, 345
Bavaria, Elector of, 310, 341
Beachy Head, 187
Beaumont, 22, 23
Beaurepaire, Lieutenant-Colonel, 192
Beer, 107
Bellefonds, Marshal, 297, 302, 303, 341
Bellew's regiment, Lord, 143, 267
Bermingham (family), 340
Berwick, Duke of, 24, 28, 29, 32, 47, 48, 54, 57, 59, 114, 131, 137, 138, 144, 146, 147, 155, 158, 159, 163, 176, 183, 187, 191; describes siege of Limerick, 194-6; 199; recalled by James, 200; 206, 224, 225, 250, 289, 291, 293, 307, 310; describes La Hogue, 301-3; on Steinkerk, 313; 320, 322; at Landen, 325-6; his capture, 329; describes bombardment of Brussels, 341; visit to London, 343-4; marries Sarsfield's widow, 357
Berwick's Memoirs, 88
Berwick regiment, 360
Bethune-Charost, Duc de, 20
Biddulph, Mr., 29
Bietagh, Thomas, 291
Bir Castle, 206
Body-guard, the (James's), 159
Boileau, 310
Boisseleau, 48, 57, 93, 120, 121, 136; defends Limerick, 187 et seq.; his report, 191-3; 201, 330
Boisseleau regiment, 192
Bonneuil, Count, 349
Bophin, Lord, 109, 243
Boufflers, Marshal, 308, 309, 313, 320, 321, 323, 330; surrenders Namur, 342; field conferences with Portland, 350-3
Bouillon, Cardinal de, 362
Boulger (different members of this Leinster sept), 57, 210, 211, 288
Boulogne, 21, 22, 29
Bourbonnais Brigade, the, 311, 312
Bourg la Reine, 51
Bouridal, M., 216

Bourges, 214
Bourk, Colonel David, 243
Bourk, Colonel Ulick, 243
Bourk, Colonel Walter, 233, 239
Bourke, Colonel, 360
Bourke, Colonel Miles, 227
Bourke, Colonel Thomas, 79
Bourke regiment, 360
Boyne, Battle of the, see Chapter VI; summarised by a French wit, 148; strength of armies, 148, 151; won by foreigners, 148; a mist conceals first movements, 150; James's order of battle, 151; Council of War at, 151; James's vacillation at, 152; Macaulay's description of, 153-4, 156-7; R. Hamilton's part in the battle, 155, 157-8; described by five participants in the battle, 158; no fortifications, 159; heroism of the Irish Guards, 160-1; Oldbridge long held by Irish infantry, 161; Schomberg's death at, ibid.; William crosses at Donore, 162; Dumont's evidence, 161-3; Irish cavalry charges, 163; James's narrative, 164-6; Plunkett's description, 166-70; losses at, 170; fresh French evidence on, 171-5; Zurlauben's report, 173-5; Irish troops retreat, 177; a foreign victory on British soil, 372
Boyne, the (river), 111, 144, 149
Boynton, Miss, 66
Braganza, Catherine of, 66
Brasil, 176
Bray, 177
"Breda," the, 205
Breda, 64
Brenan, John, 267
Brest, 56, 177, 283, 285, 339
Breteuil, 24
Brindijonc, 340
Brittany, Irish in, 340
Brittas, Lord, 57
Broadside, a notable, 82-3
Broghall, Edward, 292
Browne, Dominic, 247
Browne, Captain John (Neal), 103
Browne, Colonel John, 263, 268, 271

Bruges, 287, 288
Brussels, 65, 69, 308, 341, 342
Bulkeley, Lady Sophia, 10, 32
Bulkeley, Miss Anne (afterwards Duchess of Berwick), 10
Burel, M., 349
Burgh, Honora de, (Lady Lucan and Duchess of Berwick), 357
Burgundy, Duke of, 348
Butler, Colonel Edmund, 104
Butler, Edward, 104-5
Butler, Colonel Richard, 210
Butler, Colonel Thomas, 244
Butler, Sir Toby, 263, 272
Butler regiment, the, 209, 210, 214, 215
Butler, Walter, regiment, 106

Cabre, 318
Cannon, Colonel, 75, 111, 112, 287
Callières, M., 349
Caillemotte, 155, 160, 161
Calais, 9, 20, 35, 287
"Campaign of the Ladies," the, 308
Carlingford, Earl of, 55 ; killed at Boyne, 163
Carlingford (town), 124
Carny, Sir Charles, 164
Carrickfergus, 124, 140
Carroll, Brian, 291
Carroll, Francis, 292, 334
Carroll, William, 79
Carryll, Secretary of State, 343
Carter, Vice-Admiral, 295, 299, 304
Casaubon (Cambon) regiment, 163, 193
Cashell, Archbishop of, 263, 267
Catalonia, 217
Catholics deprived of arms, 74-5 ; again stripped of lands, 202 ; rights granted to, 268-9 ; rights cancelled, 272-8
Catinat, Marshal, 217, 218, 219, 309, 317, 318, 319, 320 ; checks Duke of Savoy, 331 ; wins battle of Marsaglia, 333-5, 349
Cavalry at Aughrim, misconduct of, 242
Cavan, 137, 138
Cevennes, Protestants in the, 335
Chalandières, 318
Chambéry, 219
Chamerade, 174, 176, 177

Charce, Mdlle. de la, 318
Charlemont, 138, 141
Charlemont regiment, 291
Charleroi, 330
Charles I, 60
Charles II, 11, 61, 64
Charles XI (Sweden), 348
Charles XII (Sweden), 348
Charnock, Mr., 346
Charters, calling in the, 73
Chartres, Duc de, 311, 323
Château Renaud, Admiral, 56, 93, 94, 105, 121, 260, 261, 265, 283, 288
Chatou, 23
Chaulnes, Duc de, 51
Cherbourg, 298
Churchill, Arabella, 37
Churchill, Brigadier, 325
Churchill, John, 68, 69. See Marlborough
Civil Articles of Limerick, 266-80
Clancarty, Earl of (first), 69
Clancarty, Earl of (third), 205, 207, 213, 267
Clancarty, Countess of, 68
Clancarty regiment, 204
Clanrickarde, Earl of 209, 247
Clanrickarde, Ulick Marquis of, 209 ; his daughter, ibid.
Clanrickarde's regiment, 151, 159, 167, 243
Clare, Viscount (various), 199, 209, 317, 334, 371
Clare's regiment, 162
Clare regiment, 317, 318, 319, 331, 359
Clarendon, Earl of, 70, 71
Clarendon's History, 207
Clark, Captain, 9
Clarke, Rev. J. S., 16n, 179
Clifford, Brigadier, 257, 258, 259, 266
Colclough, Colonel Dudley, 257
Coleraine, 90
Colgrave, Colonel, 210
Collier, Sir David, 263
Colonel's poundage, 213, 363
Commons, House of, 62
Compounders, the, 338
Coningsby, Mr., 264, 271
Connel, Brigadier, 243
Conty, Prince of, 348

Cook, Matthew, 291

Cork, 83, 84, 85, 86, 87, 139, 183, 185, 202, 203

Cork, garrison, cruel treatment of the, 204, 287–8

Coulanges, 105

"Courageux," the, 57

Courtassier, 135

Coverent, 131

Crafton, Felicité, 211

Crafton, Colonel Henry, 211

Crane, Mr., 58

Craven, Earl of, 27

Creagh (Bishop of Cork), 199

Creagh regiment, 106

Creagh, Sir Michael, 88, 89

Crécy, Count de, 349

"Criaghts," the, 137

Croissy family, 363

Cromwell confiscates the estates of the Irish, 60–1, 65

Cromwell Fort, 188

Cross, Mr., 296, 297

Crum Castle, 108, 109

Culmore Fort, 91, 103, 110

Cusack, Colonel Nicholas, 263, 292

Curragh, the, 121, 141

Cutts, Lord, 263

Cutts regiment, 193

Dalrymple, Sir J, 18, 179

Danes, the (troops), 148, 162, 193

Dangeau, Marquis de, and his diary, 15, 23, 32, 48, 76, 128, 136, 178, 205, 206, 207, 219, 290, 334, 353

Danish Court, the, 337

Dartmouth, Lord, 29

"Dartmouth," the, 110

Dastier, Lieutenant, 105

Dauphin, the (Monseigneur), 321, 322, 330

Dauphiné, 217, 318, 331

Dauphiness, the, 31, 32, 33, 177

Davia, Madame, 18. *See* Countess d'Almonde

Declaration of James, the, 296–7

Delft, 349

Dempsey, Colonel Lawrence, 143

De Rannes Dragoons, 316

Dicconson, Captain, 57, 334

Dichult, Mr., 349

Dieppe, 340, 341

Dillon, Colonel Arthur, 209, 211

Dillon, Colonel Garrett, 263

Dillon, Maurice, 291

Dillon, Thomas, 247

Dillon, Viscount (Henry), 129, 246, 247, 263

Dillon, Viscount (Theobald), 209, 243

Dillon regiment, a, 215

Dillon regiment, the, 209, 210, 211, 215, 317, 359

Dinant, 309

Donore, 152, 162

Doran, Dr., 244

Dorington, Colonel, afterwards General, William, 57; at the Boyne, 160; 188, 199, 234, 236, 243, 291, 324, 326, 355

Dorington regiment, 355, 360

Douglas, Lieutenant-General, 167, 186, 206

Douglas regiment, 193

Dover, Lord, 35, 52, 108, 115, 139

Drogheda, 64, 111, 124, 143, 144, 149, 185

Drogheda regiment, 193

Dromore, 90

Drummond, Captain, 79

Dublin, 42, 44, 64, 82, 88, 89, 111, 124, 128, 144; panic in, 176

Dublin Corporation, the, 73

Dublin, Parliaments in, 273, 276, 278

Dublin regiment, 291, 324

"Duc," the, 58

Dufour, 10, 18, 19

Duleek, Lord, 243, 244

Duleek Pass, 155, 159, 162, 174

Dumbarton, Lord, 35, 75, 93

Dumont de Bostaquet, 150, 152, 158, 161, 162, 163, 197, 231, 233, 241

Duncannon, 177, 185

Dundalk, 124, 141, 142

Dundee, Viscount, 58, 111; death of, at Killiecrankie, 112

Dungan, Lord, 56, 131–2; at the Boyne, 158, 162, 168; 213

Dungan, Sir John, 63

Dungan, Walter, 63, 64

Dungan, William (Earl of Limerick), 63

Dunkeld, 112

Dunkirk, 340
Du Quesne, Admiral, 94, 111, 115, 177

"Eagle," fireship, 29
Edinburgh Castle, 58
Elizabeth, Queen, 60
Embrun, 318
Emperor Leopold, 349
England, a veiled conquest of, 13, 373; humiliating position of, 40
English recruits, mortality in Ireland, 128
Englishry, fresh plantation of, 61
English troops at Cork, 203; at Steinkerk, 312-4; at Landen, 326; at Brest, 339
Enniskillen, 44, 109
Enniskillen, Lord, 247
Enniskilleners, the, 163
"Entreprenant," the, 57
Escots, Chevalier d', 93, 120, 121, 146
Espinguen, d', 150
Estates, Irish, restored, 97-8
Estrades, M. d', 50
Estrées, Chevalier d', 298, 299
Estrées, Marshal d', 50, 57
Etiquette, questions of, 33-4
Eustace, Maurice, 220
Eugene, Prince (of Savoy), 218, 317, 318, 332, 333
Evelyn's diary, 69, 72, 76, 82, 117
Everard, Sir John, 243

Fagon, Dr., 341
Faméchon regiment, 135, 201
Faméchon, Colonel, 174, 176
Farlow, Captain, 143
Farrell, Colonel Roger, 105
"Faucon," the, 58
Faversham, 27, 28
Feilding, Colonel Robert, 209
Feilding regiment, 209, 210, 212, 214, 215
Fenwick, Sir John, 347
Feuquières, General, 314, 317
Feversham, Lord (Duras), 26
Fisher, Captain, 346
Fitzgerald, Captain Maurice, 92
Fitzgerald, Colonel, 188, 190
Fitzgerald, Colonel Nicholas, 228, 229

FitzJames, Henrietta (Lady Waldegrave), 55
FitzJames, Henry (Lord Grand Prior), 29, 57; scene with Lord Dungan, 131-2; 155, 176, 291; see Albemarle
Flag in France, Irish, 217
Fleming, Captain Richard, 105
Fleurus. 175, 179, 180, 187
Fontainebleau, 354
Foran, 177
Ford, Matthew, 68
Forest regiment, 135
"Fort," the, 57
Four Mile Pass, 142, 143
Foyle, Lough, 94, 110
France, 284, 288, 292
François, Guttier, 10
"François," the, 57
French army, reduction of, 358 et seq.
French contingent at the Boyne, 151 et seq.
French influence in England, 11; opinion of England, 13
French troops return to France, 201
French War Department, archives at, 171-5, 207, 216, 220
"Furieux," the, 57
Furstenberg regiment, 218
Fumeron, M., 226, 227, 241, 247

Gabaret, Admiral, 49, 56, 83, 136, 139, 140, 141
Gacé, Count de, 93, 120, 140, 141
Galway, Lord, 213, 243
Galway regiment, the, 209
Galmoye, Lord, 199, 209, 234, 238, 263, 267, 292, 297, 307, 360
Galway, 174, 178, 183, 198, 233, 245, 246, 247
Garter, Order, conferred by James on Lauzun, 49; on Tyrconnell, 200
Gaydon, John, 292
Gembloux, 309, 321
Gendarmes, regiment, 68, 69
Germany, Emperor of, 11, 349
Gibraltar, 298
Gilbert's Jacobite Narrative, 80-1
Ginkel, General, 204, 227, 229, 231, 232, 234, 235, 236, 237, 246, 248, 249, 256, 258, 262,

263, 264, 265, 266, 271, 283, 285

Girardin, Marquis de, 48, 57, 136, 142, 146, 178

Giuduci, Father, 10

Golding, Captain, 340

Gordon, Duke of, 58

Gosworth, Lord, 176, 249, 267

Grace, Captain Richard, 105

Grace, Colonel Richard, 186, 231

Grafton, Duke of, 200, 204

Gramont, Count de, 68

Gramont, Countess de, (Elizabeth Hamilton), 37, 362

Gramont memoirs, 66, 67

Gravesend, 11

Greder regiment, 217

Grenoble, 218, 219, 318, 331

Griffin, Lord, 28

Guard, the English, 213

Guards, the Irish, 121, 125, 161; its losses at the Boyne, 163; at Aughrim, 236; at Landen, 327-8; abolished, 355

Guildford, 17

Guillestre, 317, 318

Hacket, Mr., 177

Hague, the, 349

Hales, Sir Edward, 26

Ham House, 27, 28

Hamburg, 267

Hamilton, Anthony, 68, 69, 71, 77; commands cavalry, 109; conduct at Newtown Butler, 110, 158, 199, 362

Hamilton, Duke of, 58

Hamilton, Elizabeth, 65, 68

Hamilton, Sir George (first), 67, 68

Hamilton, Sir George (second), 66, 67-9

Hamilton, John, 47, 57, 68, 158, 188, 234, 243

Hamilton, Lady, 66, 67-9; see Frances Jennings and Duchess of Tyrconnell

Hamilton, James, 68

Hamilton, Richard, 48, 68, 69, 71, 75; charge against, 76; 84, 85, 90, 91, 92, 103, 104, 105, 110; at the Boyne, 155, 157-8, 159; 297, 362, 363

Hamilton, Thomas, 68

Harcourt, Marquis d', 315, 316, 323, 327, 344

Havre, de Grace, 297

Heidelberg, 323, 330

Henrietta Maria, Queen, 33, 34

Henry VIII, 60

Herbert, Admiral, 93, 94

Herbert, Sir William, 176, 296

Hocquincourt, Marquis d', 93, 120, 161

Hoguette, Marquis de la, 136, 146, 158; his first letter on the Boyne, 171; his conduct, 172-3; his full report, 174-5; 176, 177; sent to Savoy, 201, 331, 332; his death, 334

Holmes, Major, 346, 347

"Home Rule," an early definition of, 80-1, 87, 96-7

Hore, Gilbert, 79

Hore, Captain W., 257

Horse Guards (James's), 291, 316

House of Commons, the, 128

House of Lords, Irish, 276-7

Howard, Lord Thomas (of Worksop), 57, 117

Huguenots at Marsaglia, 334, 335; in Ireland passim

Hungary, 217

Hungate, Captain, 346

Huxelles, Marquis d', 316

Huy, 323, 326, 327

Inchiquin, Lord, 84

Independent Companies, the, 292-3

Ireland, James's chances in, 41; "money scarce in," 54; at time of James's accession, 62; Protestants v. Catholics in, 70-1, 72, 73, 74, 80-1, 96-7, 98-9, 99-103; Stuart cause dead in, 180-2; a poor country, 201; changed position in, 202

Irish army, defects in, 106-7; after Aughrim, 247

Irish Brigade, achievements of the, 335-6; its status in France, 336; reduction of, 358-60; speak English, 361; sufferings of, 362-8

Irish Catholics lose estates, 61

Irish Cavalry in the Ardennes, 316

Irish Confederation, the, 60

Irish, unfortunate view of the English of the, 221-2

Irish Parliament, the, 93, 95-6, 97, 98

Irish and French, relations between, 83

Irish sent to Hungary, 267

Irish in French navy, 215

Irish regiments sent to England, 75-6

Irish regiments in France, 291

Irish officers in German regiments, 214

Irish at the Marsaglia, 333-5

Irish troops, condition of the, 216; demand red coats, *ibid.*

Irish receive "*la petite solde,*" 290

Iveagh, Lord, 149, 185, 263, 267

Iveagh, Lady, 247

Jacobite plot, a, 343-5

Jamaica, 84

James I, 62

James II, accession of, 11; his position, 12, 13; failure of, 14; entrusts his papers to Terriesi, 16; prepares for flight, 17, 18; his flight, 24-30; visits Versailles, 32; position of, 39-41; not keen on Irish adventure, 41-6: prepares to leave for Ireland, 49-51; sails for Ireland, 56; his affection for Scotland, 58; his views, 59; accession to throne, 61; his religion, 61-2; serves under Turenne, 64; living in Brussels, 69; travels about, 70; sends Talbot to Ireland, 71; his verdict on Tyrconnel's rule, 72; his intentions in Ireland, 81, 86; his arrival in Ireland, 82-8; judged by d'Avaux, 83; makes Tyrconnell a duke, 85; forms Council, 89; marches to Ulster, 90; opens Irish Parliament, 93, 95, 96; excuses English fleet, 94: dissents from Irish policy, 98; his views of Ireland, 99; his conversations with d'Avaux, 101-2; cancels Roze's order, 107-8; his part in the Melfort controversy,

112-7; his views of Ireland, 118; marches against Schomberg, 125; offers battle, 126; defends his inaction, 127; requests French troops, 128; his lenity, 128-9; his measures to benefit soldiers, 130; his requests of France, 134; lets Lord Dover depart, 139; requests Gabaret to attack William's fleet, 140; moves to Dundalk, 142; his talk with Farlow, 143; his weak decision, 143-4; confronted with possibility of losing Dublin, decides to fight, 144-5; desire to leave Ireland, 145-6; a Unionist, 147; at the Boyne, 151-70; flight of, 175; leaves Ireland, 176-80; views of his conduct, 180-2; his account of Aughrim, 239-41; on the oath taken by garrison at Limerick, 260; on the Treaty of Limerick, 281-2; letter to Irish troops, 289; inspects them, 290; his Irish army, 292; design to recover England in 1692, 294-303; his responsibility for La Hogue, 299, *et seq.*; describes battle, 303-5; on Melfort, 338; corresponds with English friends, 338-9; informs Louis of Brest expedition, 339; issues letters of marque, 340; alarmed at approach of peace, 342; sends envoys to England, 343; collects army at Calais, 344; his last attempt, 346-8; his consistency, 352; change in his style and state, 354-5; his comment on William's banishments, 364-5; his religious fervour, 366

James, Prince of Wales (afterwards James III or the Old Pretender), 10, 13, 16, 18, 23, 25, 38, 348, 351, 352, 356

Jamestown, 127

Jeannin, M., 49

Jennings, Frances, 65, 66   *See* Hamilton, Lady, and Tyrconnell, Duchess

Jermyn, Lord, 66

Joyeuse, Marshal, 344

Kaunitz, Count, 349
Kavanagh, Colonel Charles, 205, 220
Kavanagh, Morgan, 205, 220
Kavanaghs (three), 288
Kavanagh regiment, the, 121, 125, 185, 204
Keating, Lord Chief Justice, 97
Kenmare, Lord, 243, 244, 267, 277
Kenmare regiment, 243, 247
Kilconnell, 233. *See* Aughrim
Kilkenny, 204
Killaloe, 189, 226
Killarney, 206
Killiecrankie, 112 ; Irish at, *ibid.*
Kilmallock, Lord, 188, 190, 191, 213, 267, 317, 334, 335
Kingsale, 56, 83, 177, 178, 183, 203, 205
King's regiment (cavalry), 292, 316
Kingsland, Viscount, 129
Kingsland, Lady, 200
Kirke, General, 108, 110, 190
Knightly, Captain, 346

L'Abadie, Mr. de, 17, 26
L'Abadie, Mrs. de, 10, 17
Lacy, James de, 334
Lagos Bay, 337
La Hogue, Cape, 273, 297 ; battle of, 299–305
Lally, Count, 211, 361, 372
Lamarche regiment, 135
Lambay, 227
Lambecq, 308
Landen, 324–7
Landrecies, 15
Lanier, Sir John, 76, 312, 314
La Roche, 316
Larray, Marquis de, 218, 219, 318, 331
La Rue, Colonel Francis, 291, 307
La Rue, 346
La Tour, Colonel, 225, 242, 257, 258
La Trappe, 366
Lauzun (Count, afterwards Duke), 10, 15, 16, 17, 18, 19, 20, 21, 30, 48, 49, 51, 115, 128 ; his appointment, 133–4; leaves for Ireland, 139 ; lands at Cork, *ibid.*; reaches Dublin, 141 ; forgotten his knowledge of war, 144; at the Boyne, 151, 152, 158, 163–6 ; at Galway, 183–4 ; reception in France, 200–1
"Lauzun," the, 177
Lavalin, Captain, 110
Lee, Sir Andrew (Marquis), 217, 286, 293, 335, 341
Lee regiment, 359
Leixlip, 176
Le Moulineau, 362
Leopold, the Emperor, 55
Léry. *See* Girardin
Leyburn, 10, 19
"Light to the Blind, A," 80, 87, 96–7
Lille, 288
Limerick regiment, 291, 319, 331
Limerick Stone, 369
Limerick, 77, 145 ; Irish army retreats to, 183 ; Lauzun's opinion of, 184 ; defended by Boisseleau, 187 *et seq.*; description of, 187 ; garrison in, 188; 220, 225, 226, 238; second siege of, 245–62; Convention of, 263–80
Limerick Treaty, its text, 268–71 ; breaches of, 271–8
List of James's companions to Ireland, 57–8
Lloyd, Mr., 299, 338
Londonderry, 44, 78, 86, 89; William proclaimed at, 90; siege of, 91–4 ; 103–5, 107, 110–1
Londonderry Corporation, the, 73
Lorges, Marshal, 315, 316, 319, 320, 341
Lorraine, Duke of, 218, 363
Loughreagh, 237, 238, 246
Louth, Lord, 263
Louvain, 321, 323
Louis XIV, 11, 12, 14, 21, 22 ; his hospitality to the Stuarts, 22–3 ; receives Queen Mary 23–4 ; receives King James, 24–5 ; his opinon of Queen Mary, 34 ; his allowance to the Stuarts, 35 ; farewell to James on leaving for Ireland, 49–51 ; sends aid to Ireland, 54 ; his correspondence with D'Avaux, 100–3; anxious at disputes in Ireland, 112–3; prepared to send troops to

Ireland, 119; his comparison of his troops, 135; the most loyal champion of the Stuarts, 140; receives and thanks Colonel Zurlauben, 175; receives James on return from Ireland, 179–80; his arrangement for Irish troops, 221; receives Mountcashell, 215; sends help to Ireland, 223; sends St. Ruth, 225; sends large supplies, 260; disappointment of, 261; lends officers of the Maison du Roi, 291; sanctions English scheme, 295; fatal order to Tourville, 299–300; compliments Tourville, 305; his undiminished hospitality to the Stuarts, 306; takes the field, 308; reviews his army, 309; Captures Namur, 310; provides Irish troops with shoes, 319; takes the field in person, 320; changes his plans, 321; desire to exalt the Royal House, 322–3; pleased with Irish, 334; desire for peace, 337; orders bombardment of Brussels, 341; secures the mediation of King of Sweden, 348; refuses to banish Stuarts from St. Germains, 351, 352-3; reduces his army, 358–9; his dealings with the Stuarts, 368

Louise Mary, Princess, 306
Louvois, Marquis de, 12, 14, 15, 36, 41, 45, 53, 83, 85, 90, 91, 105, 115, 118, 119, 133, 180, 183, 214, 224; death of, 261, 319
Lowestoft (battle), 66
Lundy, Colonel, 74
Luttrell, Henry, 199, 229, 234, 238, 242, 245, 247; arrested, 248; saved by Ginkel, 249; receives English pension, *ibid.*; assassinated, *ibid.*; 266
Luttrell's dragoons (Henry), 176, 188, 234
Luttrell, Simon, 124, 188, 199, 291, 324
Luxemburg, Marshal, 175, 180, 308, 309; a spy of, 310-1; wins battle of Steinkerk, 311-5; 321,

323; wins battle of Landen, 324-7, 330; death of, 342

Macarty Mor regiment, 204
Macaulay, attack on Talbot, 62, 74; attack on Hamilton, 76; attack on D'Avaux, 99–103; his misquotation, 100; his description of the Boyne, 153-4; errors in it, 155, 156-7; blindly follows Story, 158; partial quotation of, 171-3; misquotes evidence on Limerick, 196-7; purely imaginary description of, 198; mistake as to age of Barbezieux, 319
McCarthy, Captain, 10, 16, 19
McCarthy, General, 84, 85, 86, 92. *See* Mountcashell
McCarthys, the, in France, 208
McCarthy, Owen, 79
McCarthy Mor, Colonel, 134
Macdonald, Captain Ronald, 28, 111
Macdonnell, 28. *See* Macdonald
MacElligott, Colonel, 204, 205
MacElligott, Colonel, killed at Athlone, 231
MacElligott regiment, 204
Macguire, Colonel C., 243
Mackay, General, 112, 231, 271, 312, 314
Maclean, Sir John, 111
Macmahon, Colonel A., 230
Macmahon regiment, the, 188, 192
Macnamara, Captain Hugh, 124
Macpherson, Sir James, 72, 124, 164, 340
Madden, Colonel E., 244
Madrid, 63, 64
Maestricht, 11, 324
Mahan, Cornelius, 79
Mahony, Colonel, 243
Maine, regiment, 331
Maintenon, Madame de, 36; her friendship with Queen Mary, 37; 133, 306, 308; wrongly blamed for Louis's change of plans, 322; 344, 345, 348
Maison du Roi, the, 35, 36, 310, 311, 320
Marigny, Captain, 109, 110

Marche, 316

Marine regiment, 291

Marlborough, his campaign in Ireland, 202-5; 296, 338, 339; sends intelligence of Brest expedition, 339-40; drops correspondence, 347

Marly, 47, 139, 206, 357

Marsaglia, the stream, 333; battle of, 333-5

Marshals, French, 371

Martinien, M., 171

Mary Beatrice d'Este of Modena (Queen), her escape from England, 9-11, 16-22; arrives at St. Germains, 23-4; her visit to the Dauphiness, 31-3; decides question of etiquette, 33-4; described, 34-5; her friendship with Madame de Maintenon, 37; her ambition, 40; believed to be enceinte, 49; grief at James's departure, 52; her letters to James in Ireland, 114, 145, 175; glad at Lauzun's appointment, 128; induces French Minister to send a fleet, 177; her regret at King's absence, 180; gives birth to a daughter, 306; and Talbot, 345; and her dowry, 352-4

Mary (Princess and Queen), 187, 296, 340

Massé, 106

Maumont, Maréchal de Camp, 48, 53, 54, 57, 92

Maxwell, General Thomas, 165, 183, 188, 199, 200, 230, 231, 292, 317, 334

Maxwell's Dragoons, 153, 176, 188, 193

Mayo, Captain, 138

Meath, Bishop of, 97

Meath regiment, 193

Mediterranean, the, 298

Medway, battle in the, 207

Melfort, Earl, afterwards Duke of, 51, 57; his character, 86; James's Chief Councillor, 89, 98; and d'Avaux, 112-7; leaves for France, 117; his character, 117-8; 297, 338

Melfort (second), Duke, 132

Melfort, Countess, afterwards Duchess of, 51, 52, 57, 117, 118

Mérode, Colonel, 174, 176, 201

Mérode-Westerloo, Count, 312-3

Mérode regiment, 135

Metz, 293

Middleton, Earl of, 27, 28, 337, 338, 343, 355

Milan, 348

Military Articles of Limerick 264-6

Militia in Ireland, 74

Moerdyck, 321

Money, base, 98

Mons, 307, 308

Monseigneur (the Dauphin), 23, 24, 32, 34

Monsieur (Duc d' Orléans), 23, 24, 32, 34

Mont Cenis, 219

Montchevreuil, Lieut.-General, 325, 326

Montecuculli, Marquis, 10

Montpensier, Mdlle de (la Grande Mademoiselle), 15, 30, 49

Moore, Colonel Charles, 243

Morgan, Lieutenant-Colonel, 243

Morris, Mr. O'Connor, 285

Moselle, 316

Mountcashell, Viscount, 69, 77, 93, 108; taken prisoner, 109-10; his escape, 125; his early career in France, 207; escapes, 208; to command brigade, ibid.; recruits his regiment, 209; goes to France, 210; received by Louis, 215; marches to Savoy, 217; wounded there, 219; sent to Roussillon, 220; his services, 221-2, 307; death of, 341

Mountcashell Brigade, the, see Chapter VIII; increased, 286, 293

Mountcashell regiment, the, 210, 215

Mountgarret, Viscount, 104, 209

Mountjoy, Lord, 44, 45, 74, 77, 78, 79, 129, 297, 312, 314

Mouskry, 207

Mousquetaires, the, 311

Moustiers, 219

Mullingar, 78

Murray, Sir, 57, 58, 84

Muskerry, Lord, 207
Muskerry regiment, a, 215

Nagle, Sir R., 176, 249, 267, 284
Namur, siege of, 309–10 ; retaken by William, 342
Nancy, 363
Nantes, 214, 215, 217 ; Edict of, 11, 14, 45–6
Nassau, Count, 265
Neerwinden, 324, 325. *See* Landen
Nenagh, 137
" Neptune," the, 58
Nesmond, Chevalier de, 225, 226
Netherlands, the, 60
Netterville, Alison, 63
Netterville, Viscount, 103
Newcomen, Lady, 137
Newcomen, Sir Thomas, 137
Newtown Butler, 109, 110
Newry, 136
Nimeguen, Treaty of, 52, 69
Noailles, Marshal (first), 217, 218, 220, 221, 307, 319, 320
Noailles (biographer of Madame de Maintenon), 322
Non-Compounders, the, 338
No Popery Bill, 279
Northumberland, Duke of, 52
Notre Dame, 49, 327
Nottingham, 75
Nugent, Brigadier Patrick, 137, 138
Nugent, Colonel A., 291, 326
Nuncio, Papal, 363

Oaths, unfair, 278–9
O'Brien, Charles (afterwards Viscount Clare), 10, 292, 317, 334, 335, 346
O'Brien, Charlotte (afterwards Lady Clare), 10
O'Brien, Daniel (afterwards Lord Clare), 209, 212
O'Brien, Sir Donogh, 68
O'Brien, Edward, 292
O'Brien regiment, the (Clare), 209, 210, 212, 215, 217
O'Callaghan's list, 291
O'Connel, Colonel, 244
O'Connor, General G., quoted, 279–81, 285–6
O'Donnell, Baldearg, 224, 246

O'Gara, Colonel, 230
Oldbridge, 143, 144, 149, 150, 151, 157, 158, 162, 166, 174
O'Mor, Anne, 327
O'Mor, Rory, 327
O'Neil, Sir Neil, 58, 150, 151, 152, 164, 167, 168, 209
O'Neil, Colonel Gordon, 188, 236, 244, 291
O'Neil, Colonel Felix, 243
O'Neil, Brigadier H. MacJohn, 243
O'Neils, the Two, 60
Orange Celebration of the Boyne, unjustified as history, 148
Order of Battle, James's, 125
O'Regan, Sir Thady, 138
Orléans, Duc d' (Monsieur), 323
Ormonde, Duke of (first), 66, 68
Ormonde, Duke of (second), 97, 329
Ostend, 205, 287
O'Toole, Sir Charles, 161
Ourthe, 316

Palatinate, plundering of 39, 55
Parc, 321, 324
Paris, Archbishop of, 49
Parker's regiment, 159, 162, 234
Parry, Garret, 79
Passage, 177
Pay, proposed for Irish soldiers, 78 ; to Irish troops in France, 212–3
Pembroke, Earl of, 349
Penniburn Mill, 92
Perkins, Sir William, 346
Perth, Earl of (afterwards Duke), 58
Petersfield, 16
Pignerol, 331, 332
Piper, Colonel, 263
Plowden, Mr., 199, 249, 267, 284
Plunkett, Captain Christopher, 136
Plunkett, Edward, 292
Plunkett, Captain John, 104
Plunkett's Jacobite Narrative, 104, 130, 166, 229, 233, 246, 249, 256. *See* Gilbert
Po, the, 218
Pointis, Marquis de, 43, 44, 45, 46, 48, 53, 54, 57, 79, 105, 106

Poissy, 52
Poland and Saxony, King of, 288
Polish Throne, 348
Pope, the, 55, 278
" Popish Champion," the, 80
Porter, Sir Charles, 264, 271
Porter, Sir George, 55, 115, 136
Portland, Earl of, 150, 190, 346, 350-4, 355, 356
Portland's regiment, 235
Portsmouth, 16, 17
Portsmouth, Duchess of, 22, 50
Portugal, 66
Powell, Mr., 343
Prendergast, Captain, 346
Prendergast, Colonel Edmund, 233
Preston, Lord (General), 64
Preston, Lord, 55, 296
Preston, Robert, 291
Protestant Succession, the, 40
Protestants, retained by James, 82
Powis, Marquis, and subsequently Duke of, 10, 16, 17, 31, 51, 57, 89, 176
Powis, Marchioness and Duchess of, 10, 16, 17. 23, 31, 32, 51
Prussia, 334
Pyrenees, 341
Purcell, Captain, 104
Purcell, Colonel Nicholas, 199, 229, 242, 245, 263, 266
Purcell's Dragoons (unmounted), 161
Purcell's Dragoons (mounted), 176, 234
Purcell, Major, 243, 258
Pusignan, General, 48, 57, 90, 92

Queen's regiment (Cavalry), 292, 316
Queen's regiment (Dragoons), 292, 317, 331
Queen's regiment (foot), 291, 331

Rabutin, Count, 133
Ramsay, Brigadier, 103
Ramullin, 150, 158, 162
Raumont à Pic, 316
Red coats for Irish troops, 216
Red Sand buoy, 29
Regiments, list of Irish, 121-3
Regiments for France, Irish, 208-9
Reilly, Colonel Luke, 247

Reilly, Philip, 247
Reynolds, Colonel, 307
Reynolds, Commissary, 64
Rheims, Archbishop of 46-7, 366
Rhue, 47
Richard II, 88
Richards, Colonel, diary of, 250-6
Rice, Sir Stephen, 44, 57
Rienan, George, 291
Richmond, Duke of, 50, 344
Rivers, Sir Richard, 73
Riverston, Lord, 199
Riva, Francesco, 10, 17 ; narrative of, 18-20
Roche Bernard, 51
Rochefort, 220
Rochester, 28
Rochefoucauld, Duc de, 356
Rome, 55
Roscrea, 68
Rosmadek, M. de, 56
Rosse, Viscount, 129
Rossnaree, 149, 151, 168, 174
Roth, Captain (afterwards Colonel) Michael, 41, 42, 43, 44, 210, 326
Rouen, 338
Roussillon, 220, 221, 307
Roussillon regiment, the, 69
Roy, 221
" Royal Charter," the, 207
Royal regiment (Dragoons), 292, 317, 331
" Royal Sun, The," 304
Roze, General, 48, 49, 53, 57, 90, 91, 105, 106 ; his cruel plan to reduce Derry, 107 ; censured by James, 107-8, 110, 126, 127, 128, 140
Rubantel, Lieutenant - General, 324, 325, 326
Rumilly, 219
Russell, Admiral, 295, 299, 300, 338
Ruvigny (Marquis), 233, 237, 241, 242
Ryswyck, 349 ; peace of, 345

" Sage," the, 57
St. Brigette, Fort, 331
St. Clément, 318
St. Cyr, 322, 348
St. Didier, M. de, 57, 117

St. Frémont, General, 316

St. Germains (Château of), 21, 22, 23, 24, 33, 35, 36, 38, 44, 179; Irish delegation to, 199; 244, 245, 291; endeavour to eject Stuarts from, 351-4

St. John's Gate (Limerick), 192, 193

St. Malo, 285, 340; Irish privateers of, 293

"Saint Michel," the, 57, 58

Saint Pater, General, 93, 120

St. Patrick's Cathedral, 94

St. Ruth, General, 201, 219, 220; correct name of, 225; sent to Ireland, ibid.; brings supplies, 226; moves to Athlone, 228; dependent on his lieutenants, 229; angry at loss of Athlone, 232; decides to fight, 233; at Aughrim, 233-43; killed, 241, 242

Saint Simon, Duc de, and his diary, 15, 300, 303, 322

Saint Vians, Lieut., 35, 36

Saint Victor, M., 18, 19, 20, 26

Sales, Marquis de, 219

Salisbury, Earl of, 17

Salt in Ireland, no, 138

Sandys, Capt., 231

Sarsfield, Patrick (Earl of Lucan), 58, 116, 120, 127, 142, 144, 165, 176; James's opinion of, 146, 147; his opinion of James, 182; at Limerick 183; his exploit at Ballineedy, 189-90; 199, 213, 234, 238, 248, 259, 263, 266, 284, 285, 286, 291, 292, 297, 307; praised by Luxemburg, 315; 320; at Landen, 324-7; death of, 327-9

Sarsfield's regiment, 153, 176, 234, 242

Saverne, 69

Savoy, 217, 218, 219, 307, 331

Savoy, Duke of, 218, 317, 331, 332, 333; makes peace, 348

Scattery, 283, 285

Schomberg, Marshal, 124, 125, 126; his letter of explanation to William, 126-7; goes into winter quarters, 127-8; 130; opens campaign, 138; 141, 142; at the Boyne, 149, 150, 152, 155, 160, 161, 169, 170

Schomberg, Duke (Charles), 317, 318, 335

Schomberg, Count M., 150, 158, 164, 166

Scot, John, 79

Scotland, Jacobite party in, 58-9

Scott, Sir E., 93, 205, 317, 318, 319, 331, 335

Scravenmore, General, 258, 271, 329

Sebastian, 248

Sedley, Miss, 37

Seignelay, 133, 177

Seilern, Baron, 349

Sevigné, Madame de, 22; quoted, 25-6, 30, 34, 35, 41, 45, 51, 52, 69, 223

Shannon, 145, 260; English fleet in the, 250

Sheerness, 29

Sheldon, Dominic (General), 10, 155, 183, 199, 234, 238, 239, 242, 257, 263, 292, 297, 307, 320, 360

Sheldon, Mr. Ralph, 27

Sion House, 28

Sisteron, 318

Six Mile Bridge, 248

Skelton, George, 12, 13, 14, 55

Slane Bridge, 149

Slane, Lord, 243, 244

Sligo, 116, 127, 265

Smyrna fleet, 337

Sole Bay, 66

"Soleil d'Afrique," the, 56

Solmes, Count, 27, 160, 312

Somerset, Lady Elisabeth, 10

Spain, 60

Spain, Queen of, her death, 49

Spires, 316, 317

Spithead, 297

Sourches, Marquis, 139, 334

Staffarde, 219

Stafford, Dean Alexius, 243

Stapleton, Colonel, 258

Stapylton, Colonel, 124

Steinkerk, battle of, 273, 310-15

Stone Fort, the, 190

Story, Rev. G. W., 76, 158, 160; on Limerick, 196-7

Strafford, 62

Strickland, Lady, 10

Stuart regiment, 193

Stuarts, penury of the, 35
Sullivan regiment, 204
Sunderland, Earl of, 11, 12, 13, 267
Susa, 219
Stratmann, Count, 349
Sutherland, General, 28, 57, 291
Sutherland's regiment, 159, 163
Swale, the, 29

Taaffe, Major John, 92
Taaffe, Count, 363, 364
Talbot, Buno, 63
Talbot, Capt., 79
Talbot, Lady Charlotte, 66, 267
Talbot, Garret, 63
Talbot, Gilbert, 63
Talbot, Griffith, 63
Talbot, James, 63
Talbot, John, 63
Talbot, Sir John, 28
Talbot, Colonel James, 243
Talbot, Mary (Lady Dungan), 63
Talbot, Peter, 63, 64, 67
Talbot, Colonel Richard (Bastille), 63, 188, 193, 195, 291, 307, 317, 319, 335, 341; sent to the Bastille, 345
Talbot, Sir Robert, 63
Talbot, Thomas, 63
Talbot, Capt. William (Wexford.), 105
Talbot, Sir William, 62, 68, 77, 85, 116, 267
Talbot, Lieut.-Colonel William (Templeoge), 103
Talbots of Cartown, the, 62
Talmash, General (also Talmach and Tollemache), 230, 271, 279, 312, 339, 340
Tangy, Chevalier de, 105
"Tapissier de Notre Dame," le, 327
Tarentaise, 219
"Tempest," the, 117
Tenneville, 316
Tessé, Chevalier de, 225, 234, 241, 297
Terriesi, Marquis, 16
Tettau, General, 190
Thionville, 317
Thomond Bridge, 256, 258
Thomond, Marshal, 371
Thurles, Lord, 67
Tiffin, Colonel, 263

Titus Oates, 67, 275
Torbay, 16, 140
Torcy, Marquis de, 353
Tournaisis regiment, 135
Tourolle, 24
Tourville, 187, 298, 299, 300, 302, 303; praised for his valour, 305-6; captures Smyrna fleet, 337
Tower, the, 12, 13, 62, 205
Trahern, Major, 138
Trevanion, Captain, 28, 29
Trinder, Mr., 57
Trimlestown, Lord, 263, 267, 284, 291, 316
Trinity College, Dublin, 79
Tubize, 310, 351
Turenne, 11, 16, 64, 68, 173
Turini, M., 10
Turini, Madame, 10
Turnham Green, 346, 347
Tyrconnell, Duchess, 129, 200
Tyrconnell regiment, the, 159, 162, 233
Tyrconnell, Duke of (Richard Talbot), 42, 43, 44, 45, 54; birth and youth of, 63-4; joins James in Belgium, 64-5; known as Goliath, 64; early adventures of, 65-6; in James's household, 65-6; sent to Tower, 66; to Portugal, ibid.; marries Miss Boynton, ibid.; imprisoned in Dublin, 67; escapes and marries F. Jennings, ibid.; as James's companion, 70; proposes restoration of Irish estates, ibid.; sent to Ireland, 71; appointed Lord-Deputy of Ireland, ibid.; his age against him, 72; his first measures, 73; deals with the army, 74-5; raises Irish army, 77; removes Protestant troops, 78; calls in arms, 79; rouses Irish confidence, 80; receives King James, 84; makes his report, 84-5; created a Duke, 85; proposes to reduce the army, 86; long illness of, 89; returns to Dublin, 113; demands Melfort's removal, 116; favours stand at the Boyne, 144; his relations with James, 147;

his courage at the Boyne, 155; defends Oldbridge, 159; at Galway, 184; reinforces Limerick, 197; appoints Berwick his deputy and goes to France, 199; his reception in France, 200–1, 223–4; position on his return, 224; goes to Athlone, 228; opposes a battle, 232; resumes command, 245; orders *Levée en masse*, 247; arrests Luttrell, 248; exacts public oath, 249; sudden death of, *ibid.*, different opinions of, 250; spurious will of, 259

Tyrone, Earl of, 205, 267
Tyrone regiment, 204

Ulster, position in, 84, 87
Ulstermen, described by d'Avaux, 137
Uniform, the Irish, in France, 216–7
Union of England and Ireland indispensable, 182
Usson, Marquis d', 225, 226, 228, 229, 232, 245, 246, 247, 249, 265

Valence, 221, 318
Vauban, Marshal, 41, 45, 46, 91, 310, 339
Vendôme, Marshal, 349
Versailles, 12, 13, 21, 29, 30, 31, 46 *passim*
Vernon, Secretary, 353
Vienna, 55, 349
Villars, memoirs of, 173, 309
Villeroi, Marshal, 218, 323; 340, 341, 342
Villiers, Viscount, 349
Vincennes, 14, 21

Waldeck, Duke of, 187
Waldegrave, Lady, 55
Waldegrave, Lord, 55
Waldegrave, Sir William, 10
Wall, John, 131
Wallace, Sir Thomas, 51
Warwick, Earl of, 335

Wassenaer, Mr., 356
Waterford, 183, 190, 204
Wauchope, Colonel, 57, 137, 138, 232, 259, 263, 291, 297, 317, 320, 333
Westmeath, Lord, 263
Westminster Abbey, 207
Weston, William (printer at St. Germains), 293
Wexford, 185
Wight, Isle of, 76
William, Prince of Orange (afterwards William III), 11, 13, 15, 16, 27, 39; lands in England, 78; lands in Ireland, 142; his army, *ibid.*; at the Boyne, 148–50, 152, 161–2, 170; marches to Limerick, 185–6; lays siege to it, 188; repulsed at, 191–3; his excuse for Limerick defeat, 195–6; anxious for peace in Ireland, 262; changes his views on Irish policy, 273–4; consequences of his breach of faith, 275; 308, 310, 311; at Steinkerk, 312–5, 321; fights at Landen, 324–7; and the Duke of Berwick, 329; plot against, 346–7; his lost opportunity, 373
William's army, 142
Williamson, Mr., 349
Wilson, Major, 175
Wine, duty on French, 114
Whitehall, 17; occupied by the Dutch, 27
White, George, 292
Wogan affair, the, 65
Wolseley, Brigadier William, 109, 137, 138
Woodstock, Lord, 356
Wool trade in Ireland, 54, 114
Würtemberg, Duke of, 190, 230, 258, 312, 313, 330

York regiment, the, 65

Zurlauben, Colonel, 158; his report on the Boyne, 173–5
Zurlauben regiment, 135, 175

Lightning Source UK Ltd.
Milton Keynes UK

175681UK00002B/31/P